The Junkers
Ju 87 Stuka

A Complete Guide to the Luftwaffe's Famous Dive Bomber

by Richard A. Franks

Airframe & Miniature No.14
The Junkers Ju 87 Stuka
A Complete Guide to the Luftwaffe's Famous Dive-bomber
by Richard A. Franks

First published in 2020 by Valiant Wings Publishing Ltd
8 West Grove, Bedford, MK40 4BT
+44 (0)1234 273434
valiant-wings@btconnect.com
www.valiant-wings.co.uk
Facebook: valiantwingspublishing

ISBN: 978-1-912932-06-1

Acknowledgments

The author would like to give a special word of thanks to George
Papadimitriou & Bryan Ribbans for their invaluable help with
photographs. Special thanks must go to Steve A. Evans & Libor
Jekl for their excellent model builds and Richard J, Caruana,
Jerry Boucher and Juraj Jankovic for their superb artwork.

We would also like to thank the following companies for
their support of this title.
• Aires Hobby Models – www.aires.com
• Eduard M.A. – www.eduard.com
• CMK & MPM Production s.r.o – www.cmkkits.com

Note

There are many different ways of writing aircraft designation,
however for consistency throughout this title we have stuck
with one style (e.g. Ju 87 V1 and Ju 87G-2 etc.)

Author's Note

There are many contradictions in documentation about the
Junkers Ju 87 series, both genuine German as well as all
written accounts since the end of WWII. As a result of this,
throughout the title you will find details of contradicting
information that was discovered by myself during the
compilation of this book. I have done this to give you as much
data as possible, so that you can make your own decision as to
the most likely scenario.

Cover

The cover artwork depicts a Ju 87B-1 from 5./St.G 77. On
the 18th August 1941, Stukas attacked the radar station at
Poling and were intercepted by Spitfires from B Flight, No.602
Squadron. S2+UN was damaged by Sgt Basil Whall (flying
LO•G, L1019) and subsequently landed at Ham Manor
Golf Course near Angmering, West Sussex. This artwork was
specially commissioned for this title. ©Jerry Boucher 2020

Hermann Pohlmann
the designer of the
Stuka with Junkers pilots
photographed at Dessau
with a Ju 87B-2 as a
backdrop

Contents

Airframe Chapters

Miniature Chapters

Appendices

2 sets 1/48th Scale Plans Fold-out

Glossary

Italian pilots ferrying newly delivered Ju 87Bs CM+AA and CM+AE

BK 3.7 . . . . *Bordkanone* 3.7 (on-board cannon 3.7cm)
BMW . . . . Bayerische Motorenwerke (Bavarian Motor Works)
DB . . . . Daimler-Benz
ETC . . . . *Elektrische Trägervorrichtung für cylinder bomben*
      (Electrically operated carriers for cylindrical bombs)
Feldwebel (Fw.) . . . . Sergeant (RAF) or Airman 1st Class (USAAF)
Fliegerkorps . . . . Air Corps
Funkgerät (FuG) . . . . Radio or Radar Set
General . . . . Air Marshall (RAF) or Lieutenant General (USAAF)
Generalleutnant . . . . Air Vice-Marshall (RAF) or Major General USAAF)
Generalmajor . . . . Air Commodore (RAF) or Brigadier General
      (USAAF)
GM-1 . . . . Nitrous Oxide injection system
Geschwader . . . . Squadron
Gruppe . . . . Group
Hauptmann (Hptm.) . . . . Flight Lieutenant (RAF) or Captain (USAAF)
IFF . . . . Identification Friend or Foe
Jumo . . . . Junkers Motorenbau
Kommandeur . . . . Commanding Officer
Kommodore . . . . Commander of a Geschwader
Lehrgeschwader . . . . Training Squadron
Leutnant (Lt) . . . . Pilot Officer (RAF) or 2nd Lieutenant (USAAF)
Luftflotte . . . . Air fleet
Major (Maj.) . . . . Squadron Leader (RAF) or Major (USAAF)
MG . . . . Machine Gun
Oberfeldwebel (Ofw.) . . . . Flight Sergeant (RAF) or Master Sergeant (USAAF)

Oberleutnant (Oblt.) . . . . . . Flying Officer (RAF) or Lieutenant (USAAF)
Oberst . . . . Group Capitan (RAF) or Colonel (USAAF)
Oberstleutnant (Obstlt.) . . . . Wing Commander (RAF) or Lieutenant Colonel
      (USAAF)
OKL . . . . (*Oberkommando der Luftwaffe*) Luftwaffe High
      Command
Rb . . . . Reihenbildner (aerial reconnaissance camera)
Revi *(Reflexvisier)* . . . . Reflector Gunsight
RLM . . . . *Reichsluftfahrtministerium* (Third Reich Air Ministry)
Rüstsätze . . . . Modification Sets
SC . . . . *Sprengbombe-Cilindrisch* (Explosive bomb –
      cylindrical) GP bombs
SD . . . . *Sprengbombe-Dickwandig* (Explosive bomb thick
      walls) fragmentation bomb
SG (*Schlachtgeschwader*) . . . . Battle squadron
Stabsfeldwebel (Stfw.) . . . . . . Warrant Officer (RAF), Master Sergeant (USAAF)
Staffel . . . . Equal to Squadron in RAF
Staffelkapitän . . . . Commander of a squadron
Stammkenzeichen . . . . Primary identification (code letters)
StG (*Sturzkampfgeschwader*) . . Dive-bomber Squadron
Technisches Amt . . . . Technical Department of the RLM
Unteroffizier . . . . Corporal (RAF & USAAF)
Versuchs or *Versuchsmuster* . . . Research or test aircraft (V-series)
Werknummer (W/Nr.) . . . . . . Works (construction) number

Ju 87D-5 T6+TU of 10.t(Pz)/SG2 surrendered at Litzingen in May 45

Preface

During WWI German military thinking had proved the worth of the dive-bomber with types such as the Junkers J.1 and so it was that WWI ace Ernst Udet strongly supported the idea of adding such a type to the re-born Luftwaffe, having seen Curtiss biplanes undertaking dive-bomber exercises in the USA in the interwar period. The development of the *Sturzkampfflugeug* (dive bomber) concept progressed in Germany during the interwar period and Hermann Pohlmann of Junkers, alongside Dipl. Ing. Karl Plauth (until his death in a flying accident in November 1927), felt that such a type had to be simple and robust, dispensing with such complex niceties as retractable undercarriage. From this came the Junkers A 48 design, which was given the military designation of K 47. Once the Nazis came to power in Germany such a type was given priority, with the *Sofort-Programm* (Immediate Programme) announced in 1933 that required a new type of dive-bomber to replace the existing Heinkel He 50 and from this came the Henschel Hs 123 biplane (*See Airframe Detail No.7 ©2019 ISBN 978-1-912932-04-7*). The Hs 123 was only an interim design as it was dated even then and would be very much so when it actually entered service (regardless of a call during WWII to put it back into production), so the RLM approached Pohlmann and began trials with the K 47, which featured the double-spar inverted gull wing platform that would become

Contenders for the Sturzbomber Programm (dive bomber programme) included the Blohm and Voss Ha 137 D-IUXU

Heinkel He 50A

Heinkel He 118 V1 D-UKYM

Ernst Udet runs up the engine of Curtiss F11C-2 D-3165, marked as D-IRIS

Junkers K 48dy (D-2012) fitted with a Siemens Junkers Sh-20 engine, although it was later fitted with a BMW 132 and became D-ITOR in 1933

The mock-up of the Ju 87, showing the twin tail configuration only used by the first prototype

A close-up of the Ju 87 mock-up showing the clean lines initially intended for the nose, with the coolant radiator set at a steep angle underneath

synonymous with the Ju 87. The K 47 lead to the A 48, which was registered as D-ITOR, powered by a BMW 132 radial engine and featuring dive brakes, which were viewed favourably when tested. Ernst Udet's fascination with the dive bomber concept had led to him purchasing two Curtiss F11C-2 biplanes in 1933 and he shipped them to Germany aboard the passenger liner *Europa*. Once there they were re-assembled and given the civil registrations D-3165 and D-3166 (later changed to D-IRIS and D-ISIS), they were then transported to the Luftwaffe test facility at Rechlin where their potential was clearly demonstrated by Udet himself on many occasions. His love of the concept was not held by high-ranking Luftwaffe officials though, who felt that the type of skilled flying needed to fully utilise the type, was beyond that which could be expected from the average pilot.

Work on the new Ju 87 began in 1933 and

The Ju 87 V1 in its initial form during ground-runs of the engine. The canopy sections are not installed, affording us a view of the heavy framework between the front and rear cockpits that acted as a safety frame in case the aircraft rolled over

because German aero engines of the time had insufficient power, it was decided to use the British Rolls-Royce Kestrel V engine, ten of which were purchased by Junkers on the 19th April 1934 for £20,514,10s,6d. Due to the restrictions imposed by the Versailles Treaty, the first prototype was built in Sweden by AB Flygindustri and secretly shipped to Germany in 1934. This airframe was found to be too weak though, so it was not completed until October 1935 and it undertook its first flight, marked as D-UBYR, on the 17th September 1935. The RLM was still unimpressed by the type, especially as it used an engine that was not of German origin, so in late 1935 Junkers suggested the adoption of the Daimler-Benz DB600 inverted V12 for future prototypes and the Junkers Jumo 210 for the production variant, to which the RLM agreed. Reworking of the design began on the 1st January 1936 but on the 24th the first prototype crashed at Kleutsch near Dresden. Its pilot *Hptm.* Willy Neuenhofen and engineer Heinrich Kreft were both killed and the crash was caused by the failure of the twin fin and rudder units, which developed flutter and collapsed during testing of terminal dynamic pressure in a dive. The second prototype, the V2 therefore had its twin tail unit removed and replaced with a conventional vertical fin and rudder, but with no DB600 engine available it was delayed until the Jumo 210Aa engine became available. In March 1936 the V2 joined the flight test programme alongside the other three potential designs for the *Sturzbomber Programm* (dive bomber programme), the Arado Ar 81 V2 (D-UPAR), the Blohm und Voss Ha 137 V4 (D-IFOE) and the Heinkel He 118 V1 (D-IKYM) at the Rechlin test facility. The Heinkel and Junkers designs proved to be the best options, but *Generalfeldmarschall* Wolfram von Richthofen told Junkers representatives that the type stood little chance against the He 118, as he felt the Ju 87 was underpowered for a bomber.

To that end he issued a confidential directive to cease all work on the Ju 87 in favour of the He 118 in June 1936, but the next day Ernst Udet cancelled it and reinstated development of the Ju 87. Things were compounded when Udet crashed the He 118 V1 on the 27th July 1936, having ignored Heinkel's warning about the fragile nature of the type's propeller Udet dived it and this resulted in the engine over-revving and the propeller disintegrating, thus causing the crash. Immediately afterwards, Udet cancelled the He 118 and announced the Ju 87 as the winner of the *Sturzbomber Programm*.

Development of the Ju 87 continued with the V3 (D-UKYQ), which had the thrust line of

The Ju 87 V2 marked as D-UHUH at E Stelle Rechlin in January 1936

The Ju 87 V3 D-UKYQ in flight

A lovely high-level shot of the Ju 87 V4 D-UBIP

The Ju 87 V5 seen here with its braking parachutes on each wing tip for steep diving trials

the engine dropped slightly to improve forward visibility over the nose. The V4 (D-UBIP) first flew in the autumn of 1936 and it acted as the prototype for the production variant with larger tail surfaces and was armed with a single MG 17 in the leading edge of the starboard wing. Later it was revised further with a new wing to ease production in which the taper of the leading inboard wing edge was replaced with a straight-line version with a rounded tip. In turn the taper at the trailing edge of the wing was increased to maintain the total wing area.

Production & Service

Ten pre-production A-0 series airframes were started in the summer of 1936 and they differed little from the V4 in its revised form.. Full production started with the A-1 (ten built), which started to come off the production line in early 1937 and these were followed later that year by the A-2, which had the Jumo 210Da engine and broader blades to the Junkers-Hamilton propeller.

The Ju 87A-1 first entered Luftwaffe service with I./St.G.162 'Immelmann' in the spring of 1937 and in December that year a flight of three,

A Ju 87B displayed in a diving stance at the Aero-Salon in Brussels in July 1939; a few months later, the type would go to war

known as the *Jolanthe-Kette*, was sent to Spain for operational evaluation during the Spanish Civil War. In Spain the three aircraft were flown by I./St.G.162 crews that were constantly rotated to ensure as many as possible got operational experience with the new type. The V4 preceded the pre-production machines' arrival in Spain, as it was sent in 1936, arriving in Cádiz in August. It is assumed that it went there to do manufacturer's tests in an operational environment, much as other types did during the Spanish Civil War, and although it was assigned the service number 29•1 it is unlikely this was ever applied to it and no photographs of it in Spain are known to exist.

Development of the type continued and in early 1938 a Ju 87A-1 was taken off the production line and fitted with a Jumo 211A engine in revised cowlings to become the V6 in preparation for the next production series. This was followed by a more extensively modified airframe, the V7, which also had an extensively modified cockpit canopy, enlarged tail, new undercarriage with streamlined spats instead of the large aerodynamic 'trousers' of the A-series, and a MG 17 added in the port wing. The V8 (W/Nr.4926) and V9 (D-IELZ) finalised all the changes for the new type. From this came the B-series and ten pre-production B-0 airframes (D-IELX being the first) were built in late 1938, followed by the basically similar production B-1 variant. This type was built by both Junkers at Dessau (from W/Nr.0217) and Weser-Flugzeug GmbH at Berlin-Tempelhof (from W/Nr.5070) and the variant saw a series of improvements throughout production, as well as application of *Umrüst-Bausätze* sets to upgrade existing airframes, along with a tropical version for use in the Middle East (see Chapter 2 for more details). The B-1 was replaced by the B-2 on the production lines in late 1939. This was basically similar to the B-1 but used the Jumo 211Da engine with direct fuel injection driving an HPA III metal propeller with automatic rpm governor. The radiator featured revised flaps and the rake of the undercarriage was increased slightly and larger tyres used to reduce the type's tendency to nose-over on landing. Again, this series adopted a number of

Ju 87A-1 D-IEAU seen in the pre-war three-colour upper camouflage. This image was used for propaganda, so you will find modified examples showing it with what look like service codes

This Ju 87A-1 was built by Weserflug in Bremen and left the Lemwerder production line in October 1937

The A-series had a long life, serving in many second-line duties such as this A-2 used by the Medical Department (Sanitätsabteilung) of the Luftwaffe (note their badge on the fuselage). The bulge underneath is probably a camera, used to look back up through the sighting window in the floor and determine the effects on the the pilot during dive trials etc.

An early Ju 87B-1 is inspected by Luftwaffe personnel in the summer of 1938. The external hinges for the rear radiator flaps can clearly be seen

Ground crew take a rest whilst undertaking engine maintenance on a Ju 87B-1 of 9./StG 77 at Flers, France in July 1940

To War

Having tested a small number of A-series airframes operationally in Spain, the Ju 87B series first went to war with the Luftwaffe during the invasion of Poland on the 1st September 1939. All nine *StukaGruppen* took part, with three in the north and remaining six in the south. Operating with total aerial superiority over Poland the Stuka was able to wreak havoc and the wailing siren and screamers fitted to their bombs had a massive psychological effect, not just on those who suffered from its attacks, but on those that saw it portrayed on newsreels around the globe – the legend of the Stuka was born.

The type next saw service during the invasion of Norway and Denmark on the 9th April 1940, although only I./St.G.1 at Keil and later Stavanger operated the Ju 87R-1 during the campaign. The invasion of France started before operations in Norway and Denmark were completed and 320 Ju 87Bs and 38 Ju 87Rs were used to support the tanks as they moved forward. Because the majority of the aircraft of The Netherlands, Belgium and, to a lesser degree, France, were obsolete, the speed of the attack meant that most of them were destroyed on the ground and as such the Ju 87 once again operated with almost total air superiority and the legend of the 'invincible' Stuka remained intact with only fourteen Ju 87s being lost during the first four days of the campaign.

The legend was not to remain completely intact though, because as the British Expeditionary Force was encircled at Dunkirk the Luftwaffe was tasked with preventing the evacuation, as it was

of *Umrüst-Bausätze* sets and a tropical version was created for operations in the Middle East (see Chapter 2 for more details). The final version based on the B-series was the R '*Reichweite*' (range) version. The prototypes for this series were the V15 (D-IGHK), V16 (DGT+AX), V17 and V18, although it is not known if the latter two were actually ever built. The R-1 was basically externally identical to the B-1 but it had a

A Ju 87B-2 of 3./StG 2 forced down in England during the Battle of Britain

150lt fuel tank fitted in each outer wing panel, plus revised fuel system to allow a 300lt drop tank to be carried under each outer wing panel (all of which meant only a 205kg bomb could be carried). The R-2 version was the same as the R-1 but lacked the 150lt tanks in the wing and was based on the B-2 variant. The R-3 is a bit of an anomaly, as some sources don't mention it while others do, stating that only a few were built and it was the same as the R-2 but fitted with a towing bridle behind the tailwheel to act as a glider tug (all variants from the B-2 onwards could be modified to tow gliders though?). The R-4 was identical to the tropical version of the R-2 except all the tropical-related equipment was fitted on the production line instead of at the field depots prior to squadron allocation, and it had a modified lubrication system to cope with the higher engine wear associated with long flights over the desert. The R-series never adopted any *Umrüst-Bausätze* sets as far as can be told, but tropical versions of the R-1 and R-2 were produced.

A Ju 87B-2 of StG 76 with the yellow nose characteristic of the Balkans campaign in 1941

a task that Göring felt his Stukas could easily achieve. For the first time though the Stuka came within the range of the RAF's modern fighters. Although the Stukas continually bombed the beaches and the ships assembling there, Spitfires and Hurricanes gave them a good mauling and the Stukas for the first time suffered heavy losses when they operated alone over the battlefield. Once the French campaign was concluded operations against Britain began and although isolated bombing of shipping around the east and south coast of the UK had previously occurred it was not until the 8th August 1940 that the first major Stuka sortie was made against a convoy. Even with Bf 109Es flying to protect them, the Spitfires and Hurricanes once again wreaked havoc amongst the cumbersome Ju 87s. Five days later on the 13th August *VII Fliegerkorps* tried to attack RAF Middle Wallop, but many Ju 87s were shot down or damaged by No.609 Squadron's Spitfires. On the 15th RAF Hawkinge and Lympne were attacked, causing widespread damage to the latter, and the next day St.G 2 attacked Tangmere but suffered heavy losses and on the 19th St.G 77 attacked the radio masts at Poling and lost twelve aircraft – the 'invincible' Stuka was no more and the *StukaGruppen* were withdrawn to the Pas de Calais area.

Balkans & Russia

On the 6th April 1941 the campaign against Greece and Yugoslavia was launched with three *StukaGruppen* transferred from France to support it, later joined by St.G 77. With Athens falling less than a month later, attention turned to Crete with St.G 2's Ju 87s operating against the Royal Navy, where they sunk the cruiser HMS Gloucester along with several destroyers. Once again though, these successes saw the Stuka usually operating in an environment where the Luftwaffe had almost total air superiority. Now Nazi

Germany turned its attention on Russia with Operation Barbarossa on the 22nd June 1941 and seven *StukaGruppen* were operated by II and *VII Fliegerkorps*, with IV.(St)/LG1 (redesignated I./St.G 5 in February 1942) operating the type from northern Norway. Once again the Stuka had good success during the initial stages of the invasion, mainly due to the fact that the Russian Air Force operated outdated machines and most of them were destroyed on the ground during the initial onslaught (first day claims by the Luft-

A Ju 87B-2 of StG 77 with personnel studying maps etc. prior to sortie. This B-2 has adopted the additional armour plate in the lower quarter of the rear canopy and has the later (armoured) gun-ring

A Ju 87B-2 Trop having the oil tank topped up via the hinged panel forward of the cockpit. The small hole in the port wing leading edge, between the gun and landing light is for a camera, the larger hole on its right is a fresh air intake for cockpit ventilation

A Ju 87B-2 with the U4 installation of skis in place of the standard (wheeled) undercarriage

Ju 87B-2s on final approach for landing at a Russia airfield in the winter of 1941, both displaying the temporary white winter distemper applied to cover the otherwise dark camouflage of the Stuka

Sicily for a proposed attack on the British Mediterranean convoys. On the 10th January the first two *Gruppen* attacked and nearly sunk the carrier HMS Illustrious and on the 11th II./St.G 2 sank HMS Southampton. A further attack was made on HMS Illustrious in Valletta harbour, Malta, by I./St.G 1 a few days later, but the 2nd *Staffel* of the unit lost all bar its *Staffelkäpitan's* aircraft in the process. In December 1941 *Luftflotte* 2 moved to the Mediterranean with its main objective being to destroy the island of Malta and drive British forces out of North Africa. With it came fifty Ju 87s operated by I and II./St.G 3 (a third Gruppe was added in the spring of 1942) and a further twelve from *Einsatz-Staffel* of Erg./St.G 1.

Stuka Upgrade

Throughout 1940 an extensive redesign of the Ju 87 took place using the lessons learned during the first years of conflict. The main revision was the adoption of a more powerful Jumo 211 engine, which resulted in a more refined nose profile, the relocation of the oil cooler from on top to below the engine and the movement of the coolant radiator from under the nose to two separate radiators, one under each inboard wing stub. The cockpit canopy was also extensively revised and rearward defensive armament was now via the twin MG 81Z machine-gun. The new type had extensive armour plating and it could now carry up to 1,800kg under the fuselage and either four 50kg or two 250kg bombs, anti-personnel bomb pods or a 300lt drop tank beneath the wings. The type also had the option to use the WB 81 weapons container in either A or B configurations or the WB FF cannon pod, with one of either weapons underneath each wing. The first prototypes for the new D-series (the C designation was used for the aborted carrier-based variant – see elsewhere) were the V21

waffe were 1,811 Russian aircraft destroyed for the loss of 35 of their own, while Russia eventually admitted to actually losing 1,200 aircraft by noon on the first day!).

Mediterranean

In early January 1941 the Stukas of I./St.G.1, II./St.G.2 and Stab/St.G 3 were sent to Trapani,

The Ju 87 V21 D-INRF was originally built as a B-1 (W/Nr.0536) but was fitted with the Jumo 211P, and later Jumo 211F, to act as a prototype for the new D-series

Ju 87D-1s seen during night-time operations on the Eastern Front, such harsh conditions played havoc with both men and machines

Ju 87D-3, S2+NM of 4./StG 77 in formation with others from its unit in 1943

A Ju 87D-3 of I./StG 77 in Russia in the spring of 1943 with the leather cuff on the starboard leg damaged and only SC50 bombs on the wing racks

A Ju 87D-3 of 6./StG 2 starts to taxy out for another mission in Russia in 1943

A Ju 87D-1 (J9+RR) of 7./SG1 being loaded with a bomb under the fuselage at Kursk

Ju 87D-3 S2+LT of III./StG 77 with the trapeze down and SC70 and SC500 bombs laying alongside

Ju 87D-5s of III./StG 2 prior to a mission with Hans Ulrich Rudel's aircraft (T6+AD) nearest

(W/Nr.0870536) and V22 (W/Nr.0870540), which both flew at some stage in early 1941, followed by the V23 (W/Nr.0870524) that flew in April 1941. Some accounts state each had the Jumo 211J, but it is more likely they initially used the Jumo 211F and it was not until the type entered production that the proposed 211J was adopted. The V24 (W/Nr.0870544) joined the development programme in May 1941, while the V25 (W/Nr.0870538) was mainly used for tropical trials before finally being used to develop the torpedo-carrying capacity that would ultimately result in the D-4.

The first production variant was the D-1, which adopted the Jumo 211J engine and had all the fuselage and cowling revisions seen on the prototype, but retained the wings of the B-series, along with its undercarriage because initial trials with a revised undercarriage leg proved it to be weak, so the older unit was retained until the problems could be sorted (resulting in the overlapping fairings of the B, instead of the two fairings separated by a canvas cover as would later be seen). Late production D-1s saw the adoption of the new undercarriage legs, which were intended to have explosive bolts to allow either or both legs to be ejected in an emergency, however these proved to be very unreliable, so it was not until the D-5 that this feature became standard. The D-2 is somewhat of an anomaly, as some sources state it was a D-1 with revised armament and others state it was a D-1 with the ability to tow a glider via a bridle fitted aft of the tailwheel, however all D-variants had this latter capability, so it seems unlikely the D-2 series was ever adopted. The D-3 was the first specifically designed for ground-attack and was a D-1 with increased protection via bulletproof (50mm) glass added (externally) to windscreen and armour plates to the fuselage and engine undersides plus the use of armoured coolant hoses and armour plate on the two coolant radiators under the wing stubs. When fitted for night operations the type became the D-3N (or D-3(N)) and this initially used the standard gunsight, but later adopted the Revi C/16DN, had muzzle blast suppressors on the wing guns and flame dampers fitted the exhausts. The D-3Ag (Ag = *Agentenflugzeug* [agent's aircraft]) was only ever an experimental design, when the Graf Zeppelin Research facility at Stuttgart-Ruit tested the fitment of a two-man (seated in tandem) gondola fitted above the centre-section of either or both wings. Intended to carry agents behind enemy lines, then to carry personnel or wounded as the need for agents became less important, the concept proved bulky and impractical, so the whole project was abandoned. The D-4, as already mentioned had the V25 as a prototype, but the few production airframes built were all based on the D-3 and combined this with the torpedo-carrying capacity trialled with the V25. It is claimed that none were ever used operationally and most were later converted back to standard D-3s. The D-5 was the first to feature

the extension to the wing span from 13.81m to 14.98m along with elongated 100% mass-balanced ailerons and MG 131/20 cannon in place of the MG 17s in the wings. The type also dispensed with the dive brakes, as dive-bombing was officially abandoned on the 10th October 1943, although the mounting stubs for them remained under the wings. The type was also field modified for night operations, when it became the D-5N (or D-5(N)),and these were similar to the D-3N in that they used the Jumo 211P (1,118kW) engine with flame dampers fitted to the exhausts (four styles are known), the dive brakes were removed and muzzle blast suppressors were fitted to the wing MG 151/20 cannon, while the radio was upgraded to the FuG 16ZY and later machines could use the Revi C/16DN gunsight. In all 771 D-5s were built from 1,178 ordered, with production ceasing in July 1944, and it was the last true Ju 87 variant built. The D-6 was never produced, as it was intended to be a 'rationalised' version. The D-7 and D-8 were 300 D-3 and D-5 airframes modified by *Metallwerk Niedersachsen, Brinkmann und Mergell* at the end of 1943 and beginning of 1944 for night operations. Just like the field-modified D-3N and D-5N these had the more powerful Jumo 211P (1,118kW), flame dampers were fitted to the exhausts and muzzle blast suppressors fitted to

Ju 87D-5 S7+LH of 1./SG3 taxies past another D-5 from the unit at Immola on the 28th June 1944 (©*SA Kuva*)

Ju 87D-3 and D-5 production in the large terminal (A2) building at Berlin-Tempelhof airport in mid-1944

Towards the end of the war the Stuka turned more and more to ground-attack and night-harassment sorties, this Ju 87D-3N (E8+GL) was operated by 3./NSGr.9 in the latter role and was captured in Austria in 1945 *(©USAAF)*

A Ju 87D-7 of NSGr 5 in Romania with fuselage cross, theatre band and swastika all painted out in black

Ju 87D-8 W/Nr.142097 of NSGr 4 captured at Milovice airfield Czechoslovakia, May 1945. Some sources list this as a D-5N

Ju 87D-8 W/Nr.100323 after capture by American forces in 1945 *(©USAAF)*

the MG 151/20 cannon, plus the type used the FuG 16ZY radio and the Revi C/16DN gunsight.

The D In Action

The D-series started to phase out the B-series in service in late 1941 and one of the first units to receive the type was I./St.G 2 near Leningrad, St.G 1 receiving the type in February 1942, with St.G 77 getting the type in April and St.G 3 in May. This latter unit used the D-series during the second Battle of El Alamein but by 15th November 1942, the unit had just thirty aircraft left and was therefore withdrawn shortly afterwards. The Stuka was no longer the vaunted aircraft it had been just three years previously and by this stage the Luftwaffe, RLM and Nazi German aircraft industry was struggling to find a replacement. In the end though, they all failed and the Ju 87 had to remain in service until the end of WWII. The Allies launched their offensive against Rommel on the 15th January 1943 and Tripoli fell on the 23rd. The Ju 87D-1 Trop was used by III./St.G 3 and I./Sch.G 2 in the region alongside the Henschel Hs 129 of 8./Sch.G 2 but losses were high and by May all Luftwaffe units had been withdrawn to Sicily, Italy and Sardinia, with St.G. 3 then moving to Russia shortly afterwards.

With the surrender of the 6th Army at Stalingrad between the 31st January and 2nd February 1943, Ju 87D units were brought forward in an attempt to hold the Donetz line under the control of *Fliegerdivision Donetz*. Alongside II./St.G 1, all of St.G 2 and I and II./St.G 77, was the new *Störkampfstaffel*, but they all failed to stop the Russian advance, which crossed the Donetz on the 5th February 1943. The Germans fought back retaking Kharkov on the 15th March and then the Luftwaffe turned its attention to the Kuban Peninsula. This offensive failed though and as a result German forces moved North to positions either side of the Russian salient at Kursk. On the 5th July 1943 Operation Citadel was launched, with the whole of St.G 2 and St.G 77 plus III./St.G 3 operating the Ju 87D-1 alongside the Fw 190A-4s and Hs 129Bs. Here the newly-arrived G-variant was used to attack the Soviet armoured divisions, while the Ds were used against communication targets.

On the 5th October 1943 the Luftwaffe's

ground-attack formations were rationalised with all dive-bomber, ground-attack and fast bomber groups formed as new ground-attack wings and the *General der Schlachtflieger* was established, commanded by *Oberst*. Hubertus Hitschold. Much effort was giving to replacing the Ju 87D with the new Fw 190F and G variants and in February 1944, II./St.G 2 re-equipped with the Fw 190, followed by II./SG 77 in March, although the Ju 87D was not fully phased out until August 1944.

The G-series

Although the F-series was proposed, this eventually metamorphosed into the Ju 187 and finally the Ju 287 (not the jet-powered bomber, this type number was first allocated to a development of the Ju 187). The next, and final, version of the Ju 87 was to be the G-series. This was developed towards the end of 1942 and it was intended specifically from the outset for the ground-attack role. The G-1 and G-2 variants were D-3 and D-5 airframes reconditioned and fitted with a BK 3.7cm Flak 18 cannon in a gondola underneath each wing. This weapon fired a tungsten-cored, armour-piercing round, twelve of which were carried by each gun. Initial tests with the weapon were carried out under existing D-series airframes at both the Rechlin and Tarnewitz facilities and some sources state that there was

A Ju 87G-2 captured in 1945 is inspected by Allied troops, some source this as having been at Salzburg, Austria, others Pilsen, Czechoslovakia

An early Ju 87G-1

Col. Hans-Ulrich Rudel is seen on the wing of his Ju 87G-2 after he surrendered to US forces at Kitzinen in May 1945. The undercarriage was deliberately ejected on landing to ensure the aircraft was not left in an airworthy condition

a pre-production G-0 series, although we have found no evidence to support this. *Hptm.* Hans Ulrich Rudel was present at the trials at Rechlin and in May 1943 he took one of the first Gs back with him to his unit in the Crimea. He first used it against Soviet armour in the Krymskaya and Temryuk areas, but it was during Operation Citadel that the type really proved its worth. During an attack on Soviet armour on the 5th July 1943 Rudel was able to destroy all twelve tanks and as a result he was asked by Luftwaffe officials to form a special *Panzerstaffel* within St.G 2. This unit was 10.(Pz)/St.G 2 and it initially used the new G-1. Rudel took over III./St.G 2 after the death of its commanding officer on the 17th July 1943 and re-equipped it with the G-series. Although a good aircraft in the hands of expert crews, the Ju 87G was not for the novice, so only III./St.G 2 and 10.(Pz)/*Staffel* of SG 1, SG 2, SG 3 and SG 77 ever used the G-series, with the *Staffeln* of SG 1 and SG 3 later being re-designated I.(Pz)/SG 9.

Final Days

Although the G-series remained in use in Russia, then moved back into Germany as the Soviet advance could not be halted, the remaining older Ju 87s also saw continued service right up to the end of WWII. Operating at night, due to the air supremacy of the Allied forces, the D-3N, D-5N, D-7 and D-8s were used by NSGr 1 and 2 in the west and NSGr 4, 8 and 10 in the east, with

NSGr 9 in northern Italy. Here they were used to harass troop and armour concentrations, along with attacking any other targets of opportunity. The situation for the Luftwaffe at this stage in the war though was such that these sorties were often little less than suicidal. *Oberst* Hans Ulrich Rudel led the last of his Geschwader on its final mission in May 1945, when a formation of three Ju 87G-1s and four Fw 190s flew to the American-occupied airfield at Kitzinen. Here, on landing, they either taxied into one another, or the explosive bolts on the undercarriage legs were activated, effectively writing off each aircraft in a fitting end for a truly infamous aircraft.

The Stuka at sea, as a trainer & 'Super Stuka'
Ju 87C

The use of the Stuka on the planned *Kriegsmarine* Graf Zeppelin-class aircraft carriers was envisaged right from the start with each initially going to have twenty Fi 167s, ten Bf 109Ts and thirteen Ju 87Cs. This was later changed to thirty Bf 109Ts and twelve Ju 87Cs once their role was seen as offensive instead of as seagoing reconnaissance platforms.

Development of the Ju 87C-series started with the V10 (W/Nr.4928, D-IHFH), which was built for the *Trägerflugzeug* (carrier fighter) programme in 1938. It was only a basic proof of concept though, as it featured only the arrestor hook and fuselage strengthening associated with deck landings. It was followed by the V11 (W/Nr.4929, D-ILGM) which was the first to feature outer wing panels that would fold up and backwards electrically (reducing the overall span from 13.80m to 5.00m). It also had the arrestor hook and fuselage strengthening associated with deck landings. Both were used at *E-Stelle See* Travemünde to test the suitability of the type for carrier operations including catapult launches and deck (wire arrested) landings. They were followed by the pre-production C-0 airframes, which were virtually B-series airframes with the outer wing panels modified to fold up and backwards electrically. The aft fuselage was strengthened to withstand the loads of an arrested carrier deck landing and a retractable arrestor hook

A poor but historic photo showing the V10 during catapult-launch tests. Only the pilot was on board, for safety

The Ju 87 V10, D-IHFH, acted as a basic prototype for the C-series and had the arrestor hook, but no wing fold

was fitted under the tail, while catapult launching gear was fitted under the stub wings and the fuselage was locally strengthened. Two rubber floatation bags were fitted in the fuselage with two more inside the leading edge of each wing. The type also carried survival equipment including life rafts and there was no ventral D/F loop or IFF mast. The undercarriage legs were fitted with explosive bolts, so they could be jettisoned individually in an emergency (and thus make for safer landing in water). They undertook extensive service trials at both Rechlin and Travemünde, including catapult launches and simulated deck landings. The pre-production machines were to have been followed by 170 production Ju 87C-1 and C-2a, but only a few were ever completed, as suspension of work on Graf Zeppelin in May 1940 resulting in cancellation of the entire order. The C-1s were basically B-1s with all the features seen in the C-0 pre-production series, while the C-2s were B-2s upgraded in the same way. Any existing aircraft and those airframes in process of being built when the order was cancelled were converted back into standard Ju 87B-2s.

Carrier Units
The first carrier-based squadron was formed by the Luftwaffe some four months before the Graf Zeppelin was to have been launched. It was designated *Trägergruppe I./186* and was based at Rugia Island near Burg. It comprised three *Staffeln* (squadrons) and was to have served aboard both carriers (*Flugzeugträger* A [broken up] and B [later named Graf Zeppelin]) once built. By 1938 construction delays led to the unit being

Pilots intending to operate the Ju 87C-1 off the Graf Zeppelin-class carriers used other versions of the Ju 87s like this B-1 (J9+AM) of 4./(St) TrGr186 photographed in East Prussia in September 1939

One of a series of views of a Ju 87C-1, shown here with the wings fully folded

A Ju 87B fitted with a Jumo 213E as part of the Ju 87F programme, seen here having landed at Kirchheim Teck airfield, which was near the Hirth aircraft facilities

Although not of great quality, this shows a close-up of the cockpit area on the mock-up for the Ju 287 Stuka project

This shows the initial Ju 187 project wind tunnel model, note the Jumo 213 with revised cowl and external bomb load

disbanded but on the 1st November a single fighter squadron (*Trägerjagdstaffel*) 6./186 was formed, commanded by Kpt. Heinrich Seeliger. This was later joined by a dive bomber squadron (4./186) commanded by Kpt. Blattner. In July 1939 a second fighter squadron was formed (5./186), commanded by *Oblt.* Gerhard Kadow and partially manned with pilots taken from 6./186. By August 1939 these three squadrons were reorganised as *Trägergruppe II./186* commanded by Maj.Walter Hagen in readiness for Graf Zeppelin's service trials that were expected to start in the summer of 1940. However, when all work was suspended in 1940 on both carriers (with one being broken up), the whole air unit was disbanded.

Ju 87E

Work on developing a torpedo-carrying Ju 87D for anti-shipping work in the Mediterranean started in early 1942, once work on Graf Zeppelin started again and it looked as if the carrier might actually be completed. Because the Fieseler Fi 167 originally intended for this role was now considered obsolete, the *Technische Amt* of the RLM asked Junkers to modify the Ju 87D into a carrier-borne torpedo-bomber/reconnaissance variant. The concept was initially tested with the V25, then a small number of production D-3 airframes were converted to carry a torpedo and were thus designated the D-4. These were used for training purposes, but never deployed operationally. The full production 'navalised' Ju 87D was designated the Ju 87E-1,

but when all work ceased on Graf Zeppelin in February 1943, the entire order was cancelled and all existing D-4s were converted back to standard D-3s.

Trainer

By the time the D-series was being produced the need for a trainer version of the Stuka had become such that the H-series was created. Each variant was based on an existing D-series variant and they were all intended for pilot training. In each the rear gunner's seat was removed and replaced with a forward-facing one taken from an Arado Ar 96 (pilot's seat). The rear-facing MG 81Z was removed along with all its associated ammunition storage and the GSL-k 81Z mounting was also removed and blanked off. Full dual controls were installed with a second instrument panel in the former gunner's compartment, the mid/rear canopy was revised and bulged to improve forward visibility and additional armour plate was added aft of Bulkhead 5. So converted D-1s became the H-1, D-3s the H-3, D-5s the H-5, D-7s the H-7 and D-8s the H-8. The exact number thus converted is unknown and to date we must admit to never having seen a period image to confirm the existence of the series.

The Super Stuka

By the time the D-series started to go into production it was obvious that the type needed to be replaced. The initial proposal was the Ju 87F, which was basically to have been an improved D-series with the more powerful Jumo 213 engine and a new wing. This proposal was rejected however and was then further modified to such an extent that it was given a completely new designation, the Ju 187.

Here things get a bit confused, as there are a couple of models of the Ju 187 and Ju 287, but most credit them the wrong way around. We believe that the Ju 187 used the 1,325kW Jumo 213A engine in a revised cowling and featured a revised wing with a retractable undercarriage whose legs rotated through 90° back into underwing fairings. A remote-controlled gun turret was to be installed aft of the two-seat cockpit canopy

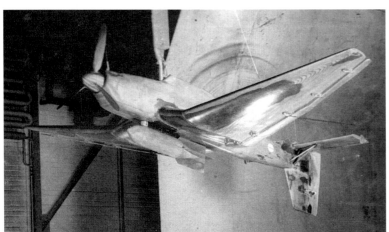

that would house two MG 151/20 cannon or a single MG 131 13mm cannon. It also had a vertical fin and rudder assembly that could be in the conventional position or rotated through 180° so it was underneath the rear fuselage (presumably to improve the turret's arc of fire). Fixed armament comprised a forward-firing 20mm cannon (maybe a motor-cannon) and the type retained the external bomb carriage system like the Ju 87, with what looks like a 1,000kg bomb on the only wind tunnel model image that we have ever seen.

This design was further modified to become the Ju 287, which is not to be confused with Junker's two-jet engine bomber programme, as the designation for that was re-allocated to it once work on the Stuka-based Ju 287 was cancelled in 1943. This design is the one most shown as the Ju 187, and featured the Jumo 213 engine in a set of standard cowls much like that of the D/G series, with a steeply sloping top cowl to improve forward visibility. The cockpit was still two-seat but the canopy was greatly reduced, had a single hinged access panel and heavily armoured framework. The remote-controlled gun turret was the same as the Ju 187, with a sighting unit much like that seen on the Ju 388 situated on the dorsal spine immediately behind the canopy. Wing armament is quoted as being a single MG 151/20 in each, but if developed further it may have ulti-

mately used the MK 101 or MK 103 cannon instead. It still had the rotatable tail unit, but had an internal bomb bay that could carry 250kg of bombs. Wind-tunnel models soon showed, however, that the type was incapable of attaining the necessary 400km/h and its bomb load was too light, so the whole (Ju 187/287) programme was abandoned in 1943.

These models show the Ju 287 Stuka project, with the reversible tail evident in the bottom two images

---

Test Airframes

Stuka airframes undertook a number of test programmes outside of those directly related to the evolution of the design or its equipment. The following selection of images show a couple of such programmes for which we believe there was no further development or direct operational use/adoption.

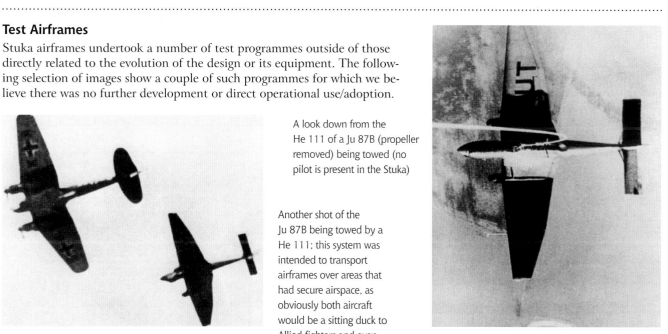

A look down from the He 111 of a Ju 87B (propeller removed) being towed (no pilot is present in the Stuka)

Another shot of the Ju 87B being towed by a He 111; this system was intended to transport airframes over areas that had secure airspace, as obviously both aircraft would be a sitting duck to Allied fighters and even anti-aircraft batteries!

This close-up shows the fitment of an aerofoil-shape container fitted under fuselage of a Ju 87B-2 Trop that could carry various loads, even a small artillery (anti-tank) peice

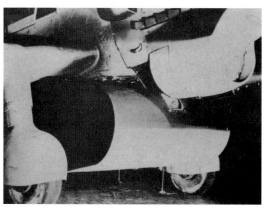

This Ju 87B was used by Heinkel for ejector seat trials

Foreign Service

Austria

in November 1937 Capt. Hans Schalk of Flieg-erregiment 2, Austrian Air Force visited several German aircraft manufacturers to test fighters, reconnaissance and dive bomber aircraft. Even though the Ju 87 seemed underpowered to him, it had far greater development potential than the Hs 123 biplane, so a request was made by the Austrian Ministry of Defence to purchase twelve Stukas. Nine people, under the leader-shio of Engineer 1st *Lt* Joshann Hoffmann, were sent to Junkers at Dessau and Köthen to gain

Bulgarian Air Force Ju 87D-5s over the Osogovo Highlands in Macedonia with 'White 30' nearest

experience with the maintenance of the Jumo engine. The twelve machines (W/Nrs.361-372) were to reside at St Pölten airfield at Wörschach air base and the Austrian Ministry of Defence wanted the deliveries to be competed by 1938. The first two were delivered on the 31st December 1937, with the transfer of the reminder planned by 31st December 1938. However, with Nazi German annexation of Austria on the 12th March 1938 the undelivered machines were never sent and the two already in Austria were taken over by the Luftwaffe.

Bulgaria

Although the Bulgarian Air Force (Vazdushni na Negovo Velichestvo Voyski – often shortened to just Vazdushni Voyski) operated a small number of Bf 109 fighters alongside Caproni medium bombers in the early stages of WWII, the Three Powers Pact of 1st March 1941 allowed for 'sympathetic' deliveries of weapons and ammunition from Germany. On the 13th August 1943 after many failed requests for more modern equipment, the first six ex-Luftwaffe Ju 87R-2s and R-4s arrived, followed by a further six Rs on the 6th September 1943. These machines were used by 1st Jato, 2 Pulk Szturmovy as well as for crew training. Later forty operational Ju 87D-3s and D-5s were supposed to be supplied to Bulgaria, but by the end of 1944 only twenty-five had arrived, with the remaining fifteen arriving in batches in May (8), June (5) and July (2). Crew training commenced and it was intended to equip three Jatos (Squadrons) with the type to form the 1st Shturmovi Orliak (Ground-attack Group), which were used to support its army in its action against partisan activity in Bulgaria and Yugoslavia.

On the 5th September 1944 the Soviet Union declared war on Bulgaria, with the pro-Western Government replaced with a pro-Soviet one, and on the 6th the new regime broke off diplomatic relations with Germany, declaring war on Nazi Germany on the 9th. The Red Army occupied the capital Sofia on the 16th September and on the 25th the whole Bulgarian army was put under Soviet command, followed on the 28th by the signing of an armistice in Moscow. All the Ju 87Rs and Ds still remaining at this stage, about thirty, were seized by the Soviets, who intended to use them with their Bulgarian crews against their former allies. Further details of their potential use and ultimate fate are unknown.

Croatia

The Air Force of the Independent State of Croatia (Zrakoplovstvo Nezavisne Države Hrvatske [ZNDH]) was the air arm of the puppet state

A Bulgarian Ju 87D-5 operated by 1/2 Storm Orliak

created on the 10th April 1941 with Axis support over the territory of the Kingdom of Yugoslavia during WWII. This new state joined the Three Powers Pact on the 15th June 1941 and fought alongside Germany in Russia. In January 1944 the Lucko Bomber Gruppe was formed within the Croatian Legion of the Luftwaffe and was equipped with six Ju 87Bs and R-2s and Fiat CR.42s to undertake initial training. In February 1944 3(Croat)./KGr 1 was created from the basis of the Lucko Bomber Gruppe and under the control of *Luftflotte* 6 it began ground-attack operations against Russian partisans, but by October 1944 the unit was disbanded and all aircraft were returned to the Luftwaffe.

Hungary

Three Royal Hungarian Air Force (Magyar Királyi Honvéd Légierö – MKHL) pilots trained at the Stukaschule 2 at Graz-Thalerhof in the summer of 1940 and returned home with two Ju 87B-2s, coded B.601 and B.602 (B = Bombazo – bomber). Once tested at the Experimental Aviation Institute both aircraft were issued to 3/1 Bombazo Osztaly at Börögond. These were supplemented in early 1942 by four Ju 87A-1s, coded B.602 to B.606, which were used a trainers. The Ju 87B was operated by the 2/2 Zuhanbombazo szazad (2nd Dive Bomber Squadron) but by February 1943 they were being used by 102/1 Zuhanbombazo szazad from Gomel airfield, near Kiev. A total of eleven D-3s and one D-5 coded B.631 to B.642 were used and they undertook their first sortie on the 1st August 1943, then moved to an airfield near Poltava, Ukraine on the 10th August. Here they were subordinate to 4 *Staffel* of II./St.G 77 and they sustained their first loss (B.636) on the 29th August. The next day the unit moved to Oyriatyn airfield, east of Kiev, flying their first mission there on the 1st September and lost two aircraft (B.637 and B.648) in a mid-air collision on the 14th September. Another aircraft (B.638) was lost on the 20th September, followed by another on the 14th October and two more on the 22nd October, leaving only four airworthy machines, so the unit was withdrawn from the front.

A new unit 102/2 Zuhanobombazo Szazad (dive-bomber squadron) was formed at Kolozsvár in Transylvania in March 1944. It operated three old 3/1 Bombazo Osztaly machines (B.601, B.606 and B.607) plus ten refurbished Ju 87B-1s delivered by the Luftwaffe. These were supplemented on the 14th May 1944 with twelve brand new Ju 87D-5s (B.701 to B.712), however, B.712 was lost on the 2nd June 1944 in a landing accident, so a replacement was supplied and coded B.713. The unit moved to Kuniowo airfield in south-east Poland on the 16th June 1944 and was subordinate to III./St.G 77. It began operations on the 30th June 1944 and moved to Rzeszów on the 6th July, where it suffered its first operational loss (B.701) on the 9th. Soviet advances were such that the unit had to move many times and by the 20th July it had

only eight serviceable aircraft left. On the 23rd two of these were shot down by VVS Bell P-39 Airacobras and by the end of August 1944 its remaining aircraft were passed to 102/1 Zuhanobombazo Szazad (dive-bomber squadron) at Kraków. They did not remain there long though, relocating to Börgönd in Hungary in September 1944, where all the remaining Stukas were destroyed on the ground during a USAAF air raid on the 12th October 1944.

Italy – Regia Aeronautica

A few weeks after Italy declared war on France and Great Britain on the 10th June 1940 the Italian High Command via its Air Attaché, Col. Giuseppe Teucci, placed an order with the RLM for the supply of one hundred Ju 87B-2s and R-2s. Training of the first crews was undertaken at Stukaschule 2 (Dive Bomber School 2), Graz-Thalerhof, Germany under the command of Capt. Ercolano Ercolani. The first ten (some sources state five) Ju 87B-2 Trops were flown by Capt. Ercolani and nine other pilots, going from Udine and Forli to Ravenna, then on to Rome-Ciampino, before transitting on the 20th August 1940 to Naples-Capodichino then via Catania to Comiso in southern Sicily. The remaining, previously promised, balance of five aircraft were ferried by pilots of 96° *Gruppo* Bombardemento a Tuffo (Dive-Bomber Group) on the 25th August. From then until July 1941 a total of fifty-two were supplied and allocated serial numbers MM.7047 to MM.7098. The first units to use the type were 236^ and 237^ *Squadriglia*

A Ju 87B in Hungarian Air Force markings, either whilst with the Experimental Aviation Institute, or once issued to 3/1 Bombazo Osztaly at Börögond

Ju 87s of 209 Squadriglia on a Sicilian airfield in 1941. Note the underwing fuel tanks which gave the 'Picchiatello' a respectable range enabling it to venture far into the Mediterranean to harass Allied convoys running the gauntlet in order to keep Malta supplied

Ju 87B-2s of 230 ^ Squadriglia, 97° Gruppo with 'Red 11' nearest, March 1941

of 96° *Gruppo* Bombardemento a Tuffo, when they attacked Malta in late August, and on the 2nd September both squadrons attacked shipping to the south of Malta, while on the 15th they attacked the airfield at Hal Far. Although Italian operations in North Africa had come to a standstill at Sidi Barrani, in late October 1940 Italian forces launched its attack on Greece. On the 27th October Ju 87s of 96° *Gruppo* attacked targets in the Balkans from their base at Lecce and on the 2nd six Ju 87R-2s of 96th *Gruppo* attacked Ioannina, returning to the same target two days later. All was to no avail though, as by mid-November the Italian forces had been pushed back to their starting point in Albania.

A second Stuka *Gruppo*, 97°, was created at Comiso, Sicily on the 20th November with 238 ^ and 239 ^ *Squadriglia* subordinate to the *Gruppo*. A part of 96° *Gruppo* was used as instructional staff and to form the core of both units. On the 28th November (some sources state 27th November) 96° *Gruppo* attacked shipping off the island of Gozo and from the beginning of December 97° *Gruppo* went into action over Greece. On the 6th December 96° *Gruppo* moved from Trapani to Lecce, south of Brindisi, and from the 14th December was ready for action, with six

Ju 87s from 238 ^ *Squadriglia* attacking Pigerasi. On the 20th the fortress of Borsch and the area around Kiepara were attacked, while on the 19th December Italian forces attacked Edda. The first Italian Ju 87 loss occurred two days later, when W/Nr.5769 whilst attacking a point target at Malvezzi was shot down by anti-aircraft fire, killing both its crew. Attacks continued and in the meanwhile more crews trained at Graz-Thalerhof were arriving with the squadrons.

On the 8th January 1941 twelve Ju 87Bs were loaded with 500kg bombs at Comiso with the intention of attacking a British convoy under way from Gibraltar to Alexandria. This it achieved south of Pantellaria, with two hits on freighters. This was followed by an attack by the Ju 87s of 236 ^ and 237 ^ *Squadriglia* against the aircraft carrier HMS Illustrious west of Gozo, albeit without success. On the 10th the carrier was once again attacked by Ju 87s from I./St.G 1 and II./St.G 2 of the Luftwaffe and as a result it had to be towed into Valetta harbour badly damaged. 97° *Gruppo* continued operations over Greece, while 96° *Gruppo* was rushed to Libya where the Italian front was crumbling. The *Gruppo* was operational there from the 30th January 1941 attacking Allied naval forces between Sicily and

Two new units with the Ju 87D were formed in 1943, these being 103° and 121° Gruppo operating from Sardinia, with a machine of the latter squadron seen here marked as 'VIII' in August 1943

Ju 87D-3 'Yellow 11' of 121º Gruppo at Lecce in October 1944

North Africa, where ten Ju 87s of 238^ *Squadriglia* were sent via Lecce and Puglia to Trapani to operate from various forward bases in Sicily. On the 6th April 1941 the German offensive in the Balkans began and this allowed the Italian forces to move forward again. Nine Stukas of 97º *Gruppo* joined the German-led Operation Marita by bombing Yugoslavian Navy bases at Kotar and Dobrota, although one Stuka was shot down and two limped home damaged. Operations in the Balkans led to the creation of another new *Gruppo*, 101º, which comprised 208^ and 238^ *Squadriglia*. Throughout April the *Regia Aeronautica* lost six Ju 87s over Yugoslavia, all of them to anti-aircraft fire.

Operations in North Africa also intensified, with 96º *Gruppo* operating in the theatre for the first time on the 11th April 1941 by attacking ships in Tobruk harbour. A further fifty Ju 87s (MM.8009 to MM.8058) were delivered to Italy between July 1941 and October 1942, most of them ex-Luftwaffe stock that were refurbished before delivery. By mid-July 1941 209^ *Squadriglia* went into action in Libya and 236º *Squadriglia* was sent from Lonato Pizzolo to North Africa. Attacks against Malta became intensive and in November 1941 Ju 87s of the 208^, 238^ and 239^ *Squadriglia* attacked the port area around Valletta. The last sortie by 238^ and 239^ *Squadriglia* over Malta took place on the 10th November 1941, thereafter the squadrons were brought to North Africa. The Italian forces were once again retreating in Cyrenaica in late December 1941 and the defence of the Mersa Brega began on the 20th January 1942 before another attack on Cyrenaica could begin (lasting up to the end of February 1942). 209^ *Squadriglia* was withdrawn from North Africa on the 16th February 1942, while the 102º *Gruppo* formed on the 1st May 1942 with 209^ and 239^ *Squadriglia* subordinate to it. The fighting in North Africa continued, with operations against Tobruk, and on the 29th June 1942 the fortress at Mersa Matruh was finally conquered. The fighting in North Africa had claimed a number of Italian Stukas, some to enemy action and others to accidents caused by operations from

One of the Ju 87Ds used by the NVST (Nucleo vola servizio tecnico) complete with the stylised 'NSVT' on either side of the vertical fin

basic forward airstrips. To that end eight more Ju 87s were supplied to the *Regia Aeronautica*, but this was far too few to deal with the losses.

With the Axis forces in retreat after the Battle of El Alamein in November 1942 only 101º *Gruppo* was still in Sicily. From mid April 1943 the first twelve Ju 87D-3s were sent to Italy from Graz-Thalerhof, followed by another six on the 20th April and by the 28th there were forty-one Ju 87D-3s at Siena-Ampugnano airfield. Between March and May 1943 the fighting in Tunisia ended with the complete retreat of Axis forces from Africa. At this time more Ju 87D-3s were being delivered and by June 1943 forty-nine had arrived. On the 9th July 1943 a new training unit Nucleo Addestramento Tuffatori was formed at Lonate Pozzolo with eight Ju 87Bs, but the very next day Allied forces landed in Sicily. On the 11th Stukas of 103º *Gruppo* (formed 1st February 1943) attacked the Allied fleet. The last Italian Ju 87 unit was 121º *Gruppo* based at Chilivani, Sardinia, where they joined the battle on the 12th July 1943, followed by similar sorties on the 13th. Heavy losses to British fighters in both operations led to the change to night sorties.

The end was coming though and on the 24th-25th July 1943 Benito Mussolini was deposed, followed on the 8th September by Italy capitulating. The nine airworthy Stukas that existed after the surrender were formed into a unit of the new Co-belligerent Italian Air Force. They were never used operationally though, being retained for training purposes until they with withdrawn from use due to damage and/or lack of spares.

A Ju 87A-1 (K-1) on public display in Tokyo, Japan in 1940. The aircraft lacked any armament and the pitot has been rotated through 180º, probably to stop it hitting those viewing the aircraft!

Japan

The Imperial Japanese Army Air Force received two Ju 87A-1s with a view to ordering and operating the type. If it had, they would have been designated the Ju 87K-1 and would basically have been a Ju 87A-1, but in the end the Japanese decided not to purchase or operate the type. Both aircraft were tested by the Mitsubishi company and were eventually destroyed during air raids on Tokyo.

OK, an interesting photo, as this shows a Ju 87A-1 in the Far East, this is probably one of those sent for tests in that country, but note the Chinese Air Force roundel on the aircraft next to it? One assumes this is some sort of test establishment or with a manufacturer, as Mitsubishi certainly tested one of the Ju 87A-1s sent to Japan

This other view of the Ju 87A-1 (K-1) displayed in Tokyo clearly shows the lack of any armament and the fuel filler point access panels missing on each wing root

Rumania

The Royal Rumanian Air Force (Forele Aeroenne Regale ale Romaniei [FARR}) received its first Ju 87D-3s and D-5s in August 1943. These were assigned to Grupul 3 Bombardement Picaj (Bomber Group) with tactical numbers 1 to 45, of which 37 to 45 were held in reserve. The remaining thirty-six flew with Escadrila 73 (Nos.1-12), Escadrilia 81 (Nos.13 to 24) and Escadrila 85 (Nos.25 to 36). When Ju 87Ds became part of Grupul 6 with the Corpul 1 Aerian in 1944 they were numbered 178 to 204 and 862 to 872. Here they were operated by Escadrila 74 (Nos.193 to 204), Escadrila 86 (Nos.862 to 872) and Escadrila 87 (Nos.178-192). All of these machines were only loaned from the Luftwaffe though and were never truly owned by Rumania.

Operations began with Grupul 3 Bombardement Picaj in the spring of 1943, subordinate to Flotia 3 Bombardement as part of Corpul 1 Aerian. From 6th July 1943 it moved to the Kerch Peninsula where it gave support to German and Rumanian divisions in the region. The Rumani-

ans were quite aggressive in their operations and by 9th August 1943 forty-five Ju 87Ds had been damaged. By the end of October 1943 Soviet units were completely cut off in the Crimean Peninsula and when the offensive began again on the 4th November the 3rd Romanian Mountain Division and the 6th Romanian Cavalry Division were given support by the Stukas. In mid-April 1944 Grupul 3 Bombardement Picaj was withdrawn from the Crimea, as the Russian counter-attack had reached as far as the eastern Rumanian frontier.

On the 20th May 1944 Grupul 6 Bombardement Picaj was formed with the Ju 87D, with just two squadrons initially (Escadrila 74 and 87). It went into action on the 30th June 1944 as part of Corpul 1 Aerian. Escadrila 86 joined as the third squadron of the group on the 16th June 1944, flying operations over the weakening eastern Rumanian front and by the 23rd August 1944 just twenty-five Ju 87s remained available with Grupul 3 Bombadement Picaj and only eighteen were airworthy. The situation was not any better with Grupul 6 Bombardement Oicaj, who by this date had lost twenty-eight of the fifty-five aircraft assigned to it.

On the 23rd August 1944 King Michael gave notice that his country would immediately separate from the Axis powers and all operations against Russia would cease. Some of the Romanian machines at Husi airfield in Moldavia were taken over by Hans Ulrich Rudel's unit and were flying for the Luftwaffe once again just a day later. Bombing of Bucharest on the 25th August 1944 led to a declaration of war with Nazi

Germany and this cost the Luftwaffe dearly as 376 machines were lost in various repair depots in Rumania. This included twenty-seven relatively new Ju 87D-3s of Grupul 3 Bombardement Picaj, which were all thus taken over by Rumania. The two Rumanian Ju 87 groups were combined to make Grupul 3/6, with the D-5s of Escadrila 74 and 81 making up the bulk and these undertaking the first actions against their previous Allies during the liberation of northern Transylvania.

Russian troops entered Bucharest on the 31st August 1944 and the Red Army occupied the whole of Rumania, except northern Transylvania, by the beginning of September. The Rumanian Stuka units however suffered heavy losses during the battles in Moravia, Slovakia and Austria. At the start of 1945 a new unit was formed, Escadrila 74 from the two squadrons of Grupul 3 and 6 Bombardement Picaj. Alongside the Henschel Hs 129s of Escadrila 41, this unit formed part of Grupul 8 Asalt/Picaj and undertook a mix of anti-tank and ground-attack sorties before being fully re-equipped with Russian Ilyshin Il-10s.

Russia

The Russian Liberation Army Air Force, also known as the Vlasov Army, was created by Nazi Germany and commanded by Gen. Vlasov. It was expanded to include its own air force and 2 Eskadrilla Bombardirovshchikov flew under the Luftwaffe designation of Schlacht*Staffel* 8. It operated twelve Ju 87Ds but because many of the pilots were trained to fly on instruments on the 28th March 1928 it was re-designated Nachtschlacht*Staffel* 8. Declared ready for combat in April 1945 and commanded by Kpt. Antilevskij the unit was based at Deutsch Brod in the Protectorate of Bohemia and Moravia. It flew its first mission on the 13th April 1945 bombing the bridgeheads over the Oder River. The unit was only to exist until the end of the month though, when all aircraft were returned to Germany (albeit one crew defected to the British occupation zone). Kpt. Antilevskij was captured by American forces on the 30th April 1945 and in September 1945 was passed back to the Soviets, who tried, sentenced and executed him on the 25th July 1946.

Slovak Republic

Negotiations for the purchase of Ju 87s began in 1940, however a contract was not signed until 1943. This specified that the Mraz plant at Trencianske Biskupice would undertake licence production of the D-5 variant. To do this workers from Mraz were trained at the Weser Flugzeugwerke in Bremen from February 1943 and on the 19th March 1943 the Slovakian Ministry of Defence placed an order for twenty Ju 87D-5s with a delivery date of 1st February 1944. This order was later extended on the 16th August 1943 to include a further thirty aircraft. The initial batch of machines built by Mraz, though, were supplied to Rumania and it was not until early June 1944 that Stukas started to be

Ju 87D-3, 'White 34' of Grupul 6, Rumania Air Force, 1943

supplied to Slovakia. These first machines were originally intended for Luftwaffe service, but they were diverted and civil registrations applied (OK-XAA, OK-XAB, OK-XAC, OKO-XAD and OKO-XAE). They were based at Piestany airfield and were to serve as trainers for I. Bombardovaci Perute (I. Bomber Group). Six more aircraft were collected from the Mraz factory on the 6th and 10th July 1944 and they were W/Nrs.666011, 666012, 666013, 66015, 66015 and 66017. The first training syllabus was not completed

before the Slovak National Uprising began on the 29th August 1944 and when the country was occupied by Nazi German forces after defeating the resistance, all the remaining Ju 87D-5s were passed to the Luftwaffe.

Ju 87D-3s of Grupul 6 with 'White 32' and 'White 33' visible, taking off on a mission, Rumania, 1943

Yugoslavia

In early 1945, Yugoslav Partisans led by Marshal Tito liberated a large portion of Yugoslav territory from the occupying forces. The army included air units that had been trained by and equipped with British and Soviet types as well as a number of ad-hoc units equipped with captured ex-Luftwaffe and Air Force of the Independent State of Croatia types. On the 5th January 1945 all these various air elements were formally incorporated into the new Yugoslav Air Force (Jugoslovensko Ratno Vazduhoplovstvo [JRV]) and at the same time, the Yugoslav fighter group that had been at Zemun airfield undergoing Soviet instruction became operational. On the 12th February 1945 a Ju 87B-2 (5B+ER) of NSGr 10 flown by *Ofw*. August Pautz with *Ofw*. Hermann Kübel as gunner, landed in error at Sanski Most in Bosnia while on a flight from Butmir in Sarajevo to Zagreb. The aircraft was quickly repainted with Yugoslavia markings and operated against German ground forces. On one mission it was hit by flak, knocking the entire rear canopy and MG 15

Ex-NSGr 10 Ju 878B-2 5B+ER was hastily put into Yugoslavian partisan markings as seen here, with the theatre band and 'ER' part of the original Luftwaffe markings still in place

Captured & Evaluated

United Kingdom

The Royal Air Force never operated the Ju 87, however a number of incomplete and complete airframes were captured and evaluated during WWII. The first complete Stuka to fall into British hands was Ju 87B-2, S2+LM of II./St.G 77 that crash-landed near Ventnor on the Isle of Wight on the 8th August 1940. It was too badly damaged to put back into the air though and was just studied from a technical point of view.

Other machines captured by British forces include the following:

• Ex-*Regia Aeronautica* Ju 87B-2 Trop (W/Nr.5763) of 209° *Squadriglia* made a forced landing in British-controlled territory in Libya on the 8th September 1941 when it ran out of fuel. It was repainted (and given the serial number HK827) and tested before being used by No.39 Squadron, an RAF bomber unit that operated the Martin Maryland. It remained in use from December 1941 to September 1944, after which it was grounded when corrosion was found in the wing structure and it is assumed it was scrapped shortly afterwards

• Ju 87 captured at Sidi Haneish after the Battle of El Alamein and painted with No.601 Squadron codes ('UF') and operated by that unit until March 1943

• Ju 87D unidentified machine photographed at Castel Benito, Tripoli in 1943

off, but it was soon repaired although a replacement MG 15 was never found.

From 17th August 1944 until the end of the war in Europe, Yugoslav aircraft undertook 3,500 combat sorties and accumulated 5,500 hours operational flying. By 25th May 1945 the Ju 87B-2 had undertaken 34 combat missions and accumulated 33hr and 15mins flight time. It is said that it undertook its last mission on the 28th May 1945, making it the last combat sortie of the Ju 87. It was then used by the new Yugoslavia Air Force for a short while before being passed to the Faculty of Mechanical Engineering in Belgrade. Today large parts of this airframe still exist and are held by the Yugoslav Aviation Museum in Belgrade.

The remains of Dornier 17s and a Junkers Ju 87 in a scrapyard in Britain, 2nd October 1940

(©British Official)

Ju 87D S7+?L captured by British troops in Libya and seen here with RAF roundels and fin flash replacing the Luftwaffe markings

Ex-Regia Aeronautica
Ju 87B-2 Trop W/Nr.5763
captured by British troops
in September 1941

Ju 87B-2 Trop W/Nr.5763
being flight tested after
capture by British troops
in North Africa

Ju 87R-2 T6+AN of 5./StG2
captured intact at Tmimi, Libya
in 1941

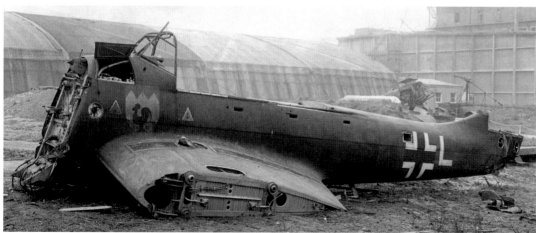

Ju 87B-2, S2+LM,
W/Nr.5600 was shot
down over the Isle of
Wight on the 8th August
1940 and the fuselage
is seen here at RAE
Farnborough where it was
examined

Ju 87R-2 W/Nr.5954 not long after arrival in the USA from North Africa as a gift from the UK for War Bonds work. Today this aircraft is displayed in the Museum of Science & Industry in Chicago, but this image gives you some idea of how battered it originally was, and how much was subsequently replaced and/or mocked-up

Ju 87R, GN+WX abandoned in North Africa being examined by US personnel
(©Life)

A Ju 87G-2 captured at Pilsen, Czechoslovakia in May 1945 being examined by USAAF personnel – many sources state this aircraft was captured at Salzburg, Austria

A typical GI's snap for the album, as he stands alongside the 3.7cm cannon of a wrecked Ju 87G

Ju 87D-8 W/Nr.100323 captured by American forces in May 1945

As Russian forces pushed towards Germany they captured many Luftwaffe aircraft on abandoned airfields, such as this Ju 87D-3

• Ju 87D captured in the Western Desert – use unknown, still retained the 'LT' part of its original Luftwaffe codes

• Ju 87G-2 (converted from D-5) W/Nr.494083, this was captured at the end of the war and held for 'Museum purposes' at various locations, but today resides in the RAF Museum, Hendon, North London.

USA

Although never operating the Stuka a number of incomplete and complete airframes were captured and evaluated by the USA during WWII. The first was Ju 87R-2 A5+HL of I./St.G 1 captured in North Africa by British forces and shipped to the USA for War Bond promotions. This aircraft exists to this day, being displayed at the Museum of Science and Industry in Chicago.

A Ju 87D-3 was captured in Tunisia and repainted in USAAF markings to be used for towing sleeve targets. It was eventually written off in a crash landing, though.

USSR

One Ju 87A-1 was sold to Russia in 1940, while the first captured machine was Ju 87D-1 (W/Nr.2754) of St.G 77 that was found at Bolszaja Rossoszka during the latter stages of the battle of Stalingrad. It was extensively tested with various bomb loads and in the summer of 1943 was part of a war trophies display in Moscow. An-

Although a Ju 87 can't be seen in this view, this is the type of war trophy display put on in Gorky Park just after the end of WWII – what would collectors pay for that lot today, not to mention the hundreds of tanks, AFVs and artillery pieces that were displayed alongside the Volga, which you can see on the right!

other Stuka eventually displayed in Moscow was the Ju 87G-1 (W/Nr.1097) mistakenly landed in error at Briansk by *Oblt*. Hans Trenkmann of Versuchsverband für Pazerkampf (Panzerjagd-kommando Weiß) in the spring of 1943.

Ju 87B, W/Nr.5670 is seen here on display at one of the many war trophies exhibits in Moscow, this time in the winter of 1941

Chapter 1: Evolution – Ju 87 Prototypes & A Series

The Ju 87 V1 in flight, the initial layout of the radiator under the chin can clearly be seen

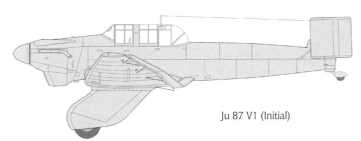

Ju 87 V1 (Initial)

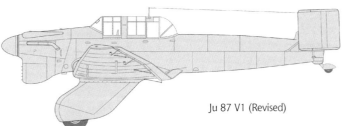

Ju 87 V1 (Revised)

The enlarged and vertical style of the new radiator can be seen on this shot of the Ju 87 V1 in its revised form

Note: Due to the large number of airframes we have to cover in this title we will not be duplicating data between sub-variants, instead we will only identify those changes in relation to the main version.

Prototypes

Ju 87 V1 (Initial)

W/Nr: 4921
First Flight: 17th September 1935
Registration: D-UBYR
The design featured a twin-spar W-cranked wing with closely-spaced ribs and smooth duralumin skin. The root stubs were built as part of the fuselage and the undercarriage legs were attached to the outer ends of these stubs, with the wing panels attached outboard. The undercarriage legs were covered by large aerodynamic spats to reduce drag and these were supported by a strut inboard and attached to the fuselage underside.

Control surfaces comprised slotted ailerons on the outer wing panels and slotted flaps on the inner section. These were attached slightly below and behind the wing trailing edge. The prototype lacked the Junkers-designed dive brakes underneath the outer wing panels, although the stubs for their attachment were present.

The tail had twin fins and rudders to give the rear gunner a wide field of fire. All control surfaces on the tail and wings were duralumin covered. A Reifendruck Schi tailwheel (180° swivel) with canvas gaiter and tear-drop shaped cover was fitted under the rear fuselage.

The fuselage had an oval cross-section formed in two halves and joined horizontally. These were built on z-section frames and hat-section stringers with a smooth duralumin covering. The pilot and gunner were seated back-to-back under a glass-house canopy with the access panels above each, hinged to starboard. A strong bulkhead/truss was located between the crew stations to protect them in case the aircraft turned over. The forward fuselage carried the mounts for the Rolls-Royce Kestrel V engine. This was a liquid-cooled, mechanically supercharged V12 that offered a maximum take-off power of 532hp and drove a two-blade, fixed-pitch wooden propeller. The initial radiator type was under the nose with angled (back) front and shutters (this was later replaced – see V1 (Revised)).

Ju 87 V1 (Revised)

W/Nr: 4921
Registration: D-IFKQ
The only revision made to the airframe was the enlargement of the water cooler radiator in the front of the chin cowling that resulted in the front being vertical in profile, rather than at an angle as per the original design. The side engine cowlings and lower cowling were revised to accommodate the new radiator.

Ju 87 V2

W/Nr: 4922
Registration: D-IDQR – Re-registered as D-UHUH 4th June 1937
First Flight: 25th February 1936
This airframe was significantly redesigned to change the tail layout, the failure of which was the cause of the fatal crash of the V1. It therefore had a large vertical fin (with a long leading edge angle) and rudder that was very similar to that used by the Ju 160. The tail was fitted with a hand-operated trimming tab, while the tailplanes were fitted with a hydraulically-actuated trimmer device. The tailplanes retained the V strut fitted at two points to the rear fuselage and its underside as seen on the V1.

It was powered by the 455kW Junkers Jumo 210Aa V12 inverted, liquid-cooled engine in completely revised cowlings with open exhaust ports and a Junkers-Hamilton HPA III three-blade, adjustable-pitch (10° adjusting range), metal propeller with revised spinner.

The wings were fitted with the Junkers-designed dive brakes, that could rotate through 90°.

Ju 87 V3

W/Nr: 4923
Registration: D-UKYQ
First Flight: 27th March 1936
This prototype was similar to the V2 with the same Jumo 210Aa engine but with thrust-line lowered slightly to give better view over the nose. The engine cowling was redesigned due to the lower thrust-line and the shape of the ventral radiator

The V2 with revisions to the engine cowls, radiator and (not visible) tail, plus it later carried armament in the rear canopy as seen here

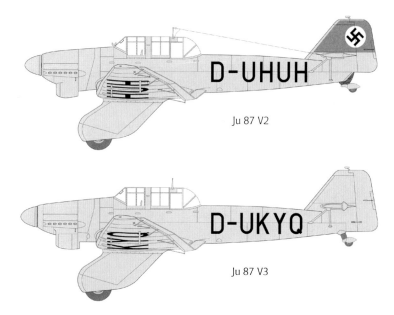

Ju 87 V2

Ju 87 V3

There are not too many images of the V3, this shows it in flight and allows you to see the slightly revised cowl top profile, enlarged tail and the landing light in the port wing

From this angle you can clearly see the original wing with the new straight leading edge, as well as the revised lower profile of the rudder and the pitot in the port wing

was also changed, having a vertical edge to the rear, whilst the V2 had this portion at an angle.

The rudder and vertical fin were enlarged to increase stability (resulting in it projecting aft of where the rear fuselage ended on the V2) and the tailplanes were now squared off (the V2 had rounded ends), with the end plates that would be common to the design now fitted on the tips at the tailplane/elevator hinge.

A landing light was installed at mid-span in the leading edge of the port wing.

It was the first prototype to be fitted with FuG VIII radio.

Ju 87 V4

W/Nr: 4924
Registration: D-UBIP
First Flight: 20th June 1936
This was basically the master for the pre-production A-0 series and it had the same Jumo 210Aa engine but with the thrust-line lowered a further 25cm and a small intake on the upper edge with revised shape to the ventral radiator (deeper).

Oblong Plexiglas viewing window added in the underside between the pilot's feet and a Zeiss-Jena Revi C/12A collimator reflector sight was installed above the instrument panel.

Revised vertical tail and rudder that was squarer and more like the production version, but with the base of the rudder at 90° to the hinge. Trim trim tabs on the rudder and the aerial leads now went to the leading edge of each tailplane, not the top of the rudder. Revised tailwheel unit that lacked a fairing over the wheel itself.

It was also fitted with armament for the first time comprising a fixed forward-firing Rheinmetall-Borsig 7.92mm MG 17 machine gun in the leading edge of the starboard wing, with 1,000 rounds of ammunition in a box in the starboard undercarriage leg spat. A flexible-mounted 7.92mm MG 15 was fitted in the rear canopy and this traversed up and down via a slot in the canopy.

Bomb trapeze arms were added under the centreline of the fuselage at the bottom edge of the engine firewall bulkhead, the upper arms incorporated a retaining/release mechanism that ensured the bomb fell clear of the propeller arc before release – it could carry a single 250 or 500 kg bomb.

It also had the semi-automatic device that initiated a pull-out from a dive after bomb release, thus helping the pilot cope with the grey- or black-out caused by the intense g-forces. This was later improved so that during pre-flight manual adjustment of the altimeter it set itself automatically to pull-out at a barometric height of 450m – this could be overridden manually by the pilot in an emergency by pushing the control column forward.

Fairing added at the base of the rear canopy to produce a vertical end to the rear canopy framework and an angled element to blend it in with the rear fuselage.

Ju 87 V4 (Revised)

W/Nr: 4924
Registration: D-UBIP
In 1937 the engine was replaced with the 477kW Jumo 211Ca, as tests had proven the original engine to be of insufficient power to fully exploit the potential of the design.

The wing was revised to make it easier to produce with the taper of the leading inboard wing edge being replaced with a straight-line version with a rounded tip. In turn the taper at the trailing edge of the wing was increased to maintain the total wing area.

Two additional oil cooling intakes added on either side of the nose, while the radiator under the chin was now squarer.

The rudder was revised with an extension at the bottom and an enlarged fairing for the tailwheel.

An angled pitot tube was added to the leading edge of the port wing.

This aircraft was used in the winter and spring of 1937 to determine the optimum bomb pattern with 250 and 500kg bombs as well as SC10 anti-personnel bombs.

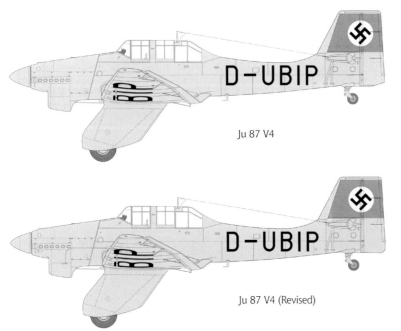

Ju 87 V4

Ju 87 V4 (Revised)

In this shot of the V5 you can clearly see the parachute pods above each wing tip, plus on the starboard side you can just make out the 'rails' added along the centreline of the upper wing surface

Ju 87 V5

W/Nr: 4925 (some sources state 4955?)
Registration: None
First Flight: 14th August 1936
This prototype tested the installation of the Junkers Jumo 210Da two-stage supercharged engine that used 87 octane fuel. It was also fitted with cameras and braking parachutes in pods above each wing tips and a series of metal tubes like grab rails were attached along the main spar on the upper surface of each wing, presumably for testing stress on these spars during diving trials. The upper surfaces of the wings also had tuffs attached in numerous places, probably to look at air flow during diving trials.

Ju 87A-0

Ten built – W/Nrs: 0001 to 0011
Registrations: D-IEAA to D-IEAK
This pre-production series were the same as the Ju 87 V4 (Revised) except some used the Junkers Jumo 210Aa, while others used the Jumo 210Ca engine.

The only other revision was that early machines had a ring-type control column top (KG 11), while later this was replaced with a straight type (KG 12).

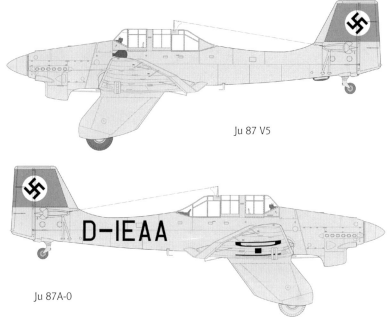

Ju 87 V5

Ju 87A-0

Ju 87A-1

Ten built – W/Nrs: 0012 to 0021
Registrations: D-IEAU to N/K
This first production series was similar to the Ju 87A-0 except they used the Junkers Jumo 210Ca (476kW) engine (*some list the Jumo 210D*) driving

This is the fourth A-0 series airframe produced (D-IEAD) and is it basically identical to the V4 externally, the only changes being the engine and control column type

This shot of Ju 87A-1 52+A11 as it warms up its engine somewhere in Germany in 1938 nicely illustrates the MG 15 machine-gun in the rear canopy

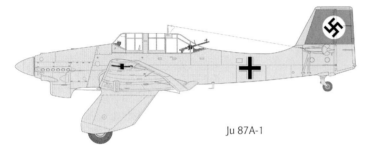

Ju 87A-1

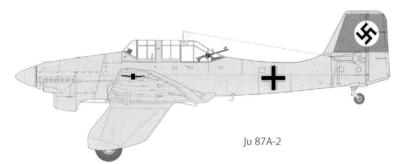

Ju 87A-2

drums, fourteen of which were carried.

The series had an ETC 500/A bomb rack under the fuselage centreline and two ETC 50 racks under each outer wing panel. This gave a centre-line bomb capacity of 500kg if flown solo (ballast required in gunner's position to retain CofG) or 250kg with two crew.

Ju 87A-2

This series was basically the same as the Ju 87A-1 except it used the Junkers Jumo 210Da (507kW) engine with two-speed supercharger driving a three-blade, two-position, Junkers-Hamilton 10° adjusting range HPA II (up to W/Nr.0870156) or three-blade, two-position, Junkers-Hamilton 20° adjusting range HPA III (from W/Nr.870157) propeller.

The undercarriage had heavier undercarriage spats.

There was a slight revision to the trailing edge of the vertical fin, resulting in it being more rounded plus the trim tabs were in a revised layout and there was a revised fairing at the base of the rudder stern post (aft of the tailwheel).

An improved radio installation saw the fitment of an Ei V intercommunication system between pilot and gunner with speech/transmitting for the pilot and speech/telegraphy for the gunner.

Photographed at Franconia in early 1940, this A-2 also has the fronts of each spat cut away, this was quite common when operating from muddy runways

a three-blade, two-position, Junkers-Hamilton 10° adjusting range HPA II propeller.

The type was armed with a fixed forward-firing Rheinmetall-Borsig 7.92mm MG 17 machine gun in the leading edge of the starboard wing, with 500 rounds of ammunition in a box in the under-carriage leg spat. It also had a flexible-mounted Rheinmetall-Borsig 7.92mm MG 15 in the rear canopy, traversing up and down via a Junkers slot-ted mount and using 75-round metal ammunition

Specifications		
	Ju 87 V4	Ju 87A-1
Span	13.00m	13.80m
Length	10.80m	10.82m
Height	3.77m	4.23m
Weight – Empty	2,273kg	2,300kg
Weight – Maximum	3,324kg	3,400kg
Maximum speed		
Level flight	320km/h	320km/h
Dive	550km/h	449km/h
Range	995km	1,000km
Ceiling	9,430m	7,000m

Chapter 2: **Evolution – Ju 87B & R Series**

Note: For camouflage and marking details for this series please see Chapter 4.

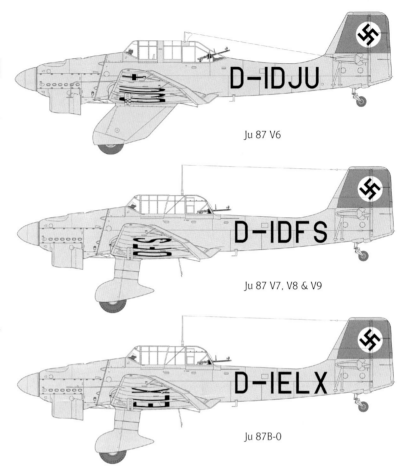

Ju 87 V6

Ju 87 V7, V8 & V9

Ju 87B-0

Prototypes

Ju 87 V6

W/Nr: 087-0027
Registration: D-IDJU
First Flight: 14th June 1937
This was basically an A-1 series airframe fitted with the Junkers Jumo 211A1 (708kW) inverted-V, liquid-cooled engine. This was not a true B-series prototype, it was just the first test installation of the Jumo 211. The fitment of the engine did however mean that everything forward of the engine firewall was redesigned.

Ju 87 V7, V8 & V9

W/Nrs: 087-0028, 087-4926 & 087-4927
Registration: D-IDFS, None & D-IELZ (some state D-IDLX)
First Flight: 23rd August 1937 (V7), 11th November 1937 (V8) and 16th February 1938 (V9, which was re-registered as WL-IELZ 16th October 1939)
These were the first true B-series prototypes and they were all like the V6 in that they used the Jumo 211A engine with its associated changes forward of the firewall. The glycol cooler under the chin was deeper and rounded and had vertical rather than horizontal shutters. An oil cooler was added above the engine with air fed into it via an asymmetric intake, this intake was wider on the port side and the air was controlled by a flap at the rear. The air for the supercharger was fed via a protruding intake on the starboard side of the engine cowling.

The undercarriage was completely revised comprising a cantilever leg with telescopic upper cover and lower streamlined spats without support struts. The undercarriage shock absorber was hydro-pneumatic and the fairings were identical, so they could be swapped port for starboard and vice versa.

A new canopy and windscreen assembly was installed, this was now in four sections with access for the pilot and gunner being achieved with the section above each sliding aft. The new cockpit and canopy resulted in changes to the dorsal spine. A single radio mast was fitted in the upper/rear of the (fixed) mid canopy section and there was a tube for the trailing aerial on the underside.

The cockpit interior was revised as was the instrumentation and the new KG 12A control column was standard (replacing the older KG 11 version). The Revi C/12A sight was replaced with the Revi C/12C. In the gunner's position the MG 15 mount and gunner's seat were relocated. The radio equipment remained unchanged as FuG VIII with Ei V intercommunication. The truss/overturn frame between the pilot and gunner's position was replaced with a new one cast from magnesium for extra strength.

Armament was upgraded with the addition of a second MG 17 in the port wing and the ammunition boxes for each gun were accommodated in the inner wing structure. An ETC 50 rack could be fitted under each outer wing panel and bomb capacity doubled to 500kg.

B-Series Production

Ju 87B-0

W/Nrs: N/K
Registration: D-IELX (first)
The ten pre-production B-0s incorporated all the revisions seen in the V6 to V9, about the only visual change was the angled pitot, which was replaced with a straight one in the leading edge of the starboard wing.

D-IELX was the first pre-production B-0 series airframe and at the time this photograph was taken it did not have the MG 15 installed

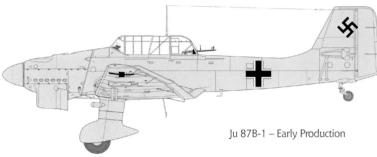

Ju 87B-1 – Early Production

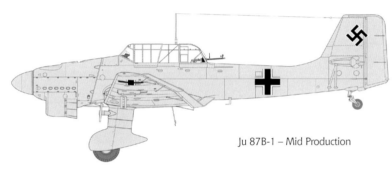

Ju 87B-1 – Mid Production

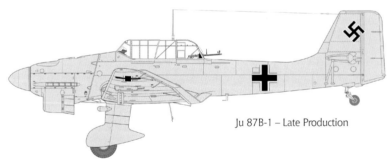

Ju 87B-1 – Late Production

T6+JS of 7./StG2 is seen here in 1939 and it exhibits all the traits of the early production B-1 series, although it lacks the siren stubs on the undercarriage legs and does not have any wing guns fitted, as their fairings are blanked off

Ju 87B-1 – Early Production

Built – 311 by Junkers (from W/Nr.0217), Weser built 386* (from W/Nr.5070)
*These included R-1 variants

This first main production series incorporated all the revisions seen in the V6 to V9 prototypes and B-0 pre-production machines but they adopted the Jumo 211Da 820kW 12-cylinder, 60° inverted-vee, liquid-cooled engine driving a Junkers-Hamilton three-blade, two-position, 20° adjusting range propeller. The type also had provision to fit a camera in the leading edge of both wings (faired over when not in use) and the radio equipment was upgraded to the FuG VIIa with Ei V intercommunication.

The segmented flaps at the rear of the radiator with the hinges visible on the outside mark this down as a mid-production B-1 airframe

Ju 87B-1 – Mid Production

Same as Ju 87B-1 – Early Production
The only change seen at this stage was the fitment of segmented, hinged, movable cooling flaps on the rear underside of the radiator cowling.

Ju 87B-1 – Late Production

Same as Ju 87B-1 – Early Production
These last production machines adopted ejector exhausts with associated revisions to the surrounding cowling area.

Ju 87B-1 Trop

These machines were modified for operations in the Middle East and as such had a sand/dust filter fitted to the supercharger intake and desert survival equipment carried in the fuselage/wings.

Ju 87B-2

This version was basically similar to the Ju 87B-1 except it used the Junkers Jumo 211Da (908kW) engine with direct fuel injection driving an HPA III metal propeller with automatic rpm governor. From the start the series used the ejector exhausts with associated revised cowling area as seen on late production Ju 87B-1s. The radiator had a deeper intake and the segmented, hinged, movable cooling flaps on the rear underside of the radiator had the hinges inside, so they were not visible externally. The engine starter point on the lower port side of the engine cowling now had a hinged cover.

To reduce the tendency to nose-over the forward rake of each undercarriage leg was increased slightly. The lower undercarriage covers were enlarged to deal with larger 815mm x 290mm tyres and a new version of the wind-driven siren was fitted to each.

A small diameter air intake was created in the leading edge of the wing between the MG 17 and landing light, to take fresh air to the cockpit.

Muzzle brakes were often fitted to the wing-mounted MG 17s.

Ju 87B-2 (Late production)

Same as Ju 87B-2
Late production machines featured revised armour around the rear gun position (2 styles). The propeller changed to a wooden 3.4m diameter VS 5 or 11 unit with broad-chord, adjustable-pitch type blades The trailing aerial mast was removed from the underside and these machines all seem to have had the Peil G.IV D/F loop in the blister in place of the trailing aerial mast.

FuG 25 IFF was installed, with associated flexible rod antenna under the aft fuselage (offset slightly to port).

This late production B-1 of II./SG 2 is being loaded with a 250kg bomb, but you can clearly see the late style ejector exhausts and single-piece rear radiator flap without visible hinges (the rear upper cowl flap is also open)

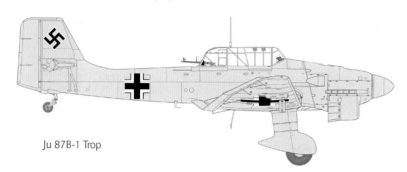

Ju 87B-1 Trop

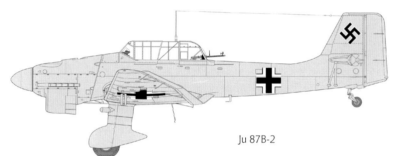

Ju 87B-2

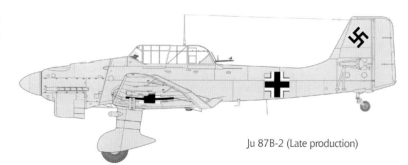

Ju 87B-2 (Late production)

S2+LM of 4./StG77 is a typical production B-2 series and is seen here serving in Russia in 1941

S2+MM of 4./StG 77 is a later production B-2 and has the compressed wood propeller blades and, just visible, has adopted additional armour plate in the lower quarter of the rear (gunner's) canopy

The big (squarer) tropical filter over the supercharger intake is a good indicator of the 'Tropical' modification

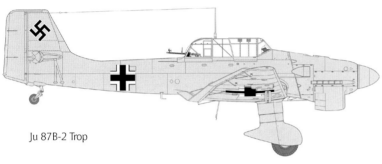

Ju 87B-2 Trop

Ju 87B-2 Trop

These machines were modified for operations in the Middle East and as such had a sand/dust filter fitted to the supercharger intake and desert survival equipment carried in the fuselage and wings.

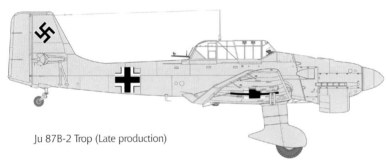

Ju 87B-2 Trop (Late production)

Ju 87B-2 Trop (Late production)

These were the same as the B-2 (Late production) combined with all the desert equipment seen in the B-2 Trop.

R-Series Prototypes

Ju 87 V15, V16, V17 & V18

Ju 87 V15, V16, V17 & V18

W/Nr: 087-031 (V15), 087-0279 (V16) & N/K (V17 & V18)
Registration: D-IGHK (V15) & None (V17 & V18)
Stammkennzeichen: GT + AX (V16)
Little is known about these prototypes for the R-series, but we suspect they tested the fitment of additional fuel tanks in the outer wing panels and/ or the carriage of a 300lt drop tank under each wing. The V15 was destroyed in a crash in 1942 and it is not known if the V17 & V18 were ever actually built.

R-Series Production

Ju 87R-1

Although of poor quality, this is the only known image of the V15 in its initial form that related to the R-series (it later went on to be a D-series prototype), oddly though it carries no drop tanks under the wings at this stage

Developed alongside the Ju 87B-1 and being externally identical the type had a 150lt fuel tank fitted in each outer wing panel. The fuel supply system was revised to allow the carriage of a 300lt drop tank under each outer wing panel – the tank was only ever filled to 295lt though). The weight of the additional fuel meant that bomb capacity was reduced to just 250kg.
Note: R = Reichweite (range)

Ju 87R-1 A5 + HK of I./StG 1 nicely illustrates the carriage of a 300lt drop tank under each outer wing panel

Ju 87R-2

Based on the Ju 87B-2, this was similar to the R-1 but did not have the 150lt tanks in the outer wings seen in that type.

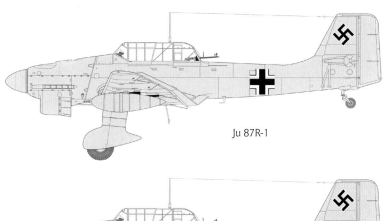

Ju 87R-1

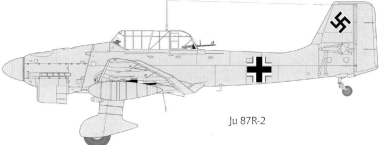

Ju 87R-2

Groundcrew pose alongside a Ju 87R-2. somewhere in Russia

A Ju 87R-2 of III./StG_2 during operations in Greece in 1941

Although this Ju 87R-2 (6G+CB) from Stab I./StG1 does not have tanks fitted, you can see the dark area in the lower quarter of the rear canopy, where additional armour has been installed – it is photographed here being escorted by a Fiat G.50 of 350° Squadriglia in North Africa in 1941

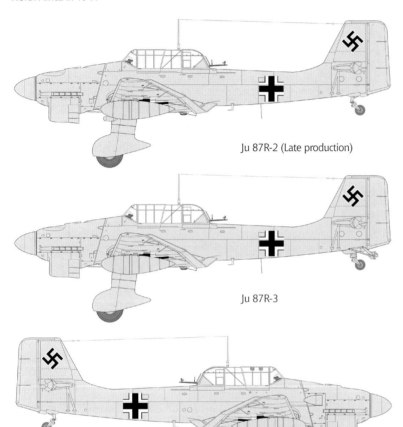

Ju 87R-2 (Late production)

Ju 87R-3

Ju 87R-4

Ju 87R-2 (Late production)

These late production machines had revised armour around the rear gun position (2 styles). The trailing aerial mast was removed from the underside to make way for the Peil G.IV D/F loop under its Plexiglass cover. The type also had FuG 25 IFF installed, with its associated flexible rod antenna under the aft fuselage (offset slightly to port).

Ju 87R-3

It is claimed that only a small number of this variant was produced, they were the same as the Ju 87R-2 but were used to tow gliders, with a tow-cable pick-up via a bridle mounted to either side of the rear fuselage.

Ju 87R-4

These were identical to the Ju 87R-2 Trop but they had all the desert/survival equipment installed on the production line instead of being fitted retrospectively. The type also featured a modified lubrication system to cope with the high engine wear associated with operating for long periods.

Ju 87R-1 Trop

These machines were retrospectively modified (at manufacturer or unit level) for operations in the Middle East and as such had a sand/dust filter fitted to the supercharger intake and desert/survival equipment carried in the fuselage/wings.

Ju 87R-2 Trop

These were the same as the Ju 87R-2 with a sand/dust filter fitted to the supercharger intake and desert/survival equipment carried in the fuselage/wings.

Ju 87R-4 A5+HR of I./StG 1 in North Africa with a 250kg bomb under the fuselage and bundles of fragmentation bombs under each outer wing panel. Both the wing guns and siren have been removed and their fairings blanked over

Although this may in fact be an R-2, 6G+KS of 8./StG 51 was based in Sicily in 1942 and has the supercharger filter associated with the tropical upgrade

Umrüst-Bausätze sets (Ju 87B-1 & R-1)

- U1 – Fighter-bomber with one ETC 500/IXb centreline bomb rack fitted
- U2 – Revised FuG radio equipment
- U3 – Extra armour plates added to protect both crew and engine. Some fitted with a special rear gun armoured mounting with bulbous ring as seen on the Ju 88
- U4 – Modified for carrier-born Tägergruppe experiments in 1941

Umrüst-Bausätze sets (Ju 87B-2 & R-2/R-3/R-4)

- U1 – Various modifications made during B-2 production was retrospectively covered by this U-number
- U2 – Improved internal radio equipment, with adoption of EiV 1a intercom
- U3 – Extra armour plates added to protect both crew and engine. Plates fitted below the cockpit and rear gun position, as well as a plate that could be rotated to cover the open area in the overturn framework behind the pilot's head
- U4 – Replacement of wheels with skis for operations in the Arctic areas of Norway and northern Russia

Specifications

	Ju 87B-1	Ju 87B-2	Ju 87R-2
Span	13.8m	13.8m	13.8m
Length	11.00m	11.00m	11.00m
Height	4.23m	4.23m	4.23m
Weight – Empty	2,750kg	2,750kg	2,750kg
Weight – Maximum	4,340kg	4,340kg	5,650kg
Speed			
Cruising	325km/h	280km/h	280km/h
Maximum	380km/h	380km/h	340km/h
Service ceiling	8,000m	8,000m	8,000m
Range	800km	600km	1,450km

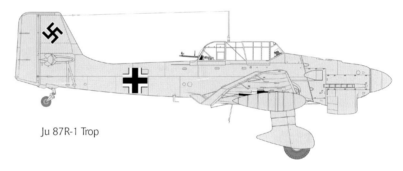

Ju 87R-1 Trop

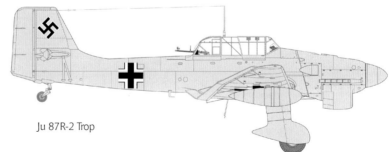

Ju 87R-2 Trop

Ju 87R-2 T6+M of 4./StG2 is seen in flight over the Mediterranean coastline of North Africa and is fitted with the Umrüst-Bausätze 3 set comprising a Ju 88A-style armoured rear gun ring, plus additional armour plates along the lower edges of the rear and mid-canopy sections

Chapter 3: Evolution – Ju 87D & G Series

This is a Ju 87 V21 an ex-Ju 87B-1 fitted here with the Jumo 211P, but later fitted with a Jumo 211F

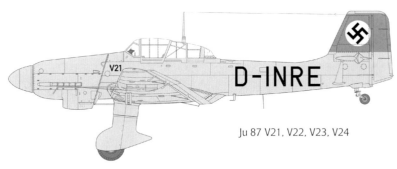

Ju 87 V21, V22, V23, V24

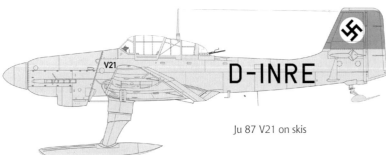

Ju 87 V21 on skis

This is the Ju 87 V21 after suffering the collapse (and shearing off) of the starboard undercarriage leg and ski during trials

D-Series Prototypes

Ju 87 V21, V22, V23, V24

W/Nrs. 087-0536, 087-0540, 087-0542 and 087-0544

These prototypes were based on the Ju 87B airframe but were fitted with the Junkers Jumo 211F 1,144kW engine in a revised cowling, with no oil cooler on the top (it was moved underneath the nose), so the top profile followed a smooth line. The engine drove a Junkers VS 11 3.46m diameter, variable-pitch, three-blade metal propeller (initially tested the Heine wooden unit, but this was found to split). The supercharger air intake was made more streamlined and was moved forward on the starboard engine cowling.

The glycol cooler was moved to two shallow units fitted under each inboard wing stub.

The canopy was streamlined with a tapered rear section with a GSL-k 81Z mount for a Mauser MG 81Z machine-gun. The pilot's seat, cockpit sides, floor and bulkhead behind the pilot were improved and became standard for all future variants.

The horizontal tailplane support was revised with the area between the 'V' of the original variants now solid to create a streamlined bracing strut, and the vertical fin was enlarged.

Ju 87 V21 on skis

W/Nr. 087-0536

This airframe (along with a number of production D-series airframes) tested the fitment of skis in place of the standard main and tail wheels. This particular airframe had a multi-head test probe in the leading edge of the port wing and although unarmed it did retain the multi-function racks under each outer wing panel.

D-Series Production

Ju 87D-1

The first production variant was the same as the V21 to V24 but used the Junkers Jumo 211J engine that could be fitted with exhaust flame dampers. An MG 81Z twin machine-gun was fitted in the GSL-k 81Z mount in the rear canopy, with 2,000 rounds fed by belts from bins mounted on each fuselage side. The Peil G.IV D/F loop was relocated under a clear panel on the dorsal spine behind the canopy. The pilot's seat was reinforced with 4mm (side) and 8mm (rear), while the rear gunner was protected by 5mm (floor) and 8mm (transverse bulkhead) armour plate

Initial machines had a revised undercarriage but after trials they proved to be weak, so were replaced with the leg and yoke of the B-series, so the covers retained the wind-driven siren.

The type was suitable for tropical conditions from the outset and additional auxiliary oil tanks were installed in the cockpit and near the engine.

The type could also carry a Waffenbehälter WB81A or B under each wing containing three MG 81Zs inclined downwards at 15° (WB81A) or firing forward at 0° (WB81B) with trays of 250rpg, or an WB FF pod with a 20mm MG FF cannon. The maximum offensive payload was increased – a PC 1800 (1,800kg) bomb could be carried under the centreline via a revised rack/bridle, while the outer wing panels featured a new type of triple bomb rack under a single cover that could carry either two 50kg or a single 250kg bomb, a wooden (AB250 or AB500) container for SD 2 or SD 4 anti-personnel bombs or a 300lt drop tank.

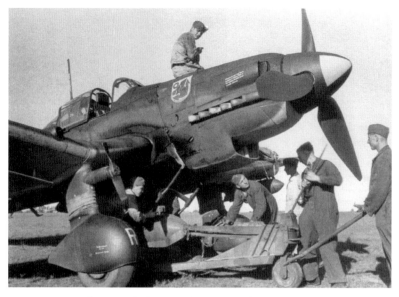

Ju 87D-1 J9 + RR of 7./SG1, which operated at Kursk in July 1943

Ju 87D-1 (Late production)

These later machines were the same as the main production D-1 except a small (air) exhaust bulge was added to the side of the lower starboard engine cowling, aft/below the exhausts.

An improved and strengthened undercarriage was incorporated, which was intended to have explosive bolts to allow either or both legs to be ejected in an emergency, however these proved to be very unreliable, so it was not until the D-5 that this feature became standard. The lower covers were smaller and the gap over the sliding oleo was protected by a canvas cover, and they no longer incorporated the wind-driven siren.

Ju 87D-2

Was intended to be as per the D-1 but with revised armament – not proceeded with (note some sources state this was a glider-towing variant, but all D-series could be modified to two gliders)

Ju 87D-3

This variant came about due to the increased use of the Stuka in the ground-attack role. It was the same as the D-1 (Late production) but it had increased protection via bulletproof (50mm) glass added (externally) to the windscreen and armour plates to the fuselage and engine undersides, plus the use of armoured coolant hoses and armour plate on the two coolant radiators under the wing stubs.

The series also featured revised exhaust stacks with the fairing removed from the front.

This Ju 87D-3 (S7 + EP) from 6./StG 3 was captured by US forces at El Aouina, Tunisia in November 1942 (©USAAF)

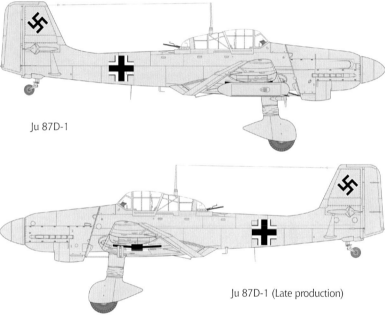

Ju 87D-1

Ju 87D-1 (Late production)

Ju 87D-3

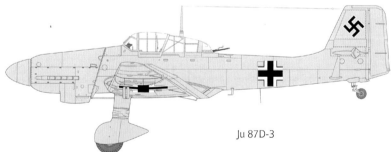

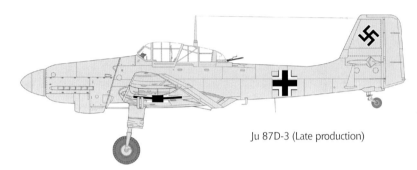

Ju 87D-3 S2+NM of 4./StG 77 in Russia in 1943

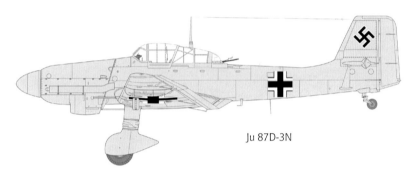

Ju 87D-3 (Late production)

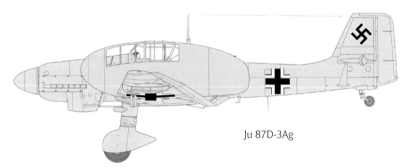

Ju 87D-3N

Ju 87D-3Ag

Ju 87D-3 (Late production)

These later machines were the same as D-3 except the wing walkways were simplified via metal strips and 100% mass-balanced ailerons were installed instead of original three-position system.

Ju 87D-3N

Field modified D-3 airframes fitted with the more powerful Jumo 211P (1,118kW) engine with flame dampers fitted to the exhausts (four styles are known). The dive brakes were removed and muzzle blast suppressors were fitted to the wing guns. The radio was upgraded to the FuG 16ZY and later machines used the Revi C/16DN gunsight.

Ju 87D-3Ag

A series of airframes were used by the Graf Zeppelin Research facility at Stuttgart-Ruit to test the fitment of a two-man (seated in tandem) gondola fitted above the centre-section of either or both wings. The unit was streamlined with a curved top and oval-section bodies. Each was equipped with a parachute and could be jettisoned in an emergency. A series of square glazed panels had to be added along both sides of the top of each gondola to improve lateral vision for the pilot. The system was impractical and the whole project was abandoned. *Ag = Agentenflugzeug (agent's aircraft)*

This Ju 87D-3N from NSGr 1 was captured by British troops in Northern Germany at the end of the war

This starboard side view of one of the D-3s used by the Graf Zeppelin Research facility clearly shows just how bulky the two-man pods were and how much of the pilot's vision they obscured

Ju 87 V25

W/Nr. 087-0538 (some state 48928)
Stammkennzeichen: BK + EF

This prototype was converted from a D1 and was fitted with the revised fuel system of the R-series and a 300lt drop tank under each outer wing panel.

Note: Some state this was designated the Ju 87D-3 To

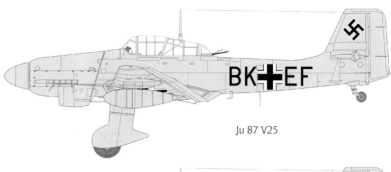

Ju 87 V25

Ju 87 V25

W/Nr. 087-0538 (some state 48928)
Stammkennzeichen: BK + EF

This prototype was converted from a D1 and was fitted with an ETC 2000 XII bomb release between the bridle under the centre-section for the carriage of a LT-5w (765kg) torpedo for the proposed D-4 series.

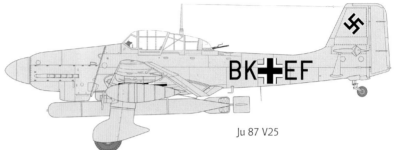

Ju 87 V25

Ju 87D-4

These were the same as the V25 but were based on the standard D-3 airframe.

This June 1941 requirement, was not proceeded with and all airframes were converted back to their original configuration.

In this shot of the Ju 87 V25 (BK + EF) you can see the LT-5w torpedo under the fuselage and one of the the 300lt drop tanks under the port wing

Aircrew of I./SG3 awaiting briefing at Immola in June 1944 with one of their Ju 87D-5s in the background *(©SA-Kuva)*

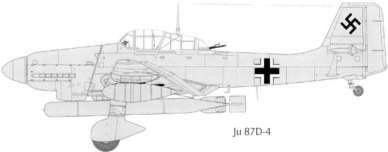

Ju 87D-4

Staffelkapitän Hans Hannes Topfer and his gunner in the cockpit of Ju 87D-5 S7 + AH of 1./SG 3 at Immola in June 1944 *(©SA-Kuva)*

Although not the greatest quality image it does show what seems to be a squadron of D-4s, although the stripes on the torpedo warheads probably indicate they are inert and thus this was only a training unit

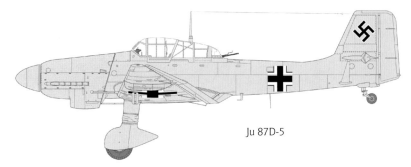

Ju 87D-5

Ju 87D-5

Production of this variant started in early 1943 and was basically the same as the D-3 except the wing span was increased from 13.81m to 15.00m (some sources state 14.98m) by extending and tapering the outer wing panels, and this new wing featured elongated 100% mass-balanced ailerons.

Having sorted out the problems associated with it, the undercarriage oleo legs now featured the explosive bolts, initially intended for the D-1, that allowed either or both legs to be ejected in an emergency (some early production machines did not have this installed though).

The MG 17 in each wing was replaced with a Mauser MG 131/20 cannon with 500rpg.

The ventral vision panel between the pilot's feet was reinforced and the auxiliary oil tank was moved to the engine bulkhead.

The automatic pull-out and bomb-release system were separated and the fuel consumption system and accessibility switch was replaced by an rpm selection lever.

The bomb racks were enlarged.

771 built of 1,178 ordered – production ceased in July 1944 (last true Ju 87 variant built).

Ju 87D-5 (Stuvi)

Same as Ju 87D-5 except:
• Top of windscreen bulged to clear Stuvi 5B dive-bombing sight that was fitted inside the top of the canopy frame.

Ju 87D-5 6G+IM of 4./SG1 showing that it still retained the dive brakes, even though the type was rarely used in that role by this time and the new wing bomb racks allow the carriage of 50kg or 240kg (as here) bombs, fitted here with fuse extenders

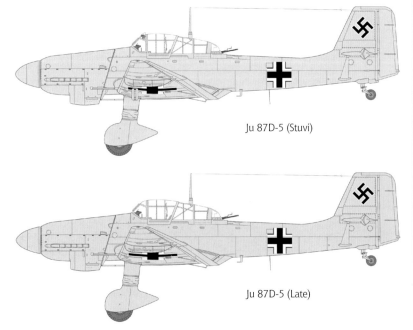

Ju 87D-5 (Stuvi)

Ju 87D-5 (Late)

Ju 87D-5 S7+EH of 1./SG3 at Immola in July 1944 has the bulge in the upper windscreen associated with the fitment of the Stuvi 5B sight (©SA-Kuva)

Ju 87D-5 (Late)

The dive brakes were removed when dive bombing was officially abandoned on the 10th October 1943, just their support stubs remained under each wing. The Peil G.IV D/F loop was installed under a clear panel on dorsal spine, aft of rear canopy.

Ju 87D-5N

Field modified D-5 airframes fitted with the more powerful Jumo 211P (1,118kW) engine with flame dampers fitted to the exhausts (four styles are known). The dive brakes were removed and muzzle blast suppressors were fitted to the wing MG 151/20 cannon. The radio was upgraded to the FuG 16ZY and later machines could use the Revi C/16DN gunsight.

Ju 87D-6

Was intended to be the 'rationalised' version – not proceeded with.

Ju 87D-7

D-3 airframes were modified at the end of 1943 and beginning of 1944 by Metallwerk Niedersachsen, Brinkmann und Mergell. The engine was upgraded to the more powerful Jumo 211P (1,118kW) and flame dampers were fitted to the exhausts (three styles are known). The dive brakes were removed and muzzle blast suppressors were fitted to the MG 151/20 cannon. The radio was upgraded to the FuG 16ZY.
Note: Some sources list these as Ju 87D-3N

This Ju 87D-5, W/Nr.142103, V8+TD operated NSG1 (Nord) was captured at Neubiberg in 1945 and you can clearly see how it had the dive brakes removed, just resulting in their brackets remaining under the wings

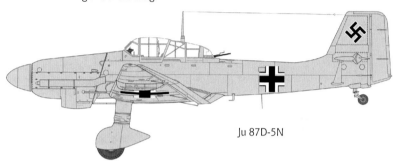

Ju 87D-5N

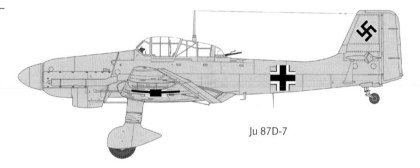

Ju 87D-7

A Ju 87D-7 of NSG9 flown by Hans Wolfsen and Hans Wilk and photographed in Italy in August 1944 – note the exhaust flame damper style and the squiggle pattern of RLM 76 applied over the upper surface colours

A partially burnt-out Ju 87D-5N found on an airfield in 1945

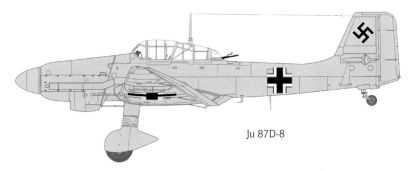

Ju 87D-8

Some sources list this as a Ju 87D-5N, but this D-8 (W/Nr.141084) was operated by NSG4 and was abandoned in Czechoslovakia in May 1945

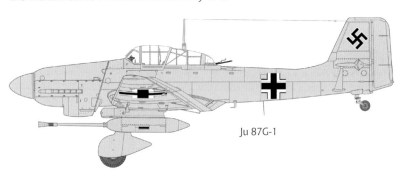

Ju 87G-1

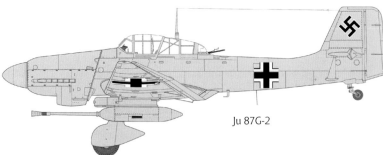

Ju 87G-2

Ju 87D-8

D-5 airframes were modified at the end of 1943 and beginning of 1944 by Metallwerk Niedersachsen, Brinkmann und Mergell. The engine was upgraded to the more powerful Jumo 211P (1,118kW) and flame dampers were fitted to the exhausts (three styles are known). The dive brakes were removed and muzzle blast suppressors were fitted to the MG 151/20 cannon. The radio was upgraded to the FuG 16ZY.
Note: Some sources list these as Ju 87D-5N

Ju 87G-1

These were all rebuilt from the D-3 and had a BK 3.7cm Flak 18 cannon (with twelve tungsten-cored, armour-piercing rounds) fitted in a gondola under each wing; the wing itself had the armament and capacity to have bomb racks removed, plus the dive brakes were also removed. The removal of the wing armament resulted in the streamlined fairings for these in the leading edge remaining, but being faired over. The type also had the additional oil tank and oxygen equipment of the D-3 series removed. The exact number of G-1s built is unknown.
Note: The Flak 18 installation was first tested under the wings of a Ju 87D-1 at Rechlin in December 1942

Ju 87G-2

These were all rebuilt D-5s and featured all the revisions seen on the G-1 but utilising the extended span of the base variant. Sometimes you will find period images of the type with flame dampers on the exhausts. A total of 174 G-2s were built.

Specifications	
	Ju 87D-1
Span	13.80m
Length	11.00m (some sources state 11.50m)
Height	4.23m
Weight	Empty 3,900g; Maximum 6,600kg
Speed	Cruising 320km/h; Maximum 400km/h
	Diving 550km/h* or 650km/h**
Ceiling	7,300m
Range	1,530km
*Over 2,000m **Under 2,000m*	

This Ju 87G-1 (GS+??) was one of the first production prototypes and was used by 10.(Pz)/SG3 for trials with the new cannon installation

Chapter 4: **Evolution – Ju 87C, E, F, H & Ju 187 Series**

As some of the types in this section were only produced in a very limited number, whilst others were a single prototype or never got any further than the drawing board, we have decided to cover them all together in this single chapter.

C-Series Prototypes

Ju 87 V10

W/Nr: 4928
Registration: D-IHFH (later TK+HD)
Built for the *Trägerflugzeug* programme in 1938, this machine featured only the arrestor hook and fuselage strengthening associated with deck landings.

Ju 87 V11

W/Nr: 4929
Registration: D-ILGM (later TV+OV)
Like the V10, this machine was also built in 1938 for the *Trägerflugzeug* programme. It was the first to feature outer wing panels that would fold up and backwards electrically – the overall span was reduced from 13.80m to 13.00m. It also had the arrestor hook and fuselage strengthening associated with deck landings.

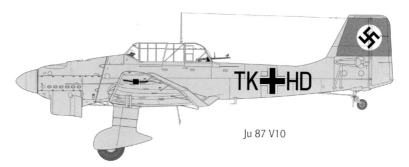

Ju 87 V10

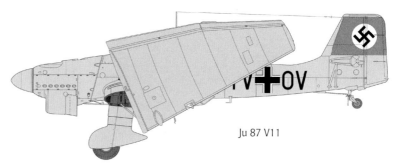

Ju 87 V11

C-Series Production

Ju 87C-0

Ten of these were built and they were virtually B-series airframes with the outer wing panels modified to fold up and backwards electrically – the overall span was reduced from 13.80m to 13.00m.

A nice overall shot of the Ju 87 V10, you can just make out the arrestor hook under the rear fuselage

This is one of a series of official images of a Ju 87C-1, note the arrestor hook under the tail and the access panel open on the inboard upper wing associated with the swivel joint for the wing fold

The aft fuselage was strengthened to withstand the loads of an arrested carrier deck landing and a retractable arrestor hook was fitted under the tail, while catapult launching gear was fitted and the fuselage was locally strengthened. Two rubber floatation bags were fitted in the fuselage with two more

inside the leading edge of each wing. The type also carried survival equipment including lift rafts and there was no ventral D/F loop or IFF mast.

The undercarriage legs were fitted with explosive bolts, so they could be jettisoned individually in an emergency (and thus make for safer landing in water – this was later introduced in the D-1 series).

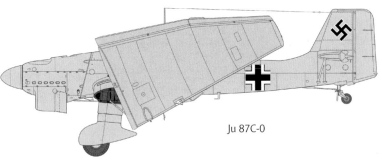

Ju 87C-0

Ju 87C-1

Based on the Ju 87B-1 with all modifications seen on the Ju 87C-0, once work on the carrier *Graf Zeppelin* was stopped, these aircraft were converted to B-2 standard.

Ju 87C-2

These were to be based on the Ju 87B-2 with all modifications seen on the Ju 87C-0. 170 were ordered, but only a few completed before all were cancelled and any actually completed would have been converted back to B-2s as per the C-1.

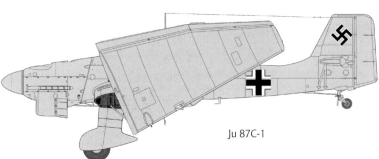

Ju 87C-1

Projects

Ju 87E-1

This was a projected variant that was basically to have been a 'navalised' version of the D-series with the same modifications seen in the C-series. It was never proceeded with.

Note: The Ju 87 V25 acted as the prototype for the series, see Chapter 3 for more details.

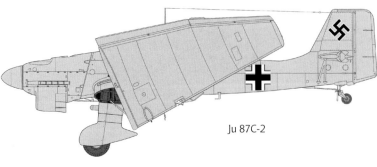

Ju 87C-2

Ju 87B with Jumo 213

(Ju 87F related)
This was part of the improvement programme for the D-series (Ju 87F), where an existing B-series airframe was fitted with the Jumo 213 engine in a revised cowl with a huge ventral radiator unit. The installation was only to test the feasibility of installing the engine in the Ju 87 airframe, so it was never intended as a true prototype for the projected F-series.

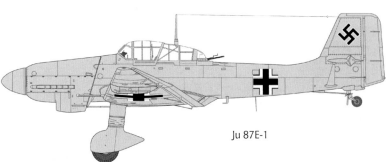

Ju 87E-1

Ju 87F

This was intended to be an improved version of the D-series with the more powerful Jumo 213 engine and incorporating a new wing. Modifications of the initial design led to this later being given a whole new designation: Ju 187 (see elsewhere).

Ju 87H-1

This was the D-1 converted for pilot training. The rear gunner's seat was removed and replaced with a forward-facing one (Ar 96 pilot's seat). The rear-facing MG 81Z was removed along with all its associated ammunition storage and the GSL-k 81Z mounting was also removed and blanked off. Full dual controls were installed with a second instrument panel in the former gunner's compartment and the mid/rear canopy was revised and bulged to improve forward visibility. Additional armour plate was added aft of Bulkhead 5.

Ju 87H-3

This was the D-3 with the modification as per the H-1.

Ju 87H-5

This was the D-5 with the modification as per the H-1.

Ju 87H-7

This was the D-7 with the modification as per the H-1.

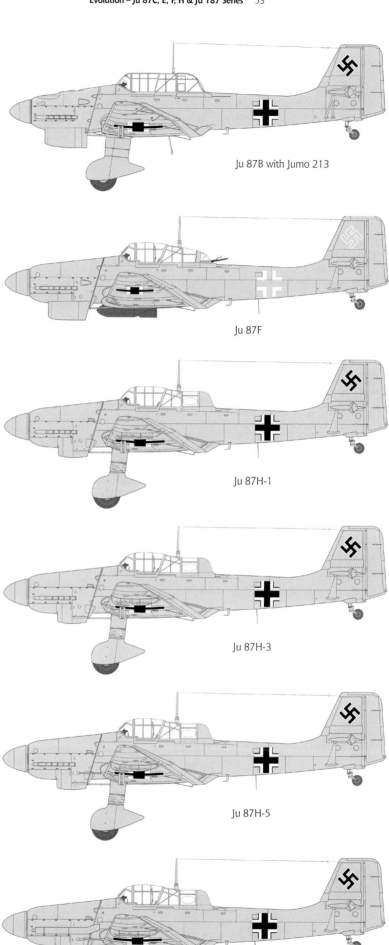

Ju 87B with Jumo 213

Ju 87F

Ju 87H-1

Ju 87H-3

Ju 87H-5

Ju 87H-7

The only photograph we have ever seen of the Ju 87B fitted with the Jumo 213E engine, taken when it landed in a field at Kirchheim Teck near the Hirth aircraft factory

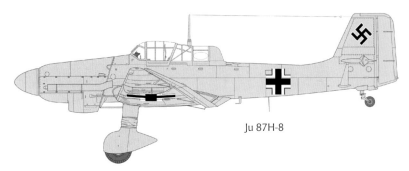

Ju 87H-8

There are few images of the original Ju 287 Stuka project, this one shows the mock-up of the cockpit area, so you can see how foreshortened the two-seat canopy was and how heavily armoured it was to have been

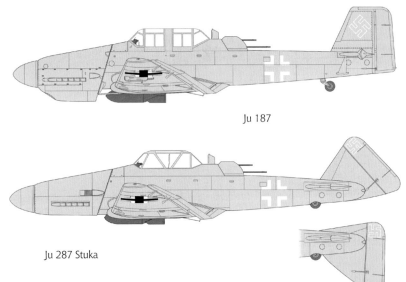

Ju 187

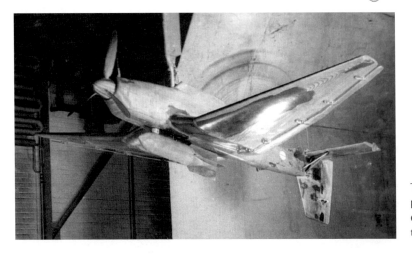

Ju 287 Stuka

Ju 87H-8

This was the D-8 with the modification as per the H-1.

Ju 187

This was developed from the aborted Ju 87F, using the 1,325kW Jumo 213A engine with a revised radiator. It was to have a retractable undercarriage, the legs rotating through 90° back into underwing fairings. A remote-controlled gun turret was to be installed aft of the two-seat cockpit canopy that could house two MG 151/20 cannon or a single MG 131 13mm cannon. The vertical fin and rudder could be rotated through 180° so it was underneath the rear fuselage (presumably to improve the turret's arc of fire). Fixed armament comprised a forward-firing 20mm cannon (mounted firing through the propeller shaft?) and the bomb load is shown externally.

Ju 287 Stuka

This was a development from the Ju 187, using the 1,325kW Jumo 213A engine but in a highly revised cowling that was steeply angled at the front to improve forward visibility. As with the Ju 187 it had a retractable undercarriage, with the legs rotating through 90° to fit flat in underwing fairings. A remote-controlled gun turret was to be installed aft of the heavily armoured and foreshortened two-seat cockpit canopy, again housing two MG 151/20 cannon or a single MG 131 13mm cannon. The design retained the rotatable tail assembly but the bomb load was all contained within an internal bomb bay that could thus carry only 250kg of bombs. The type was to have the heavy armour protection similar to that seen on the Ilyushin Il-2 Sturmovik. The wind-tunnel models soon showed however that the type was incapable of attaining the necessary 400km/h and its bomb load was too light, so the whole project was abandoned.

Specifications

	Ju 87C
Span	Full 13.00m; Folded 5.00m
Length	11.00m
Height	4.23m
Weight	Empty 2,900g; Maximum 4,510kg
Speed	Cruising 325km/h; Maximum 380km/h

This wind tunnel model shows the initial Ju 187 project with the revised cowl of the Jumo 213, external bomb load and the tail, shown rotated through 180° in this instance

Chapter 5: **Camouflage & Markings**

Let us first start by saying that nothing is certain when trying to deduce colours from old black and white photographs. The best you can make is an educated, and with luck, intelligent guess using both photographic and documentary evidence. The regulations with regard to the camouflage and markings of Luftwaffe aircraft during the war period are well known and most survive, the problem is that at the front line when the regulations changed it was highly unlikely that the ground crew rushed out to paint every aircraft in their charge, it was simply not practical. This whole subject is massive, you can write volumes on the subject, with some publishers having done just that, but we will try and keep it concise. Just remember, nothing is an absolute when it comes to camouflage and markings, and nothing illustrates that more graphically than late-war Luftwaffe C&M!

For the C&M applied to the various prototypes, please see their individual entries in the previous chapters.

Although we all use the term 'RLM' to prefix Luftwaffe colours it should be noted that in period documents the only colour designated in this manner was RLM 02, the rest were simply prefixed 'Farbton' (shade/tone/ hue of a colour). The confusion lies in the fact that the main paint manufacturer (Warnecke und Böhm) issued paint charts that prefixed all colours with 'RLM', followed by Farbton 65, 70, 71 etc. However for consistency throughout this book we will prefix all colours with 'RLM'

Luftwaffe Service

Throughout its career, the Stuka only ever used a couple of colour combinations, so we will break them down into eras and/or theatres

Pre-war & Spanish Civil War

The V4 was initially sent for evaluation purposes to Spain in August 1936 (assigned the codes 29•1) and it was followed by three pre-production A-0s in January 1938. These were allocated codes 29•2 to 29•4 and allocated to *Versuchsjagdstaffel*/88 (VJ/88). They were in the then standard military scheme of RLM 61 *Dunkelbraun*, RLM 62 *Grün* and RLM 63 *Hellgrau* in a splinter pattern for the upper surfaces and undercarriage spats, with RLM 65 *Hellblau* on the undersides. This scheme had been adopted for all bombers at the end of 1936 and was applied in two patterns, the latter being a mirror-image of the former. Although applied to official regulations there were variations in application by manufacturer and the three colours could be transposed, resulting

in a potential to create six patterns. The markings carried by the Ju 87A-0s in Spain comprised the type number ('29') in black characters to the left of the black dot on the mid-fuselage, with the individual aircraft number in the same style/size black characters to the right of that dot (this remained the same regardless of which side it was applied). The rudder was white with a diagonal cross in black applied over it and black discs with a white cross on them were applied above and below each wing. The wing tips were

Not how they were usually applied, as German aircraft manufacturers in WWII tended to use mats to mask off things like national insignia etc., this period image does shows the original Type B1 cross being extended to the wider Type B2 style on the fuselage of an early Ju 87B-2

An unidentified Ju 87A-1 in Spain, the contract between the RLM 63 and RLM 62 on the nose is very evident, while the spinner tip looks to be yellow and the propeller blades are polished aluminium (the backs were painted matt black)

Ju 87A-0, 29•2, 5./VJ88, Condor Legion , Spain, 1938
RLM 61/62/63 upper surfaces with RLM 65 undersides. All fuselage markings in black.
White underside of wing tips. White rudder with black cross superimposed.
Unit badge on wheel spats

Ju 87A-1, 29•5, St.G 163 'Jolanthe-Kette', Condor Legion, Spain 1937-38
RLM 61/62/63 upper surfaces with RLM 65 undersides; codes and fuselage marking in
black. White wing tips; RLM 02 spinner with black tip. White rudder with black cross
superimposed. Unit badge on wheel spats

painted white, their inner edge being alongside the outer arc of the black disc/white cross marking. Initially these machines sported a badge comprising an umbrella and bowler hat within a white diamond outlined in black (in reference to the crews' pseudo-civil status) was applied on the outer face of the port undercarriage spat, but this was frowned upon by officials so it was replaced by the 'Jolanthe the Pig' artwork on a white oval in the same location. This was from the cartoon of the same name and was a reference to the Ju 87's ungainly looks and resulted in the three aircraft being known as the 'Jolanthe Kette'. When 29•4 was damaged in the autumn of 1938 it was replaced with another machine, which received the codes 29•5, but was in the same camouflage and markings as the previous machines. Three B-1s

were sent in January 1939, but these were in the new two-colour upper scheme (see 'New Scheme' section elsewhere).

The Stuka entered Luftwaffe service in the spring of 1937, first equipping I./StG 162, then II./StG 162, I./StG 165 and a tactical development wing created from I./StG 165 and designated IV(Stuka) *Lehrgeschwaer* 1 (IV.(St)/LG 1). All of these machines were finished in the RLM 61/62/63 over 65 scheme applied to the A-0s in Spain, the only differences being in regard the national insignia. From the spring of 1936 the cross (*Balkenkreuz*) had been reintroduced and this was applied on either side of the mid-fuselage and above and below the wings. The swastika (*Hakenkreuz*) was applied across the fin and rudder on a white disc that lay atop a wide

This image of the replacement Ju 87A-1, 29•5 operated by VJ/88 in Spain shows how contrast and exposure of a negative can make it look completely different, as this looks neither in an A or B pattern, but obviously is three colours simply down to the light (RLM 63) patch mid-fuselage

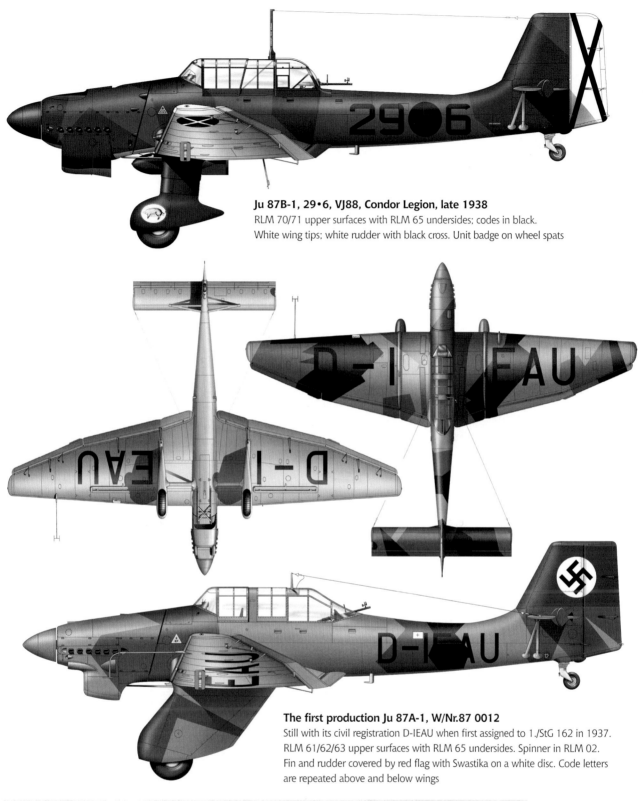

Ju 87B-1, 29•6, VJ88, Condor Legion, late 1938
RLM 70/71 upper surfaces with RLM 65 undersides; codes in black.
White wing tips; white rudder with black cross. Unit badge on wheel spats

The first production Ju 87A-1, W/Nr.87 0012
Still with its civil registration D-IEAU when first assigned to 1./StG 162 in 1937.
RLM 61/62/63 upper surfaces with RLM 65 undersides. Spinner in RLM 02.
Fin and rudder covered by red flag with Swastika on a white disc. Code letters
are repeated above and below wings

This shot of Ju 87A-1
D-IEAU allows you to
see the camouflage
pattern (pattern A in this
instance), as well as how
the civil registration was
applied above the wings

Ju 87A-1, W/Nr.87 0012, now marked as 52+C1 with III./StG 165 in 1937
RLM 61/62/63 upper surfaces with RLM 65 undersides. Spinner in RLM 02.
Balkenkreuz in six positions; codes in black. White '12' on rear fuselage

Sadly, all you can see of the codes on this Ju 87A-1 are +C26, however you can determine the Pattern A scheme by looking at the areas of the canopy affected by the darker shade

red band. Unit and aircraft identification used a complex five-character system, with two to the left and three to the right of the cross on each fuselage side and two under the starboard and three under the port wings, inboard of the cross and orientated so that they were read from the trailing edge, looking forward. These numbers were broken down as follows: first number was the *Luftkreiskommando* (Local Air command); the second number was the position of the *Geschwader* (Group) within the *Luftkreiskommando*; the third was a letter and denoted the individual

This underside view of Ju 87A-1 52+C13 operated by 3./ StG 165 in 1939 nicely shows how the codes were applied under the wings; note that if a colour had been used for the individual aircraft letter, that would have been repeated under the wings as well, sometimes thinly outlined in white to give contrast with the RLM 65

aircraft within the *Staffel* (Squadron) ; the fourth number was the *Gruppe* (Wing) within the *Geschwader*; and the fifth number was the *Staffel* within the *Gruppe*.

This shot of 1./StG 165 Ju 87A-1s being refuelled in Germany in 1938 does allow you to see what looks to be the aircraft at left (562+A11) in the new RLM 70/71/65 scheme, whilst the aircraft on the right (52+B11) is still in the older RLM 61/62/63/65 scheme. Note also what looks to be white horizontal bar/s on the rudder of both?

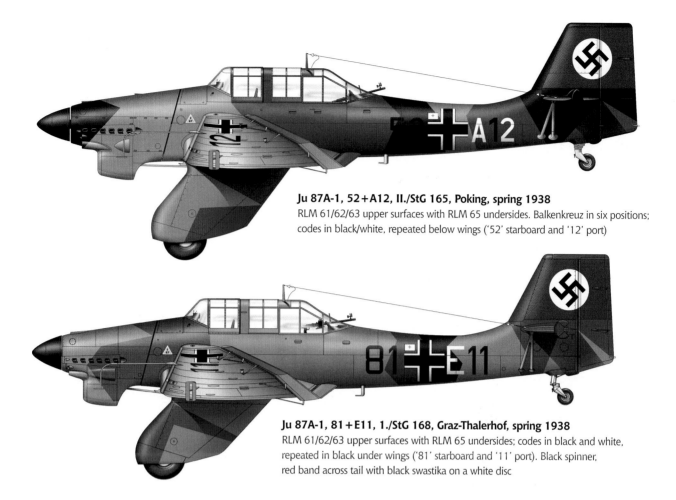

Ju 87A-1, 52+A12, II./StG 165, Poking, spring 1938
RLM 61/62/63 upper surfaces with RLM 65 undersides. Balkenkreuz in six positions; codes in black/white, repeated below wings ('52' starboard and '12' port)

Ju 87A-1, 81+E11, 1./StG 168, Graz-Thalerhof, spring 1938
RLM 61/62/63 upper surfaces with RLM 65 undersides; codes in black and white, repeated in black under wings ('81' starboard and '11' port). Black spinner, red band across tail with black swastika on a white disc

New Scheme

During 1938 a new two-colour scheme was adopted to be more suitable for operations in a European environment. This comprised RLM 70 *Schwarzgrün* (Black Green) and RLM 71 *Dunkelgrün* (Dark Green) in a splinter-pattern on the upper surfaces and RLM 65 *Hellblau* on the undersides. The demarcation between upper and lower colours was always way down at the bottom of the fuselage, taking a hypothetical line from the trailing edge of the wing straight back to the rudder stern post, as it never went onto the rudder itself. The demarcation for the front took another hypothetical line projected forward from the lowest point on the leading edge of the wing demarcation (e.g. at the bottom of the gull-wing). Once again, the upper pattern had two options, the latter being a mirror-image of the former. This scheme was applied to the three Ju 87B-1s sent to Spain in January 1939, otherwise these machines had the same markings as the previous A-0s and received the codes 29•6, 29•8, , 29•10, 29•11 and 29•13 (the missing numbers were just a ruse so as not to alert everyone to the true number of machines sent). They only remained in Spain for a short time though, and all returned to Germany in April 1939.

The expansion of the Luftwaffe led to certain re-organisational changes and in February 1939 the new *Luftflotten* (Air Fleets) were created. These comprised *Luftflotte 1* covering Northern and Eastern Germany plus East Prussia; *Luftflotte 2* covered North-West Germany; *Luftflotte*

3 covered South-West Germany; and *Luftflotte 4* (created in March 1939) covered South East Germany, Austria and Czechoslovakia. Within each was a *Luftgau* (Air District) that took over the role previously done by the *Luftkreiskommando* and operational functions were undertaken by the *Fliegerdivision* (Air Divisions – later renamed *Fliegerkorps* (Air Corps)). All this reorganisation led to a new coding system for bombers, dive-bombers and multi-engine aircraft. The new system used four characters, two each side of the fuselage cross, and was introduced in the spring of 1939. This system comprised two characters (either a letter/number or number/letter combination) to the left of the cross that identified the unit, usually the *Geschwader* or for smaller units, the *Gruppe*. The first of the two characters to

This Ju 87A-2 at Graz-Thalerof in 1939 seems on initial inspection to be RLM 70/71 over 65, but look at the light areas on the wings, which would suggest RLM 61/62/63 over 65 – isn't using B&W images to determine colours a treat!

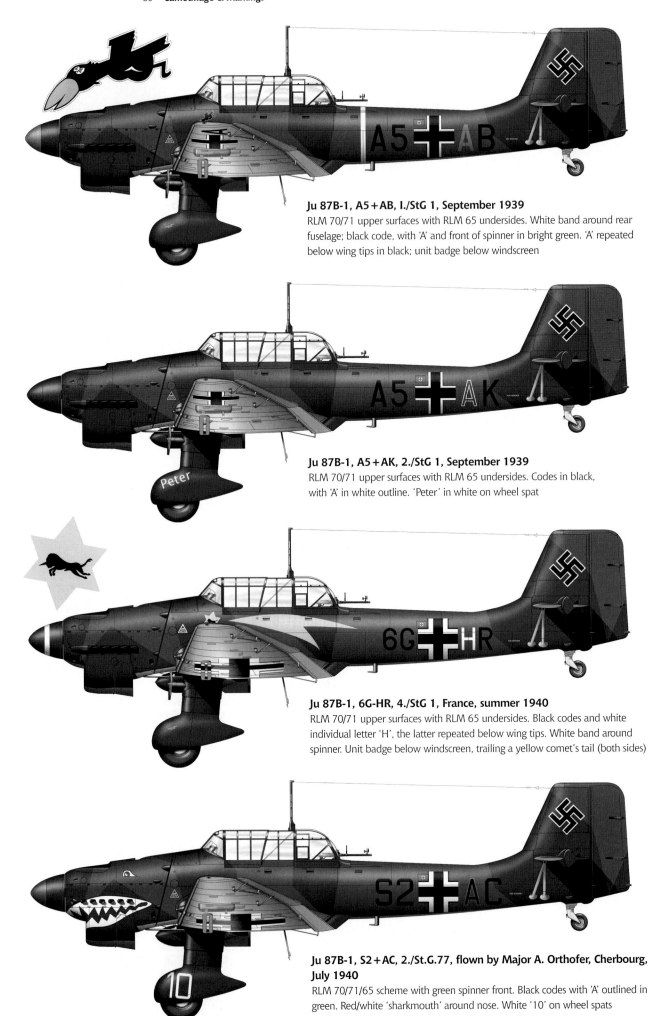

Ju 87B-1, A5+AB, I./StG 1, September 1939
RLM 70/71 upper surfaces with RLM 65 undersides. White band around rear fuselage; black code, with 'A' and front of spinner in bright green. 'A' repeated below wing tips in black; unit badge below windscreen

Ju 87B-1, A5+AK, 2./StG 1, September 1939
RLM 70/71 upper surfaces with RLM 65 undersides. Codes in black, with 'A' in white outline. 'Peter' in white on wheel spat

Ju 87B-1, 6G-HR, 4./StG 1, France, summer 1940
RLM 70/71 upper surfaces with RLM 65 undersides. Black codes and white individual letter 'H', the latter repeated below wing tips. White band around spinner. Unit badge below windscreen, trailing a yellow comet's tail (both sides)

Ju 87B-1, S2+AC, 2./St.G.77, flown by Major A. Orthofer, Cherbourg, July 1940
RLM 70/71/65 scheme with green spinner front. Black codes with 'A' outlined in green. Red/white 'sharkmouth' around nose. White '10' on wheel spats

Ju 87B-2, W/Nr.3360, T6+HL, 3./St.G 2 'Immelmann', St Malo (France), summer 1940
RLM 70/71 upper surfaces with RLM 65 undersides. Black codes with yellow 'H' (repeated on front of wheel spats in yellow and below wings in black). Yellow front tip of spinner. Unit badge below windscreen

the right of the cross was invariably painted in the *Staffel* or *Stab* (Staff) colour and identified the individual aircraft, whilst the final character identified the *Staffel* within the *Gruppe*. The three *Staffel* within each *Gruppe* were identified by colour; the first was RLM 21 Weiss (white), the second was RLM 23 Rot (red) and the third was RLM 04 Gelb (yellow). Because there were cases when there were more than three *Staffel* in the *Gruppe*, colours such as RLM 24 *Dunkelblau* (dark blue) and RLM 25 *Hellgrün* (light green) were also used, even though these were basically *Stab* (Staff) colours.

On delivery aircraft would usually have the *Stammkenzeichen* (primary identification code letters) applied in black on either side of the fuselage and although once in service these were painted out and replaced with the unit codes, some training units retained them and even added an individual aircraft letter to the beginning (e.g. ANO+HP of Pilot's School (C) 12 at Prague/Ruzyne airport); this individual letter was usually in colour and that colour was often used for the propeller spinner tip (also the case with

squadron machines).

The *Balkenkreuz* initially applied to the A and B-series in the new RLM 70/71/65 scheme was the thin Type B1, with a corresponding Type H2 swastika, but as wartime operations progressed experience showed that these needed to be revised. The fuselage and lower wing crosses were therefore made more visible, to aid ground-to-air recognition (something learned the hard way in

A nice in-flight image of Ju 87B-1 29•11 of the Condor Legion over Spain on the 30th May 1939. Its RLM 70/71/65 scheme is evident, and the wing in the foreground nicely illustrates the application of the national insignia and white wing tips

A nice example of a 'Pilot's Monument' (e.g nose-over) allows you to see the way in which the Stammkenzeichen was applied under the wings on the Stuka

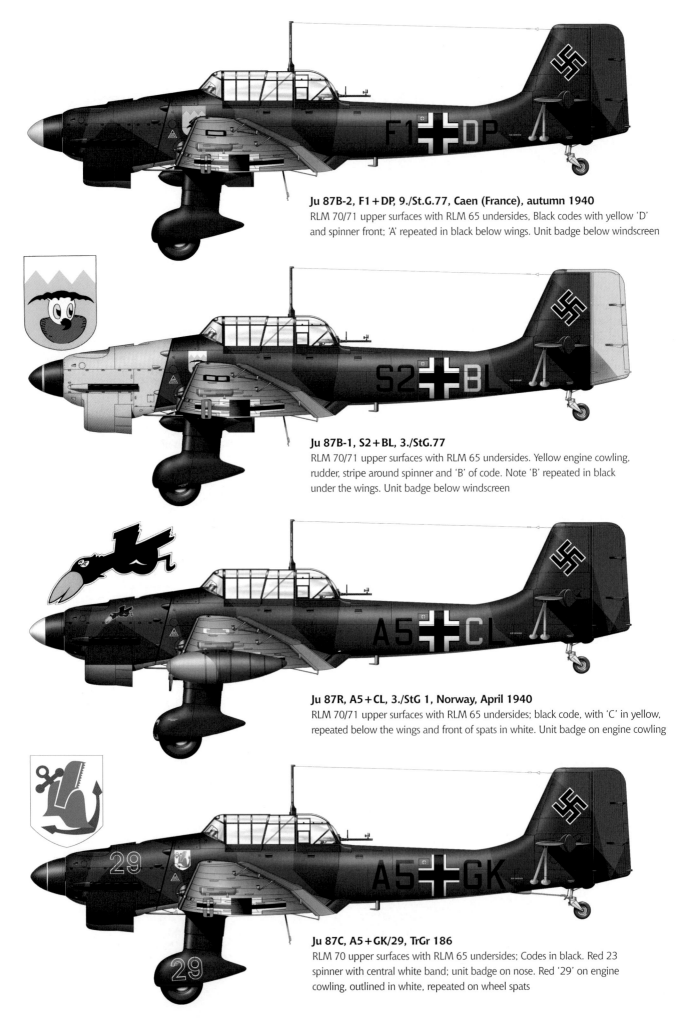

Ju 87B-2, F1+DP, 9./St.G.77, Caen (France), autumn 1940
RLM 70/71 upper surfaces with RLM 65 undersides, Black codes with yellow 'D' and spinner front; 'A' repeated in black below wings. Unit badge below windscreen

Ju 87B-1, S2+BL, 3./StG.77
RLM 70/71 upper surfaces with RLM 65 undersides. Yellow engine cowling, rudder, stripe around spinner and 'B' of code. Note 'B' repeated in black under the wings. Unit badge below windscreen

Ju 87R, A5+CL, 3./StG 1, Norway, April 1940
RLM 70/71 upper surfaces with RLM 65 undersides; black code, with 'C' in yellow, repeated below the wings and front of spats in white. Unit badge on engine cowling

Ju 87C, A5+GK/29, TrGr 186
RLM 70 upper surfaces with RLM 65 undersides; Codes in black. Red 23 spinner with central white band; unit badge on nose. Red '29' on engine cowling, outlined in white, repeated on wheel spats

This shot of Ju 87B-1 12+A11 nicely illustrates early markings in that you have the Type B1 cross with its thin white borders, the old style of identification codes but what looks like a Type H2 swastika. The white aerial mast and pennant probably identify this as the group leader and may have been there for an exercise

This ex-StG 1 Ju 87B-2 was used by an unidentified training unit and therefore has a 'fleet' number applied in large white characters on either side of the nose, a fairly common practice for such machines

Ju 87B-1 S2+EP of 6./StG 77 exhibits the yellow nose seen on many Stukas during the Battle of Britain era

Ju 87Bs over Poland in September-October 1939, note the aircraft letter repeated above the wings, inboard of the crosses, in the same colour as it is on the fuselage

operations in Poland). This resulted in the Type B2 cross being applied in each location, those under the wings being much larger and placed inboard as a result (so the front arm crosses over the dive brake).

The *Werke Nr.* was not always applied to the Stuka, but when it was it was usually done in small black or white characters along the top of the vertical fin, directly above the swastika. You will find some photographs that show the number applied in white at the top of the rudder, although this seems to be restricted to the B and R series. Early machines only carried the last four of the number (e.g '0540' for 087-0540), while later machines carried the full six-digit number (e.g 494194).

Emblems

This Ju 87B carries the emblem of 8./StG 51 which later became 6./StG 2

This Ju 87A-2 has the emblem of the medical department (Sanitätsabteilung) of the Luftwaffe applied on either side of the forward fuselage

Ju 87B-1 6G+AR carries the comet emblem on the mid-fuselage region

Sadly, the identity of this Ju 87B with the Popeye cartoon artwork on the spats is unknown, but was obviously a unit that operated in Finland (©SA-Kuva)

Ju 87B-2, 2./StG 2, Balkans, 1941
RLM 70/71 upper surfaces with RLM 65 undersides; yellow spinner front, nose section, underside of wing tips and rear fuselage band. Codes in black with 'C' repeated in black below wing tips and in white on front of wheel spats. Unit badge below windscreen

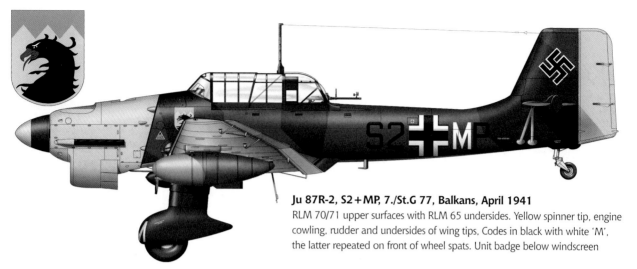

Ju 87R-2, S2+MP, 7./St.G 77, Balkans, April 1941
RLM 70/71 upper surfaces with RLM 65 undersides. Yellow spinner tip, engine cowling, rudder and undersides of wing tips, Codes in black with white 'M', the latter repeated on front of wheel spats. Unit badge below windscreen

Balkans

The Stukas that supported operations in the Balkans and Crete retained the standard RLM 70/71 over 65 main scheme, but the engine cowlings and the rudder were painted RLM 04 Gelb (yellow). No clear regulations were issued with regard to the application of these yellow areas, so you will find wide variation in surviving images, with some having just a band around the nose while others have the entire front end, back to the engine bulkhead painted in yellow, and some with just the rudder painted or the entire vertical fin and rudder or even both tailplanes and elevators.

Wings and fuselage crosses tended to all be Type B2 with a corresponding Type H2 swastika on either side of the vertical fin. Unit codes were applied in the usual manner in black either side of the fuselage cross, with the individual aircraft character (3rd one) in colour. Spinner tips were also often in the unit colour and the individual aircraft letter was often repeated under each wing, outboard of the cross in black. There are examples with the individual aircraft number under the wings and in whatever colour it was on the fuselage above each wing.

Ju 87R-2s of III./StG 2 in Greece in 1941, with the yellow nose of the theatre, but applied only up until the aft cowl panel lines, not to the firewall bulkhead. Note the III./StG 2 badge just aft of the yellow cowling

Ju 87R-2s S1+HK and S1+AK of 2./StG 2 seen over Rhodes, Greece

This Ju 87B-2 of 3./StG 3 shows the yellow nose markings of the Balkans campaign, while the aircraft in the background has the yellow rudder also associated with this campaign

Ju 87R-2 A5+EL of 3./StG 1 abandoned at El Daba in November 1942 exhibits what look like either RLM 79 with RLM 80 mottle or, more likely, Giallo Mimetico 3 with a mottle of Verde Mimetico, as the contrast on the mottle is too consistent for it to be the underlying RLM 70/71, plus you can see how it has been applied around the existing markings (overlapping the 'E' in places). You can also see the older Type B1 crosses above the wings, whilst the fuselage ones are the wider Type B2, a common practice with the B and R-series

This shot of Ju 87R-2 Trop A5+BH of 1./StG1 returning to its base in North Africa shows the application of RLM 79 overall to create 'scales' of either the underlying RLM 70/71 or newly-applied RLM 80 (some sources state the 'scales' were RLM 71). Note the diving pelican motif of the unit

Ju 87R-2 T6+CP of 6./StG 2 flown by Hubert Polz based at Tmimi, Libya in 1941. This is the famous 'snake' Stuka and there is much debate on the colour of the snake's scales, as it has been depicted as red, tan, sand, yellow etc. Note the rough mottle (applied with a brush) of green applied to the tip of the spinner

A closer look at the snake along the port side of Ju 87R-2 T6+CP of 6./StG 2 flown by Hubert Polz at Tmimi, Libya in 1941. The scales and details are not the same as the underlying camouflage, so may well have been one of the quoted (red, tan, sand or yellow) colours?

A badge applied on the nose of a Ju 87D-3 in North Africa

Ju 87R-2 S1+GK of 2./StG3 after nosing over in 1941, this machine looks to be either Giallo Mimetico 3 or RLM 79 on the upper surfaces, with most likely RLM 65 underneath

Ju 87D-1, S7+EM of 8./StG 3 at Trapani (Sicily) in May 1942
Still in the European scheme of RLM 70/71 upper surfaces with RLM 65 undersides;
red/white spinner and red individual letter 'E'; white band around rear fuselage

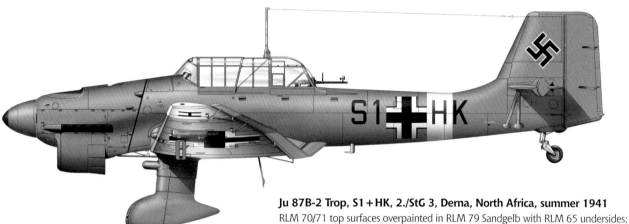

Ju 87B-2 Trop, S1+HK, 2./StG 3, Derna, North Africa, summer 1941
RLM 70/71 top surfaces overpainted in RLM 79 Sandgelb with RLM 65 undersides;
white wing tips and rear fuselage band. Code in black with 'H' in red (RLM 23),
repeated in red outlined in white on front of wheel spats and in black below wings;
red front of spinner

North Africa & the Mediterranean

When Stukas moved to support Italian forces
in Sicily in early 1941 they were still painted in
the European RLM 70/71/65 scheme. The first
recognition marking to be applied was the white
band around the rear fuselage, similar to the
marking carried by *Regia Aeronautica* machines.
The size and location of this band varied hugely,
so you will find them right up against the rear
arm of the fuselage cross, or nearly up against
the leading edge of the horizontal tailplane!
Some aircraft, not all, also had the undersides

This Ju 87B-2 Trop (xx+PW) is seen in service in North
Africa still in the 'European' scheme of RLM 70/71/65,
although the fuselage cross is applied on top of the white
theatre band

Wrecks of Ju 87s including S7+HL and S7+IH on a scrap
heap at El Daba in November 1942. Note the variations in
the upper camouflage colours and patterns, the nearest had
sufficient shades in the dark areas for it to be RLM 79 applied
over the existing RLM 70/71, whilst the next one is probably
Giallo Mimetico 3 with a mottle of green, and S7+IH looks
to be Giallo Mimetico 3 or RLM 79 overall. You can also see
the variation in the size and location of the white fuselage
band and S7+IH has the original Stammkenzeichen painted
out but still visible under the codes

Ju 87R-2, W/Nr.6146, S7+AB, I./StG 3, June 1942, flown by Hauptmann Heinrich Eppen, Libya (North Africa), June 1942

RLM 79 with RLM 80 mottles on all upper surfaces; RLM 65 undersides. White rear fuselage band. Codes in black with 'A' in green. W/Nr. in white above swastika on fin. Spinner is green/white

Ju 87D-1 Trop, S7+AA flown by Oberstleutnant Walter Sigel, Geschwaderkommodore of St.G.3

Participated in the thrust towards Bir Hacheim, the second siege of Tobruk, transferred to Fuka and then El Alamein. Standard RLM 70/71 upper surfaces overpainted in part with RLM 79 Sandgelb. Undersides in RLM 65; spinner front and 'A' of code in RLM 24 Dunkelblau. 'A' repeated in white on wheel spats

The Ju 87D-1 of Obstlt. Walter Sigel of StG 3 in Libya in June 1942, note the two tones in the camouflage area on the top of the nose, visible on the extreme left, clearly showing this aircraft had RLM 79 (or Giallo Mimetico 3) applied over the base RLM 70/71

of the wing tips also painted in white. Some of the dark upper surfaces were broken up by the application of RLM 79, with those machines initially sent to the theatre it is most likely that the areas of 'RLM 79' were in fact from Italian paint stocks and were thus *Giallo Mimetico 3*. This could be applied in a variety of ways, as blocks with hard edges to create a 'third' colour in the splinter scheme, or airbrushed on in mottles or loose bands or even squiggles. The fuselage and wing crosses tend to be Type B2 with a match-

ing Type H2 swastika either side of the vertical fin. Sometimes the fuselage cross was applied directly on top of the white theatre band, others had this aft of the cross with the last character of the codes applied partially on top of it. Some machines dispensed with the lower wing crosses. The unit codes were applied in black either side of the fuselage cross, with the individual aircraft character (3rd one) in the unit colour, outlined in black. The spinner tip was often also in the unit colour, while the rest of the spinner and propeller blades were in the usual RLM 70. It is possible that some Stukas had the upper surfaces repainted entirely in *Giallo Mimetico 3* with a light or dense mottle of *Verde Mimetico* (Camouflage Green). By early 1942 stocks of the new RLM desert colours started to be readily available and the upper surfaces were overpainted with RLM 79 *Sandgelb* (Sand Yellow) and either left in that single colour or with a mottle of RLM 80 *Olivgrün* (Olive Green); some machines were painted as such at the factory, but this was very limited.

Some Ju 87B-2 Trops that were delivered later and some of the early Ju 87D-1 Trops were apparently supplied painted RLM 79 on top and RLM 78 *Hellblau* (Light Blue) underneath.

Eastern Front

Stukas operating in support of Operation Barbarossa retained the standard RLM 70/71 over RLM 65 scheme, but had the lower wing tips in yellow, along with a similar coloured band around the rear fuselage. This band varied in size and location and you will see some Stukas with it applied under, and to the same width, as the cross. The codes were applied in the usual manner either side of the fuselage cross in black, although some units applied the first two in a very small size. The first character of the second two numbers (individual aircraft identification) was usually applied in the colour that related to the *Staffel* and these were also often thinly outlined in white to give contrast with the underlying dark RLM 70/71. You will find a mix of national insignia styles on Stukas in this region, and there is no real system to this. The most common cross is the Type B2, but you will also find D and G-series machines with Type B3 or Type B5 on the fuselage, whilst the wing crosses remained Type B2. The same applies to the swastika, with Type H2 being the most common, but you will also find some adopting the later simplified Type H4, usually combined with a similarly simplified Type B5 fuselage cross. The changes to these simplified types of national marking came into affect at the end of 1943. Whilst the tip of the spinner was often applied in the unit colour you will also find that Maj. H-J Rudel had his G-series

machines with a spinner spiral like a fighter, he also adopted fighter markings on the fuselage instead of codes, these being a black arrow head and horizontal line ahead and another horizontal line behind the cross, all with a thin white border to them.

During the winter months on the Eastern Front the Stuka adopted water-based white distemper (Ikarin A2515.21 or 7126.21) on the upper surfaces to reduce the stark (dark) nature of the base RLM 70/71, whilst operating over a snow-covered landscape. This could be applied

A Ju 87D of an unidentified unit on the Eastern Front clearly exhibits just how easily the temporary white paint soon became worn, originally this had been applied with an airbrush, as seen by the soft edge demarcation around the chin radiator

Ju 87B-2, F1+AR, 7./St.G 77, Russia, 1941
RLM 70/71 upper surfaces with RLM 65 undersides. Yellow fuselage band.
Black codes with white 'A' (outlined in white). White spinner front.
Unit badge below windscreen

Ju 87B-2, T6+JK, 2./St.G 2, Russia, 1941
RLM 70/71 upper surfaces with RLM 65 undersides. Yellow rear fuselage band.
Black codes with red 'J'. Red spinner front. Unit badge below windscreen

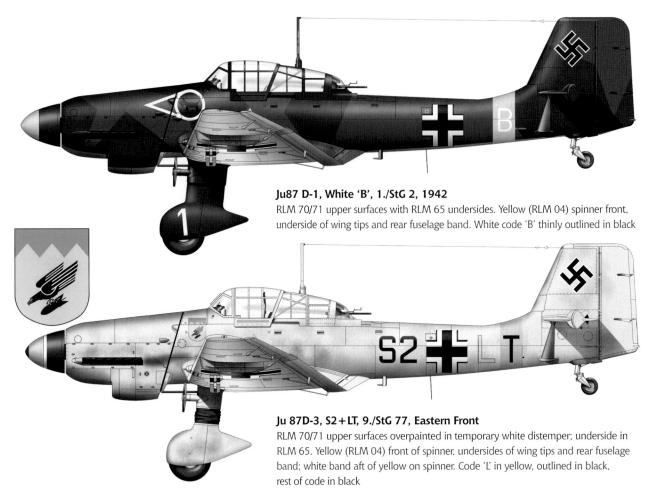

Ju87 D-1, White 'B', 1./StG 2, 1942
RLM 70/71 upper surfaces with RLM 65 undersides. Yellow (RLM 04) spinner front, underside of wing tips and rear fuselage band. White code 'B' thinly outlined in black

Ju 87D-3, S2 + LT, 9./StG 77, Eastern Front
RLM 70/71 upper surfaces overpainted in temporary white distemper; underside in RLM 65. Yellow (RLM 04) front of spinner, undersides of wing tips and rear fuselage band; white band aft of yellow on spinner. Code 'L' in yellow, outlined in black, rest of code in black

roughly with a wide brush or broom, resulting in a streaky effect, or more commonly it was airbrushed on, resulting in a much softer finish. Around the national insignia and swastika the white would either be hard-edged (brush applied) or soft (airbrushed) and the latter often resulted in overspray onto the marking itself; you will also see instances of the black centres of the crosses and swastika also being overpainted in white. There are many variations in just how much white was applied, with some machines having the area around the cockpit left unaffected, while other machines had the white applied in dots to produce a spotty effect. There are also examples where the white was applied to produce a sharksmouth effect on the nose, although that is very rare.

A Ju 87D-5 of 1./SG 1 has the winter white distemper sprayed on freehand, resulting in it covering the outer edges of the upper wing cross – a D-3 can be seen in the background

Ju 87D-5 S7 + A of 3./SG3 at Immola in July 1944, note how the rear fuselage band does not go up onto the dorsal spine and the fighter-style chevron added quite a distance ahead of the individual aircraft letter. The crosses are the simplified type B5 on the fuselage and B3 under the wings, with a Type H4 swastika (©SA-Kuva)

Ju 87D-5 A5+KJ of Stab SG1 in Russia in 1943-44. You can see how dirty the mid region became, as well as how quickly the white was removed from that region, plus how the lower (wide) frames of the canopy sections were treated with the white, while the rest of the frames and aerial mast were not. Note how airbrush application resulted in fairly broad clear regions around the markings, and the 'A5' codes seem to have been on a lighter patch to start with

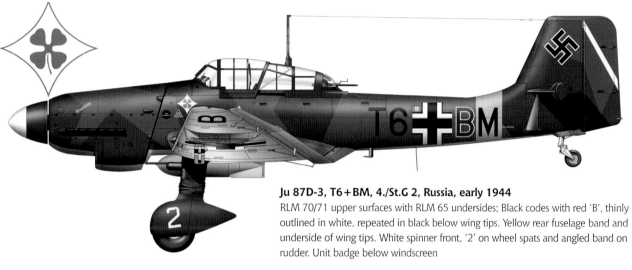

Ju 87D-3, T6+BM, 4./St.G 2, Russia, early 1944

RLM 70/71 upper surfaces with RLM 65 undersides; Black codes with red 'B', thinly outlined in white, repeated in black below wing tips. Yellow rear fuselage band and underside of wing tips. White spinner front, '2' on wheel spats and angled band on rudder. Unit badge below windscreen

Ju 87D-5, 'Yellow A', flown by Staffelkapitän Lt Teo Baurle, 3./St.G 3, Immola (Finland), summer 1944

RLM 70/71 upper surfaces with RLM 65 undersides. Yellow spinner tip, underside of wing tips and rear fuselage band. Code and rank pennant in yellow. 'A' repeated, also in yellow, on front of wheel spats

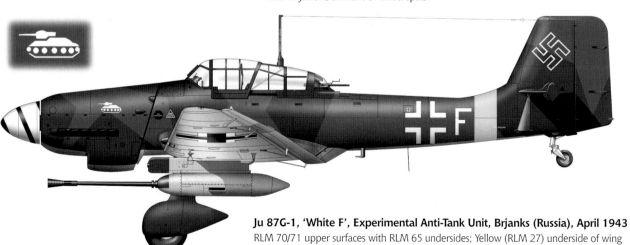

Ju 87G-1, 'White F', Experimental Anti-Tank Unit, Brjanks (Russia), April 1943

RLM 70/71 upper surfaces with RLM 65 undersides; Yellow (RLM 27) underside of wing tips and rear fuselage band. National markings in white only over the top colours; white 'tank' marking on nose. White/black spiral spinner

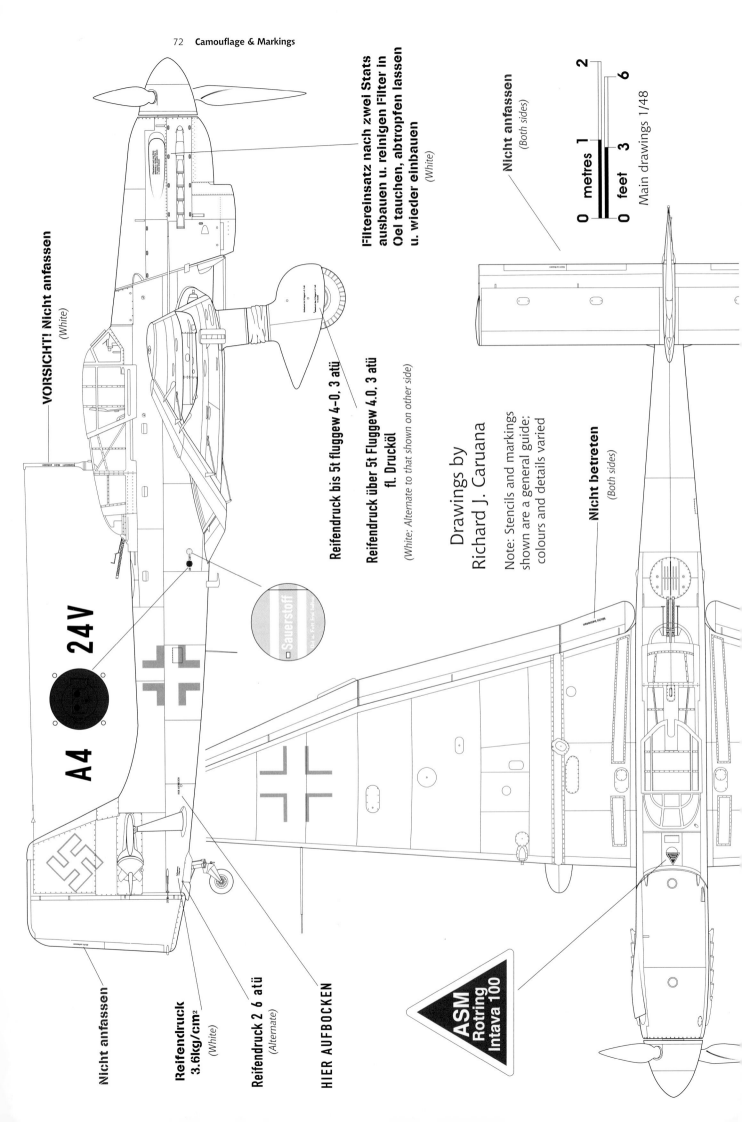

VORSICHT! Nicht anfassen
(White)

Filtereinsatz nach zwei Stats ausbauen u. reinigen Filter in Oel tauchen, abtropfen lassen u. wieder einbauen
(White)

Reifendruck bis 5t fluggew 4–0, 3 atü

Reifendruck über 5t Fluggew 4.0, 3 atü fl. Drucköl
(White: Alternate to that shown on other side)

24V

A4

Sauerstoff

Nicht anfassen

Reifendruck 3.6kg/cm²
(White)

Reifendruck 2 6 atü
(Alternate)

HIER AUFBOCKEN

Nicht anfassen
(Both sides)

Drawings by
Richard J. Caruana

Note: Stencils and markings shown are a general guide; colours and details varied

Nicht betreten
(Both sides)

ASM
Rotring
Intava 100

0 metres 1   2

0 feet   3   6

Main drawings 1/48

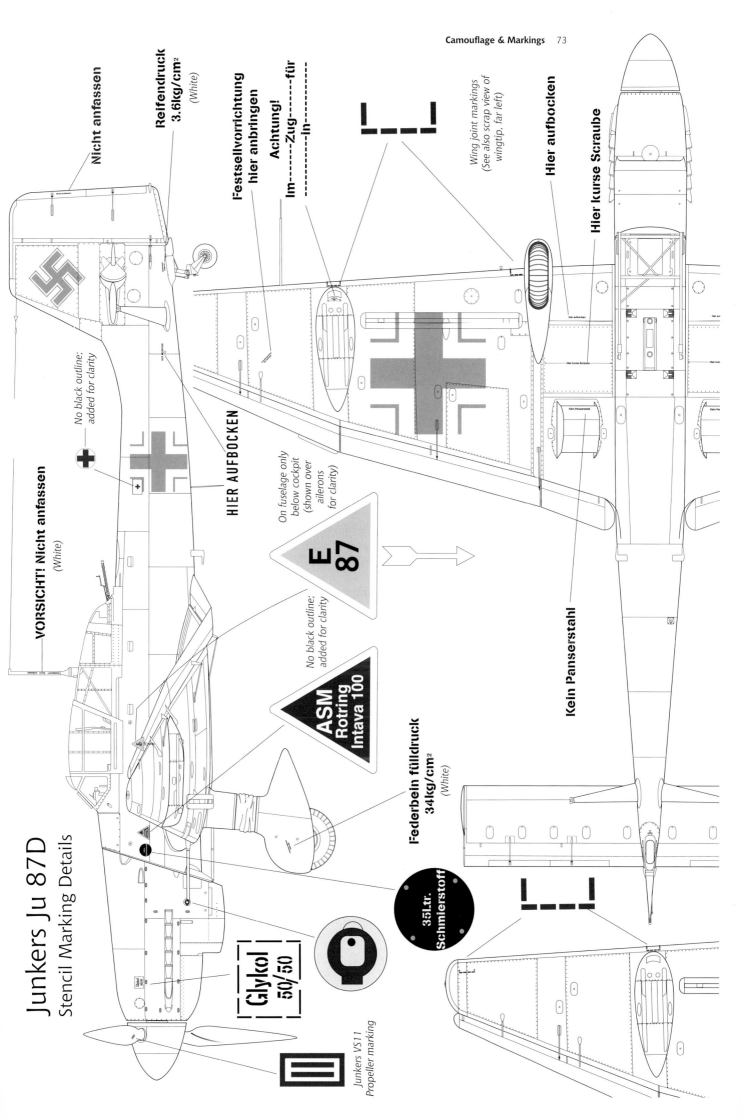

Junkers Ju 87D
Stencil Marking Details

Nicht anfassen

Reifendruck 3.6kg/cm² (White)

Festsellvorrichtung hier anbringen

Achtung!
Im------Zug------für------In------

Wing joint markings (See also scrap view of wingtip, far left)

Hier aufbocken

Hier kurse Scraube

No black outline; added for clarity

VORSICHT! Nicht anfassen (White)

HIER AUFBOCKEN

On fuselage only below cockpit (shown over ailerons for clarity)

E 87

No black outline; added for clarity

ASM Rotring Intava 100

Federbein fülldruck 34kg/cm² (White)

Kein Panserstahl

Glykol 50/50

35Ltr. Schmierstoff

Junkers VS11 Propeller marking

Ju 87D-5N, E3+SH, 1./NSG 9, Tuscania, April 1944
RLM 70/71 upper surfaces overpainted with a wavy pattern (Mäander) of brown/grey;
RLM 65 undersides also overpainted in 'tiger stripes' of grey. White national markings
on top colours; white extreme tip of spinner and 'S' on wheel spats. Code in black
with 'S' outlined in white

The high contrast of this image of Ju 87D-8 E8+CH operated by 1./NSGr 9 clearly shows the squiggle (Mäander) of RLM 76 on the upper surfaces

Night Operations (*Nachtschlachtgruppen*)

As the war progressed the Stuka was used more and more for night harassment against troops and other ground installations and as a result, they would often have the undersides painted black. This would extend to painting out the underwing crosses although there are examples of later D-series machines with the lower engine cowling still in RLM 65 or with the fuselage crosses, swastika and even the theatre (white) bands also roughly painted out in black.

Stukas operating in Italy in 1944-1944 as well as the D and G-series machines used on the Eastern Front by the *Nachtschlachtgruppen* often adopted the squiggle (*Mäander*) pattern of brownish-grey or RLM 76 *Lichtblau* (Light Blue) applied all over the upper surfaces. This sometimes even extended over the national markings and even the first, second and last characters of the codes, just leaving the individual aircraft character exposed. Some machines also had the undersides painted in stripes of grey, the exact shade is unknown and may have been locally-produced?

Late-War Revisions

In late 1944 the *Geschwader* (or *Gruppe*) codes were reduced to 1/5th the size of the remaining characters and this coincided with the re-designation of all Stuka units to *Schlachtgeschwader* (Ground Attack Group). The new *Schlachtgeschwader* also adopted in late 1944 the large yellow 'V' underneath the outer wing panel and these often had the forward arms running up and onto the upper surface as well. Those on the Eastern Front had the width of the yellow under each wing tip reduced to fit the new marking in between it and the cross and in 1945 a wide yellow band was also applied around the nose of *Schlachtgeschwader* machines to aid in ground-to-air recognition.

This Ju 87D-7 from NSGr 9 was flown by Hans Wolfsen and Hans Wilk in Italy in August 1944 and you can clearly see the Mäander pattern applied over the existing upper surface camouflage. The aircraft has flame dampers on the exhaust and the spinner has segments of white only on the front half, with squiggles applied over the rear (RLM 70) half

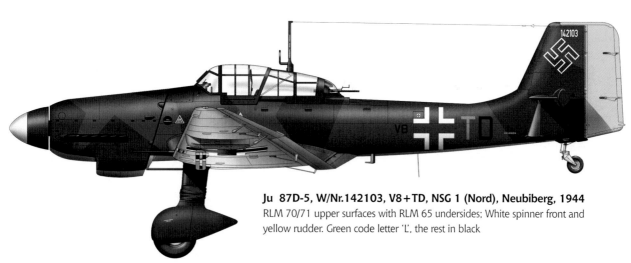

Ju 87D-5, W/Nr.142103, V8+TD, NSG 1 (Nord), Neubiberg, 1944
RLM 70/71 upper surfaces with RLM 65 undersides; White spinner front and
yellow rudder. Green code letter 'L', the rest in black

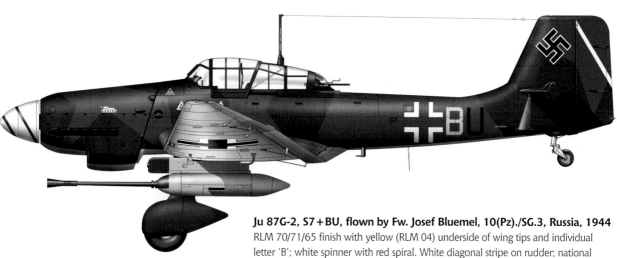

Ju 87G-2, S7+BU, flown by Fw. Josef Bluemel, 10(Pz)./SG.3, Russia, 1944
RLM 70/71/65 finish with yellow (RLM 04) underside of wing tips and individual
letter 'B'; white spinner with red spiral. White diagonal stripe on rudder; national
markings in white only on upper surfaces

**Ju 87G-2, W/Nr.494193, flown by Oblt. Hans Rudel, Stab/SG 2,
Seregélyes (Central Hungary), late 1944**
RLM 70/71 upper surfaces with RLM 65 undersides; Yellow (RLM 27) rear fuselage
band, underside of wing tips and 'V' below port wing. National markings in white
only on top colours; black/white spiral on spinner. Chevron and bar markings in black,
outlined in white. Note the misalignment of the W/Nr. on the port side of the fin

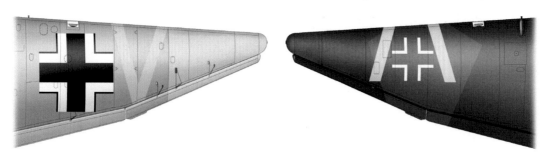

This colour image of US personnel inspecting Ju 87D-5N, W/Nr.141286, 5B+LK of NSGr 10 at Fürth clearly shows the yellow band around the cowl adopted for all ground-attack aircraft in the final stages of WWII. This machine also has the spinner spiral usually associated with fighters and the W/Nr. in large stencil-style white characters on the top of the vertical fin *(©USAAF)*

Ju 87G-2, W/Nr.484231, S7+EN, 10(Pz)./SG.3 , September 1944
RLM 70/71/65 finish with yellow (RLM 04) underside of wing tips; white spinner with red spiral. Codes and serial in white. Force-landed near Kekava (Latvia) after being hit by Soviet ground fire

Ju 87G-2 W/Nr.494200 previously operated by 1./StG2 captured at Pilsen, Czechoslovakia in May 1945. Again, the yellow nose band of ground-attack aircraft is applied and you can just make out the light-coloured rudder, which is yellow as well. The big Type B2 crosses are still applied under the wings. Note that there are colour versions of this image about, but they have been coloured via modern computer technology and are not original

Ju 87D-5, 'White 13', 1/2 Orljak, Royal Bulgarian Air Force, summer 1944
RLM 70/71 upper surfaces with RLM 65 undersides; Yellow underside of wing tips
and fuselage band. National markings in six positions; '13' in white. Rudder in green
and red; red/white spiral on spinner

Foreign Service

Bulgaria

The Bulgarian Air Force (*Vazdushni na Negovo Velichestvo Voyski* – often shortened to just *Vazdushni Voyski*) operated approximately twelve ex-Luftwaffe Ju 87Rs as trainers in the summer of 1943, although these most likely retained their Luftwaffe C&M. They also operated the D-3 and D-5 variants in 1944-45. These were supplied in standard Luftwaffe camouflage of RLM 70/71 in a splinter pattern on the upper surfaces and RLM 65 underneath with the demarcation in the usual position low down on the fuselage and engine cowling sides. The Luftwaffe markings were painted out and replaced with the national insignia (black cross in a white box) applied either side of the fuselage and above and below the wings. Initially the mid-fuselage band was yellow (48cm wide), as were the wing tips, to denote the Eastern Front theatre, but when Bulgaria changed sides in September 1944 these were over-painted in white (the lower wing tips remained yellow). Individual aircraft numbers were applied in large white characters aft of the national insignia, either side of the rear fuselage, although note should be made that the national insignia was aft of the fuselage band, so this individual marking was well towards the rear

of the fuselage. The rudder was often painted in light green at the top (76cm) and red below. Some machines you will find, once Bulgaria had changed sides, were oversprayed with large blotches of RLM 76 (some state light grey) over the upper surface camouflage.

Croatia

The Croatian Luftwaffe Legion (3(Croat)./KGr 1) operated six B and R-series in support of the Luftwaffe in Russia during 1944 and these all retained the standard Luftwaffe RLM 70/71 over

Bulgarian Air Force Ju 87D-5s over the Osogovo Highlands in Macedonia with 'White 30' nearest, note the fuselage band forward of the national insignia and wing tips plus the fighter-style white spinner spiral

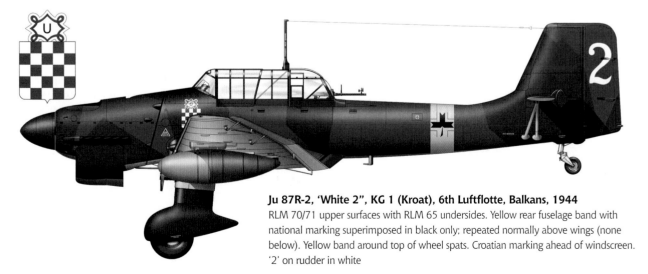

Ju 87R-2, 'White 2", KG 1 (Kroat), 6th Luftflotte, Balkans, 1944
RLM 70/71 upper surfaces with RLM 65 undersides. Yellow rear fuselage band with
national marking superimposed in black only; repeated normally above wings (none
below). Yellow band around top of wheel spats. Croatian marking ahead of windscreen.
'2' on rudder in white

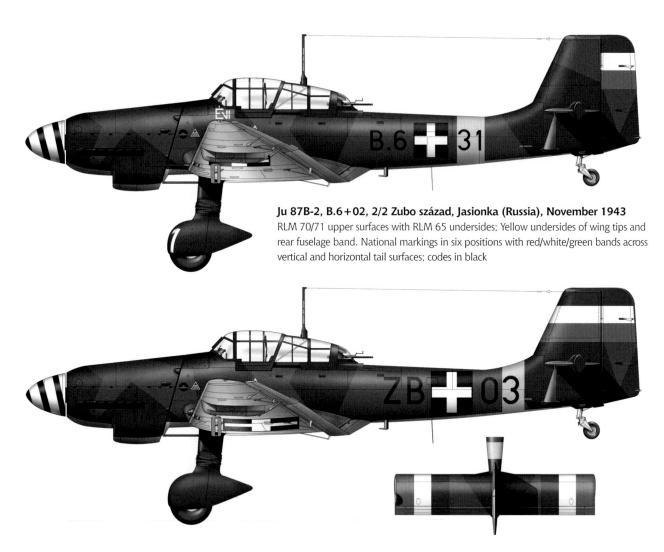

Ju 87B-2, B.6+02, 2/2 Zubo század, Jasionka (Russia), November 1943
RLM 70/71 upper surfaces with RLM 65 undersides; Yellow undersides of wing tips and rear fuselage band. National markings in six positions with red/white/green bands across vertical and horizontal tail surfaces; codes in black

Ju 87D-3, ZB+03, 102/1 Zubo Szazadm Hungarian Air Force, autumn, 1944
RLM 70/71 upper surfaces with RLM 65 undersides. Yellow undersides of wing tips and rear fuselage band. Black/white spiral on spinner. National markings in six positions. Codes in black. Red/white/green upper section of rudder; the same colours cover the horizontal tail surfaces up to mid span from tip, upper and lower surfaces, green to tip both sides

Ju 87B B6+02 of the Hungarian Air Force, not the best quality image, but it does clearly show the fuselage markings and coloured bands around the fin/rudder and tailplane/elevator

65 scheme, but with the fuselage and wing crosses painted out and the Croatian cross applied in their place. Usually the wing ones were applied on top of a white cross, to give contrast with the surrounding dark paint, while the fuselage one was often applied on the yellow band at the midpoint. The Coat of Arms of the fascist State of Croatia (*Nezavisna Drzava Hrvatska* – NDH) was sometimes applied on either side of the forward fuselage just below the windscreen, while an individual aircraft number was applied in a stylised white font on either side of the upper portion of the rudder.

Hungary

The Royal Hungarian Air Force (*Magyar Királyi Honvéd Légierö* – MKHL) first had two ex-Luftwaffe Ju 87B-2s (B.601 and B.602), which were tested by the Experimental Aviation Institute and then issued to 3/1 *Bombazo Osztaly* at Börögond; these probably retained their RLM 70/71 over 65 scheme. Four Ju 87A-1s (B.602* to B.606 – *confusion exists here as some sources only state three [B.603 to B606], because B.602 was a B-2?) operated from 1942 with the Dive Bomber Training Squadron based at Kolozsar. There seems to be some dispute as to their overall scheme, as some sources state they adopted the pre-war scheme of RLM 61/62/63 over 65, others say they were delivered in RLM 70/71 splinter camouflage on the upper surfaces and RLM 65 underneath, while others state they were overpainted with Stone Grey, Earth Brown and Dark Green (which may in fact be some assuming the RLM colours were produced locally?). The Hungarian national insignia (wide white cross on a black square) was applied in place of the Luftwaffe crosses on the fuselage sides and below and above each wing. A yellow

Hungarian Ju 87D-5s and a B-1 in flight in 1944. Although not the greatest quality, it does allow you to see the size and location of the upper wing markings and the variation in the coloured bands on the tail between that visible on the B-1 (all across top of fin/rudder) and that seen on the D-5 (top 1/3rd of rudder only)

theatre band (48cm wide) was applied around the rear fuselage, just ahead of the vertical fin fillet and the underside of each wing tip was also yellow. Most of the upper surface of the vertical fin and rudder was covered with equal wide bands of red (top), white and green and this was also repeated across the entire horizontal tailplane and elevator (red being inboard). The individual aircraft identification codes were applied in yellow (some sources state black) with the first two (B.6) on the left and the aircraft number (e.g. 06) to the right – this remained the same regardless of the side it was applied.

The MKHL operated the Ju 87B with 2/2 *Zuhanbombazo szazad* (2nd Dive Bomber Squadron) and these were all in the original RLM 70/71/65 scheme, although again some sources state they were partially repainted in the Stone Grey, Earth Brown and Dark Green scheme as the A-1s. By mid-1943 the MKHL started to operate the D-3 and D-5 and these were also in the standard RLM 70/71 over 65 scheme and carried the same national marking as the A-1s. The bands across the tail were applied on the B-1s in the same manner as the A-1, but the D-series had this applied only on the upper 1/3rd of the rudder (plus above and below the tailplanes/elevators). The D-3 and D-5s used the same type number 'B.6' (see accompany colour profile for a machine with 'ZB' codes), although the twelve new D-5s supplied in May 1944 used 'B.7' (B.701 to B.712). These codes were usually applied in black over a painted-out area where the original Luftwaffe codes used to be (some quote RLM 76 for this,

others, a light grey). The individual aircraft number was once again on the right of the cross on the fuselage and also in black, but some aircraft has this outlined in white (thus crossing into the white theatre fuselage band [48cm wide]). Yellow wing tip undersides were also applied and the D-3 and D-5 usually carried the 102/1 squadron badge on either side of the forward fuselage, just below the windscreen.

Italy – *Regia Aeronautica*

Known to the *Regia Aeronautica* as the *Picciatello* ('Little Woodpecker') after the cartoon character, the Ju 87Bs and Rs operated by them were in standard Luftwaffe camouflage of RLM 70/71 splinter camouflage on the upper surfaces and RLM 65 underneath. All the Luftwaffe markings were painted out (in a darker shade than the underlying paint, so this means it was done with Italian Verde Oliva Scuro) and the Italian fasci

Not great quality but included as this clearly shows how the existing wing crosses have been painted out in a darker shade than the surrounding RLM 70/71

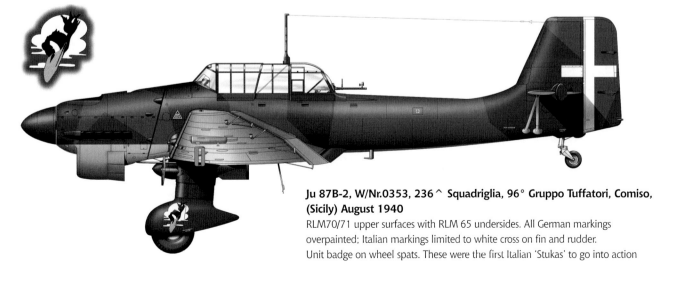

Ju 87B-2, W/Nr.0353, 236^ Squadriglia, 96° Gruppo Tuffatori, Comiso, (Sicily) August 1940
RLM70/71 upper surfaces with RLM 65 undersides. All German markings overpainted; Italian markings limited to white cross on fin and rudder.
Unit badge on wheel spats. These were the first Italian 'Stukas' to go into action

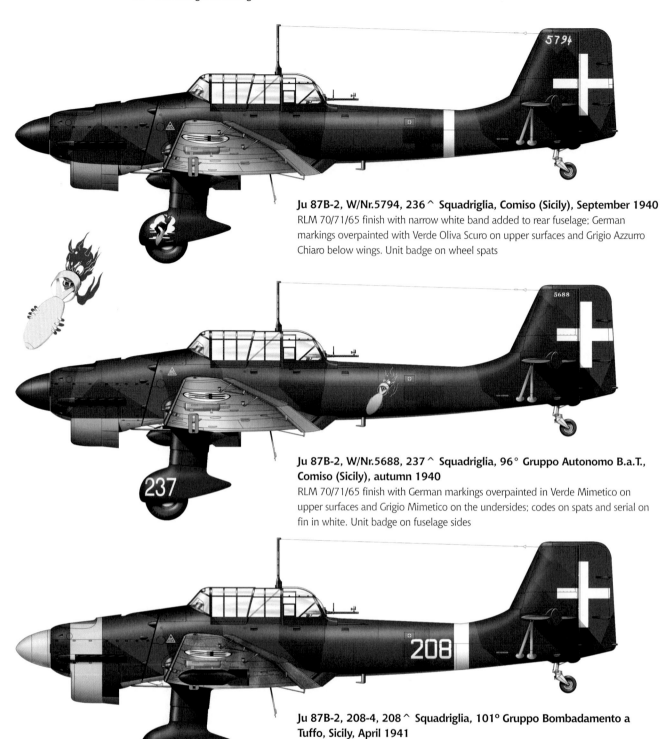

Ju 87B-2, W/Nr.5794, 236^ Squadriglia, Comiso (Sicily), September 1940
RLM 70/71/65 finish with narrow white band added to rear fuselage; German
markings overpainted with Verde Oliva Scuro on upper surfaces and Grigio Azzurro
Chiaro below wings. Unit badge on wheel spats

**Ju 87B-2, W/Nr.5688, 237^ Squadriglia, 96° Gruppo Autonomo B.a.T.,
Comiso (Sicily), autumn 1940**
RLM 70/71/65 finish with German markings overpainted in Verde Mimetico on
upper surfaces and Grigio Mimetico on the undersides; codes on spats and serial on
fin in white. Unit badge on fuselage sides

**Ju 87B-2, 208-4, 208^ Squadriglia, 101° Gruppo Bombadamento a
Tuffo, Sicily, April 1941**
RLM 70/71/65 finish with German markings overpainted in Verde Mimetico on top
and Grigio Mimetico on undersides; dark green roughly brushed on undersides.
Giallo Cromo spinner, band around engine cowling and '208' on fuselage. Red '4'
on wheel spats; White cross on tail and rear fuselage band

208a Squadriglia re-equipped with the Ju 87B-2 in
March 1941 and two examples are here seen in flight,
note the relatively small white cross on the fin/rudder,
the squadron number ahead of the white fuselage
band and the yellow (Giallo Cromo(band around
the nose denoting those aircraft operating in Albania,
Greece and Yugoslavia (©R.J. Caruana)

Ju 87 W/Nr.5688 of 237a Squadriglia, 96° Gruppo based at Comiso, with W/Nr. on the fin in white, Squadriglia number on wheel spats and the unit badge of the bomb-riding devil on the fuselage

(©R.J. Caruana)

Ju 87R-2, '208', flown by Capitano Raul Zucconi, Commander of the 101° Gruppo Autonomo Bombadamento a Tuffo

RLM 70/71/65 finish with German markings overpainted in Verde Mimetico on top and Grigio Mimetico on undersides. Giallo Cromo spinner and band around engine cowling. White cross on tail, '208' on fuselage and rear fuselage band; command pennant on wheel spats

Ju 87R-2, 209-8, 209 ^ Squadriglia, 97° Gruppo Autonomo Bombardamento a Tuffo, Derna (Libya), summer 1941

RLM 70/71/65 with previous German markings overpainted in Verde Mimetico on upper surfaces and Grigio Mimetico on undersides. Giallo Cromo band around engine cowling, '8' on wheel spats and '209' on fuselage. White band around rear fuselage and cross on tail

Ju 87B-2, W/NR.5763, 209-18, 209 ^ Squadriglia, 101° Gruppo Bombardamento a Tuffo

RLM 70/71/65 with all German national markings overpainted in Verde Oliva Scuro; Giallo Cromo nose and '18' on wheel spats. White tail cross, rear fuselage band and '209'; national markings with a white background below wings, black only above wings

**Ju 87B-2, W/Nr.7061, 239-7, flown by Cap. Giuseppe Cenni, Commander of 97°
Gruppo Bombardamento a Tuffo**

RLM 70/71/65 with previous German markings overpainted in Verde Oliva Scuro; national
markings with a white background below wings, black only above wings. Red spinner front, rank
pennant and unit badge on wheel spats; '7' repeated in red on front of spats. White cross on tail,
white fuselage band with '239' in black. Note 250kg Italian bomb on ventral cradle

insignia was applied under the wings (none on top). The white Savoy Cross (from the House of Savoy's coat of arms) was applied at the midpoint of the rudder, with the inner arm extending about 1/4 way across the vertical fin, plus a white band aft on the rear fuselage. Most *Regia Aeronautica* Stukas that operated in Albania, Greece and Yugoslavia also had a wide yellow (*Giallo Cromo*) band painted around the nose, as the Luftwaffe ground-attack forces would adopt in the final stages of WWII. Those operating

in North Africa could have the front 1/3rd of the cowling and the entire spinner in the same yellow. The *Squadriglia* (squadron) number was applied in white, red or yellow on each fuselage side, this was sometimes aft or ahead of the white band, while some had it on top in a contrasting colour. 237^ *Squadriglia* had their number applied on the outer face of the undercarriage lower cover. An individual aircraft number was often applied in smaller characters on either side of the mid-fuselage (again in white, red or

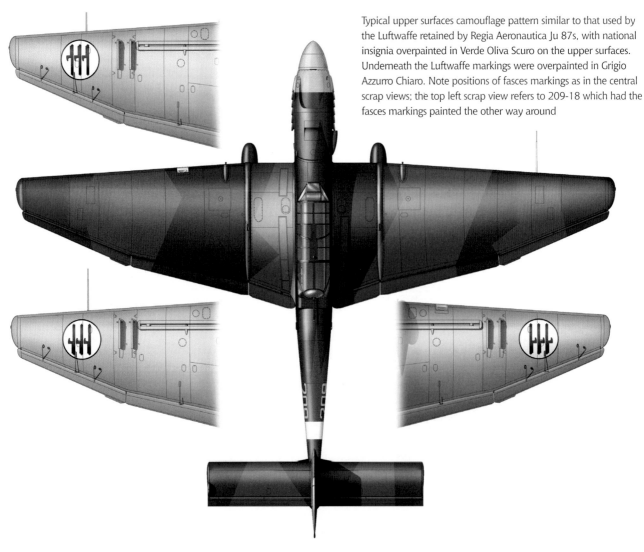

Typical upper surfaces camouflage pattern similar to that used by
the Luftwaffe retained by Regia Aeronautica Ju 87s, with national
insignia overpainted in Verde Oliva Scuro on the upper surfaces.
Underneath the Luftwaffe markings were overpainted in Grigio
Azzurro Chiaro. Note positions of fasces markings as in the central
scrap views; the top left scrap view refers to 209-18 which had the
fasces markings painted the other way around

yellow), while others had this applied on the outer face on the lower part of each undercarriage cover; 216^ *Squadriglia* used Roman (not Arabic) numerals in red for this applied on top of the fuselage band. Other markings included red propeller blade tips by 239^ *Squadriglia*, while unit badges such as the bomb-riding devil of 237^ *Squadriglia* and dive-bombing goose of 239^ *Squadriglia* were often applied either on the forward fuselage, or on the outer face of the lower undercarriage cover. Some machines retained their W/Nr., while others adopted a military serial number (MM.xxxxx) in its place.

Close-up of the diving-bombing goose emblem on the undercarriage spat of a 239a Squadriglia, 97° Gruppo machine

Ju 87D-3, 207-1, 207^ Squadriglia, 103° Gruppo Autonomo Tuffatori, Regia Aeronautica, Chilivani, June 1943

RLM 70/71 upper surfaces with all German markings and codes overpainted in Verde Oliva Scuro; RLM 65 undersides with German markings overpainted in Grigio Azzurro Chiaro. Red spinner front; codes in black with '1' in red

Ju 87D-3, 237-10, 237^ Squadriglia, 103° Gruppo Autonomo Tuffatori, Regia Aeronautica, Chilivani, May 1943

RLM 70/71 upper surfaces with all German markings and codes overpainted in Verde Oliva Scuro; RLM 65 undersides with German markings overpainted in Grigio Azzurro Chiaro. Yellow spinner front; codes in black with '10' in yellow repeated on wheel spats

Ju 87D-3, 216-VIII, 216^ Squadriglia, 121° Gruppo Autonomo Tuffatori, Regia Aeronautica, Capua, August 1943

RLM 70/71 upper surfaces with all German markings and codes overpainted in Verde Oliva Scuro; RLM 65 undersides with German markings overpainted in Grigio Azzurro Chiaro. White rear fuselage band and '216'; red 'VIII' over the white band (reason with the smaller 'V' is unknown). Aircraft fitted with flame damper exhausts

Ju 87D-3, 'Red 11', 121° Gruppo Autonomo Tuffatori, Lecce Galatina, autumn 1944
Verde Oliva 1 upper surfaces with Grigio Azzurro Chiaro 2 undersides. Spinner had white segments. Red '11' on fuselage sides ahead of roundel. National markings in six positions. Note the rear section of the canopy removed and the white 'E' on front of wheel spats

The Co-Belligerent Air Force Ju 87Ds were only used operationally for a very short time, then relegated to training duties, as seen here with 'Yellow 6', which has the Italian roundel on the fuselage and what's left of the fuselage band aft of that, plus the little '6' in yellow on the vertical fin on a darker patch that is the shape of the original Savoy Cross that used to occupy that area

Italy – Co-Belligerent Air Force

From the armistice of the 8th September 1943 a small number of ex-Luftwaffe Ju 87D Stukas were found on the Allied side, so those that could be made airworthy were. These were repainted Verde Oliva 1 upper surfaces, with Grigio Azzurro Chiaro 2 undersides, although you will see some with the demarcation on the nose quite high up the cowling sides. All Luftwaffe markings were painted out and the new Italian roundel was applied on either side of the fuselage and above and blow the wing, these were the same diameter in all six locations. Most seem to have adopted white bands on the spinners, these encompassed the blade root cut-out (thus determining their width), then tapered to the spinner tip. Some machines can be seen with a two-digit identification number applied in small white or red characters ahead of the fuselage roundel on both sides, while those used by the NVST (*Nucleo vola servizio tecnico*) carried 'NSVT' in small characters on either side of the vertical fin about 1/3rd from the top and with the 'S' in a very stylised form (as if stretched out length-wise). The service serial number (e.g. MM.100410) was applied on either side of the rear fuselage, low down, below the vertical fin fillet and in small white characters (not applied on all airframes). Note that none of these machines carried armament and the NVST machine was equipped with the glider towing bridle aft of the tailwheel.

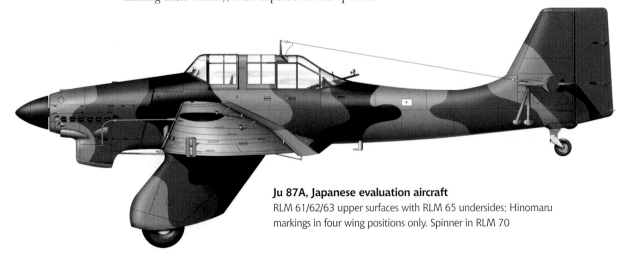

Ju 87A, Japanese evaluation aircraft
RLM 61/62/63 upper surfaces with RLM 65 undersides; Hinomaru markings in four wing positions only. Spinner in RLM 70

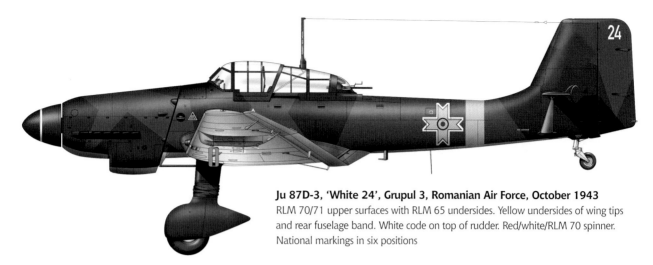

Ju 87D-3, 'White 24', Grupul 3, Romanian Air Force, October 1943
RLM 70/71 upper surfaces with RLM 65 undersides. Yellow undersides of wing tips and rear fuselage band. White code on top of rudder. Red/white/RLM 70 spinner. National markings in six positions

Japan

This nation never actually operated the Stuka, although two A-series airframes were sent to them for evaluation by both the military and aircraft manufacturers, before being used for public display and finally destoyed in a bombing raid on Tokyo.

Rumania

The *Fortele Aeriene Regala ale României* (Royal Rumanian Air Force – FARR) operated the D-series from the summer of 1943 and these were all ex-Luftwaffe stock, so retained their RLM 70/71 splinter camouflage over RLM 65 scheme. All Luftwaffe markings (often including radio call-signs) were painted out (again in what looks like original Luftwaffe paints) and the 'Michael the Brave' national insignia was applied either side of the rear fuselage and above and below the wings. A yellow theatre band (48cm wide) was applied around the rear fuselage, with yellow also applied underneath each wing tip. No codes etc. seem to have been applied, although an individual aircraft number would often be applied in white characters at the top of the rudder, or below the blue (front), yellow and red stripes

that can often be found applied at the very top of the rudder (often these were hand-painted, so were not precise).

When the coup occurred on the 23rd August 1944 the existing national markings were painted out and the pre-war style red/yellow/blue roundel was applied on either side of the fuselage and underneath the wings; none were applied above the wings. The top 1/3rd of the rudder usually had the blue/yellow/red stripes and the individual aircraft number was applied below it, usually in a script style font and either in white or yellow.

Ju 87D 'White 34a' of Rumanian Air Force with the initial style of 'Michael the Brave' insignia and yellow fuselage band

Ju 87D 'Hai noroc' with the later (simplified) 'Michael the Brave' national insignia plus '861' in yellow on the rudder with bands of blue/yellow/red across the top of the rudder. Note the original Luftwaffe codes and cross painted out in a darker shade on the fuselage

Individual aircraft names were also often applied in script-type white characters, usually applied on the upper, rear of the engine cowling and usually confined to the port side only.

Although of poor quality, this is one of the few images that show a Rumanian Ju 87D in post-coup markings, with the pre-war style roundels, those under the wings being positioned right on top of the original Luftwaffe crosses, which you can probably just make out as having been overpainted with a slightly lighter colour than the original RLM 65

Ju 87D-5, OK-XAC, Slovak Air Force, summer 1944
RLM 70/71 upper surfaces with RLM 65 undersides. Codes in white, with a small '3' at the base of the rudder. National markings in six positions

Ju 87D-5, B-6, 11th Squadron, 3rd Air Regiment, Slovak Air Force, based at Piestany, 1944
RLM 70/71 upper surfaces with RLM 65 undersides. Yellow wing tips and rear fuselage band. Slovak marking carried on fin and above wings; Luftwaffe cross retained underwing. B-6 is white

Slovakian Ju 87D-3 bearing the civil registration OK-XAC along with the Slovak cross on the tail

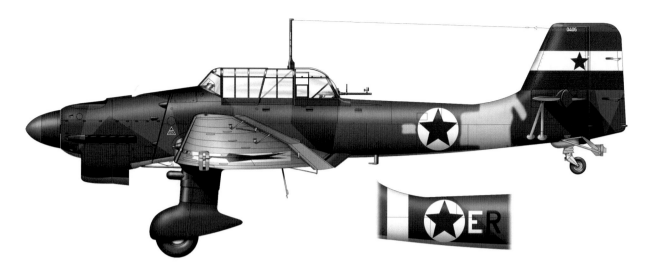

Ju 87B-2, W/Nr.0406, ex-5B+ER of NSGr.10, captured by Yugoslav partisans, Mostar, May 1945
RLM 70/71 upper surfaces with RLM 65 undersides. Markings overpainted in a light grey. Red stars added on a disk on the rear fuselage and on white rectangles above and below wings. Original code letters 'ER' and rear fuselage white band on starboard side retained. Note non-standard shape of the five-pointed red stars

Slovakia

The *Slovenské vzdušné zbrane* (Slovak Air Force – SVZ) operated a small number of D-series Stukas (initially given pre-war civil registrations registered OK-XAA to OK-XAE, although images of only XAA, XAB and XAC are known to exist) and these were all in tended for Luftwaffe use, so retained their RLM 70/71 splinter camouflage over RLM 65 scheme. All Luftwaffe markings were painted out (again in what looks like original Luftwaffe paints) and the Slovak national insignia (white cross on a blue background with a red dot in the centre) was applied above and below each wing and on either side of the vertical fin, mid-way up and with the rear arm of the cross just inboard of the rudder hinge line. A coding system (e.g. OK-XAA = 1, OK-XAB = 2 etc.) saw this number applied at the outer edge of the base of the rudder as a small white character. A later scheme saw the retention of the Luftwaffe cross on the underside of the wings and the codes were applied in white on either side of the fuselage, comprising 'B' followed by a number separated with a hyphen (see accompanying colour profile of B-6). These machines also adopted the yellow theatre band around the rear fuselage and yellow undersides to each wing tip.

Yugoslavia

Although this nation never received the type, partisans obtained at least one ex-Luftwaffe Ju 87B-2 (5B+ER previously of *Stab* NSGr 10) and this was hastily repainted in Yugloslavia markings. These comprised a red star on a white circle either side of the rear fuselage and those on the wings comprising the red star but in a large white square that we assume was that size simply to cover the Luftwaffe cross originally there. The upper half of the vertical fin and rudder was painted in equal width bands of blue (top), white and red, with a small red star in the middle of the white band. No other markings were carried and the original

Luftwaffe codes and yellow theatre band on the fuselage seem to have been roughly painted out in what is assumed to be grey.

Further Reading
We would also recommend the following titles for those wishing to read more on this complex subject:
- Luftwaffe 1935-1945 Camouflage and Markings Part 1 by Jaroslaw Wróbel and Janusz Ledwoch (AJ Press 1994, ISBN: 83-86208-08-2)
- Luftwaffe 1935-1945 Camouflage and Markings Part 2 by Jaroslaw Wróbel (AJ Press 1995, ISBN: 83-86208-14-7)
- Luftwaffe Colours 1935-1945 by M. Ullmann (Hikoki Publications Ltd 2002/Crécy Publishing Ltd 2008 ISBN: 9-781902-109077)
- Luftwaffe Emblems 1935-1945 by Barry Ketley & Mark Rolfe (Fight Recorder Publications 2012)
- The Official Monogram Painting Guide to German Aircraft 1935 – 1945 by Kenneth A. Merrick & Thomas H. Hitchcock (Monogram Aviation Publications 1980 ISBN: 0-914144-29-4)

The single ex-Luftwaffe Ju 87B-2 operated by the Yugoslavian (partisan) Air Force, the painted-out Luftwaffe markings and hastily applied Yugoslavian star can be seen on the fuselage and under the wings, as well as the horizontal bars with the small red star across the fin/rudder

Chapter 6: Ju 87 Kits

The Ju 87 has been a very popular subject with kit manufacturers over the years, so once again we thought we would have a look through a selection of kits and give you our assessment of them (*).

The list below is arranged by scale, then by manufacturer and variant

*With so many kits to cover, we have opted to go with those kits that remain in production as we write (February 2020). We would have done more but there are simply too many and fitting them within the available space would have been impossible.

Please note, although we initially wanted to use commercially produced and published scale plans in the below assessments, we have found that many are at odds when you convert the real measurement from the official manuals to scale and then compare that with the drawings. To make matters worse it should also be noted that the manual dimensions don't agree with published data either, especially the length of the D/G series, which some published sources incorrectly list as 11.5m, while all the manuals correctly state 11.00m We have therefore worked from the following scale conversions (to one decimal place) for the major dimensions based on the dimensions in the General Arrangement diagram in each type's manual:

1/144th Scale

Eduard, Czech Republic

Ju 87B
This kit was first released in 2004 as #4414 and reissued as a 'Dual Combo', with two complete kits in the box, (#4431) in 2014. We have the latter here for assessment.

Plastic: Dark grey-coloured with engraved panel lines and access panels but no fasteners or rivets.

Wings: These are solid units for each side, the control surfaces are separate and the dive brakes are supplied as etched brass. The panel lines and access panels match scale plans and the overall length is correct.

Fuselage: This is split vertically and the overall length is spot on. The panel lines seem to match most scale plans, the supercharger intake is a little short though. The exhausts and radiator flaps depict a late production version. The crew access steps on either side of the main fuselage are supplied as etched parts.

Ju 87A-1	1/72nd	1/48th	1/32nd	1/24th
Span (13.80m)	154.2mm	287.5mm	431.3mm	575mm
Length (10.82m)1	150.3mm	225.4mm	338.1mm	450.8mm
Height* (3.915m)2	54.4mm	81.6mm	122.3mm	163.1mm

1 – Tail up (in flight) position
2 – Tail up (in flight), bottom of wheel to top of propeller blade (pointing upwards)

Ju 87B/R	1/72nd	1/48th	1/32nd	1/24th
Span (13.80m)	154.2mm	287.5mm	431.3mm	575mm
Length (11.00m)3	152.8mm	229.2mm	343.78mm	458.3mm
Height (4.23m)4	58.8mm	88.1mm	132.2mm	176.3mm

3 – Tail up (12º ground angle), tip of spinner to tip tail light
4 – Tail up (12º ground angle), bottom of main wheel to top of rudder

Ju 87 D/G (short span)	1/72nd	1/48th	1/32nd	1/24th
Span (13.80m)	154.2mm	287.5mm	431.2mm	575mm
Length (11.00m)3	152.8mm	229.2mm	343.8mm	458.3mm
Height (4.23m)4	58.7mm	88.1mm	132.2mm	176.3mm

Ju 87D/G (long span)	1/72nd	1/48th	1/32nd	1/24th
Span (15.00m)	208.3mm	312.5mm	468.8mm	625mm
Length (11.00m)3	152.8mm	229.2mm	343.8mm	458.3mm
Height (4.23m)4	58.8mm	88.1mm	132.2mm	176.3mm

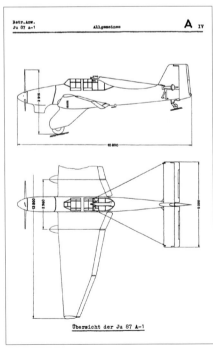

GA for Ju 87A-1

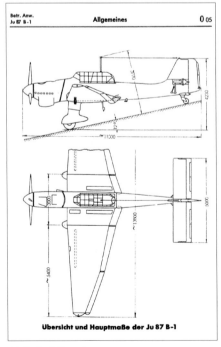

GA for Ju 87B-1

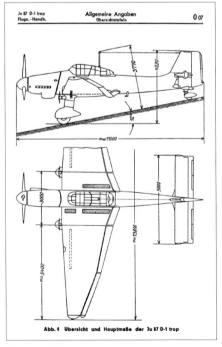

GA for Ju 87D-1

Eduard 4431

Undercarriage: These are supplied as single units, with the spats and wheels all moulded as one. The overall size is correct, but the thick nature of the moulding means that there is a slight sink mark on the left side of each leg. The tyres have tread detail, but the mould line around the circumference means you will have to take care cleaning. Fitment to the wings is achieved via big sockets in the wings to ensure a strong fit. The tailwheel is supplied as a separate part with yoke and wheel moulded as one.

Tailplanes: These are moulded with the elevators, the end caps with the vertical plates are separate parts, while the support V strut is etched, so a little 'flat'.

Engine: None is supplied.

Propeller: Separate spinner and blades, the length of the latter is correct but the profile is a little too wide.

Interior: None is included, the area in each fuselage is blanked off, only the outer elements of the MG 15 is supplied and then as etched, so again this is all 'flat'.

Details: The twin 50kg bomb racks are included as separate parts, there are no bombs for them though. The bomb trapeze is supplied as photo-etched and the centreline bomb is a single piece, so its fins are a little thick. The sprues also include 300lt drop tanks, but these are not mentioned in the instructions.

Canopy: This is one-piece, the framework is very fine, but the windscreen has external armoured glass. The rear gun position has the centre of the mounting as an etched part, although overall, it's not very effective.

Decals: The kit comes with three options as follows:

• Ju 87B-1, S2+AC, 'White 10' flown by Maj. Alfons Orthofer of II./JG27. This is RLM 70/71 over 65 with a sharkmouth on either side of the nose

• Ju 87B-2 Trop, A5+MK of 2./St.G 1, Derna, Libya, October 1941. This is RLM 79 over RLM 65 with a white theatre band around the rear fuselage

• Ju 87B, 29•6, 5.J/88, Legion Condor, Catalonia, Spain, January 1939. This is also RLM 70/71 over 65 with white rudder and wing tips

The decal sheet includes all the national and unique markings with the swastikas in two parts, although this element may be removed in certain countries. No stencils are included

Verdict:
This is certainly the choice for the type in this small scale, as the Revell one is a little too old and basic to consider now, while the Zvezda example is

intended for wargaming and thus is over-simplified and lacks detail.

Eduard, Czech Republic

Ju 87G
This kit was first released in 2004 as #4417 and reissued as a 'Dual Combo', with two complete kits in the box, (#4430) in 2014. We have the latter here for assessment

Plastic: Dark grey-coloured with engraved panel lines and access panels but no fasteners or rivets.

Wings: These are solid units for each side and the control surfaces are separate (dive brakes are not applicable to the G). The panel lines and access panels match scale plans and the overall length is about 1-2mm short. The ventral radiators are supplied as separate one-piece units.

Fuselage: This is split vertically and the overall length is spot on, but the ventral radiator is slightly too shallow with the intake lips also far too thick. The panel lines seem to match most scale plans, the supercharger intake looks to be too long, ending too near the spinner. The exhausts are a little flat, with an oblong raised surround that does not really reflect that area on the real thing. The crew access steps on either side of the main fuselage are supplied as etched parts.

Undercarriage: These are supplied as single units, with the spats and wheels all moulded as one. The overall size is correct, but the

Eduard 4430

thick nature of the moulding means that there is a slight sink mark on the left side of each leg. The tyres have tread detail, but the mould line around the circumference means you will have to take care cleaning them. The canvas gaiter on each leg is nicely depicted. The tailwheel is supplied as a separate part with yoke and wheel moulded as one.

Tailplanes: These are moulded with the elevators, the end caps with the vertical plates are separate parts, while the support strut is etched, so a little two-dimensional.

Engine: None is supplied.

Propeller: Separate spinner and blades, the length of the latter is correct with the wide profile of the later type.

Interior: None is included, the area in each fuselage is blanked off, only the outer elements of the MG 81Z is supplied and then as etched, so again this is two-dimensional.

Details: The twin 50kg bomb racks are included as separate parts (but no bombs), as are the BK 3.7 Flak 18 guns and gondolas although their ammunition magazines are

etched, so a little flat (even the folded up etched version).

Canopy: This is one-piece, the framework is very fine and the windscreen has the correct external armoured glass. The aerial mast is supplied as etched .

Decals: The kit comes with three options as follows:

• Ju 87G-2, W/Nr.494193, flown by Hans Ulrich Rudel, SG 2, Eastern Front, 1944-45. This is RLM 70/71 over 65 with yellow fuselage theatre band and the yellow 'V' under the port wing seen on ground-attack aircraft in the latter stages of WWII

• Ju 87G-2, W/Nr.491216, T6+BU, SG2, Eastern Front, 1944-45. This is RLM 70/71 over 65 with yellow lower wing tips

• Ju 87G-2, 'White F' of *Versuchskommando für Panzerbekanpfung*, 1943. This is RLM 70/71 over 65 with yellow rear fuselage and lower wing tips.

The decal sheet includes all the national and unique markings with the swastikas in two parts, although this element may be removed in certain countries. No stencils are included. Pre-cut self-adhesive masks are included for the main wheel hubs plus the fuselage and wing tip bands

Verdict:
This is certainly THE choice for the type in this small scale.

Note: We have not included the Zvezda Ju 87B kit (#6123) here because it is intended for wargaming use and as a result is very simplified (just a few components), so it would be unfair to assess it as if it were intended for the scale modelling market in general.

1/72nd Scale

Academy, Korea

Ju 87G-2
This kit was first release as a 'Kanonen Vogel' (#12404) in 2005 and was then reissued with the ex-Zvezda JS-2 (#12539) in 2016 as a Limited Edition. We have the former here for assessment.

Plastic: Light grey-coloured plastic with engraved panel lines and fasteners, but no rivets.

Wings: These are moulded as a single-piece lower and two separate upper halves. The span and chord are spot on and the panel lines match most scale plans. The raised wing walkways also match scale plans/period images. The tip lights are moulded with the wings, so are not clear. The control surfaces are all moulded with the lower wing half, making securing them not an issue. Because the wing tips are obviously done via separate tooling inserts, there is a visible line on the upper halves, while the lower one seems to not only have the line, but is shiny when compared to the rest of the wing? All lower linkage arms to the control surfaces are separate. The kit includes two styles of fairing for the wing guns, one when they were installed, the other blanked off, only the latter apply to the G-2. The radiators are separate units, but moulded as one, so there are no separate flaps etc., plus each unit is about 2mm too short.

Fuselage: This is moulded in two halves including the rudder and stopping at the engine firewall. The overall length is OK but its cross-section is about 1mm too shallow. Nearly every assessment of this kit you will read will tell you that the fuselage is woefully short in the engine region, however if you actually measure it and not just put it on scale plans, you will find it is almost spot on the correct 152.8mm? This is almost certainly caused by the fact that nearly all the published plans we have seen are about 48 scale-centimetres too long (often an error like this is just repeated and it becomes 'law'). The nose section has good overall detail, but the radiator is slightly too shallow (marginal).

Academy 12404

Undercarriage: These are supplied as two-part legs and separate main wheels. The overall length of the former is OK, but their overall height is too short, the front lower section does not look bulbous enough and the rear sections are too pointed plus the canvas gaiters are too long and depicted with basic deep lines; thankfully Quickboost do corrections (#QB72328). The upper legs also have the stubs for the siren, but that is not applicable to the (later) D or G-series (again the Quickboost set corrects this). The main wheels have nice tread pattern but if you use the Quickboost set, they are better examples. The tailwheel is depicted with a gaiter on it, this is rarely seen in wartime images.

Tailplanes: The tailplanes are moulded with the elevators and are the correct span and chord. The tips are separate and the trim tab linkage is moulded in situ on the underside. The support struts are separate parts.

Engine: None is supplied.

Propeller: This is made up of a spinner, propeller, cap and backplate. The spinner diameter is good, but it's too long/pointed. The propeller diameter is about 1mm short on each blade, but the profile is acceptable.

Interior: This comprises a floor, separate seats, mid and aft bulkheads, radio equipment and MG 81Z (oversimplified) with spent cartridge pipe and collector bag. Sidewall detail is also moulded in situ within each fuselage half and the instrument panel has basic moulded detail and a decal overlay. The lower section of the gunsight is moulded with the instrument panel, the upper clear lenses are not depicted. You can get a resin and etched interior from Aires (#7093).

Details: The gondolas are multi-part, although there is a better alternative set in resin from Aires (#7095).

Canopy: This is supplied either as a closed one-piece or four-part open version. The panel

frames are nicely depicted (although all are external, when some were only inside) and the windscreen has external armoured glass. The clear fret also includes the lens for the landing light in the port wing and the Pfeil G.IV D/F loop in the dorsal spine. The aerial mast is a separate (grey) component.

Decals: #12404 came with the following option:

• Ju 87G-2, W/Nr.494193, flown by Maj. Hans-Ulrich Rudel, *Kommodore* SG2, Russia, summer 1944. This is in an RLM 70/71 over 65 scheme.

The decal sheet includes all the national and unique markings, but no swastikas. Some airframe stencils are included along with the yellow fuselage band and 'V' that wraps around the port wing, although most will mask and paint these.

Verdict:

In the box this looks a nice kit, cleanly moulded with good overall detail, however most write it off due to the supposed dimensional errors as far as the nose goes, but that is not the case. This builds into a nice model (see Libor's build in Section 7) and there are loads of aftermarket products to update, correct and superdetail it, so it's well worth the time and effort.

Airfix, UK

Ju 87B-1

This kit was first released in 2016 (#A03087) and remains in production.

Plastic: Moulded in their blue-grey coloured plastic with engraved panel lines and access panels but no fasteners or rivets.

Wings: These are moulded as two upper halves with the lower section done as two outer panels and combined inner sections that include a section of the lower fuselage and a spar unit. The span and chord match scale plans, as do most of the access panels, the long oval one on the port wing, just by the join should not be there, though, and is just duplicated from the starboard. Not 100% convinced by the two close-together panel lines near each tip. Wing walkways are depicted as raised areas and the wing-mounted machine gun blisters are separate parts that fit into holes in the wing. The control surfaces are separate and include all linkage rods and even the two balance weights on the outer region.

Fuselage: This is moulded in two sections with the mid and rear fuselage stopping at the engine firewall. Overall length is good, the rudder is separate and the panel lines etc. match scale plans. The cowlings are made up in three parts, the upper one has the asymmetric oil cooler intake and its exhaust area is correctly depicted oblong. The oil cooler matrix is depicted via a separate insert, which also doubles as the exhaust flap. The exhausts depict the early oval outlets and there are separate inserts from the inside of each cowl half. The lower radiator has the front lip and radiator detail as a separate part, but the latter is a bit too far forward, resulting in a lip that is too shallow. The aft area of the radiator unit is moulded with the cowl halves and it depicts the early version without the flaps.

Undercarriage: The main legs are depicted

as four-part legs/spats and separate main wheels. The overall shape of all of these is very good and the upper section comes with the siren stubs (blanked off) as separate parts. The main wheels have a very finely engraved simple tread pattern and are 'weighted', but can be used for on-the-ground or in-flight via a tab that locks into the inside of the undercarriage spat, one way puts the flat at the bottom, or rotate it so it is hidden up inside the spat (clever). The tailwheel is moulded as one piece, but you get two styles, one with and one without a fairing over the wheel.

Tailplanes: These are moulded with the elevators and are the correct size and chord. The two upper access panels are depicted raised, while those underneath are missing. The end plates are separate parts and the trim tabs lack any linkage. The support struts are separate and include the aerodynamic fairings at each end.

Engine: None is supplied.

Propeller: This is made up of a spinner, propeller, backplate, bush/bearing and shaft. Going by scale plans the propeller is too great in diameter and the blade shape is too narrow with a blunt tip (I think Quickboost make a corrected B/R propeller for the Fujimi kit that might work here).

Interior: Sidewall detail inside each fuselage half is via separate parts, so no worries about sink marks. The cockpit floor is part of that spar section that fits to the lower fuselage and inboard lower wing halves. You have the option of a pilot's seat with or without seat belts, the latter used if you install the supplied separate figure. The separate instrument panel lacks any moulded detail, it relies entirely on a decal. The sight support frame and sight itself is supplied as a clear component. The mid

Airfix A03087

bulkhead has all the radio equipment moulded with it and the rear gunner's seat and MG 15 spent cartridge bag is also supplied. You not only get the clear panel in the floor between the pilot's feet, you also get the box structure around it inside.

Details: Four 50kg bombs are included as single-piece mouldings, so the fins are a little thick, their accompanying racks are separate and quite nice considering their small size. You get a multi-part 250kg and 500kg bomb for the centreline rack (the fins are quite thin) and you even get the ETC rack itself plus the trapeze as separate parts; the latter item comes in 250kg or 500kg versions.

Canopy: This comes in open or closed versions, each being three-part, however the problem with that is painting the framework for the overlapping mid portion if you go with the open option. The canopy frames are clearly defined and the round panel in the rear gun position is a separate part. The gunsight and landing light lens are also on the clear sprue. The aerial mast is a grey-coloured component, as is the pitot tube.

Decals: The kit (#A03087) came with the following options:
• Ju 87B-1, 6G+AT, 9./St.G 51, Norrent-Fintes, France, August 1940
• Ju 87B-1, 29•8, *Kampfgruppe* 88, Legion Condor, Spain 1938

Both options are RLM 70/71 over 65, while option 2 has a white rudder and wing tips. The decals are nicely printed although a little matt looking. The sheet includes all unique and national markings plus a series of airframe stencils, walkways and that decal for the instrument panel. No swastikas are included.

Verdict:
This the THE choice for the B or R-series in this scale nowadays, as Airfix revised this as the B-2/R-2 (#A03089/#A50179) in 2017. Hopefully Airfix may also consider the D or G version one of these days.

HobbyBoss, China

Ju 87D-3 (#80286)
G-1 (#80287)
Both kits were released in 2013 and have remained in production ever since. They are both within the 'Easy Assembly' range with limited parts and partially solid fuselage etc. Although both the D-3 and G-2 should be different, they share common parts, so we will cover them together.

Plastic: Moulded in a medium grey-coloured plastic with finely engraved panel lines and fasteners, but no rivets.

Wings: This is moulded as a solid unit complete with the lower region of the entire fuselage. Whilst the control surfaces are separate both the D-3 and G-2 kit have the extended tips, so with the former you can't actually build that variant, only a D-5. The span is about 1mm over but the chord is correct. The main panel lines match most scale plans and whilst the majority of access panels are correct, there are a number at odds with plans in that they are in the wrong place, wrong size or are oval when most show them as round etc. The landing light in the port wing leading edge is not depicted, either as engraved lines or a separate clear component.

Fuselage: This is one-piece and partially solid, with the lower region moulded with the wings. Overall length is fractionally too great, but it's marginal. Overall the main panel lines are good, but again some of the access panels are at odds with scale plans. The rudder lacks any linkage for the trim tabs and the small bulges on the upper/top edge of the engine cowls look too pronounced. The supercharger intake is a little too long and is solid without definition of the flap at the front. The exhausts are separate and the correct length/style for the D-5 and later, albeit each outlet is solid (OK, a lot to ask for an 'easy' kit in this small scale). The chin radiator is depicted with the front section separate, to allow the internal detail to be depicted, but as moulded the lip

HobbyBoss 80286

of the unit is too shallow, making the radiators inside far too near the front of it; the lip is also too thick. The D/F loop is moulded into the dorsal spine with a separate clear cover.

Undercarriage: These are moulded as two-part leg/covers and separate wheels. The overall length of the units looks good and whilst the profile of the lower cover matches some plans, others depict it more bulbous/deeper. The wheels are the correct diameter and have the right crosswise style tread pattern. The hubs lack any detail though. The tailwheel is moulded as one unit and although the wheel size is good, the overall length of the yoke arms is slightly too great, so once attached the wheel will actually sit too far aft. The oleo leg itself is not that accurate either.

Tailplanes: This is moulded as a single unit with the elevators moulded in situ. Span and chord are correct and the end caps are the correct shape. The linkage arms for the elevator trim tabs are too long and the access panels underneath the tailplane depict the style (e.g. five of them) of the B-series, not the four oval and one rectangular of the D and G series. The access panels on the upper surface are confusing, as the manual shows them running fore and aft on the port and side to side on the starboard(?), while this kit depicts them side to side on both.

Engine: None is supplied.

Propeller: This is made up of the backplate, spinner and three-blade propeller unit. The spinner diameter and profile are good, while the propeller is way undersize, being short at least 2mm on each blade. The blade profile is also odd, although that's of little consequence considering the diameter error.

Interior: The floor is moulded into the partially-solid fuselage, the only other details you get are separate control column, pilot's seat (the gunner's is not included) and a rather odd partial depiction of the rear MG 81Z. The instrument panel is depicted via a decal that is applied to the bulkhead moulded inside the fuselage half, while the sighting glass in the floor between the pilot's feet is a separate clear component.

Details: The 250kg bomb for the centreline rack is multi-part and quite nice, although it depicts the fragmentation bomb with the 'blast' ridge around the nose. The wings have no racks, either moulded in situ or separate and you thus have no options to fit anything on them either. Whilst the aerial mast is depicted separately, the crew access steps are moulded with the lower wing/fuselage and are just stubs, lacking the horizontal (forward)

elements, plus they are also at 90° to the fuselage underside, not splayed outwards as they should be. The kit also completely fails to include the pitot for the starboard wing, although separate barrels for the MG 151/20 cannon are included. Both kits include, but only the G-2 uses, the BK 3.7cm Flak 18 gondolas, which are multi-part but the gondola body is undersize (too short and thin) and the gun barrel is about 5mm short. Whilst the upper pylon is a separate part for some reason HobbyBoss have completely omitted the ammunition feed/ejection unit on either side.

Canopy: This is a single-piece moulding with all the frames as raised detail, even though a number of them are inside the glazing. The clear sprue also includes the ventral sighting window and the cover for the DF loop on the dorsal spine.

Decals: Each kit offers the following options:
#80286
• Ju 87D-3, S2+NM of 4./StG 77 – This is RLM 70/71 over RLM 65 with yellow rear fuselage band (supplied as a decal) and underneath each wing tip
• Ju 87D-3, S2+LT of 9./StG 77, Winniza, Ukraine, winter 1943-44 – This is in the RLM 70/71/65 scheme but with white winter distemper applied to all the upper surfaces

The decal sheet includes all the unique and national markings, with the swastikas in four parts. There is also a good set of airframe stencils and a decal for the instrument panel.

HobbyBoss 80287

#80287
• Ju 87G-2, GS+MH of 10.(Pz)/SG 1, Dubno, Ukraine, June 1944 – This is RLM 70/71 over 65
• Ju 87G-1*, S7+EN of 10.(Pz)/SG 3, Jakobstadt, Lithuania, July 1944 – This is RLM 71 over 65

The decal sheet includes all the unique and national markings, with the swastikas in four parts. There is also a good set of airframe stencils and a decal for the instrument panel.
*You can't make a G-1 from this kit, as it was based on the D-3 and thus has the short-span wings

Verdict:
Whilst these kits are crisply moulded with excellent engraved detail and offer straightforward construction, the errors and omissions are such that I can't see anyone wanting to make either kit, plus of course 'either' is inappropriate, as BOTH depict the long-span D-5/D-8/G-2.

Italeri, Italy

Ju 87B/R

This kit was first issued as a Ju 87B-2/R-2 (#079) in 1997 and reissued as #1292 in 2010. It was also released as a special limited edition in 1992 as 'Speciale Italia' (#6805). We have both #1292 and #6805 kits here for assessment.

Plastic: Light-grey coloured with engraved panel lines and hatches, but no fasteners or rivets.

Wings: These are moulded as a one-piece lower and two upper halves, the overall span is correct but the chord is a little under. The panel lines are a mix of some that match most scale plans and others that have nothing to do with the type, such as the odd kidney-shaped one just inboard of the outer wing panel joint, while others are just the wrong size, shape and location (e.g. wing gun access panels). The roots also lack any depiction of the anti-slip panels. The lower wing half is a bit better, having the control surfaces all moulded in situ to ease assembly, although all the linkage is also moulded in situ as solid wedges. Most of the smaller access panels have been depicted as ovals that are far too elongated, plus a number are missing and some are once again depicted that don't match plans or diagrams from the manuals, The wing tip lights are not depicted in any manner and on the fuselage centre-section region included with the lower wing half, the centreline rack is depicted via four oblong holes that are the wrong way round (they would be more accurate running side to side, rather than fore and aft), while the actual rack pick-up in the centre is not depicted at all.

Fuselage: This is moulded from the rudder to the engine firewall, with the rudder itself moulded with the port fuselage half. Overall length is OK, but the profiles of the leading and trailing edges of the vertical fin and upper rudder are slightly undersize, and the top of the vertical fin has a tube moulded into it (either for the aerial lead or as a pitot, neither of which are correct). The main panel lines match most scale plans, although the First Aid kit access panel on the port side is in the wrong place and the wrong size, while the panel lines ahead of the cockpit are at odds with plans (those on the vertical tail whilst 'nearly' correct, have a few errors as far as placement and overall size of panels are concerned). The nose section is separate and moulded as four parts, comprising sides, radiator intake and upper cowling. The overall size and shape of this unit is good, with the deeper radiator depicted, but the cover for the starter handle on the lower port side is missing and the shutters in the radiator intake lacks the round bulged cover near the top. The upper cowl has the asymmetric oil cooler intake at the front and the exhaust at the rear, but the latter lacks any depiction of the exhaust flap itself. The upper cowl also lacks a number of small intake scoops associated with the B-2 series and the filler access panel on the upper/rear. For some reason Italeri have depicted the cowl fasteners as oblong indentation on the lower halves, these are not only incorrect for the round fasteners of the type, but they are positioned well below the upper

cowl edge and there are too few of them. The ventral area between the wings is moulded with the lower wing half, as already mentioned, but the in region ahead of this there is no depiction (not even an engraved outline) of the viewing panel in the cockpit floor that is so well-known with the Stuka.

Undercarriage: The main undercarriage covers are about 1mm too long overall, while the upper sections are slightly too narrow (all at the front) and the front profile of the lower spat is also too shallow (at the front lower edge). The siren mounts are moulded in situ, but the stub is one constant unit, where in reality it was two separate units (you can engrave the missing panel line). The separate siren propellers are the correct size, but lack any hub detail and the shape of the blades is incorrect with no real twist at the base and depicted as a constant (straight) unit, where in reality they tapered slightly all the way to the tip. The main wheels are moulded separately and lack any tread pattern, while the hubs have an odd series of four circular indentation in them on one side, and nothing the other. The tailwheel is moulded as one with the port fuselage half and it depicts the later style unit used by the D and G series, as the yoke is too skinny and there is no canvas gaiter.

Tailplanes: These are moulded with the elevators, but have the tips separate and span and chord are OK. The separate tips correctly depict the bulged end caps of the B-series, but the area that is attached to the elevator and thus produces a protractor-shaped unit is not depicted correctly, instead the tailplane end flares out to meet the elevator end and the

Italeri 1292

curve of the 'protractor' is shown as a raised line with the unit then tapering to the trailing edge when it should only actually project half-way along the elevator before going down to the elevator thickness. These small parts also feature a prominent ejector pin mark in the aft region. The support struts are separate and are of the correct size and shape with the fairings around each root moulded in situ.

Engine: None is supplied.

Propeller: This is made up of the backplate with shaft, spinner and three-blade propeller. The propeller blades are about 1mm too long and the profile is neither the early HPA unit, nor the compressed wooden blades of the VS unit, it's something between the VS 5 and VS 11 with the blades also lacking much in the way of twist at the root. The spinner diameter is good, but the profile is about 1.5mm too long, resulting in it having a longer taper

and less of the pronounced bulge seen in the real thing.

Interior: This comprises a floor, separate control column, seats, mid-bulkhead and instrument panel with raised detail. The pilot's seat has belts moulded in situ and the mid-bulkhead has all the radio equipment moulded into it. The turnover frame at the top of the mid-bulkhead is depicted with vertical support bars that have a horizontal and diagonal one towards the base, however the real unit only had two vertical bars that ran from the upper middle, to the lower edges with a wide frame on the sides. The control column is too short and depicted as a very odd shape, nothing like the real KG 12 unit, the rudder pedals are just wedges moulded with the floor and the spent shell bag for the rear gunner is just a simple box moulded with the floor. There is no sidewall detail, either separate or moulded within each fuselage half. The raised detail on the instrument panel is not really much like the B-series example, the shape is also off, as it's made to follow the contours of the interior of the fuselage, when the real thing had flat/tapered sides. The gunsight is moulded atop the instrument panel so it's grey-coloured plastic, plus it is not very accurate (a simple square block) with the lens also in grey-coloured plastic.

Details: The bomb trapeze depicts the late B-series unit with the adjusters half-way along each arm, but the unit is depicted with straight arms forward of this, when the real unit curved to mount at the lower/front of the engine firewall and this means that the kit part is wholly connected via its attachment to the bomb, instead of also via the underside of the fuselage. The ETC racks and 50kg bombs are included for underneath the outer wing panels, but these are moulded as one unit, the racks are just simple oblongs and the bombs themselves lack any real detail plus the fins are too thick. The centreline bomb looks to be 250kg and comes as two halves with the fins as a separate unit. The retaining strap around the middle of the bomb is depicted, but it's rather too pronounced in this small scale. The separate fins are not too bad with the bracing struts moulded in situ for each, but the rear upper profile of each is rounded, when the real thing was square, with only the leading edge having a taper (correctly depicted here). The dive brakes are separate and the correct size and shape, but the mounting brackets are all just simple lugs. The kit offers both standard and desert supercharger intake, the former is slightly undersize (too short at the rear), while the latter lacks the panel line around it at the mid-point. The exhaust stacks are a separate insert on each side, but the individual stacks are just poorly defined (solid) wedges. The R-series has the 300lt drop tanks to go under the outboard ETC racks and these are moulded in two halves with the lugs associated with this type of fitment, however the racks themselves will not be there, as they are moulded with the 50kg bombs, so it's not a very accurate depiction. The aerial mast, crew steps, mass balance weights and pitot are all separate parts – ignore the illustration for Stage 9 in the instructions though, as it shows the model with a pitot in the leading edge of both wings?

Canopy: This is supplied in three sections and is moulded to allow the forward section to be slid aft. The frames are all depicted by a slightly raised frosted effect to them, however they are all too heavy/wide as a result and the frames inside the rear section are not depicted at all, whilst those in the pilot's sliding section are depicted on the outside via the raised/frosted effect. The rear gun mount only depicts the early unarmoured style.

Decals: Each kit offered the following options:

#1292
- Ju 87B-2 Trop, T6+DP of 6./StG 2, Libya, January 1942 – this is the well-known 'snake' option in RLM 79 with RLM 70/71 patches over RLM 65
- Ju 87R-2, S1+CK of 2./StG 3, Crete, May 1941 – this is RLM 70/71 over 65 with yellow nose and rudder
- Ju 87B-2, F1+LR, 7./StG 77, France, August 1940
- Ju 87R-2, '208' of 208° *Squadriglia, Bombardamento a Tuffo, Regia Aeronautica*, Greece, December 1940 – this is RLM 70/71 with the undersides overpainted in black, except the nose, which remained in RLM 65 with the yellow band around it

The decal sheet includes all the unique and national insignia, but no swastikas. The snake artwork is depicted on both sides of the fuselage and is in pale yellow and white (other depict as red/white (or RLM 79/white) and only on the port side). The sheet also has a small selection of airframe stencils, the wing walkways and the white fuselage band for the Italian option

#6805
- Ju 87R-2, '209' of 209° *Squadriglia, Bombardamento a Tuffo, Regia Aeronautica*, Tuffatori, Sicily, 1941 – this is *Verde Scuro* over *Grigio Azzurro Chiaro* with a yellow band around the nose

Verdict:
As with so many kits this one is a mish-mash of good and bad points, and whilst it is crisply moulded and generally accurate in shape, the various errors in certain aspects coupled with the total lack of detail in others mean that nowadays it is probably not going to be on anyone's 'to do' list because there are simply better examples out there.

Zvezda, Russia

Ju 87B-2

This new kit (#7306) was first announced in 2013, but was not actually released until 2015. It is a snap-together kit, but not simplified, being more akin to a standard kit that just also happens to be snap-fit in certain areas.

Plastic: Medium grey-coloured plastic with engraved panel lines and a few attachments and fittings, but no rivets.

Wings: Moulded as upper and lower halves, with the ailerons and flaps moulded in situ with the upper half and the lower linkage arms with the lower half. The tip and one panel inboard are moulded with the upper half. Overall span and chord correct. The panel lines on the upper surface do not match published plans, the two oblong access panels towards the tip are missing, whilst the oval

one behind the gun access hatch and just inboard of the wing seam are the wrong size. No tip lights are depicted, or included as separate parts. The panel lines and access panels on the lower wing half matches scale plans. The ETC 50 racks are moulded in situ and are just very basic blocks with plugs for the bombs. The downward visible panel (clear) and dive brakes are also separate parts. The pitot is moulded in situ in the starboard leading edge and it's a bit thick. The clear cover for the landing light in the port wing is also a separate part.

Fuselage: This is broken down into two halves, but the upper section of the vertical fin and rudder are moulded as one with the starboard half. The upper nose cowling is separate from the firewall forward and the front and rear of the chin radiator are also separate. The overall length is 3mm short, all of this being forward of the firewall. The upper cowling has good overall shape, as does the oil cooler intake, having the lop-sided shape of the real thing. The rear exhaust flap is moulded in situ and partially open, so that is not as effective. The curved panel over the top engine pick-up bolts is a little 'pointed' and poorly defined,

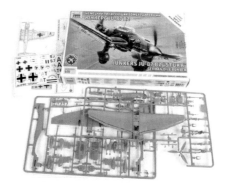

Zvezda 7306

while the small intake is depicted below on the port side but solid, as you would expect in this small scale. The front chin intake is a little shallow and two-dimensional around the lip, while the shutters are also a little 'flat'. The rear section of the chin cowling depicts the separate flaps of the mid-production. Upper and lower bulkheads for the oil cooler and lower radiator (rear) are included as separate parts. The supercharger intake is separate, but is a little shallow.

Tailplanes: These are moulded as single-piece units for each side, with the elevators in situ. The span and chord are correct, but the access panels are the wrong shape, size and location. The V-shaped support struts are separate and the correct size and shape with solid locating points into the fuselage.

Undercarriage: Each leg is moulded with a large locating lug at the top, so they will be secure. The overall size is good, but the profile at the front is a little shallow. The dive siren mounts are moulded in situ with the two-blade propeller separate and the wheels are also separate with nice tread and hub detail.

Engine: None is supplied.

Propeller: This comprises the three-blade unit, a backplate and spinner with the mounting shaft added through the bulkhead in the engine compartment. The propeller diameter

is good, but the blade profile looks too wide, being more akin to the later paddle blades.

Interior: A basic floor is moulded with the upper wing half, a separate control column, central bulkhead with radio equipment and spent ammunition bin are also included and you have the option of including the multi-part crew figures, which are moulded with their seats, or just the seats (with moulded belts) on their own. The instrument panel comes with moulded detail or plain, so you can use the supplied decal. Part of the gunsight is moulded with the upper fuselage decking, with the main body as part of the instrument panel, this does mean the lens is not clear.

Details: The kit comes with a 250kg bomb for under the fuselage, the overall shape is good but detail is lacking and it uses a large pin to secure it in place. The bomb trapeze is separate and very nicely done. The 50kg bombs under each outer wing panel are single-piece mouldings, so there is no real detail, the fins are a little thick and each locates via two sockets onto the pins of the racks that are moulded with the lower wing half. The exhaust stacks are separate items with solid outlets.

Canopy: This is a single-piece unit that snaps into place, the rear gun mounting ring is a separate piece and this, along with the gun and ammunition drum has to be secured with conventional adhesive. The overall shape of the unit is good, although the framework looks slightly over-scale.

Decals: The kit offers two decal options:
- S7+HL, 3./StG.3, North Africa, 1941
- T6+AT, 9./StG.2, Western Europe, 1940

The accompanying decal sheet is well printed with good register and colour, but whilst it offers all the unique and national markings, plus (just two) wing walkways and yellow fuselage band there are no swastikas nor any airframe stencils.

Verdict:
Overall this is a nice kit, one of the better ones in this smaller scale. Some may ignore it due to the snap-together nature, but the level of detail is very nice and having built their Yak-3 in the same format, I can assure you they look very good once completed.

1/48th Scale

Airfix, UK

Ju 87B/R Series

Airfix announced their intension to produce a new tooling of the Stuka in 1/48th in 2015, but it was not until 2017 that the first, the Ju 87B-1 (#A07114,) was actually released. This was followed the same year by the revised tooling to allow the B-2 and R-2 versions to be produced (#A07115) and in 2019 #A07114A was released, which was #A07114 with revised decal options. All three remain in production and as all share common parts with a few revisions, we will work from the B-1 (#A07114), noting any differences in #A07115 as we go along.

Plastic: Moulded in a medium grey-coloured plastic, the parts feature engraved panel lines and fasteners and some rivets.

Wings: These are moulded as separate upper and lower halves with the lower inner stubs as part of the lower fuselage section and a separate box spar unit is included to give the whole thing better strength. The span is spot on and the chord is slightly narrow, but it's marginal (and only if you accept published plans). Both the panel lines and the access panels match most scale plans (although none of them agree) and the anti-slip areas are defined by raised borders. The flat area in the stub/outer wing panel fairing is missing on both sides. The gun blisters are separate and include the gun barrel projecting from them. There is an option to open the gun bays if you so choose, and the instructions show you what areas need to be removed, the gun and ammo feed etc. are supplied for this and fit into a 'bay' created by the wing spars. The control surfaces are separate and oddly feature rivet details. All the control surface mounts are finely moulded and the linkage rods are all depicted as such (not wedges or blocks). You get the option of having the inner sections deployed via two complete sets of control surfaces, and the mass balance weights on the ailerons are moulded in situ. The landing light comes as a clear inner section depicting the light and a separate clear cover. The dive brakes are separate, good in overall size and shape and have fairly fine mounting lugs.

Fuselage: This is moulded in two halves with the cowlings and rudder separate. Overall length and profile are excellent and you have optional parts for the radiator in the form of segmented or plain rear flaps and the front intake is depicted with the shutters open or closed. The depth of the radiator intake lip looks a bit shallow when compared with period images and the two small intakes under the front cowl above it are only in partial relief. The differences in the B-1 and B-2 radiators and exhausts are dealt with via different components, with the B-1 having the original narrower/shallower radiator and the oval open exhausts, while the B-2 has the deeper/wide radiator and the ejector exhaust stacks although the breakdown of the assembly in each case is the same. The upper cowl is the same for both versions and includes the asymmetric intake with the rear exhaust flap and oil cooler itself done via a separate component. The sprues contain the segmented rear flap for the ventral radiator, although it is not used in either the B-1 or B-2/R-2 kits. The supercharger intake is separate (with the inner tube to lock it in place in the cowling) and you have the tropical version included for the R-2. Both the oval and ejector exhausts are separate, so each is very effective, especially as the former are slightly hollow at each outlet. The ventral viewing panel is supplied in clear plastic (the structure's inside as part of the cockpit interior), with the outer cover also separate so you can pose it open or closed.

Undercarriage: The main legs are made up of two-part upper struts, two-part lower leg/covers and separate wheels. The overall size and shape are very good and the shape of the opening for the wheel is correct, with it tucking back in to create the underside at the rear of the fairing; there has a raised lip around it in reality, but in this scale that's a

lot to ask. The joint between the front and rear section of the wheel covers is depicted as a raised line with the fastener bolt holes recessed. The upper portion of each leg is separate to allow the stub for the siren to be included or omitted; only the blanked-off stub (which suffers from a sink mark) is mentioned in each kit, although two stubs with propellers (#D09 & D14) are included on the sprues. The main wheels are the correct diameter and have the usual crosswise tread pattern. They are weighted, but Airfix give you the option of using this feature or ignoring it simply by rotating the wheel to a set position in the cover, where a tab on the tyre engages with a socket inside. Two styles of tailwheel are on the sprues, one depicts the B-type with the heavy cast yoke and canvas gaiter, while the other has the later version with the smaller yoke and exposed oleo strut.

Tailplanes: These are moulded as upper and lower halves on both sides with the elevators and end caps separate. The span and chord are good for each element and the end cap comes in two version so that you can have the elevators in the neutral position or deflected slightly. The linkages for the trim tabs on the elevators are not depicted in any way, probably due to the problems this would cause in deflecting them. The support struts are well moulded and have positive locating tabs on either end thanks to Airfix opting to just use elongated versions of the fairings

Airfix A07114

at that point. Airfix have not opted to show the square access panel under the starboard tailplane, as this seems a contentious issue with some plans showing it and others not (I have not personally looked up underneath the R in Chicago, so can't really comment further on this point). The trim tab linkage is on the undersides, but the rods themselves are poorly defined, even as moulded detail.

Engine: You get a whole multi-part engine complete with oil cooler, radiator, supercharger, exhausts and engine bearers. The supercharger intake tube is even included to lock into the tube that is part of the intake on the cowls and if you want to leave all the cowls off, you can, as the splines on the propeller shaft are depicted, or you can add the propeller unit as a whole. The engine bulkhead is nicely detailed, so that the engine can be exposed.

Propeller: This is made up of a shaft and collar, backplate, spinner and three-blade propeller. The B-1 kit uses the narrow HPA propeller blades, whist the B-2/R-2 has the

wider compressed wooden blades, although both propeller types are on the sprues in both kits. The spinner diameter and profile are spot on, while the blade shape and length for each version is good. The blade root profile may be a little off with the latter type and the tip is too blunt with the earlier version, but Quickboost do replacements for each (#QB48787 & QB48788) if you want.

Interior: This is made up on a floor that is part of the spar box, there is a separate rear bulkhead, correctly shaped pilot's seat with the open hoop at the top, spent cartridge bin, ammunition drum rack, gunner's seat, radio equipment, control column, sidewalls and an instrument panel that has the rudder pedals and the surround for the ventral viewing panel (with clear window) in it. The instrument panel features raised details for the dials plus there is a decal to lay over it and add the actual dial faces etc. The roll-over frame depicts the unarmoured version in both kits, although we are sure the aftermarket etched sets will have covered the armoured version/s by now? The crew seats have no seat belts, however Quickboost do seats with belts moulded in situ (#QB48794).

Details: The small ETC racks under each outer wing panel are separate and quite acceptable for the scale, the R-version includes 300lt drop tanks to hang off these (and these have the tube projecting from the front seen on many wartime images of the R-series). The centreline ETC rack is separate and has the sway braces also as separate parts. The 250kg bomb is multi-part and the fins are quite thin, although no support struts are depicted between them. The trapeze used for both versions is for the 250kg bomb, but the sprue also contains a version that has been widened to allow a 500kg bomb to be carried. The rear MG 15 is moulded with a partial chute for the spent cartridges, when some early machines had a bag, the ammunition drum is separate though (you will need to add a ring sight though). The aerial mast (correct shape), crew access steps (not convinced by their shape), pitot tube and trailing aerial tube are all included as separate parts and the kit even includes the starter handle on the port side of the engine cowls.

Canopy: This is supplied in three parts, with optional centre parts that allow it to be depicted open or closed. This sounds nice but effectively makes it impossible to paint those canopy frames on the fixed middle section that are now covered by the sliding pilot's canopy (a four-piece canopy would have been preferable). All the frames are raised on the INSIDE, yes Airfix understood how the Stuka canopy was made and thus you can paint those sections that had exterior elements on the outside and the rest on the inside, just like the real thing. The rear gun position depicts the early unarmoured ring for the B-1 and the later armoured one for the B-2/R-2, although both styles are on the clear sprue in each kit.

Decals: Each kit came with the following decal options:
#A07114
• Ju 87B-1, T6+BC, II./StG 2, Bonn-Hangelar, Germany, spring 1940 – This is RLM 70/71 over 65

Airfix A07115

- Ju 87B01, 29•8 of *Kampfgruppe* 88, Legion Condor, Spain, 1938 – This is RLM 70/71 over 65 with white wing tips and rudder

The decal sheet is well printed with good register, but with slightly 'misty' carrier film that will be very visible with a lot of the stencils and inside things like the fuselage codes. The sheet has all the unique and national marks, but no swastikas, and there is a good selection of airframe stencils including wing walkways, instrument dials and the yellow bars between the fins on the bombs.

#A07115

- Ju 87B-2, S1+HK, 2./StG 3, Greece, spring 1941 – This is RLM 70/71 over 65
- Ju 87B-2 Trop, T6+AN, 2./StG 2, Libya, May 1942 – This is RLM 70/71 overpainted with RLM 79 on the upper surfaces and RLM 65 underneath

The decal sheet is well printed with good register, but the carrier film is slightly misty once again (see above). The sheet has all the unique and national marks, but no swastikas, and there is a good selection of airframe stencils including wing walkways, instrument dials and the yellow bars between the fins on the bombs.

Verdict:

Wow, these are excellent kits that we suspect nowadays will be THE choice for the type in this scale. Sure, it is more complex than the Hasegawa ones, so not as easy to build, but it is actually cheaper than Hasegawa ones tend to be once reissued, so well worth investing in and building (at least one, but probably more).

Italeri, Italy

Ju 87B-2 Stuka

This new tooling (#2690) was first released in 2010 and is currently not in production. It was reissued as a B-2/R-2 'Picchiatello' (#2769) in 2017 and that does remain in production. We have #2690 here for assessment.

Plastic: This is light grey-coloured with engraved panel lines and fasteners but no rivets.

Wings: These are moulded as a single-piece lower and two separate upper halves. The span is correct but the chord is a little off, being about 1mm short by the root, tapering down to the correct chord by the tip. The panel lines are pretty good, although the ones at the tip are too close together. The access panels are a mix of some that do match plans, other that don't (the oval panel just inboard of the outer wing panel joint is too long and set inboard

slightly, for example). The cut-out (over the spar bolt) in the fillet that covers the inboard and outer wing panel joint is also missing, as the fillet is depicted as constant, front to back. The anti-slip panels at each wing root are depicted either as decals or via the separate photo-etched brass components. The wing guns comprise separate bulges and gun barrels, the location being defined by a fine engraved outline on the upper surface. The landing light has both a clear outer cover and the light itself (also clear) inside. The access panels on the underside are also a mix of right and wrong, with some being depicted a lot larger than most plans (or manual diagrams) show, while there are a couple shown as raised detail. The dive brakes are separate and are about 2mm short, plus the tips should be a constant curve, whilst the kit parts depict a curve that slants inwards at the rear, plus the attachment points are just basic pins (all moulded in situ). The control surfaces and hinges are moulded with the lower wing half, but all the linkage is separate, as are the mass balance weights.

Fuselage: This is moulded as two halves from the rudder hinge line to the engine firewall. Overall length is about 2mm too great (all in the mid-fuselage region) but the profile and cross-sections are good. Panel lines match most scale plans, but there is an oblong access panel under the starboard tailplane that is not depicted on any plans we have seen; the R-4 in the USA has an oval panel at the front and square one at the back in this region (so you can't always trust scale plans). The square access panel low down at mid-fuselage on the starboard side is omitted, although again this is not on any scale plans but can be seen on the R-4 in the USA. The fairing for the rudder cable on the lower port rear is too short and the cable is moulded in situ, but that is something you can remove and replace with rod/wire if you so choose. The rudder is separate and about 1mm too narrow in chord, plus the linkage for the twin trim tabs is shown as a raised fairing (front) and very thin and poorly defined linkage rod; each is depicted the same length, when in reality the upper linkage is shorter than the lower because the fairings are in different locations (they are shown in line with each other). The hole aft of the tailplane incident plate is depicted as such, but as with their 1/72nd scale kit, Italeri depict a rod at the top leading edge of the vertical fin, which we presume is supposed to be the anchor and insulators for the aerial lead, however it is not very effective or accurate and thus best removed. The whole front end is a separate sub-assembly to accommodate the supplied engine (see elsewhere) and the overall size and shape of the cowls and ventral radiator are good. The flaps at the rear of the latter depict the separate ones and are posed open but there is no detail inside or actuating linkage, which is odd considering the effort expended on offering a complete engine? The upper engine cowl correctly depicts the asymmetric intake shape and the (aft) exhaust flap is depicted, but only as engraved detail. The two small intake scoops on either side of the front of the upper cowl are there, but only in partial relief and all the various filler caps are engraved. The front lower lip region

of the radiator is a separate part, so it is deep enough, but the two intake scoops either side at the top are only in partial relief. The supercharger intake is a separate part and acceptable in overall size and shape, plus there is an etched screen to go inside. The tropical version of the intake is also included on the sprue but unused in this version (suspect it is used in #2709 though). Oddly, considering the effort expended offering the engine and including photo-etched in the kit, there is no attempt to depict the clear viewing panel in the fuselage underside.

Undercarriage: This is offered in the traditional manner of two-part legs/covers and separate wheels. Each leg is about 2mm too long for a loaded aircraft and the error is all in the upper sections. The stubs for the sirens are moulded in situ with the propeller or a blanking cap separate, so you can depict machines with or without these. The wheels are of the correct diameter and have the correct style tread pattern, plus they are 'weighted', which may appeal to some modellers but not others as no 'un-weighted' option is included. The tailwheel is separate with a two-part oleo/yoke and separate wheel. The former item is the correct overall size, but the style does not match that used for the B-series and the leg is depicted again without the canvas gaiter, albeit many in-service machines had this removed. The diameter of the tailwheel tyre and hub is too small, the tyre features the same tread pattern as the main wheels (most period images show a smooth tyre) and it is 'weighted', but in far too an exaggerated manner.

Italeri 2690

Tailplanes: These are moulded as separate tailplanes, elevators and end caps. The latter items combine an etched (forward) element and plastic (rear) component, so are very effective. The tailplane span is about 1mm short, but chord is correct and the access panels on each side match most scale plans, albeit the square one on the starboard underside is depicted large when some scale plans have it smaller (few agree on this point though). The elevators are the correct span and chord and have the twin trim tabs with the linkage correctly only on the underside. The support struts come with the fairings at each end moulded in situ and they have positive location holes in the fuselage side and tailplane underside.

Engine: A complete engine with oil and

coolant radiators is included. The engine itself is multi-part and well detailed, plus vinyl tubing is included to make the pipework for the oil cooler etc. Oddly though things like the support bars at the back of the ventral radiator unit are not depicted because really, the engine is not designed to be on show. The cowls are not supplied in a manner that allows you to have them 'removed' in a realistic manner, because the side panels are joined with the lower section and that lower section is multi-part, so it would be difficult to cut them up in such a manner that would allow the creation of the side panels and lower chin cowling as seen on the real aircraft. The overall detail on the engine is also very simplified, with much of it in only partial relief and therefore rather poorly defined. The exhaust stacks are separate, although the outlets are solid.

Propeller: This is depicted as a backplate, spinner and three-blade propeller. The propeller diameter is fractionally short, but it is marginal. The blade profile is also a bit off, being a little narrow in places (especially towards the root), but this would be difficult to correct. The spinner diameter is good and the profile has the correct bulbous shape to it.

Interior: A full cockpit interior is included via separate sidewalls, floor, crew seats, mid-bulkhead, radio equipment, aft bulkhead, spent cartridge bin, control column, instrument panel, gunsight and even ammo drum racks. The inclusion of photo-etched parts means that Italeri can include a full set of seat belts and the gunner's back strap, plus you have the option of an etched instrument panel or using decals. Going by the illustrations in the parts manual, the pilot's seat is the wrong shape, being depicted as square-edged, when it was curved with an open (tubular) top hoop. The etched belts are also incorrect, as they should have the triangular-shaped back panels behind the main strap, but they are depicted as just single straight belts (the end brackets are also wrong, as they are not the open triangular ones, they were the 'T' shaped ones, but they won't be that visible once assembled). The gunsight is in clear plastic and quite acceptable for the scale.

Details: The centreline 250kg bomb is multi-part with the fin supports also separate and you get a stencil for it as well. The wing ETC ranks are single-piece mouldings and are acceptable for the scale. The 50kg bombs are single-piece mouldings, so some may wish to replace the fins (sadly Italeri did not opt to offer alternative fins for all their bombs on the etched set included with the kit). The 50kg bombs also have a stencil decal. The 'D' sprues included in the kit also offer AB250 and 500 containers and 300lt drop tanks, although none of this is used with this particular release. The aerial mast, crew access steps, trailing aerial tube and pitot are all separate parts.

Canopy: This is supplied in four parts with the framework depicted via faintly frosted regions, although once again some frames that are inside only, are depicted externally. The rear gun sight is the original (un-armoured) version and actually, looking at it and comparing it with period images, the framing is not pronounced enough, as you need a raised in-

ner ring and (flat) outer frame, when you only get the flat outer ring (plus the upper fore/aft rear canopy frame was raised).

Decals: Each kit offered the following decal options:

#2690
- Ju 87B-2, F1+AD, Stab III./StG 77, Bulgaria, April 1941 – RLM 70/71 over 65 with yellow nose and rudder
- Ju 87B-2, T6+KL of 3./StG 2, France, August 1940 – RLM 70/71 over 65
- Ju 87B-2, T6+JK, 2./StG 2, Russia, July 1941 – RLM 70/71 over 65 with yellow theatre band around rear fuselage
- Ju 87B-2, 9J+BH, 7./StG 1, France, summer 1940 – RLM 70/71 over 65 with a heavy brush application of black on the undersides (excluding the radiator cowling)

The decal sheet is well printed although a little matt looking and contains all the national and unique markings plus stencils, including those for the bombs and those decals for both elements of the instrument panel. The decals do not include, nor do the instructions show, the swastikas

Verdict:

Overall Italeri offers a nice kit, with lots of detail but nowadays it has competition from the Airfix example and when you consider that the engine although included, can't be displayed and the various shape issues and detail errors and omissions, it has to be said that it is less appealing. Couple this with the fact that in the UK as we write #2709 is some £8 dearer than the Airfix B/R kit and you can see why we think this one is probably not the best option in the scale at present.

1/32nd Scale

Hasegawa, Japan

Ju 87G 'Kanonenvogel' (#ST25)

This kit was first released in 2006 (complete with a metal figure of Han Ulrich Rudel in the first production batch) and was reissued in 2011. Although not available as we write it is scheduled for reissue during 2020.

Plastic: Medium grey-coloured with engraved panel lines and fasteners, but no rivets.

Wings: These are supplied as a single-piece lower and two separate upper halves with the lower inboard stubs moulded with part of the lower fuselage and the upper sections as separate parts. A box spar unit fits within the wings to give strength and to aid the assembly of the inner and outer panels. The fairing that covered the inner and outer wing panel joint is moulded partially with each wing panel, so you will have to deal with the seam running along its entire length. The kit offers both short and long spans, thanks to separate tips. Overall span in both instances is good and all the control surfaces are separate, including the ailerons, so that different length ones can be included for the different spans. The linkage for the control surfaces is separate and depicted as rods while the mass balance weights for the ailerons are also separate. The main panel lines match most scale plans (the access panels are again at odds with most, but scale plans seldomly agree on this aspect anyway).

To get around some revisions with regard to panel lines on the inner upper surface of each wing (dependent on the wing gun type), Hasegawa opted to create small panel inserts and the instructions clearly show how these look and which way around they fit. The multi-function nature of the tooling means that there are a lot of flashed-over holes inside the lower wing halves, but the instructions clearly show which are to be opened up for this version. The gun fairings are on the sprues (#F17), but there are also blanked off ones (#F18) and even the MG 17 versions for the B/R series (#F19), so Hasegawa must have originally intended to do the earlier series as well? The dive brakes are supplied but not used in this version. The inner lower wing halves allow the troughs for the radiators to be included, so that the separate radiator housing plus interior can be supplied. The slightly raised lip around the side of each radiator is only shown as an engraved line (with the round access panel on each side also done in this manner), in reality though this was part of the radiator housing and would have been better moulded with that part (#D1) instead. The upper wing stubs have the wing walkways moulded as raised ribs and the landing light cover is a separate clear component with the light inside the wing itself also depicted via a separate component.

Fuselage: As with their 1/48th scale kit this is moulded in two halves up to the engine firewall. Overall length is good and the major panel lines match most scale plans, while some of the access panels are shown

Hasegawa ST25

as slightly raised detail. The control linkage for the rudder and its trim tabs are all nicely depicted with the rod going into a recess for the latter, which is correct. The tailplane incidence plates are moulded with each fuselage half and although they look a bit shallow as a result, it's still acceptable. The forward upper decking ahead of the cockpit is a separate part, split along the panel lines, to accommodate the instrument panel that is mounted inside. Appliqué armour plates are supplied separately for either side of the forward fuselage. The entire nose is separate and overall is slightly short. The radiator interior is a separate part as is the front edge and upper cowl section directly in front of it, and this results in a seam where there is no panel line.

Undercarriage: This is made up in the usual manner of separate upper leg/base, oleo/covers and wheel. The overall length is good, but the lower cover has the aft section flat, when it was curved (there being a slight step between the 'flat' open region for the wheel and the closed (curved) rear portion); nearly all depict this area in this manner and it is probably as much about tooling costs than anything else. The siren stubs are moulded in situ, although here the instructions tell you to cut them off, which is fine because the mounting flange behind the stud on the cover is not depicted in any manner so you won't have to remove/fill that. The siren propellers are actually on the sprues (#F21) though. The gaiters on each main leg are depicted via raised lines, these are acceptable in this scale but not a 100% accurate depiction of the 'uneven' nature of the real thing (the raised lines are consistent and straight). The tailwheel comprises a three-part leg and yoke with a two-part wheel. This depicts the uncovered later style leg, the flange around the lower portion was in fact the ring that the gaiter was attached to, so it's usually missing when the leg is exposed like this. The wheel has nice hub detail and the same crosswise tread pattern.

Tailplanes: These are done as separate upper and lower halves with both tailplane and elevator moulded as one and the tips and trim tab linkage arms separate. Overall span and chord are good and the access panels on the upper surface are correctly depicted running side to side on the starboard and fore and aft on the port side. Underneath the usual five panels are depicted, with the oblong panel inboard under the starboard side. It is great to see the trim tab linkage as separate parts, as they deserve to be in this scale. The support struts are separate and correctly depict the faired fuselage pick-up and exposed 'U' bracket underneath the actual tailplane.

Engine: None is supplied.

Propeller: This is made up of the back-plate, spinner and individual blade. The profile of the tip suggests that they depict the VS 11, but the blade width is too narrow. Quickboost do replacements (#QB32022), but we have to say the tip profile is too noticeably angled. They also produce a set of VS 111 blades (#QB32063) and these are a much better bet profile-wise. The spinner diameter is good and the profile has the distinctive bulge to it plus the plate on the tip is represented by a raised disc (you can drill this out if needs be, as some aircraft lost the plug fitted here).

Interior: This is made up of sidewalls with separate throttle box etc., floor, control column, rudder pedals, crew seats, multi-part crew figures, mid-bulkhead, radio equipment (with decals for some details), spent cartridge box/tube, ammunition bins, rear (armoured) bulkhead and instrument panel with decal overlay, while the gunsight is supplied as a grey-coloured plastic main body and mounting bracket and separate clear lens. Overall detail is good although the nature of moulding means that some of it is a little shallow (flat) for the scale. The pilot's seat is the correct later (square topped) shape and you have

the head armour included (#J21) as most machines had this. The mid bulkhead has the armour in only one style, although there are a few variations for the D/G-series, so check your references for the particular version you are building. The internal housing for the ventral sighting window is no longer depicted and there is a solid panel engraved on the fuselage underside to depict the cover in the closed position. The upper dorsal spine area aft of the rear canopy is separate to allow the DF loop to be depicted, and this is done via moulded detail inside the new spine insert and a separate clear cover (with a decal to go inside it to represent the conductive element moulded into it).

Details: There are no bombs or drop tanks included, just the BK 3.7cm Flak 18 gondolas. These are multi-part with the barrel and muzzle brake moulded with each gondola half and the ammo feed/ejector separate. The mounting brackets along with the external pipework are also separate. The split barrel is an issue though, so use one of the many aftermarket turned metal replacements, such as the Master set (#AM-32-014). The aerial mast, crew access steps and pitot are all supplied as separate parts.

Canopy: This is supplied in four sections and the overall shape and size is good with the external armoured glass of the windscreen supplied as a separate part. Hasegawa did their homework and have correctly depicted the framework either inside or outside via engraved lines and the instructions tell you which is which to aid painting. You can alternatively use a set of self-adhesive masks for this, as Montex do a set for both interior and exterior of the D and G series (#SM32046). The depiction of the GSL k 81Z cupola is done in a way that has it all as one unit with the rear canopy section, but you do get the armour plate inside as a separate (grey-coloured plastic) component. This is acceptable, but would have been more accurate if they had made the aft section of the rear canopy separate. The mounting frame for the ring and bead sights either side of the MG 81Z is supplied as a separate part, as are the ring sights themselves.

Decals: The kit offers the following options:
- Ju 87G-2, W/Nr.494193, , flown by Obstlt. Hans-Ulrich Rudel, Stab./SG2, autumn 1944 – This is RLM 70/71 over 65 with yellow lower wing tips and a white spinner spiral
- Ju 87G-1, GS+MD, *Versuchsverband für Panzerkämpfung* – This is RLM 70/71 over 65

The instructions include scale templates for the camouflage pattern and the decal sheet is well printed and includes all the unique and national insignia, with the swastikas off to the right so that they can be cut off in those countries that ban the symbol. Both standard (anti-slip) and later (raised) wing walkways are included, the latter not really needed as the kit parts have this detail moulded in situ and the former only applicable to the G-1. A full set of stencils along with the black/white instrument panel decal are included, plus a yellow 'V' marking and white spinner spiral, and all the decals to

represent the canopy frames done in either black or RLM 66.

Verdict:

This kit is certainly worth building if you already have it in your 'to do' pile, plus there are a wealth of excellent upgrade sets already available for it. The retricted availability and retail price are often an issue, especially when you consider the reissue of this kit planned for 2020 will see it retailing for £76.99 in the UK! So, if you have one, build it, you won't regret it.

Trumpeter, China

Junkers Ju 87A (#03213)

This A-series kit was first released in 2014 and it remains in production.

Plastic: This is light grey-coloured and has engraved panel lines and fasteners, with the rivets restricted to the major ones alongside each panel line.

Wings: These are moulded in a similar manner to the Hasegawa 1/32nd kits, with the lower inboard stubs moulded with a section of lower fuselage, two upper inboard stubs, upper and lower outer wing panels and separate wing tips. There are front and rear spar sections to go inside the wings that ensure a strong assembly. The gun access panel is separate on each side, but there is only a gun in the starboard wing. You will have to fill the oval access panel in on #B24, as that relates to the wing armament, plus the location mark for the gun fairing (#B2 and B3), as that has been done as an engraved outline on the upper wing half. Most of the other access panels depicted as engraved detail on the upper wing panels relate to the B-series, not the A and the same goes for the underside, although it's not that bad due to some commonality in this region between A and B-series. The anti-slip panels are depicted via raised outer edges, but you have two on each wing root, when in reality there was only one (rear one) on the starboard side. The separate tips are there only because the wings are basically B-series and we suspect they have been used as the basis for the long-span wings, but it does mean you get the tip lights as separate clear components. The landing light in the port leading edge is depicted as a separate part and there is also a clear cover. The control surfaces are all separate with the hinges moulded to each element and the linkage as separate parts (the mass balance weights for the ailerons are also separate). The dive brakes are separate and come with each mounting point separate, but the instructions only show them deployed (which rarely happened on the ground), however the locating point on the back of each is a slot, so you can also pose them in the more 'natural' stowed position.

Fuselage: This is moulded in two halves up to the engine firewall with the rudder separate. Overall size and shape are good and most panel lines match plans. The access hand-holds on each fuselage side are correct, but fill the forward one as the A-series only had two such hand-holds either side. The rudder is shown in two forms, parts D3 and D12 are the squarer version associated with the B-series, whilst G3 and G13 are correct for the A-series. Note that the B-series ones have linkage for the twin trim tabs on both sides, when they should be only on the port side. The linkage for the actual rudder itself is supplied as separate parts for each side. All the engine cowlings are separate and are good in overall shape. The exhaust and spark plug cooling intake scoops are separate, as are the oil cooler intakes (and exhausts) on either side of the lower front region. The small intake on either side of the upper nose region (#E33 and E34) should only be on the starboard side (#E34), the one on the port side should be removed and filled as the round filler cap engraved below it should be larger and higher up. The hole for the starter handle on the lower rear port side is too small and it was also oval, not round (the one on the starboard side should not be there). The larger intake further aft on the starboard upper cowling (#E24 or PE7) was not a flap, it was a fixed scoop with a small flange around its base, so you will need to modify #E24 accordingly and ignore the use of #PE7. The forward lip of the ventral radiator is separate, as this allows the vertical support beam to be added along with the engine first, although in truth this had an elongated hole behind it, to allow the lower cowl to be positioned with the strut in place (it's part of the radiator assembly). The First Aid kit compartment on the port mid-fuselage is depicted by engraved lines, however the A-series had this behind a clear panel.

Undercarriage: These actually have the oleo leg and rear strut inside the spats, plus a rubber tyre with a plastic hub. The rubber tyre is one of those love or loathe things, but to ensure over time the rubber does not react with the plastic, best to seek aftermarket replacements (B-series should be fine). The undercarriage spats look OK, although I am not 100% convinced by the profile at the lower/back edge. The main panel lines on the spats are OK, but there are a number of details and access panels missing and the inner starboard one lacks the oblong access panel for the ammunition box. The main wheel hubs lack any real detail, so there are no brake lines etc. The support struts are multi-part and are quite detailed. The tailwheel is made up with a two-piece leg/yoke, a separate wheel hub and a rubber tyre. The tyre has a crosswise tread pattern, but the illustrations in the manual show it had a circumferential pattern. The yoke is also more like the heavy cast one use for the early B-series, as the A actually had a simple strut and yoke once the cumbersome wheel fairing was removed (which it always seems to have been in service).

Tailplanes: These are moulded as upper and lower halves for the tailplanes and elevators, with the endplate and trim tab linkage separate. The end plates are depicted with the bulged forward section, but that only applies to the B-series onwards, as the A-series had this area flat. The access panels on both sides of the tailplanes relate to the B-series, as the A only had two oval panels running side-to-side on the upper port tailplane, and nothing on the upper starboard; the five oval panels on the underside of both tailplanes is correct for the A-Series).

Engine: A complete multi-part engine is included along with engine bearers and

bulkhead. The radiator under the nose is a separate sub-assembly and the trapeze for the bomb is slung off the mounts behind it. The exhausts come as separate parts moulded with their surround and each oval outlet is hollow.

Propeller: This is made up of a backplate, two-part hub, three blades and a spinner. The spinner diameter is OK but it is too long (about 2.5mm) and thus looks to be too pointed. Note that the round panels between each blade on the spinner edge are supposed to be holes. Whilst the blade profile is good for the early metal HPA II or III, the twist at the root is not sufficient, making them lay too 'flat' in the hub.

Trumpeter 03213

Interior: This is made up of sidewalls with separate details, floor, control column, crew seats, oxygen bottle, bulkhead with radio equipment, spent cartridge collecting bin, ammunition rack and drums, instrument panel and gunsight. The control column whilst showing the correct (ring) Type KG 11 grip lacks much of the detail on the grip and column and it is too skinny in the main shaft, which is also too long, and the canvas gaiter at the bottom is too small and too short. The instrument panel lacks the crash-pad that was situated between pilot and gunsight. The instrument panel dial layout does not match many of the images and diagrams in the manuals, but we should also point out that the diagram in the flight manual does not match that in the spare parts manual! You get a decal overlay for the instrument panel, as it just has the dials raised, no dial face detail etc. The rudder pedals are from the D/G-series, not the A (which had the same bulky pedals as the B-series). Looking at the photographs in the A-series manuals we can't help but feel most of the sidewall detail is more applicable to the B-series, but it is a starting point because there are similarities .The gunsight is not bad for the C/12, with a separate clear lens, but the ring sight in front of that is missing, so this is more akin to the C/12B of the B-series, then the C/12A of the A-series (note that early As had the gunsight offset to port, while late A-1s and A-2s usually had it offset to starboard). The radio equipment (#E48 and E49) on the mid-bulkhead (#E17) looks nothing like the sender and receiver in this region, in fact we would go as far as to say it looks like the well-known image of the mock-up of this area. There is also only

one bottle (#E52+E53) below the radio equipment, when there should be two, so the supplied bottle is also too big/long and the connector at the end is all wrong (it also lacks the two metal retaining straps – this again ties in with that image of the mock-up of this area). All the rods that radiate out from the radio equipment on #E17 were in fact actually springs with shrouds to shock-mount the radio equipment, so they used a hook and eye at each end, they are not actually part of the surrounding framework. The vertical bars in the armour plate behind the pilot (#E8) are actually made from rods, not square bars, and the outer profile of the area angles in each side at about shoulder height, then forms a hoop at the top. There are also more than four vertical bars, it's hard to see in period images, but we would guess at six and even in this scale we would say the diameter of the rods was less than the box section bars shown on #E8. The rear gun is well done, with the counter-balance arm assembly for the gun itself anchored on the starboard side, the racks for the ammunition drums on the starboard side and the ring and bead sight are depicted via etched parts (the fore sight was a complex floating vane rather than a traditional bead, though). The armour plate (#E9) is not something we have come across in period images or diagrams, so can't really comment on its accuracy. The spent cartridge bin (#E3+E4) was actually only metal around the top square opening, the rest was canvas, so never held the rigid square shape depicted in the kit parts. The ventral sighting window is made up as a separate unit and mounted to the interior of the lower fuselage/wing stub component (#E22), this has a clear upper and lower panel in it and looking at period images of the outside area, we feel that the surrounding framework was heavier resulting in a narrower oblong clear panel.

Details: The pitot is supplied in three parts, the twin fork of #E51 is incorrect though, as the horizontal element on the port side should be cut off, as that type of pitot only existed on the inner prong. The sprues include four bundles of SC50 bombs, the D/G-series outer bomb rack with 50kg bombs and Dinort fuse extenders, WB 81 weapons pods, 300lt drop tanks and what looks to be a 500kg bomb, none of which are applicable to the A-series. The ETC 50 racks (#WD2, 3, 14 & 15) can be installed, as can one 50kg bomb on each, while the centreline bomb is best replaced with an aftermarket 250kg example just to be on the safe side. The 'ram's horn' aerial masts and crew access steps are separate parts.

Canopy: This is in four sections (with the roll-over frame done in grey-coloured plastic) and the kit parts come in two styles so you can have them open (hinged to starboard) or closed. All framework is exterior and done by slightly frosted regions between engraved lines and rivets, although in this scale the rather heavy frames inside each canopy element would best have been depicted with separate structures. This last point also would allow the hinges/retainers for the hinged sections to have been depicted, as once again, these were quite big. The track for the rear gun is a separate piece, but the manner in which the MG 15 fits into it is just depicted as fitting into the slot, whereas in reality there was a mounting bracket attached inside that the gun barrel went through, so a little scratchbuilding may be called for here otherwise the gun will just 'float about' in the slot.

Decals: The kit offers the following decal options:

- W/Nr.5040, 'Yellow 6', 'Irene' of an unidentified Luftwaffe unit – This is RLM 70/71 over 65 with a yellow rudder and wing tip undersides
- S13+S29, 9 *Staffel* StG, Nuremberg, Germany, 1939 – Although depicted as RLM 79/78/65 over RLM 65, this is most likely in the pre-war scheme of RLM 61/62/63 over 65?

Don't forget that the upper surface camouflage on the A-series often wrapped slightly around the wing leading edge, so check images of the options to see if either had this feature. The decal sheet is well printed, although the yellow used for option 1 looks a bit too bright/light. Otherwise the sheet has all unique and national markings with the swastikas cut in two to get around restrictions in certain nations. There is also a good set of airframe stencils (no anti-slip for the wing walkways, oddly) and a decal for the instrument panel that is sadly black/white, so not very useful for the grey-painted panel of the A-series (the Eduard etched set #32-832 comes with a pre-painted instrument panel).

Verdict:

Although it has various detail issues, this is a mainstream kit of the A-series in 1/32nd scale and who would ever think we would be saying that! For this reason alone, it is worth buying and taking the time to build and correct, as nothing quoted is insurmountable.

Trumpeter, China

Junkers Ju 87B & R-series

Trumpeter produced the B-2 (#03214) in 2012, followed by the B-2/U4 (#03215) and R (#03216) in 2013 and they all remain in production. We have #03216 here for assessment and as it shares many common sprues with the earlier A-series kit, we will only cover here those elements that differ.

Wings: These are the same 'A' and 'B' sprues of the A-series, hence that kit having many B-series features. You do keep both MG 17s in the wing this time, along with their associated panels. Most of the engraved access panels on the upper and lower surface are applicable to the B-series, but not all, as no-one seems to agree on this aspect! The combined lower fuselage section and lower stub wings component is new though, to correctly depict the revisions in this area (it retains the capacity to have the viewing window in it and has a bigger clear panel for that as a result).

Fuselage: These parts are all new, so you get the main fuselage with the rudder and everything from the engine firewall forward separate. The overall dimensions are good and the main panel lines match scale plans as do most of the access panels. The rudder

is separate, but ignore the instructions and use #D4 and #D9, as they are on the 'new' B-related fuselage sprue. The engines cowls are good in overall shape, although the fairing at the front of the exhausts is too small/narrow and tapered, resulting in the hole at the front being too small (the fairing is flat-sided (rounded edges) with a slight taper towards the front). The starter handle point is correctly depicted as a hinged oblong cover on the port side, but is also repeated on the starboard side. The filler cap on the forward port side should only have a single engraved dot offset to one side, as it's not attached with screws, it has a clip that is activated with the 'dot' (button). The smaller intake scoop towards the back of the cowl on the port side is solid, so needs to be opened, plus is it too shallow. The upper asymmetric intake is via an insert, so we are not sure how that one will work out? The rear exhaust unit is also done in this manner. The trapeze under the nose is incorrect for the B-series though, it has only a single 'strap' across it, when the B-series had a complex series of tubular cross-members in that region. The supercharger intake on the port side is separate, but oddly the R-series kit does not include the tropical unit, just the standard one and it is open to the interior of the cowl with no mesh screen etc.

Trumpeter 03214

Undercarriage: These are all new (on the 'L' sprue) and although the overall size of each spat is good, the rear lower profile is flat, when it should go from the 'flat' alongside the wheel cut-out to the curved underside of the rear fairing, resulting in a slight up-turn in the profile of the lower spat edge as it transitions between these two regions. The struts have the siren stub moulded to them, plus the blanking cap is used in this version. The main oleo legs depict the B-series with the compression links on the back, but the slider element is exposed when it was actually covered with a canvas gaiter (there is still no brake line etc). The main wheels remain unchanged from the A-series, so see the comments there about these. The tailwheel is the later style unit seen on the later B and R-series, with the thinner yoke and the support hoops for a canvas cover, which was usually removed, and again the separate rubber tyre has a crosswise tread pattern when period diagrams show this to be circumferential.

Tailplanes: These are unchanged from the A-series, but you will recall that many of the

features there were from the B/R-series, so here the bulged end tips and access panel layout is correct for this series.

Engine: You have a complete engine, revised from the earlier version in the A-series, but it is built in a similar manner, it's just revised for the later series 211 and has the cast engine bearers, and the bomb trapeze is mounted off the firewall lower edge. The coolant radiator is revised and a separate sub-assembly with the rear cowl flaps offered either open or closed (they depict the segmented version).

Propeller: This is all new, with a two-part boss, separate blades, backplate and spinner. Nit-picky we know, but the hub part #L38 is wrong, because this actually had a dome in its centre. The blade profile looks good, as does the tip, although comparing it with period images I don't think the root is long enough (the overall blade length is fine though), so suspect the cut-back at the root will be too close to the spinner. The spinner diameter is OK but the profile is a little too skinny, resulting in the unit looking too pointy and lacking the bulbous nature of the original. The hole in the centre was usually covered with a plate, though.

Interior: This is mainly all new and comprises floor, sidewalls with separate details, crew seats, bulkhead and radio equipment, ammunition racks and drums, rear bulkhead, spent cartridge box, control column and rudder pedals. The rudder pedals are once again the later sort for the D/G series, but at least this time the radio equipment is depicted as the correct sender and receiver (pity you can't get these parts from Trumpeter for the A-series kit). The turnover frame above the armour plate behind the pilot depicts the correct 'M' shape struts that can be seen in period images, even though many illustrate this as a 'V' strut only. The pilot's seat is incorrect for the B-series, again this is another instance where you could do with this assembly from the A-series kit, which is correct for the A and B series. The instrument panel is not bad for the B-series, but ignore the decal overlay as that is done in black and white, where the real thing was RLM 66 (early B-1s were most likely RLM 02). The clear gunsight has a separate lens and is quite nice, but could do with the bead sight adding to be more like the C/12B.

Details: The sprues include four bundles of SC50 bombs, the D/G-series outer bomb rack with 50kg bombs and Dinort fuse extenders, WB 81 weapons pods, 300lt drop tanks and what looks to be a 1,000kg bomb, most of which are not applicable to the B-series. The ETC 50 racks (#WD2, 3, 14 & 15) can be installed, as can one 50kg bomb on each, because although there are images with bundles of 50kg bombs on these racks under the B and R-series, these had a collective cover on the front that is not included in the kit parts. The 300lt drop tank is seen attached to the underside of each wing via the rack only used on the D and G series, the B and R used the twin ETC 50 racks and special mounting lugs, so you may be able to create this by combining the smaller racks with the lugs (#WD11 and WD12) used on the D/G series rack? The centreline bomb is much too large for the R or B series and best replaced with an aftermarket 250kg or 500kg example. The aerial mast, pitot on starboard wing and crew access steps are separate parts. The rear MG 15 has the ring and bead sights supplied as photo-etched.

Canopy: This comes in four sections but all the frames are moulded on the outside via engraved lines and slightly frosted areas, whilst quite a few frames are actually only on the inside. The round panel of the rear gun mount is the early unarmoured version and it has the exposed 'gear' on the inside done via photo-etched brass. The sliding 'clear vision' vertical panel in either side of the rear canopy section is depicted with the runners, which are actually inside, as if they were exterior frames. The rear-view mirror offset to starboard inside the windscreen is supplied as an etched component, as are both of the grab handles up inside the top of the windscreen frame.

Trumpeter 03216

Decals: The kit we had (#03216) came with the following decal options:
• Ju 87R-2, S1+HK, 2./StG 3, Derna, Libya, 1941 – This is shown as RLM 79 over 78, but is more likely to be RLM 79 over 65 and it should have the underside of each wing tip white and carry a black 'H' in that region
• Ju 87R, A5+AH, 1./StG 1, Kuhlmey Sir Dufan, Libya, 1941 – This is RLM 70/71 over 65 but it should have the fuselage cross applied on top of a wide white band
• Ju 87R, S7+DN, 5./StG 3, Derna, Libya, 1942 – This is shown as RLM 71 with a mottle of RLM 79 over RLM 78, but is more likely to have been RLM 70/71 with a mottle of RLM 79 over RLM 65

The decal sheet is well printed and includes all unique and national insignia, but no swastikas. A full set of airframe stencils is included along with that black/white decal for the instrument panel

Verdict:
You can see the logic behind Trumpeter's approach to the Stuka series, especially with the wings, but having done new sprues for the fuselage and engine here, they would have been better off doing separate wing parts for the A-series as well. This kit is more a B than an R, due to the mix-up with the wing tanks and the lack of tropical filter, but with a little work these can be corrected. Overall the kit is much better than the old Revell example and for that it has to be the choice for the R (or B) series in this scale. Buy it and build it, we don't think you will be disappointed.

Trumpeter, China

Junkers Ju 87D & G series

Trumpeter released the G-2 (#03218) kit in 2015 and followed it with the D (#03217) in 2016, both remain in production. They also announced a D-2 and D-7 without kit numbers in 2010 and these have never been produced, so we suspect they were replaced by the D-series kit (#03217) instead. As this kit actually uses some parts from the previous A and B/R series kits, which we have already assessed, we will only cover here those areas that are specific to the D/G series.

Wings: Whilst the lower wing and control surfaces sprue remains unchanged from the A and B/R series, the upper wing sprue is new. This new sprue has the upper wing panels and stubs, the latter with the raised ribs seen for the wing walkways, plus extended wing tips, new tailplane supports and a couple of other detail parts. The panel and access lines on the upper wing outer panels match scale plans, although there are two oval access panels behind the open gun bay, when there should only be one (the nearest to the open bay). The large oval panel on the outer edge of the stub is actually shown as having more of a taper/point to the rear end in the manual. The extended wing tips looks a little off in overall profile when compared with period images, but the tip lights are supplied as separate clear parts. The plate and panel that is situated at the front of the inner/outer wing joint fairing, which covers the top of the oleo strut mount, is depicted as engraved detail, but it does not match the rather complex shape of the outline you will see on the wing of the G-2 at Hendon. The radiators under each inboard stub are separate with the radiator block inside a separate two-part item. The overall shape is good although the flange around the side/edges is not depicted (the round access panel alongside is engraved in the lower wing stub) and for some reason the front lip has been moulded partially open. This is because that is how this area is set on the Hendon example, but in plastic is just does not work because you don't have enough depth to the plastic nor do you have the linkage inside. There is no linkage inside the rear flap either and the flap is just defined by engraved panel lines, thus meaning the sides of the flap are not depicted either; all of these problems with the radiators are corrected in the Eduard etched exterior set #32378.

Fuselage: A new sprue offers the fuselage from the rudder to the engine firewall, the only real changes to these halves being the modifications for the tailplane supports. The engine cowlings are also new and look good, although the small scoop on the upper rear port side is too small (and solid). There should also be two oval access panels along the top (centreline) of the cowling. The supercharger intake on the starboard side is nicely depicted and the hinged flap at the front is a separate part. The exhausts show the fully exposed versions, so correct for the G-2 (and D-5/D-8).

Undercarriage: This is another new sprue and the overall size of the legs looks good. The two holes, one above the other, on the lower spats were actually screws, so ideally these would have been better engraved as

such, while the rivets above the gaiter look too big compared with the real thing. As usual the gaiter is done via moulded detail, so it's a little too precise compared with the real thing (straight lines and indentations), but quite understandable. The underside of the rear section of the spat is again too flat. Inside the covers you get the correct slightly angled oleo leg complete with compression linkage, while the wheel hubs are split in two and lack any detail like the brake lines etc., and the tyres are rubber. The tailwheel is the same as the B/R series, so it lacks the canvas cover seen on the preserved example at Hendon, but that seems to often have been removed in service.

Tailplanes: These are the same as in the B and R series kits, but are correct here as well and the layout of the access panels is also correct for this later series

Engine: Whilst the core of the separate engine is unchanged from the B/R series, the tanks above and on the side are new components, as are the engine bearers and the ventral coolant radiator.

Propeller: This is made up of the back-plate, three blades, two-part hub and a spinner. The blade profile is a little off, as it looks too wide, the root taper on the back edge is too pronounced and the tip profile is a little too rounded, but there are plenty of replacement aftermarket sets for this. The spinner profile looks good, although the plug in the tip is not depicted in any way, so just scribe it in place.

Interior: This is new, although a number of the parts are the same as seen in the B/R series kits. It comprises floor, sidewalls with separate details, crew seats, bulkhead and radio equipment, ammunition racks and drums, rear bulkhead, spent cartridge box, control column and rudder pedals. The rudder pedals are the correct later sort for the D/G series, while all the other detail seems to be based on the G-2 at Hendon, although the side profile of the pilot's seat is not 100% accurate (the change in direction of either side piece should be curved, not a sharp angle – the edges are also rolled, not square-cut). The box for the spent cartridges (#N52) is not really accurate, as this was a bag that was attached to the rear bulkhead (#N1), so was not a rigid shape as depicted, plus it's in the wrong place (too far forward), as the tube from the gun to it was at an angle and that tube is not a concertina type as depicted, it was a plain fabric tube of a much larger diameter. The instrument panel has raised detail plus a decal to go on top, but the decal is just black and white, so not very accurate (the Eduard etched interior set #33055 has this in colour). There seems to be a crash-pad (#Q1) fitted ahead of the instrument panel and gunsight, which I don't recall seeing in any diagrams or images of this area? It is probably down to some indicating that a well-known image of the instrument panel etc. depicts the D-series, when in fact its actually a B-series converted as one of the test airframes for the D-series canopy and it has that crash-pad in place for safety reasons during trials, it was not a feature of the production D or G-series (both series has a hot air pipe coming from the port side at the top of the instrument panel though, which is missing). The gunsight is separate and done in clear plastic and whilst a reason rendition of the Revi C 16D or D/N of the D-G series, in this scale it is probably best replaced with an aftermarket version (use the Quickboost Revi 16B #QB32006, as that's close enough). You will also have to add a cross-bar on which to mount the Revi sight, as it's not on a stem from the top of the instrument panel as depicted in this kit (it's bolted to a tube that runs ahead and across the top of the instrument panel). No seat belts are included, but once again they can be obtained from various aftermarket sources if you want.

Details: The sprues again include include all the ordnance listed with the R-series kit previously, all of which are not applicable to the G-2. Oddly the centreline bomb trapeze is actually the correct style for the B/R series, so obviously Trumpeter got really confused here. You do get the BK 3.7cm Flak 18 gondolas. These are multi-part with the barrels moulded as one with the muzzle hollow, but lacking the various perforations in this area. You get the option of a (solid) plastic ammunition magazine or by combining plastic and photo-etched brass parts you can use the supplied clips of ammunition. The aerial mast, pitot on starboard wing and crew access steps are all separate parts. The MG 81Z has separate barrels with the perforations in partial relief and the ring and bead sights are separate etched components.

Canopy: This is supplied in four sections, but you have optional versions for the windscreen and pilot's sliding canopy sections. Going by the G-2 at Hendon #X12 and #Y1 are the combination there. The framework is all engraved on the outside, but the D/G series have far fewer frames under the Perspex than the earlier version, so some careful

Trumpeter 03218

masking and painting inside and out should be acceptable. The rear-view mirror inside the windscreen is a separate etched part and there are also two etched grab rails. The rear cupola is well done, but again the rearmost section is moulded with the remainder, when it was in fact separate. The gun-profile on the outside of the rear gun frame/decking is moulded in situ, so in this scale it's a bit too 'flat' really.

Decals: The kit offered the following decal options:
• Ju 87G-2, W/Nr.494193, flown by Hans Ulrich Rudel, SG 2, Eastern Front, 1944-

45. This is RLM 70/71 over 65 with yellow fuselage theatre band, lower wing tips and the yellow 'V' under the port wing seen on ground-attack aircraft in the later stages of WWII. The W/Nr. on this machine should be white, not black
• Ju 87G-2, W/Nr.494110, flown by Hans Ulrich Rudel, Stab 10. (Pz)/SG 2, 8th May 1945 (this is the machine in which Rudel and his gunner surrendered to American forces at Kitzingen). This is RLM 70/71 over 65. Note that some show this with a yellow fuselage theatre band and the yellow 'V' under and above the port wing, while others do not. The kit does not include/depict any of the yellow markings

The decal sheet includes all the unique and national markings with the swastikas split in two. The yellow fuselage band and wing 'V' for the first option are also supplied as decals, along with a set of airframe stencils and a black/white decal for the instrument panel.

Verdict:
In this scale you have this or the Hasegawa kit, this one wins purely on price, as the projected 2020 reissue UK retail price on the Hasegawa example is some £23 more. The detail errors and omissions with this kit are such that it is still worth buying and building, as only a little extra work will be needed to result in an excellent G-2.

1/2th Scale

Trumpeter, China

Ju 87A (#02420)

Trumpeter shocked everyone by producing this A-series kit in 2017 and it remains in production.

Plastic: Light grey-coloured with engraved panel lines and fasteners and the rivets restricted to the major ones alongside each panel line.

Wings: These are moulded with the lower inboard stubs moulded with a section of lower fuselage, two upper inboard stubs, upper and lower outer wing panels and separate wing tips. There are front and rear spar sections to go inside the wings that ensure a strong assembly. The gun access panel is separate on each side, but there is only a gun in the starboard wing so fill in the port access panel (#B7). You will also have to fill in the oval access panel on #L5, as that relates to the wing armament, plus the location mark for the gun fairing (#L22 and L23, which you omit) because that has been done as an engraved outline on the upper wing half. Most of the other access panels depicted as engraved detail on the upper wing panels relate to the B-series, not the A, and the same goes for the underside, although it's not that bad due to some commonality in this region between A and B-series. The anti-slip panels are depicted via raised outer edges, but you have two on each wing root, when there should only be the aft one on the starboard side. The separate tips are only there because the wings are basically B-series and we suspect they have been used as the basis for the long-span wings, but it does mean you get the tip lights as separate clear components. The landing light in the port leading edge is

depicted as a separate part (#D31) and there is also a clear cover. The control surfaces are all separate with the hinges moulded to each element and the linkage and aileron mass balance weights as separate parts. The dive brakes are also separate and come with each mounting point separate, but the instructions only show them deployed (not likely), however the locating point on the back of each is a slot, so you can also pose them in the more 'natural' stowed position as well.

Fuselage: This is moulded in two halves up to the engine firewall and with the rudder separate. Overall size and shape are good and most panel lines match plans. The access hand-holds on each fuselage side are correct, but fill the forward one in, as the A-series had only two such hand-holds either side. The rudder is shown in two forms, parts Aa4 and Aa8 are the squarer version associated with the B-series, whilst F13 and F17 are correct for the A-series. Note that the B-series ones have linkage for the twin trim tabs on both sides, when they should only be on the port side. The linkage for the actual rudder itself is supplied as separate parts for each side. All the engine cowlings are separate and are good in overall shape. The exhaust and spark plug cooling intake scoops are separate, as are the oil cooler intakes (and exhausts) on either side of the lower front region. The small intake on either side of the upper nose region (#H11 and H12) should only be on the starboard side (#H12), the one on the port side should be removed and filled, while the round filler cap engraved below it should be larger and higher up. The hole for the starter handle on the lower rear port side is too small and it was also oval, not round (the one on the starboard side should not be there). The larger intake further aft on the starboard upper cowling (#H31 or PE7) was not a flap, it was a fixed scoop with a small flange around its base, so you will need to modify #E24 accordingly and ignore the use of #PE7. The forward lip of the ventral radiator is separate and this allows the vertical support beam to be added first along with the engine, although in truth this had an elongated hole behind it, to allow the lower cowl to be positioned with the strut in place (it's part of the radiator assembly). The First Aid kit compartment on the port mid-fuselage is depicted by engraved lines, however the A-series had this behind a clear panel.

Undercarriage: These have the oleo leg and rear strut inside the spat, plus a rubber tyre with a plastic hub. The undercarriage spats look OK, although I am not 100% convinced by the profile at the lower/back edge. The main panel lines on the spats are OK, but there are a number of details and access panels missing and the inner starboard one lacks the oblong access panel for the ammunition box access. The main wheel hubs lack details like the brake lines etc. The support struts are multi-part and are quite detailed. The tailwheel is made up with a two-piece leg/yoke, a separate wheel hub and rubber tyre. The tyre has a crosswise tread pattern, but the illustrations in the manual show it had a circumferential pattern. The yoke is also more like the heavy cast one use for the early B-series, as the A actually had a simple strut and yoke once the cumbersome wheel fairing was removed (which all in-service machines seem to have done).

Tailplanes: These are moulded as upper and lower halves for each separate tailplane and elevator, with the end plate and trim tab linkage separate. The end plates are depicted with the bulged forward section, but that only applies to the B-series onwards, the A-series had this area flat. The access panels on both sides of the tailplanes relate to the B-series, as the A had only two oval panels running side-to-side on the upper port tailplane, and nothing on the upper starboard; the five oval panels on the underside of both tailplanes are correct for the A-series.

Engine: A complete multi-part engine is included along with engine bearers and bulkhead. The radiator under the nose is a separate sub-assembly and the trapeze for the bomb is slung off the mounts behind it. The exhausts come as separate parts moulded with their surround and each oval outlet is hollow.

Propeller: This is made up of a backplate, two-part hub, three blades and a spinner. The spinner diameter is OK but it is too long (about 3.5mm) and thus looks to be too pointed. Note that the round panels between each blade on the spinner edge are supposed to be holes. Whilst the blade profile is good for the early metal HPA II or III, the twist at the root is not sufficient, making them lay too 'flat' in the hub.

Interior: This is made up of sidewalls with separate details, floor, control column, crew seats, oxygen bottle, bulkhead with radio equipment, spent cartridge collecting bin, ammunition rack and drums, instrument panel and gunsight. The control column whilst showing the correct (ring grip) Type KG 11 unit lacks much of the detail on the grip and column and it is also too skinny in the main shaft, which is also too long, and the canvas gaiter at the bottom is too small and too short. The instrument panel lacks the crash-pad that was situated between pilot and gunsight. The instrument panel dial layout does not match many of the images and diagrams in the manuals, but we should also point out that the diagrams in the flight manual do not match those in the spare parts manual! You get a decal overlay for the instrument panel, as it just has the dials raised, no face detail etc. The rudder pedals are from the D/G-series, not the A (which had the same bulky pedals as the B-series). Looking at the photographs in the A-series manuals we can't help but feel most of the sidewall detail is more applicable to the B-series, but it is a starting point. The gunsight is not bad for the C/12, with a separate clear lens, but the ring sight in front of that is missing, so this is more akin to the C/12B of the B-series, than the C/12A of the A-series (note that early As had the gunsight off-set to port, while late A-1s and A-2s usually had it offset to starboard). The radio equipment (#F10 and F12) on the mid-bulkhead (#Ea11) in fact depicts the area in the well-known image of the mock-up of this area (e.g. the radio mounting racks were there, but not the radios themselves). There is also only one bottle (#Ga3 and Ga19) below the radio equipment, when there should be two, so

the supplied bottle is also too big/long and the connector at the end is all wrong (it also lacks the two metal retaining straps and this again ties in with that image of the mock-up of this area). All the rods that radiate out from the radio equipment on #Ea11 were in fact springs with shrouds to shock-mount the radio equipment, so they use a hook and eye at each end, they are not actually part of the surrounding framework as depicted here. The vertical bars in the armour plate behind the pilot (#Ea10) are actually made from tubes, not square bars and the outer profile of the area angles in each side at about shoulder height, then forms a hoop at the top. There are also more than the five vertical bars depicted, it's hard to see in period images, but we would guess at six and even in this

Trumpeter 02420

scale we would say the diameter of the rods was less than the box section bars shown on #Ea10. The rear gun is well done, with the counter-balance arm assembly for the gun itself anchored on the starboard side, the racks for the ammunition drums on the starboard side and the ring and bead sight depicted via etched parts. The armour plate (#Ga18) is not something we have come across in period images or diagrams, so can't really comment on its accuracy. The spent cartridge bin (#Ea5+Ea6) was actually only metal around the top square opening, the rest was canvas, so never held the rigid square shape depicted in the kit parts. The ventral sighting window is made up as a separate unit and mounted to the interior of the lower fuselage/wing stub component (#Ea4).

Details: The pitot is supplied in three parts, the twin fork of #Ga10 is incorrect though, as the horizontal element on the port side should be cut off, as that type of pitot only existed on the inner prong. The sprues include four bundles of SC50 bombs, the D/G-series outer bomb rack with 50kg bombs and Dinort fuse extenders, WB 81 weapons pods, 300lt drop tanks and what looks to be a 500kg bomb, none of which are applicable to the A-series. The ETC 50 racks (#WD4, 5, 14 & 15) can be installed, as can one 50kg bomb on each, while the centreline bomb is best replaced with an aftermarket 250kg example just to be on the save side. The 'ram's horn' aerial masts and crew access steps are separate parts.

Canopy: This is in four sections (with the roll-over frame done as a separate grey-coloured plastic part) and the kit parts come

in two styles so you can have them open (hinged to starboard) or closed. All framework is exterior and done by slightly frosted regions between engraved lines and rivets, although in this scale the rather heavy frames inside each canopy element would have been best depicted with separate structures. This last point also would allow the hinges/retainers for the hinged sections to have been depicted, as once again these were quite big. The track for the rear gun is a separate piece, but the manner in which the MG 15 fits into it is just depicted as fitting into the slot, whereas in reality there was a mounting bracket attached inside that the gun barrel went through, so a little scratchbuilding may be called for here otherwise the gun will just 'float about' in the slot.

Decals: The kit offers the following decal options:
• W/Nr.5040, 'Yellow 6', 'Irene' of an unidentified Luftwaffe unit – This is RLM 70/71 over 65 with a yellow rudder and wing tip undersides
• 52+A12, 2./StG 165, Pocking, Germany, March 1938 – This is RLM 61/62/63 over 65?

Don't forget that the upper surface camouflage on the A-series often wrapped slightly around the wing leading edge, so check images of the options to see if either had this feature. The decal sheet is well printed, although the yellow used for option 1 looks a bit too bright/light. Otherwise the sheet has all unique and national markings with the swastikas cut in two to get around restrictions in certain nations. There is also a good set of airframe stencils (no anti-slip for the wing walkways, oddly) and a decal for the instrument panel that is sadly black/white, so not very useful for the grey-painted panel of the A-series.

Verdict:
This is an exact scaled-up version of the 1/32nd scale kit and has all that kit's various detail issues. It is however the only mainstream kit of the A-series in this scale and for that reason alone it is worth buying and taking the time to build and correct.

Trumpeter, China

Ju 87B-2 (#02421)
Trumpeter producing their B-series kit in 2019 and it remains in production. As it shares many common sprues with the earlier A-series kit, we will cover here only those elements that differ.

Wings: These are the same 'N' and 'P' sprues of the A-series, hence that kit having many B-series features. You keep both MG 17s in the wing this time, along with their associated panels. Most of the engraved access panels on the upper and lower surface are applicable to the B-series, but not all, as no-one agrees on this aspect. The combined lower fuselage section and lower stub wings component is new though, to correctly depict the revisions in this area. It retains the capacity to have the viewing window in it but has a complete surround to it due to revisions associated with the new cowls etc.

Fuselage: These are all new, but still broken down with the rudder and everything forward of the engine firewall. The overall dimensions are good and the main panel lines match scale plans as do most of the access panels. The rudder is separate, as is the linkage on either side of the lower/rear fuselage. The engine cowls are good in overall shape, although the fairing at the front of the exhausts is too small/narrow and tapered, resulting in the hole at the front being too small; the fairing is flat sided (rounded edges) with a slight taper towards the front. The starter handle point is correctly depicted as a hinged oblong cover on the port side, but is also repeated on the starboard side, so fill that one in. The filler cap on the forward port side should only have a single engraved dot offset to one side, as it's not attached with screws, it has a clip that is activated with the 'dot' (button). The smaller intake scoop towards the back of the cowl on the port side is solid, so needs to be opened, plus it's too shallow. The upper asymmetric intake is via an insert and the rear exhaust flap is also done in this manner. The trapeze (#M28) under the nose is incorrect for the B-series, as it only has a single 'strap' across it, when the B-series had a complex series of tubular cross-members in that region. The supercharger intake on the port side is separate and offers only the standard unit, there is no tropical option, there is also no mesh screen etc. inside.

Undercarriage: These are all new (on the 'Gb' sprue) and although the overall size of each spat is good, the rear lower profile is flat, when it should go from the 'flat' alongside the wheel cut-out to the curved underside of the rear fairing, resulting in a slight up-turn in the profile of the lower spat edge as it transitions between these two regions. The struts have the siren stub moulded to them, plus separate blanking caps. The main oleo legs depict the B-series with the compression links on the back, but the slider element is exposed when it was actually covered with a canvas gaiter and there are still no brake lines etc. The main wheels remain unchanged from the A series, so see the comments there about these. The tailwheel is the later style unit seen on the later B and R-series, with the thinner yoke and the support hoops for a canvas cover, which was usually removed, and again the separate rubber tyre has a crosswise tread pattern when period diagrams show this to be circumferential.

Tailplanes: These are unchanged from the A-series, but you will recall that many of the features there were from the B/R-series, so here the bulged end tips and access panel layout are correct.

Engine: You have a complete engine, revised from the earlier version in the A-series, but it is built in a similar manner, it's just revised for the later series 211, has the cast engine bearers, and the bomb trapeze is mounted off the firewall lower edge. The coolant radiator is revised and a separate sub-assembly with the rear cowl flaps offered either open or closed (they depict the segmented version).

Propeller: This is all new, with a two-part boss, separate blades, backplate and spinner. Nit-picky we know, but the hub part #T22 is wrong, because this actually had a dome in the centre. The blade profile looks good, as does the tip, although comparing it with

period images I don't think the root is long enough (the overall blade length is fine though), so suspect the cut-back at the root will be too close to the spinner. The spinner diameter is OK but the profile is a little too skinny, resulting in the unit looking too pointy and lacking the bulbous nature of the original. The hole in the centre was usually covered with a plate, though.

Interior: This is mainly all new and comprises floor, sidewalls with separate details, crew seats, bulkhead and radio equipment, ammunition racks and drums, rear bulkhead, spent cartridge box, control column and rudder pedals. The rudder pedals are once again the later sort for the D/G series, but at least this time the radio equipment is depicted as the correct sender and receiver (pity you can't get these parts from Trumpeter for the A-series kit). The turnover frame above the armour plate behind the pilot depicts the correct 'M' shape struts that can be seen in period images, even though many illustrate this as a 'V' strut only. The pilot's seat is incorrect for the B-series, again this is another instance where you could do with this assembly from the A-series kit, which is correct for the A and B series. The instrument panel is not bad for the B-series, but ignore the decal overlay as that is done in black and white, where the real thing was probably RLM 66 (early B-1s may have been RLM 02). The clear gunsight has a separate lens and is quite nice, but could do with the bead sight adding to be more like the C/12B.

Trumpeter 02421

Details: The sprues include four bundles of SC50 bombs, the D/G-series outer bomb rack with 50kg bombs and Dinort fuse extenders, WB 81 weapons pods, 300lt drop tanks and what looks to be a 1,000kg bomb, most of which are not applicable to the B-series. The ETC 50 racks (#WD4, 5, 14 & 15) can be installed, as can one 50kg bomb on each, because although there are images with bundles of 50kg bombs on these racks under the B and R-series, these had a collective cover on the front that is not included in the kit parts. The 300lt drop tank is seen attached to the underside of each wing via the rack only used on the D and G series, the B and R used the twin ETC 50 racks and special mounting lugs, so if you want to depict an R-series you may be able to create this by combining the smaller racks with the lugs (#WD2 and WD3) used on the D/G series rack? The

centreline bomb is is too large for the B series and best replaced with an aftermarket 250kg or 500kg example. The aerial mast, pitot on starboard wing and crew access steps are separate parts. The rear MG 15 has the ring and bead sights supplied as photo-etched

Canopy: This comes in four sections but all the frames are moulded on the outside via engraved lines and slightly frosted areas, whilst quite a few frames were only on the inside. The round panel of the rear gun mount is the early unarmoured version and it has the exposed 'gear' on the inside done via photo-etched brass. The sliding 'clear vision' vertical panel in either side of the rear canopy section is depicted with the runners, which are actually inside, as if they were exterior frames. The rear-view mirror offset to starboard inside the windscreen is supplied as an etched component, as are both of the grab handles up inside the top of the windscreen frame.

Decals: The kit came with the following decal options:
- Ju 87B-2, W/Nr.6002, T6+IR of 7./StG 2, Bulgaria, 1941 – This is RLM 70/71 over 65 with yellow lower wing tips and rear fuselage band
- Ju 87B-2, L1+AU, 10./LG1, France, 1940 – This is RLM 70/71 over 65, but the swastika is too small and going by images of other Stukas in this unit, it should be the white outline only Type H4

The decal sheet is well printed and includes all unique and national insignia, with the swastika (two sizes) cut in two. A full set of airframe stencils is also included along with that black/white decal for the instrument panel. There are no decals for the wing walkways, though

Verdict:

As with the 1/24th scale A-series, this is very much scaled-up from the 1/32nd scale kit. The common tooling elements make sense, especially with the wings, but having done new sprues for the fuselage and engine here, they would have been better off doing separate wing parts for the A-series as well. Overall it may be a more detailed (and 'modern') option than the Airfix example, but ultimately the choice is down to what the individual modeller wants/likes.

Trumpeter, China

Ju 87D & G series

Trumpeter released the D-5 (#024240) kit in 2018 and followed it with the G-2 (#02425) in 2019, both remain in production. As this kit actually uses some parts from the previous A and B series kits, which we have already assessed, we will cover here only those areas that are specific to the D series.

Wings: Whilst the lower wing and control surfaces sprue remains unchanged from the A and B/R series, the upper wing sprue is new. This new sprue has the upper wing panels and stubs, the latter with the raised ribs seen for the wing walkways, plus extended wing tips and various other detail parts. The panel and access lines on the upper wing outer panels match scale plans. The large oval panel on the outer edge of the stub is actually shown as having more of a taper/point to the rear end in the manual. The extended wing tips' overall profile is a bit off when compared with period images, but nothing that can't be easily corrected, and the tip lights are supplied as separate clear parts. The plate and panel that are situated at the front of the inner/outer wing joint fairing, which cover the top of the oleo strut mount, is depicted as engraved detail, but it does not match the rather complex shape of the outline you will see on the wing of the G-2 (converted from a D-5) at Hendon. The radiators under each inboard stub are separate with the radiator block inside a separate two-part item. The overall shape is good although the flange around the side/edges are only depicted via engraved lines, as is the round access panel alongside and for some reason the front lip has been moulded partially open. This is because that is how this area is set on the Hendon example, but in plastic is just does not work because you don't have enough depth to the plastic nor do you have the linkage inside. There is no linkage inside the rear flap either and the flap is just defined by engraved panel lines, thus meaning the sides of the flap are not depicted either.

Fuselage: A new sprue offers the fuselage from the rudder to the engine firewall, the only real changes to these halves being the modifications for the tailplane supports. The engine cowlings are also new and look good, although the small scoop on the upper rear port side is too small and solid. There should also be two oval access panels along the top (centreline) of the cowling. The supercharger intake on the starboard side is nicely depicted and the hinged flap at the front is a separate part. The exhausts show the fully exposed versions, so correct for the D-5/D-8 and G-2. The D/F loop in the upper dorsal spine is depicted via an insert with a separate clear cover.

Undercarriage: This is another new sprue and the overall size of the legs looks good. The two holes, one above the other, on the lower spats were actually screws, so ideally these would have been better engraved as such, while the rivets above the gaiter look too big compared with the real thing. As usual the gaiter is done via moulded detail, so it's a little too precise (straight lines and indentations) compared with the real thing, but quite understandable. The underside of the rear section of the spat is again too flat. Inside the covers you get the correct slightly angled oleo leg complete with compression linkage, while the wheel hubs are split in two and lack any detail like the brake line etc. plus the tyres are rubber (love or loathe them). The tailwheel is the same as the B series, so it lacks the canvas cover seen on the preserved example at Hendon, but that seems to often have been removed in service.

Tailplanes: These are the same as in the B series kit, but are correct here as well and the layout of the access panels is also correct for this later series.

Engine: Whilst the core of the separate engine is unchanged from the B series, the tanks above and on the side are new components, as are the engine bearers and the ventral coolant radiator.

Propeller: This is made up of the back-plate, three blades, two-part hub and a spinner. The blade profile is a little off, as it looks too wide, the root taper on the back edge is too pronounced and the tip profile is a little too rounded. The spinner profile looks good, although the plug in the tip is not depicted in any way, so just scribe it in place.

Interior: This is new, although a number of the parts are the same as seen on the B series kit. It comprises floor, sidewalls with separate details, crew seats, bulkhead and radio equipment, ammunition racks and drums, rear bulkhead, spent cartridge box, control column and rudder pedals. The rudder pedals are the correct later sort for the D/G series, while all the other detail seems to be based on the G-2 at Hendon, although the side profile of the pilot's seat is not 100% accurate (the change in direction of either side piece should be curved, not a sharp angle – the edges are also rolled, not square-cut). The box for the

Trumpeter 02424

spent cartridges (#U23) is not really accurate, as this was a bag that was attached to the rear bulkhead (#S19), so was not a rigid shape as depicted, plus it's in the wrong place (too far forward, as the tube from the gun to to it was at an angle and that tube was not a concertina type as depicted, it was a plain fabric tube of a much larger diameter). The instrument panel has raised detail plus a decal to go on top, but the decal is just black and white, so not very accurate. There seems to be a crash-pad (#R16) fitted ahead of the instrument panel and gunsight, which I don't recall seeing in any diagrams or images of this areas? It is probably down to some indicating that a well-known image of the instrument panel etc. depicts the D-series, when in fact it's actually a B-series converted as one of the test airframes for the D-series canopy and it has that crash-pad, but it was not a feature of the production D (or G-series). The hot air pipe coming from the port side at the top of the instrument panel is missing. The gunsight is separate and done in clear plastic and whilst a reasonable rendition of the Revi C 16D or D/N of the D-5/D-5N, so you may want to replace it. You will also have to add a cross-bar on which to mount the Revi sight, as it's not on a stem from the top of the instrument panel as depicted in this kit (it's bolted to a tube that runs ahead and across the top of the instrument panel). No seat belts are included, but once again they can be obtained from various aftermarket sources if you want.

Details: The sprues include four bundles of

SC50 bombs, the D-series outer bomb racks with 50kg bombs and Dinort fuse extenders, WB 81 weapons pods, 300lt drop tanks and what looks to be a 1,000kg bomb. The outer racks (#WD6 and WD13) can be used either with the 250kg bombs with or without fuse extenders, or a 300lt drop tank. You can also use the WB 81 weapons pods on each outer wing rack if you like, although these were mainly used for ground-attack and as such the airframe may well have had flame dampers fitted and they are not in the kit. The centreline bomb looks too large, so if you want a bomb here replace it with an aftermarket 250kg or 500kg example. The aerial mast, pitot on starboard wing and crew access steps are separate parts. The rear MG 81Z is multi-part with the breech/trigger and barrels separate plus the ring and bead sights are supplied as photo-etched. All the appliqué armour plates for the fuselage sides are also separate, check your references which were fitted though, as there are numerous variations.

Canopy: This is supplied in four sections and the framework is all engraved on the outside, although the D-series has far fewer frames under the Perspex than the earlier versions, so some careful masking and painting inside and out should be acceptable. The rear-view mirror inside the windscreen is a separate etched part and there are also two etched grab rails. The rear cupola is well done, but again the rearmost section is moulded with the remainder, when it was in fact separate. The gun-profile/track on the outside of the rear gun frame/decking is moulded in situ, so in this scale it's a bit too 'flat' really. Appliqué armour is included for the starboard side of the gunner and pilot's canopy sections, which is good, but no such armour is included for the port side. Check your references on this because the style/location of such armour differs hugely.

Decals: The kit offered the following decal options:

- Ju 87D-5, 3./SG 3, Immola, Finland, June 1944 – This is RLM 70/71 over 65 with yellow lower wing tips and rear fuselage band. Most of the D-5s with this unit at this time had the Stuvi 5B sight fitted up inside the top of the windscreen and neither the sight nor the bulged upper windscreen is depicted in the kit
- D-5, A5+AD, Stab III./SG1, Vitebsk, Russia, 7th March 1944 – This is RLM 70/71 over 65 with stripes of white distemper on the upper surfaces and yellow lower engine cowling, lower wing tips and rear fuselage band

The decal sheet includes all the unique and national markings with the swastikas split in two. The sheet includes a good set of airframe stencils plus that black and white decal for the instrument panel.

Verdict:
As with the A-series kit, this is the only game in town and for that reason alone it is worth taking the time and effort to build and undertake any necessary corrections and/or upgrades as you go. In this scale, it will be really impressive once built.

Chapter 7: **Building a Selection**

Having looked at what kits are and have been available of the Ju 87 series in the four major scales, we thought it would be a good idea to build a selection in 1/72nd, 1/48th and 1/32nd. Apologies that this is not a larger section and we have not done certain kits, but we only have a specific number of pages available.

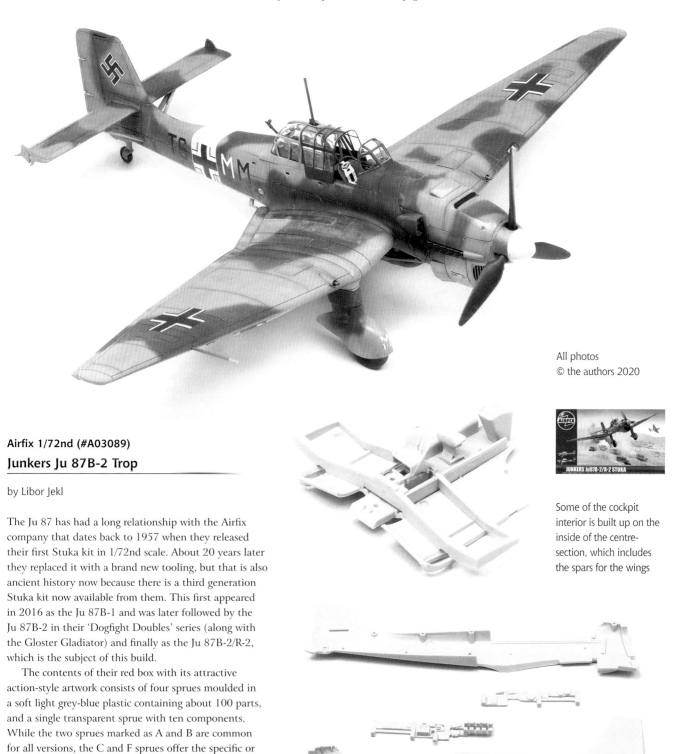

All photos
© the authors 2020

Airfix 1/72nd (#A03089)
Junkers Ju 87B-2 Trop

by Libor Jekl

The Ju 87 has had a long relationship with the Airfix company that dates back to 1957 when they released their first Stuka kit in 1/72nd scale. About 20 years later they replaced it with a brand new tooling, but that is also ancient history now because there is a third generation Stuka kit now available from them. This first appeared in 2016 as the Ju 87B-1 and was later followed by the Ju 87B-2 in their 'Dogfight Doubles' series (along with the Gloster Gladiator) and finally as the Ju 87B-2/R-2, which is the subject of this build.

The contents of their red box with its attractive action-style artwork consists of four sprues moulded in a soft light grey-blue plastic containing about 100 parts, and a single transparent sprue with ten components. While the two sprues marked as A and B are common for all versions, the C and F sprues offer the specific or alternative parts for the given variant, such as the cowling, tailwheel, siren propellers etc. The main airframe parts are cleanly moulded with minimum flash or sink marks and the engraved panel lines are quite nice, as they are reasonably thin and consistent. A nice feature is the subtly raised access panels for the weapons in the wing, however, some other surface details are omitted,

Some of the cockpit interior is built up on the inside of the centre-section, which includes the spars for the wings

The sidewalls are separate and although with some nice moulded detail they will benefit from some additional work

Once painted the interior was detailed with the pre-painted etched details from the Eduard set, including those seat belts that help cover up the 'solid' nature of the gunner's seat

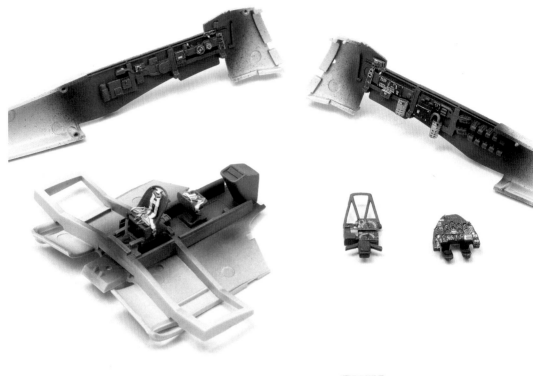

The engine cowling is multi-piece and the exhausts were replaced with the Quickboost resin version simply because they had hollow outlets

such as fasteners or rivets, and according to some scale drawings the panel lines do not seem to be complete, especially on the wing. The separately moulded control surfaces have thin trailing edges, while their attachment pins do look quite thick; on my example I also found a moulding defect in the form of sunken plastic, which had to be levelled with a fine sanding stick. Unfortunately, the flap actuating rods and balancing weights are not usable due to their crudeness and I therefore suggest you completely replace them. The cockpit details look decent though, and some parts such as seats, basket for spent ammunition or control stick are to be placed within the upper region of the centre-section, which along with the

The ventral sighting window is moulded as a clear block to represent its housing inside the fuselage, so you have to paint that before it's installed

spars, forms the cockpit floor. Separately moulded are the cockpit sidewalls with structure and various levers and control boxes, however, these details are a bit soft and vaguely defined. The rather complex cowling is split into several parts and the completed unit is then reinforced via linked exhausts, although the radiator cooling flaps would have benefited from sharper definition. The propeller probably represents the VS 5 type with the broader blades, but these look a bit wide and thick, especially at their roots. The undercarriage spats correctly show the connection seam lines on the sides, but there should be another one running along the front faces. Also provided are alternative parts allowing the sirens or their stubs blanked over. The tyres are moulded plain without any tread pattern and they could be fitted in the spats in weighted or un-weighted appearance via alternative locking points. The kit includes 250kg and 500kg bombs with their corresponding mounting braces coupled with smaller 50kg bombs along with the wing racks and drop tanks, which go with the R-2 version. The clear parts are moulded without visible defects or excessive distortion and are reasonably thin, however, the plastic

Using clamps whilst the glue dried on the wing/ fuselage assembly

used does not seem to be crystal clear and more sharply defined frames would be welcome as well. An alternative opened pilot's canopy is provided, which is moulded together with the bottom fixed part, but that does not enable you to paint the canopy framing underneath; I believe this was a good approach for less experienced modellers. Airfix did not forget the viewing panel in the bottom of the fuselage through which the pilot could observe the target, and the circular-shaped window of the gun mount is provided separately so that the armoured version can be included as an alternative part, plus it makes mounting the MG 15 itself a lot easier.

The kit captures the basic dimensions and shapes without major omissions, some may notice that the upper fuselage part is too flat, though. It's correction would be quite difficult I'm afraid, as the complete rear fuselage outline would have to be carefully sanded and reshaped. The instructions are very informative and clearly drawn and should guide you through the whole building process without any problems. The kit provides markings for the well-known machine from 6./StG 2 'Immelman' with the snake motif on the fuselage sides that operated in North Africa in 1941. In my opinion this plane was tropicalised and therefore it should be equipped with the larger supercharger intake with integral sand filter, but that is not included in the kit (I think this has only ever been included in 1/72nd scale kits by Italeri). The other option is a Ju 87R-2 from 209a *Squadriglia* of the *Regia Aeronautica* from the same theatre, along with bonus decals of it once it was captured and put in RAF markings.

Construction

The build starts with the assembly of the centre-section on which are glued the seats and spent ammunition basket along with the T-shaped spar to make a rigid base element for the subsequent attachment of the wing to the fuselage. The gunner's seat was in fact a tubular framework but is moulded in the kit as a solid piece, however, once the seat belts are added to it and if you do not intend to open the rear cockpit, it will be acceptable. The sidewalls are usable, but they will benefit from additional detail and for this I acquired the Eduard photo-etched set (#73-633), which offers the usual set of pre-painted parts, such as seat belts, instrument panel and radio transmitter/receiver faces supplemented with oxygen bottles shells and ammunition drum faces with handles, that substantially improve the look of completed interior. The cockpit could then be primed with Mr Surfacer 1500 (Black) and airbrushed with RLM 66 Black Grey

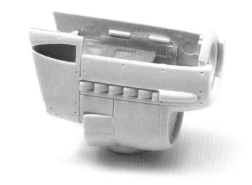

The cowling with the resin exhausts and the supercharger intake removed, so that a tropical one could be built; its interior is blanked-off with plasticard

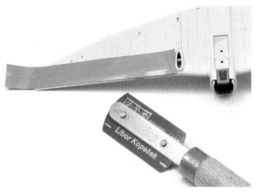

The panel lines damaged by filler/sanding along each wing leading edge are re-instated using embossing tape as a guide

(Gunze-Sangyo #H416) which in my opinion is the correct colour for Ju 87Bs manufactured at that time. RLM 02 is often mentioned for this (including the kit's instructions, which refer to Humbrol 240) but this seems to have only been used on early B-1 machines, prior to or in the very early stage of WWII.

The cowling consists of separate halves, the front part of radiator and a single-piece exhaust assembly including inner reinforcement. The latter part I eventually replaced with Quickboost resin item (#QB72595), as I preferred having the individual exhaust stubs hollowed, which would otherwise be difficult to depict because the openings were not a regular round shape. This part is designed as a straight replacement that does not need any extra surgery and the reinforcements are cast in it as well, so there is no danger the complete cowling assembly will become too soft and flexible. On the starboard cowling side there is the supercharger intake but as already mentioned, this does not correspond to the tropical version I required (it is a pity Airfix did not mould this area separately to allow optional intake types). I removed it with a scalpel, backed the area with thicker plastic sheet and scratchbuilt the intake. I used a similar

The prominent raised seam along the front of the undercarriage cover was reproduced with a thin piece of stretched sprue that was gently sanded once the glue had fully cured

The first stage of making a new tropical intake is to use the front section from one in the spares box, then build up the back with laminations of plasticard

The ventral viewing panel received an outer frame from the etched set

The rear section was then carved and sanded to shape

Not satisfied with the detail on the tailplanes and elevators, these were replaced with the Aires set that also has the benefit of having each element separate

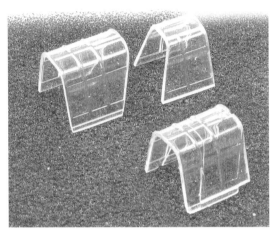

The clear canopy sections are OK, but the plastic used is not that clear and the frames are poorly defined

intake front part from my spares box and the rest of the body was built up with Atol Hobby plastic sheets and sanded to the corresponding shape. In the intake itself I glued a rolled-up piece of perforated etched strip which depicts the filter insert.

Next I joined the fuselage with the centre-section and wing upper halves, which all fitted precisely, although for better alignment I recommend you secure the joints with clamps while the glue fully cures. I used a small amount of cyanoacrylate for filling any visible seams where the bottom wing halves meet the centre-section and at the bottom of the wing leading edge I restored the panel line using embossing tape as a guide for the scribing tool. In the nose I installed the bottom clear sighting panel that is oddly moulded in the form of a clear 'tunnel'

The control surfaces have all the mounts, linkage and mass balance weights moulded in situ, so the last two were removed to be replaced later with etched examples

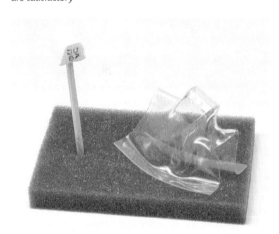

The overlapping pilot and mid-sections come either separate, or moulded together in the open position, neither of which are satisfactory

connected to the cockpit floor, so its sidewalls had to be painted black. The clear panel then received an etched frame and it was masked off before continuing with any further work. I added the completed cowling to the fuselage, which required a little trimming on the cowling sides, but then all sat in place nicely. At this point I also added the new sand filter. After completion of the wheels with their covers I prepared a length of thin plastic wire cut from heat-stretched sprue to represent the front seam line and glued it in place with extra thin cement then sanded it down a little with a fine sanding cloth. The spats could then be joined with their upper halves and the assembled units then attached to the wing. The

The oil cooler rear flap was replaced with etched, while the gun blisters came from Quickboost

A new canopy section over the pilot was crash-formed using the kit part (filled with Milliput for rigidity) as a mould

tailplanes looked a bit unconvincing having soft details and rather thick elevator balance plates, so I went for the replacement items from Aires (#7363), which also includes separated elevators. From the wing flaps I cut off their thick actuating rods and mass balance weights and marked their position with a fine drill for later replacement with etched alternatives, which had to be added after painting the model. At this step I attached the outstanding extra parts to the base airframe such as oil cooler outlet flap and replaced the wing machine gun aerodynamic (tapered) fairings with resin ones coming from Quickboost (#QB72594), as these offered finer detail with excellent machine-gun muzzles, plus the set also includes a replacement pitot tube. In the port wing leading edge between the gun and the landing lamp I drilled out two holes, one was the gun camera and the other an air inlet.

I did not like the way the centre canopy (sliding) section was moulded and therefore went for scratchbuilding a replacement. From the solid canopy part (#E05) I removed the centre section using a fine razor saw and used it as a plug for crash-forming a new one, while the inside of the original part was filled with white Milliput to avoid its deformation during the moulding process. Next I attached the windshield, which required a small amount of filler to create a smooth transition to the fuselage. The clear parts could then be masked off with a set of Eduard masks (#CX513) and the kit was primed with Mr Surfacer 1000 (Grey).

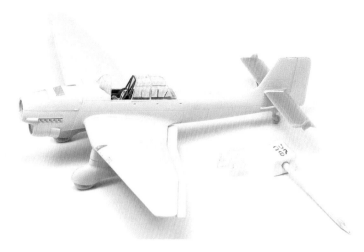

Camouflage & Markings

Since I had already built both marking options provided in the kit I opted for another Luftwaffe machine operating in North Africa that was featured on the Xtradecal decal sheet (#X72223 Junkers Ju 87B/K/R Stuka). First I airbrushed the white theatre band (H11) and continued with RLM 65 Light Blue (H67). This Stuka of 4./StG 2 (T6+MM) had the standard scheme on the upper surfaces consisting of RLM 70 and 71 (H65 and H64) oversprayed with an irregular pattern of RLM 79 Sand Brown. For the latter colour I used my own mixture of H79 Sandy Yellow and H310 Brown in a 1:1 ratio plus a drop of red for fine tuning to get a slight pinkish hue. After applying all the decals, which went on without any problems at all, I further worked to weather the surface colours in a way you would expect for an aircraft operating in such a hot environment. As the first step I applied with a tip of toothpick a series of dots of various oil paints (such as ochre, sand, light grey and white) spread over all the surface, and once they dried out a bit after a couple of minutes, they were blended with a flat brush and MIG Production's thinner, always working in the direction of the airflow on the wing, and in a vertical direction on the fuselage. The next step was to add traces of dust with an airbrush and some heavily diluted light sand acrylics, while the exhaust stains were reproduced with black and light grey.

All the canopy panels were covered with an Eduard set of die-cut masks prior to the model being primed

With the canopy plugged with foam, the model with primer to highlight any areas that needed additional attention

The theatre (white) band around the rear fuselage and the wing tip undersides were all painted first, then masked so that the lower RLM 65 could be applied

The upper scheme was done in the original RLM 70/71 splinter pattern first

Once the RLM 70/71 scheme was dry, this was broken up with a loose application of RLM 79

The kit propeller (left) is too wide, especially at the root of each blade, so it was replaced with the Quickboost example intended for the Fujimi B/R kit

The kit spinner and hub was retained, the latter modified to accept the Quickboost blades

Once glossed, the model received its decals, which all went on without fuss as they are nicely printed by Cartograf

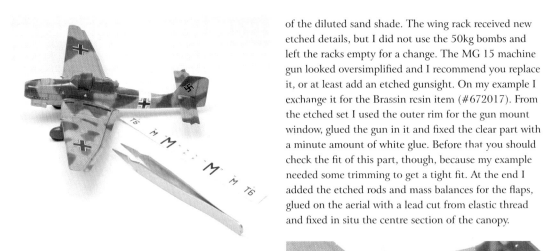

With the decal sealed by another gloss coat dots of various shades of oil paint were applied, then blended with thinner to weather the overall scheme

Final Details

On my first inspection of the propeller it looked wrong to me, especially the blades, which seemed too thick, so I replaced them with the Quickboost items intended for the Fujimi kit (#QB72422). The kit spinner was still used along with the original centre part of the propeller, which I modified to accept the new blades. This part was then sprayed Alclad II Duraluminium (ALC102) while the propeller blades were done with RLM 70 (H65), and the spinner in a combination of white (H11) and RLM 23 (H414). Now I assembled the 500kg bomb, painted it RLM 70 and weathered it with few passes

The trapeze, bomb and ETC 50 racks were all from the kit, suitably painted and weathered, although the latter racks did receive some detail parts from the etched set

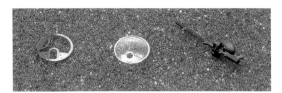

The rear gun panel received a detailed outer frame from the etched set, while the MG 15 itself was a replacement resin item from the Brassin range

of the diluted sand shade. The wing rack received new etched details, but I did not use the 50kg bombs and left the racks empty for a change. The MG 15 machine gun looked oversimplified and I recommend you replace it, or at least add an etched gunsight. On my example I exchange it for the Brassin resin item (#672017). From the etched set I used the outer rim for the gun mount window, glued the gun in it and fixed the clear part with a minute amount of white glue. Before that you should check the fit of this part, though, because my example needed some trimming to get a tight fit. At the end I added the etched rods and mass balances for the flaps, glued on the aerial with a lead cut from elastic thread and fixed in situ the centre section of the canopy.

The last details to add, once all the painting and weathering was complete, were the linkage rods and aileron mass balance weights, as the etched versions just looked more 'scale' than the original kit parts

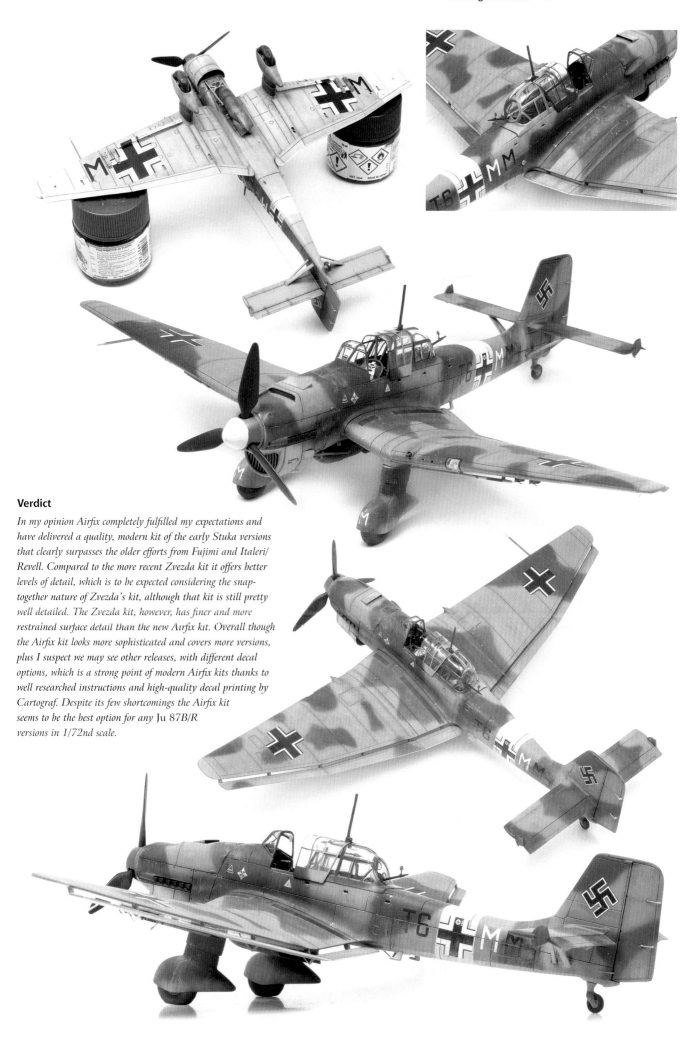

Verdict

In my opinion Airfix completely fulfilled my expectations and have delivered a quality, modern kit of the early Stuka versions that clearly surpasses the older efforts from Fujimi and Italeri/ Revell. Compared to the more recent Zvezda kit it offers better levels of detail, which is to be expected considering the snap- together nature of Zvezda's kit, although that kit is still pretty well detailed. The Zvezda kit, however, has finer and more restrained surface detail than the new Airfix kit. Overall though the Airfix kit looks more sophisticated and covers more versions, plus I suspect we may see other releases, with different decal options, which is a strong point of modern Airfix kits thanks to well researched instructions and high-quality decal printing by Cartograf. Despite its few shortcomings the Airfix kit seems to be the best option for any Ju 87B/R versions in 1/72nd scale.

Fujimi 1/72nd (#F14)
Junkers Ju 87D-3

by Libor Jekl

The cockpit interior is basic in the kit, so some plasticard additions help

This was truly the first modern Stuka kit series in 1/72nd scale, first appearing in 1986, which is a bit surprising considering the quality of the tooling. Even now these kits are comparable with more recent efforts, especially as far as the fine surface details and overall moulding quality is concerned. Obviously, there are areas in certain kits that are outdated or simplified nowadays, such as the cockpit or cowling details. Also, there are small inaccuracies, caused most likely by the universal nature of the toolings, which tried to cover all the main versions from the B-1 to the G-2, and these include omissions like the tropical equipment of the B/R versions, landing light, lack of propeller options and missing viewing panel in the cockpit floor, plus they ignored certain aspects of the late versions such as external armour plates, the different shape of undercarriage spats or the radio compass clear cover on the rear fuselage dorsal spine. Due to generally poor availability over the past years these kits seem to be still quite popular though, and certain companies specialising in re-issuing older kits seem to have taken advantage of this, such as Hobby 2000 who just reissued the D-1,

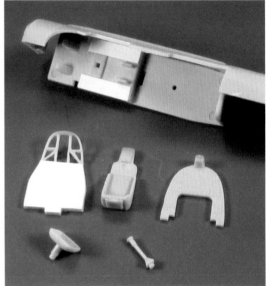

D-3N/D-7 and G-2 kits recently in their own range with new decals.

In my stash I had the D-1 kit, which I intended to upgrade to a late D-3 version used by the Rumanian Air Force during WWII. The kit consists of four sprues moulded from a hard light grey-coloured plastic and a single frame with transparencies. The interior consists of just a few components such as the floor, seats, instrument

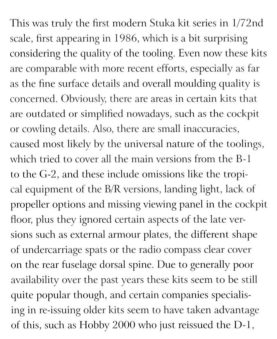

Combining plasticard and stock, along with wire and some left-over etched detail, the interior can be make to look a little better

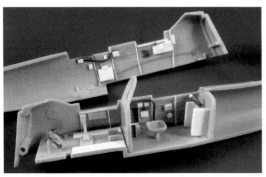

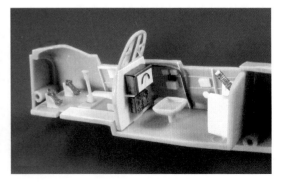

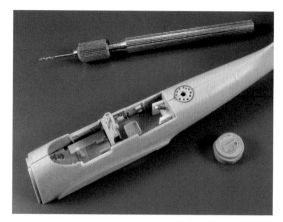

One of the major omissions in the Fujimi D and G kits is the lack of the D/F loop on the dorsal spine, so this was obtained from the Quickboost range and the area on the dorsal spine was marked, chain-drilled and then removed

The interior looks quite acceptable once painted

The new D/F loop

panel with raised dials, control column and the central bulkhead with safety framework, while the fuselage sidewalls are completely devoid of any detail. There are many ejector-pin marks that need to be addressed as well. The bottom wing halves are moulded integrally with the control surfaces, which is not so bad as it keeps the assembly and makes any handling of the model easier, however, their actuating rods are in the form of solid triangles and are thus a bit too simplified. The 50kg, 500kg and 1,000kg bombs with their mounts and racks look reasonable, while the machine-guns in the wing and the radio-operator MG 15 gun once again look oversimplified. However, the kit captures the basis dimensions and shapes with no major omissions, especially as far as the correct cowling length and shape of the wing is concerned. The construction diagrams in the instructions are common for all D-1, D-3 and D-7 kits, but the individual differences are clearly marked and the colour chart refers to Gunze-Sangyo products. There are two decal options provided in this kit: a Stab./StG.3 machine (S7+AA) with RLM 79 over the standard RLM 70/71 splinter camouflage dating from 1942 in North Africa, and a 2./StG 2 machine (T6+BK) in the standard camouflage scheme that operated on the Eastern Front. The decals seem a bit thick, they probably come from the same firm that does the decals in Hasegawa or Tamiya kits, so they may need plenty of hot water and stronger decal solutions to reasonably conform

to the surface detail. I didn't eventually used them here though, as I went for a replacement aftermarket sheet.

Construction

I used the D-1 kit as the starting point for my late D-3 build, so I started with scratchbuilding the fuselage internal structure, side consoles, machine-gun ammunition boxes and other components using Evergreen plastic stock, while brass wires and some old etched leftovers were sourced for the foot pedals, radio equipment faces and various cabling and wiring. Strips of thin plasticard were glued on the floor and bulkhead so they overlapped the ejector pin marks, which otherwise would have been filled with putty. Next, I located and drilled out the opening for the Peil G.IV D/F loop, which I obtained in the Quickboost range (#QB72327). The interior was painted in RLM 66 (H416) including the compass bay and the seat belts were added from etched leftovers as well.

I continued with modification of the wing using an old resin set from JK Resin I found in my pile of treasures (this company has been out of business for more than 15 years, but I still have some of their sets). This

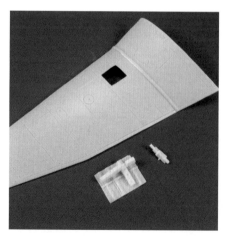

The wing MG 17 came from an old JK Model resin set, and a little surgery is required of the kit parts for its use

Once the MG 17 and bay is painted and weathered it is quite effective

The simplified wing walkways are created with plasticard strips, as is the appliqué armour; the only filler used included the blob of black cyanoacrylate on the upper cowling!

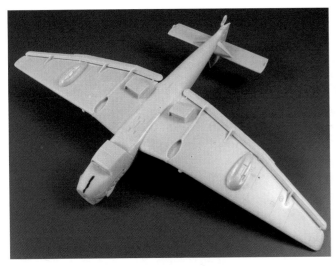

The fit of all the parts is superb, again the only 'filler' used was the blob of black cyanoacrylate under the nose

With everything in place, the model could be masked ready for some primer

Once the lower surfaces were painted RLM 65 and had dried the upper surface camouflage could be applied – here the RLM 71 has been applied and masked, ready for the RLM 70

The original Luftwaffe crosses were applied then painted out, as per the real thing – the yellow theatre band had been added before any other colour was applied

one was a relatively simple and effective upgrade allowing the port MG 17 machine-gun bay to be exposed, so first I removed its access panel from the wing using a fine razor saw and scalpel blade. The two resin pieces make the whole conversion, the gun mount with ammunition boxes and the weapon itself, so these were painted and attached to the upper part of the bottom wing half. The missing landing light in the port wing leading edge was opened with a razor saw, the lamp was bent to shape from an old etched component and the opening glazed

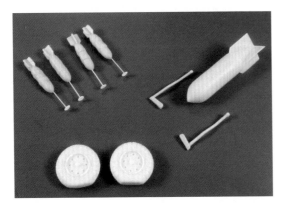

Final details included replacement resin wheels from Kora Model and a bomb load, with the 50kg bombs having fuse extenders made from scratch

with a piece of clear adhesive tape.

Now I joined the main airframe components together, which highlighted one of the strong points of this manufacturer's products, the joints were near perfection without any need for filler. I addressed a visible seam line on the nose with thicker (black) cyanoacrylate, but that was all. On the outer fuselage sides, I added the armour plates cut from thin plasticard and the walkway strips on the roots were trimmed from the same material. I continued with installation of the canopy and made a new centre section by crash-forming clear thermo-form sheet. The canopy parts matched their fuselage joints again very precisely, so I could mask them off with my own masks cut from Tamiya tape, and the model was primed with few thin coats of Mr Surfacer 1000 (Grey).

Colour & Marking

Rumanian Stukas wore the original Luftwaffe camouflage colours with overpainted national markings and yellow theatre markings. The splinter camouflage pattern of RLM 70 and 71 on the upper surface was masked off with Tamiya tape and airbrushed using Gunze-Sangyo Mr Aqueous acrylics. The corresponding shades of H64 and H65 seem to give a distinct contrast once applied, so

I gave the upper surfaces several thin coats of H64 Dark Green to blend them in a bit, while the Luftwaffe markings were oversprayed with fresh H65 RLM 70 colour. After a coat of gloss varnish I could apply the decals from the Kora Model sheet (#72.122 Junkers Ju 87 D-3 Stuka in Rumanian Service). Their decals are usually very thin with good opacity, but they are printed with a solid clear carrier film, so they have to be individually trimmed from the background paper first. They do require careful handling especially during positioning onto the model's surface.

Final Details

The wheels from the kit were replaced with Kora's resin examples that are 'flattened', and I then continued with the ordnance. From the JK Model resin set I sourced the 500kg and 50kg bombs, which offered thinner fins than the kit parts, and the 50kg bombs also received extended igniters (Dinort rods) scratchbuilt from circles punched from thin plasticard and a piece of stretched sprue. At the end I attached the centre canopy section and other outstanding small bits such as the aerial mast and lead, pitot and the propeller unit.

Verdict

The Fujimi Ju 87D kit is still a pretty sound effort that offers a satisfying and enjoyable build experience with good fit and nice surface detail. However, the level of detail is average and with areas like the cockpit interior it is almost non-existent by today's standards. Due to the lack of a truly modern kit of the late-series Stuka it seems to be a suitable starting point for any 1/72nd scale 'Dora', either from the original manufacturer or its recent reissue from Hobby 2000.

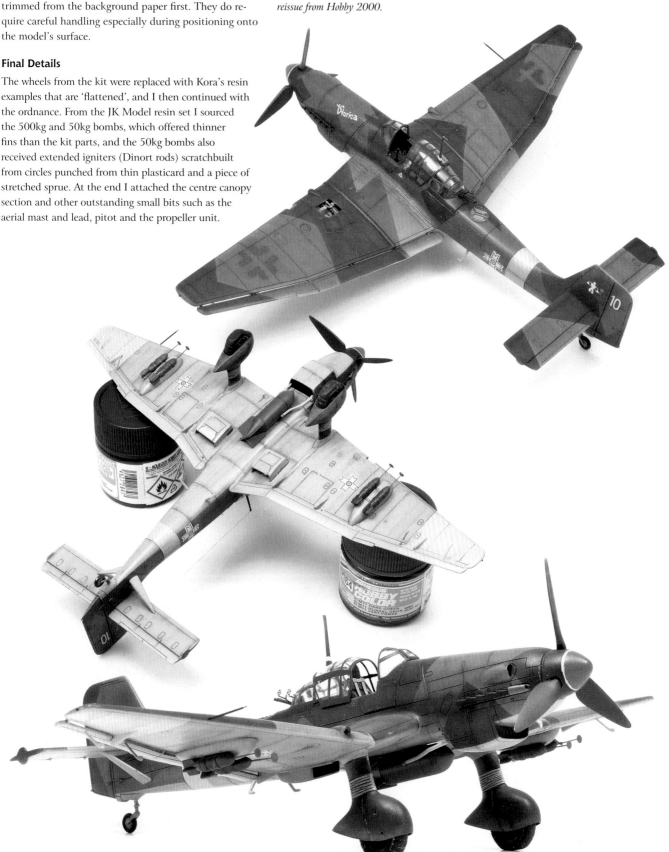

Academy 1/72nd (#12404)
Junkers Ju 87G-2

by Libor Jekl

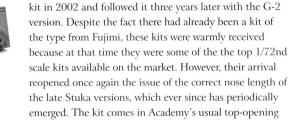

The South Korean company Academy released their G-1 kit in 2002 and followed it three years later with the G-2 version. Despite the fact there had already been a kit of the type from Fujimi, these kits were warmly received because at that time they were some of the the top 1/72nd scale kits available on the market. However, their arrival reopened once again the issue of the correct nose length of the late Stuka versions, which ever since has periodically emerged. The kit comes in Academy's usual top-opening box and consists of five sprues with 74 parts moulded in light grey-coloured plastic and seven clear parts. The moulding quality along with the fine engraved panel lines and other surface details are all excellent and despite the kit's age it still represents a very high standard that some other companies still fail to achieve. Of note is the great engineering too, resulting is a smart parts count and precise fit of all components. The cockpit interior is nicely detailed and offers all the main equipment visible through the crystal clear, though a little bit thick, canopy

The cockpit interior benefits from etched upgrade parts, especially things like the tubular seat of the gunner

that is supplied in four separate pieces. Unfortunately, the canopy sections cannot be posed open due to their thickness, but at least they may well serve as moulds for heat moulding new ones, if your feel up to the challenge. Up to now it is still the only Ju 87 kit which correctly depicts the clear cover of the D/F loop (other kits only have it engraved, if at all). Reasonably detailed 37mm gun pods are included along with their racks and ammunition boxes. The kit provides a single decal option, the personal mount of SG2 *Kommodore Major* Hans-Ulrich Rudel flown on the Eastern Front in the summer of 1944.

There are few minus points that need to be reported, though. Probably the most apparent shape error is that the radiators under each wing stub are about 2mm too short. I do not like the shape of the undercarriage spats either, as they seem to not sufficiently bulge in the front part and are too pointed at the rear. I believe they also lack some millimetres in their overall height, in other words, they do not look robust enough and look too skinny. This error was noted by Quickboost who offered a set

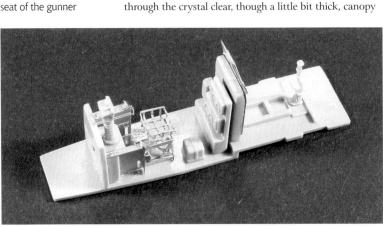

The ExtarTech set had an etched instrument panel, which is not really the right shape for a D/G (should have side sections), but it did allow the correct style rudder pedals to be depicted

The chin radiators lack any real detail, so once again the etched components in the ExtraTech set helped here

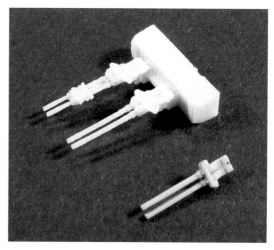

The rear MG 81Z is a little basic, so it was replaced with a resin version, although that needed the barrels shortened to their correct length first

of resin replacement units complete with separate wheels. It seems the propeller diameter is about 2mm short as well and some details such as the MG 81Z and flap actuators are simplified, but usable. My example suffered from shallow ejector-pin marks on the tailplane struts, but these could be addressed with sanding sticks. On the wing tips there is a visible seam line due to a tooling insert (the G-1 had the shorter span), but this can be corrected with a few strokes of a sanding stick.

The main reason for the often-debated cowling length was apparently caused by some older (and a few newer!) drawings that list the overall fuselage length as 11.500m, which is incorrect. In fact, the length of the fuselage with the tail up to the engine bulkhead is the same for all versions, and the introduction of the new Jumo 211J for the D/G version could not cause the quoted 50cm difference in nose length. Obviously, the cowling was modified and received cleaner lines, which along with the lack of the oil cooler inlet at the top and slightly longer spinner (references usually state approximately 100mm) may cause on some photographs (especially taken from certain angles) a much more pronounced look. The Academy kit is almost spot on with regard to the length, although some purists may consider the cowling is about 1mm short in 1/72nd, if you take 11.00m as the total fuselage length.

Construction

Despite initially wanting to do this build without much additional detailing and to build it with a closed canopy,

The floor, seats etc. once painted

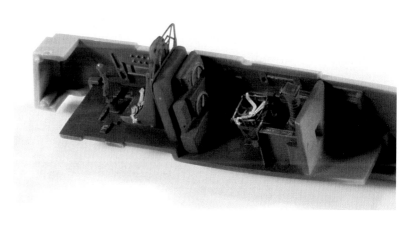

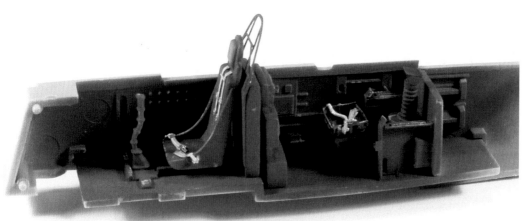

The interior looks quite busy once painted and weathered

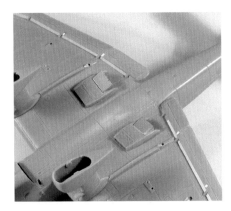

The radiators under each wing are too shallow, but the etched set at least allowed the rear flap to be depicted with a more scale thickness

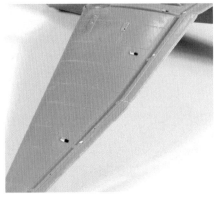

The control surface linkage as moulded was removed, these little etched fairings added and the links themselves added later, again from etched

The end plates on the tailplanes are a bit thick, so look a lot more convincing once replaced with etched examples

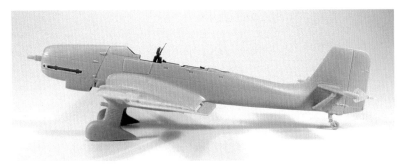

Regardless of what some may claim, the kit's length is good, being almost spot on equivalent to 11.00m overall

I found in my stash the Extratech etched set (EX72144). It contains only replacement parts that are either inferior in plastic or completely omitted in the kit, such as the thick safety framework behind the pilot, correct tubular type gunner's seat belts, the ammunition boxes, the

instrument panel with foot pedals or gunsight. In the nose I fixed the replacement radiator and intercooler screens, and then I painted the interior RLM 66 (H416), which was subsequently gently dry-brushed with a light grey oil paint. At this point I dealt with the rear MG 81Z machine-gun, which was replaced with an Aires resin example (#7109), however, the barrels needed to be shortened in order to match the correct length of the real weapon, which was 475mm.

The main airframe assembly could be managed within two short sessions thanks to the perfect fit of all the main components. The only place where I used a minute amount of putty was the attachment of the tail struts to the fuselage. The radiator outlet flaps on the wing were replaced with etched parts as well as the bulged covers of the flap actuating rods. Their thick openings in the flaps were then plugged with plastic strips and sanded smooth. The elevator mass balance weights would benefit from the etched replacements because the original plastic parts looked a little bit on the thick side. Next I assembled the 3.7cm BK cannon and added some wiring and plumbing from lead wires. The etched set also offers a couple of parts that substantially improve the look of the assembled unit, such as petite gun mounts and the ammunition boxes. The gun muzzle walls were carefully thinned with a scalpel blade to get their thickness to a more scale level.

Camouflage & Markings

This consisted of the usual splinter scheme with yellow theatre markings and was airbrushed with Gunze-Sangyo

How much filler? Exactly that much filler, none!

Now this is where the etched set comes into its own, the finesse of the mounts and the ammunition unit are just so much better in this medium

The muzzle brake on each cannon barrel was carefully opened up, although you can also go the easy route and purchase one of the many superb aftermarket turned brass replacement barrels

Aqueous acrylics from their Luftwaffe range; H64 for RLM 71, H65 for RLM 70 and H67 for RLM 65. The paint scratches were in all the usual places, such as the wing roots or along the cowling, and these were brushed on using light grey Vallejo acrylics. As with many older Academy kits the decals are probably the weakest point of their kits, and this example was no exception. They needed really hot water to release them from the backing sheet and I had to use also plenty of Mr Mark Softer to blend them into the surface. They also seemed to tend to disintegrate at their outer edges and could easily break up completely as well. The missing swastika and the fuselage code that I eventually could not save were thus sourced from older generic Tally-Ho! and Propagteam sheets respectively.

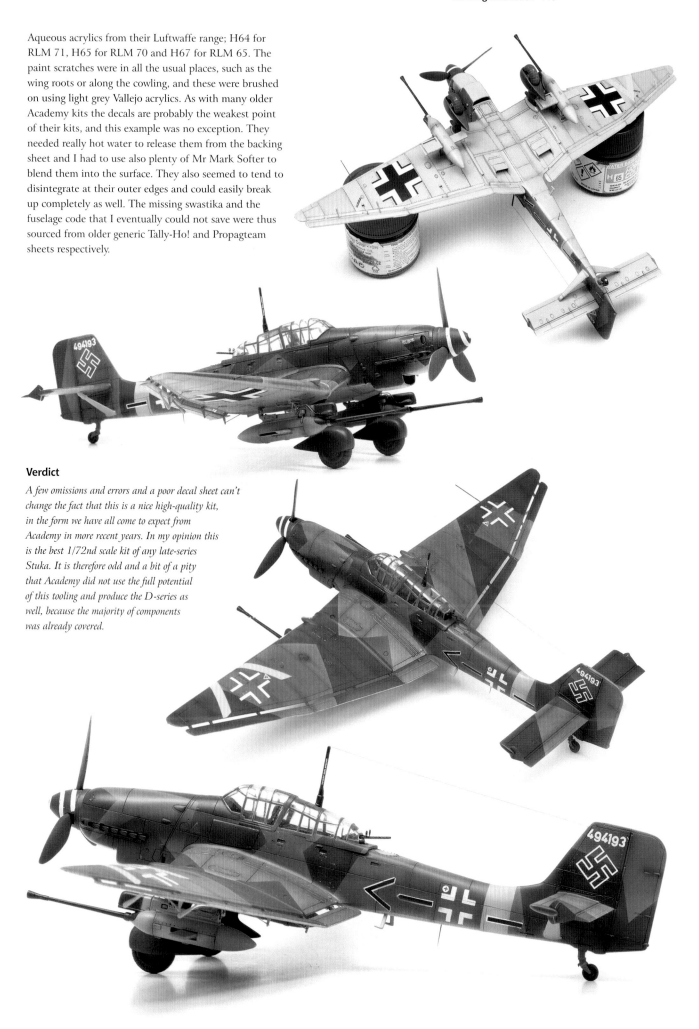

Verdict

A few omissions and errors and a poor decal sheet can't change the fact that this is a nice high-quality kit, in the form we have all come to expect from Academy in more recent years. In my opinion this is the best 1/72nd scale kit of any late-series Stuka. It is therefore odd and a bit of a pity that Academy did not use the full potential of this tooling and produce the D-series as well, because the majority of components was already covered.

Special Hobby 1/48 (#SH48007)
Junkers Ju 87A Stuka

by Steve A. Evans

This particular kit is of course one of the very first versions, the Anton, which was the start of the whole thing and at the time it wasn't a great aircraft at all. Used for the first time in anger during the Spanish Civil War, the low power of the engine, coupled with clumsy aerodynamics, gave this machine a very limited set of capabilities. Indeed, the 500kg maximum bomb load was only possible if you left the gunner and his equipment on the ground! The Germans learned quickly, however, and before long the Stuka had matured into a fearsome tool of the Blitzkrieg. This early machine is portrayed here in plastic form by Special Hobby in one of their earliest releases and a limited edition version at that. This means you get plenty of resin to play with in the box, as well as the normal plastic. There are two sprues of plastic, with fifty-six parts, all in grey-coloured shiny material. It has surprisingly little flash for a short-run kit and all the parts are very tidily moulded, with good recessed panel lines and limited rivet detail. There are no deformities and very few sink holes, although there are plenty of sprue gates and ejection pins to deal with. The resin, all forty-five bits, are very nicely cast but remember, this is old so some of it is broken and it's all brittle and needs careful handling. You also get two

Instantly recognisable as being from the early Special Hobby collection, it's a decent piece of art to entice you in

vac-form canopies that are nicely clear but incredibly thin and a small instruction sheet of ten pages that is really well drawn. The decals sheet is neatly printed and the images look quite thin, so they should work well enough, more on that later of course.

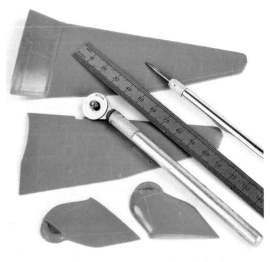

The main plastic parts in the box are shiny, hard and well formed, with good surface detail, so hopefully shouldn't come up with too many nasty surprises

I opted to ad a little riveting to the surface. The kit doesn't necessarily need it but I like it a bit busier

Construction

It all starts with the resin interior, so there's plenty of cleaning up to do, although the casting is very neat and tidy, so there's not too much of that messy job. You do have to make a number of scratchbuilt additions, including the roll-over bar, commonly called the *Vogelkäfig* or birdcage, which is nothing like the thing shown in the instructions! Thankfully the fit of the resin parts into the fuselage is good, although it's not the easiest, so you'll need trial fits and trims at all points during this build. Even at these early days in Special Hobby's foray into this scale, the plastic mouldings were very neat and tidy for the most part, so the fit of the major components is pretty good. It's nothing like the later stuff from mainstream manufacturers of course and there will be some fit problems later, but for now it's all OK. That's not to say that they got it all right because there are plenty of bits that need some care and attention, don't forget, this isn't for the novices out there. From the parts in the kit you can make an A-1 or an A-2, with the most noticeable difference being the increased radius at the top of the rudder for the A-2.

It's difficult to tell you how to progress with a kit like this because you know that you'll have to work hard at some points, even fight with it to be honest, so my advice is patience, a good supply of curse words and plenty of trial fits, which is pretty standard for this kind of kit. With that in mind, here are some of the points to watch out for:

- The parts you have to make, not only for the cockpit but also for a number of bits on the airframe itself. Check the instructions and your references to see exactly how to progress.
- The fit of the wing outer sections is pretty poor, with massive gaps at the angled joint with the inner section. You will need some serious filler at this point.
- The little resin scoops provided for the upper parts of the engine nacelle are entirely the wrong shape so just bin them and make your own
- There is no bomb load in the kit. Not that that is a great problem but it's a little annoying.
- The trailing edge flaps and ailerons are going to be massively delicate, I suggest fitting these as late as possible in the whole process to avoid breakages.
- And now for the big one: the canopy. There are two vac-formed items in the kit and although they are beautifully clear, they are painfully thin and seriously difficult to work with. One of mine was so thin at one point around the windscreen it had collapsed and was

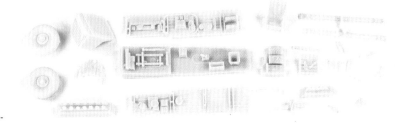

The resin is pretty good, with very neat castings but a couple of broken bits and probably the most useless resin wheels ever. They are not weighted or bulged and there are no attachment points for them in the moulded spats, so what's the point?

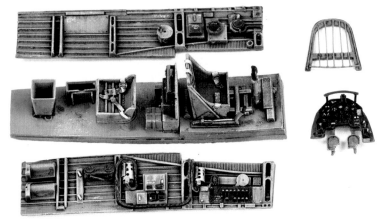

unusable. The canopy continued to cause me problems throughout the whole build, as it came unstuck at one point and I had to do some nasty looking repairs to get it into place again.

Colour & Markings

The kit decals give you two options and to be fair to Special Hobby, even though I ignored both of them, they're good choices. You get one from 1938 with lovely Spanish markings in the three-colour splinter. The second option is a Luftwaffe machine from 1944! That's not a misprint as these early machines were used right up to the end in some of the training units, giving you an idea of how reliable they were at least. This kit is not mine however and its owner opted for something entirely different, using the glorious RLM 61/62/63/65 colours and the iconic red tail and swastika for an early Luftwaffe machine. As you can imagine, this basically means lots of masking and getting the actual splinter shapes correct. There are plenty of vari-

The interior looks pretty decent once painted but please ignore the instructions that call for RLM 66. For this early machine it should be Aluminium or RLM 02

The resin exhaust stacks are separate items and you need to open out the positioning holes; fiddly stuff

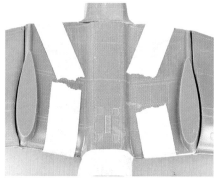

The plastic might have nice shapes and detail but the fit of some of the parts is really poor. Those are big gaps around the joint

Filler, filler, filler! You'll be using a lot of it on this one

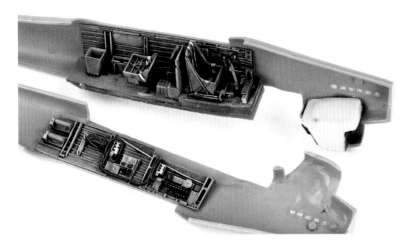

The interior parts fit into the fuselage halves without too much bother. That yellow lump at the front is the radiator of course

They look good on the sheet but in reality, they are much too thin. The one closest was already deformed around the top of the windscreen and was pretty much unusable

The birdcage affair is in place and ready to be sealed up. I had hoped this would be relatively straightforward; how wrong was I?

ations on this theme of course as they created a number of schemes by changing the orientation of the colours. The instructions have reasonable drawings of the splinters, although they are a little on the small side and don't show the inner faces of the spats, which were not the same as the outer faces. I used Hataka paints for this one as they do a very nice set of early Luftwaffe paints for the Condor Legion era. Thinned out with some Gunze Self

Levelling Thinner, they spray beautifully and the colour representation is excellent. My only caveat to that is that the RLM 65 looks a little dull to me, but that's personal taste, I guess. Thankfully the splinter shapes are all hard edged, so masking is pretty straightforward, even if it does take some time to get right. Starting with primer and the RLM 65, things quickly progressed but within minutes it all went wrong as that troublesome canopy decided to let go and split along its joint, meaning more work for me before I could get on with the colours. "Do modelling as a hobby" they said. "It'll be fun" they said. Thankfully, after a day or two of cementing, filling and sanding, the canopy joint looked acceptable and it was on with the weathering and getting a good gloss coat for the decals.

The kit decals I used, for the stencilling, crosses and such worked fine, the rest of them are a mish-mash from the spares box because I ran out of time to get the real markings. This means the codes aren't quite right for an StG.2 machine but it's not far off and does look good at least. Once settled in and weathered with some pastel dust it's onto the next bit, the final assembly and this is going to be seriously fiddly.

Final Assembly

It doesn't look like there's too much left to do but it's deceptive. An oil wash is applied and wiped away then it's on to the real messy stuff around the trailing edge, with the ailerons and flaps and all the linkages to sort out. It doesn't matter how you look at it, this area on the kit is going to remain a definite *"do not touch"* once complete as it's so delicate. You need three linkages on each side and the kit supplies only two, so there's a bit more scratch-

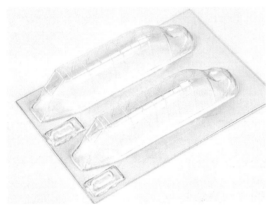

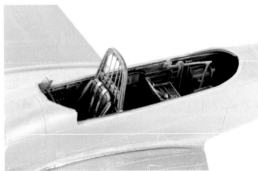

Masked and in place my hopes and dreams had yet to be cast aside on the harsh rocks of vac-form reality

The resin intake as supplied is entirely the wrong shape, which I found out after I'd glued it into place. Of course

The strutted tail section fits perfectly and at all the right angles, so well done to Special Hobby for that

There are more struts supporting the pantaloon style spats, which all fit together very well indeed

Primer on and you can see from the various shades of grey around the canopy attachment points, things were not going great at this point

The Hataka RLM 65 looks nice in this shot but under weathering it ended up looking far too dull. Something to watch out for in future

The masking/painting/ masking/painting ritual is not much fun really but the end result should be worth the trouble

The balance of the colours is just about perfect to my eyes and this does make a very striking scheme.

I hand painted the little Scotty dog and added a few faded panels as the first step in the weathering process

Mucky but not too mucky. Tamiya Smoke is the main weathering medium, along with some pastel dust of course

It looks deceptively simple at this point, not much to do right? That trailing edge collection will remain seriously delicate to the touch

building for you, but once done it does make it look like a proper Stuka wing. Then it's on to all the other little bits and apart from the small size of a lot of the parts there are no problems until it comes to fitting the aerials and wires to the canopy. Because the vac-form is so thin, the whole thing flexes alarmingly as the parts are positioned and a real delicate touch is needed for the two wires. The final item isn't perfect, so don't look too closely.

After that the matt varnish is applied and the masking very gently removed from the canopy. Thankfully nothing untoward happened and although it's not the cleanest inside (surprising after all the repairs I had to do) it's perfectly acceptable so I'm calling time on this one and leaving well enough alone.

Verdict

In its day, this kit must have been something special because it's neatly moulded, comes with some very nice resin and is a beautiful subject. These days it's showing its age and isn't a representative kit of what Special Hobby can produce now, they have progressed way beyond it. It's a bit tricky in places, even clumsy and the canopy is a nightmare, but with a bit of care and patience plus a little ingenuity you can make a pretty good-looking model from what's in the box.

Many Thanks to Simon Fairgray for providing the kit.

Paints Used
Alclad 2 lacquer:
ALC-600 Aqua Gloss
Hataka Orange Line:
HTK-CS32 Luftwaffe Legion Condor paint set
Tamiya Color acrylic:
X-19 Smoke
Xtracolor enamel:
XDFF Matt Varnish

Hasegawa 1/48 (#09307)
Junkers Ju 87D-4 'Torpedo Flieger'

by Steve A. Evans

There is something a little special about the late marks of the infamous Stuka. Gone are the angular, slightly comical shapes of the early models, replaced by a smoother, more powerful, more sinister look. That look is captured to perfection by the Hasegawa 1/48th Stuka and in this particular case, the smooth shapes are accentuated by a smooth paint job. The torpedo armed Stukas were supposed to arm the mighty *Graf Zeppelin* aircraft carrier. When that was shelved, so were the plans for a dedicated torpedo carrying type, the D-4. That meant that only a couple of this type were ever made and available photographs show it in a very mucky looking RLM 76 scheme. Hasegawa have given us the markings for the prototype and also a neat looking 'What if?' scheme as shown on the box top, supposedly from a training unit for the D-4.

What you also get in the box is a collection of twenty sprues of grey-coloured plastic with lots of detail, no flash and lovely etched panel lines. The plastic is smooth and

The box top art is a striking side profile that really stands out on the shelf. You won't miss this one!

hard, so it's easily worked, and you get six resin bits to make the torpedo. That resin is very old-style stuff, so it's brittle and a little warped but easily straightened by leaving it in hot water for a bit, then holding it straight as it cools. A couple of things to note are the facts that there are lots of duplicated and unused parts on the sprues, especially J sprue, so pay close attention to the instructions and the sprue numbering to make sure you get the right bits. Also, don't forget that as lovely as the decals look on the big single sheet, they are the older style Hasegawa decals and will need you to be paying attention when it comes to their application.

The interior is typically Hasegawa, with good detail and easy to piece together. There are no belts in the kit so you'll have to find your own, in this case they're from Eduard

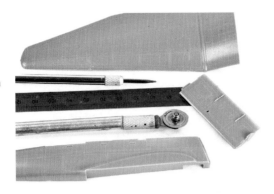

The surface detail of the kit is lovely with finely engraved panel lines but very little rivet detail, so it's time to add some with the wheel and needle

The uprated engine of the 'D' is built up as a separate unit, complete with neat little exhaust stacks

Construction

This is fairly straightforward, starting with the interior. It's nicely detailed, although there is plenty of room for additions of course and is made up of just thirteen parts. The main instrument panel gets a decal for the dials if you like, or you can paint the raised detail on the panel itself. These instructions are a little odd in that they don't mention the rudder pedals, part J2. These attach to the back of the instrument panel. They may not be the exact type for the later D models but they're better than nothing. The assembled interior fits very tightly into the fuselage halves, with good, positive location. The fuselage pieces also fit each other neatly with only a tiny step along the centre line to deal with. The same is true of the separate engine, which is made up of only six parts, not including the prop and spinner, which add another seven.

The wings, with the large single-piece lower section is also easy to build, noting the holes that need to be opened in the lower wing for the radiators, dive brakes and outer wing stores racks. As far as major parts go,

there are only the spatted wheels to build and it can all go together. These are four-part assemblies, with the main wheel trapped and movable between the two halves of the spat. The fit of all the parts is really good with almost no fettling needed anywhere. This means that putting the sub-assemblies together is quick and painless, so that before you know it, it's ready for paint.

Colour & Markings

In the box you get two versions; one is the prototype and one is a make-believe scheme as if it was being used in a training unit. Both aircraft have an overall RLM 76 or RLM 65 colour and this is a little contentious, as some people say it should be RLM 02, or even RLM 63. As there are no colour images of this aircraft, the choice is entirely up to you. I opted to use RLM 76 and use the 'What If?' markings, because the badge and extra numbering looks very interesting. I don't think they would have used this scheme in service but it should look quite striking when it's finished. We start with primer; Halfords Grey Plastic Primer is my choice here. Patches of RLM 76, applied to all the panel centres, to get the shading effect started, follow the primer. The Alclad 2 Mil-Spec RLM 76 is a grey version of the colour and should look quite effective as a single-colour paint job. Layers of RLM 76 are then added, slowly fading the shaded areas away until they can only just be seen. This is the beginning of getting the paintwork scruffy and well used. This is carried on by applying a lighter colour to a number of panels, breaking up the monotone colour, accentuated by a very thin mottling of a darker colour. All of which sounds a bit complicated but takes very little time and seriously affects the

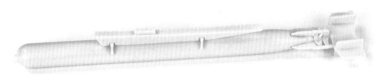

This is the resin torpedo, which is very 'old school' style resin, so it's warped and brittle but easily straightened with some hot water and patience

The interior of the wing is peppered with flashed-over holes, showing just how many variants this one moulding can be used for

The main component sub-assemblies. It takes a little while to get to this point but afterwards is remarkably quick

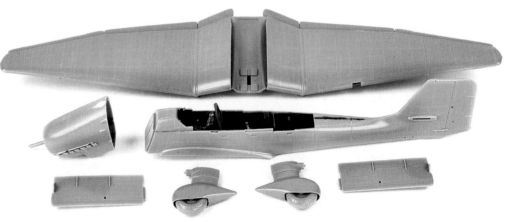

Putting it all together took less than an hour, the fit and finish of the parts is very good indeed. The tape is there to keep the wings at the right angles while the glue sets

The additional parts for the underwing stores are detailed and fit very nicely, although the drop-tank fitment later is a little bit of a pain

The clear bits are very clear indeed, with well-defined canopy frames, both inside and out

way the model looks. An application of pastel weathering dusts and some Tamiya X-19 Smoke along the panel lines is just the next layer, all of which is sealed in under some Alclad Aqua Gloss varnish. This last bit is vital for a good glossy surface to get the decals to grip onto.

Talking of decals, the sheet in the box is beautifully printed with pre-weathered white areas and very sharp edges. It looks good, with plenty of stencils and all the appropriate markings. But you have to remember that these are Hasegawa decals, from a few years ago and as such will need some special treatment. It's not that they are bad, far from it, it's just that they need hot water to release them from the backing paper and once you've got them settled and pressed into position with some Microscale setting solution, you need to let them dry out for a bit before the next steps. Hasegawa decals are pretty resistant to softening by standard solutions, even the likes of Daco Strong isn't that effective, so Gunze-Sangyo made Mr Mark Softer especially for them. Once the decal has been in position for a few minutes, apply the softer and stand back. Do NOT touch the decals once the solution has been applied because it literally melts them into place. This is also true of some types of paint, so be warned, don't let the Softer solution pool on the paintwork, as it will have detrimental effects. A quick word about the softening solutions while we wait. Mr Mark Softer has a newer type called Mr Mark Softer NEO. This is nothing like as aggressive as the original and is therefore only marginally effective on the older types of decals. I have no idea why they changed it, probably due to H&S reasons no doubt but be aware, it's not the same product. OK, once the decals have had time to settle in and dry out, they are given a coat of Aqua Gloss and an oil wash is applied to the whole model. I used 502 Abteilung Dark Mud, which was probably a little too brown and I should have used a dark grey. Not to worry, once it's been mostly wiped away it only slightly changed the overall colour it still looks pretty good.

Final Assembly

This section of the build is probably the most involved of all. The basic construction is relatively straightforward, as is the painting with just once colour. Therefore, it's down to the final details to make it all far more complicated. Let's start with the torpedo and the delicate resin needs cleaning up, building and painting. The kit has two sets of decals for the stripy nose, either red or black. The main body is metallic silver (Alclad 2 of course) and bronze acrylic for the twin propellers. Next are the drop tanks and I have to admit to hating these things with a passion because they don't fit

You get lots of gun options in the kit and no real help in the instructions about which ones to fit. Check your references is all I can advise

Paint part 1: the primer. Halfords grey Plastic Primer to be exact

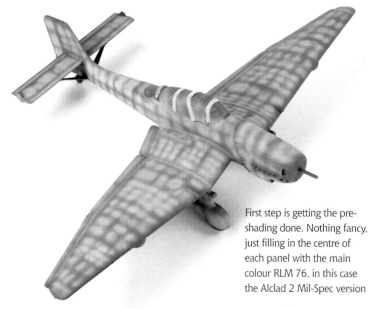

First step is getting the pre-shading done. Nothing fancy, just filling in the centre of each panel with the main colour RLM 76, in this case the Alclad 2 Mil-Spec version

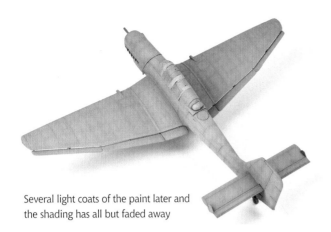

Several light coats of the paint later and the shading has all but faded away

Some of the panels are picked out in a lighter shade of RLM 76 and then a thin speckling of a slightly darker shade applied to break up the colour

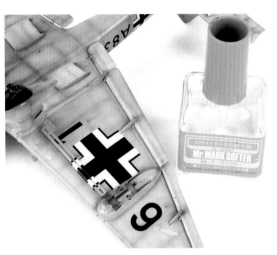

After applying the weathering comes the decals and for the older Hasegawa decals you really need this stuff: Mr Mark Softer, from Gunze-Sangyo. This decal softener was specifically designed to 'melt' Hasegawa decals into place

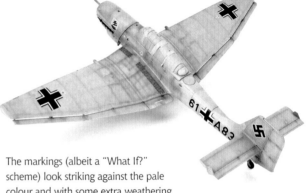

The markings (albeit a "What If?" scheme) look striking against the pale colour and with some extra weathering around the crew access areas, it also looks suitably worn

This is a lot of tricky stuff to end up with; the drop tanks and the 4 little stays for each one is a real test of patience

very well at all. The little stays, four on each one, are a total agony to all get positioned at the same time, whilst keeping it square and correctly aligned. You will also need to fit the rods to the front of the tanks, which are not mentioned in the instructions. Apart from that, it's the usual collection of aerials, pitots and wires to sort out, especially around the cockpit, which also needs positioning, after the Xtracolor XDFF flat varnish is applied.

The canopies are demasked and cleaned up and repositioned so that the front section is fully open. Luckily it fits quite neatly and with the MG 81Z machine gun positioned in the rear section it really does look the part. The final bit of all is the aerial wire running from tail to mast, which is 1lb-fishing line, with some careful painting and it's job done.

Verdict

These days Hasegawa 1/48th kits are getting to be pretty expensive. Out of production items like this one come at a premium but the flip side of that is that you will be getting the best Stuka in this scale. They are well-detailed, easy to build and as long as you can handle the decals (or are willing to replace them) they won't give you any trouble at all. It has that 'vulture' feel about it and it really does look the part sat on the shelf. Highly recommended.

Many thanks to Simon Fairgray for supplying the kit.

Paints Used

Alclad 2 lacquer:
ALCE222 RLM 76   ALC-103 Dark Aluminium
ALC-111 Magnesium   ALC-600 Aqua Gloss

Gunze Mr Hobby Aqueous acrylic:
H416 RLM 66

Tamiya acrylic:
X-19 Smoke

Vallejo Model Color acrylic:
70.973 Light Sea Grey

Xtracolor enamel:
XDFF Matt Varnish

502 Abteilung oil:
Abt130 Dark Mud

Trumpeter 1/32nd (#03217)
Junkers Ju 87D Stuka

by Steve A. Evans

Trumpeter used to be a tiny presence in our modelling world. I remember when they were a brand-new name to us all and nobody knew what they would produce. Since those early days they have figuratively and literally spread their wings and they are now one of the biggest model manufacturers on the planet! This means that their catalogue is huge and it encompasses a multitude of types and scales. This, of course, includes 1/32nd and it's great to see just about anything you want now being produced in the bigger scales. If what you want is a Stuka

Lovely little engine and it's all wasted effort because without major surgery to the kit, none of it will ever be seen again

It's a big box all right, which hints at the size of the finished model and it is stuffed with very nice-looking plastic

then Trumpeter currently has no less than six different versions on offer and this is the late model D. The box top art may not be the most brilliant out there but it's atmospheric and effective and the big sturdy box certainly looks like it could be worth your hard-earned cash. Inside it's more of the same story with a very pleasing array of big sprues, full of grey plastic, lovely transparencies and even a few etched bits for good measure. It comes with rubber tyres, which is a horrible thing to see but at least they are well moulded. There are two versions on offer in this box, both in typical late-war markings, one of which is in a temporary white distemper. The decals look to be well printed as usual from Trumpeter, all with clean lines, bright colours and good register. The paint page is a single sheet of full-colour, four-view drawings that are clear and well marked with all the colours in Gunze-Sangyo references. A nice touch is a little conversion chart for the paints with Vallejo, Model Master, Tamiya and Humbrol references. The instruction book runs to sixteen pages and is beautifully drawn and very clear, once again with paint references from Gunze-Sangyo. However, please check your own references as some of the colour call-outs are a little dubious; RLM 02 for the interior? The plastic itself

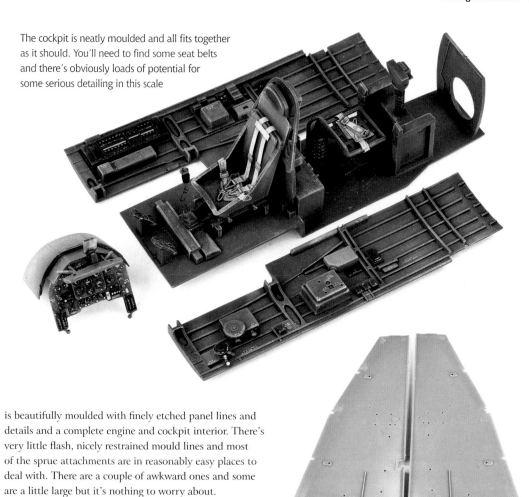

The cockpit is neatly moulded and all fits together as it should. You'll need to find some seat belts and there's obviously loads of potential for some serious detailing in this scale

is beautifully moulded with finely etched panel lines and details and a complete engine and cockpit interior. There's very little flash, nicely restrained mould lines and most of the sprue attachments are in reasonably easy places to deal with. There are a couple of awkward ones and some are a little large but it's nothing to worry about.

Construction

It all starts with the interior of course, and a very nice engine. It's made up of forty-four parts and they fit together without too much fuss to end up with a neat representation of the Jumo 211. It's a pity that the finished engine is then wrapped up in the close-fitting cowls and it will never be seen again, not even glimpsed. What a waste.

At least the excellent looking cockpit won't be wasted as that's on full show at the end, especially if you open the canopies. There's plenty of detail in there, with radio gear, sidewalls and rear machine gun to keep it looking busy but surprisingly there are no seat belts on the etched fret, so you'll have to find/make your own. I opted for the excellent pre-painted Eduard 'Steel' belts and they look very nice when it's all finished. The main instrument panel has a decal to go over the raised dial details but to be honest it's not very good, so painting is a much better option in this scale. And once it's enclosed in the fuselage,

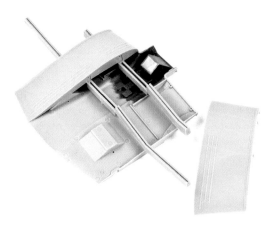

The wing lower outer-sections are literally peppered with holes, most of which are of no interest to this build but there's no hint of which ones in the instructions

The upper sections get a little bay for the wing mounted MG 151 cannons, as well as extended wing tips. The aerofoil section of the wings at the outer areas is definitely not right but thankfully it's not too noticeable on the finished thing

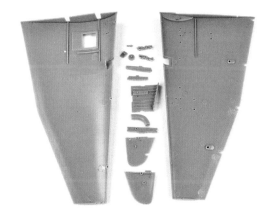

along with the gunsight and the crash bar, it's not easy to see anyway.

Talking of fuselage, this goes together very tightly, with almost zero misalignment of the centre-line joint. Some parts of it are practically invisible, which just goes to show how good the Trumpeter moulds can be. The cockpit tub fits into the little slots well enough, although a little fettling makes it much easier and once in place it's very securely positioned.

Next up are the wings and once again it's all pretty good news. They are moulded neatly enough and all of it will fit very will but there are a couple of talking points. First off are the number of flashed-over holes in the lower wing sections. There is no mention of what to do with these in the instructions and while most of them don't apply here, the ones for the outer bomb racks will need to be

The wing centre section, complete with viewing window and spars, the longer sections of which are fairly pointless

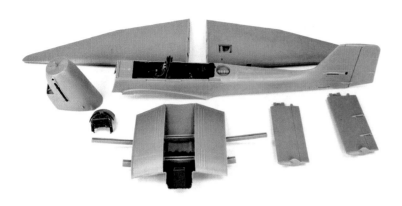

The main sub-assemblies. Most of the hard work has been done by this point; all that's left to do is slap it all together

The characteristic spats have to go and the spindly oleo leg needs some re-modelling. Plastic card and filler on standby!

opened out. The attachment holes for the dive brakes are already opened up but the dive brakes are supposedly not fitted in this kit. Towards the end of the war, many of the Stuka units removed the dive brakes because they were no longer needed but they invariably left the attachment points on the wing. It would have been nice to have this option in the kit, especially as the brake units themselves are on the sprues. I opted to make some generic looking struts and fix the dive brakes on anyway a little later in the build. Talking of parts in the box, it's also interesting to note that the 37mm Flak 18 cannon for the tank-hunting G variant is all present and correct in this box, so if you were looking for that one but could only find this boxing, then your luck is in! The wing centre-section has a large set of spars running through it to keep everything at the correct angle, which looks good but in reality, is of no real use. I say this because the slots that they fit into

on the outer wings are non-existent, so they don't actually hold anything in position. In fact, they force the wing joint apart because they're so long, so I ended up chopping them off into little stumps about 5mm long and that worked perfectly.

Perfect is the right word to describe the fit of the centre-section to the fuselage though, not a gap to be seen and the wing roots are seamless. More good stuff from Trumpeter, no wonder their newer kits are usually so good to build. It doesn't take long to get the main parts together as most of the work has been done in sub-assemblies and once the excellent canopies have been masked off and put into place it's almost time for paint. Just a couple of jobs first. The tail units, complete with support struts, slot straight into place and then it's the main wheels and it's here that I diverged a bit from the kit. The Stuka is famous for its spats but the Russian Front was pretty tough on airframes and so many had the spats removed to better cope with the mud on the airfields. The Trumpeter kit has fully separate oleo legs but sadly they are nothing like the real thing at all. I tried to get some resin replace-

ments from the net but after being let down by a supplier and with time running out, I was forced into doing a bit of scratch-building with some plasticard and lots of super-glue and talc filler. The results actually surprised me with how good they look so it's not all a loss. The spats themselves are easy to slice up with a razor saw because you just follow the raised line for the leather gaiter that covers the sliding section. A quick lick with a sanding stick to even it up and there you go, a spat-less Stuka.

Colours & Markings

As mentioned, in the box there are two options, neither of which are identified other than A and B. Both are in the classic RLM 70/71 splinter camouflage over RLM 65 undersides, but one has a white distemper over the top of that. I wanted to do something different with mine so the winter finish looked like a good option. Little did I know the trouble that would cause me but for the moment, oblivious to the pain ahead, I steamed on. Gunze-Sangyo Aqueous Mr Hobby Color is my main weapon of choice for Luftwaffe stuff and this was no exception. I started with the RLM 65 underside and once happy with that, it was masked off and the upper surface done, including the RLM 04 yellow areas of course. The splinter stuff is really easy because it's all hard edged. The Trumpeter marking sheet is quite accurate with the shapes and positioning and it's simple to follow the pattern. I sprayed fairly even coats of it, without any real thought of shading, as I knew I was going to cover it up later. I let that dry and then sprayed it with Alclad 2 Aqua Gloss to isolate the paint from what followed. I opted to add the decals to spray

Yep, that's a Stuka all right. Get the canopies on and it's almost time for paint

Some of the Ju 87's had extra armour added and Trumpeter supply it in the kit but only for the right side of the aircraft, so it was out with the plasticard once again to make a more suitable set

Let's do some painting shall we? Primer first please, Halfords' finest

RLM 65 is one of the classic Luftwaffe shades and there are any number of versions available on the market, so chose your poison

RLM 71 next and although I started doing some shading, I soon realised the error of my ways considering what I was about to do to it

The splinter camouflage is masked according to the plans, Trumpeter's are actually very good

around, just like the real thing, and they worked very well indeed. I had to alter the fuselage cross to the slightly simplified style but that was done in two seconds with a sharp pair of scissors and once they were settled down another quick coat of gloss had them sealed in.

Now the fun (nightmare) began. How to get the drastically worn and chipped look to the temporary white finish that the late war aircraft had? I opted to go down the hairspray route of applying a coat of Silvikrin, letting that dry and then covering it with a fairly even coat of white acrylic. Apparently then with a damp brush you just scrape and brush away small areas and the paint comes of in tiny streaks and patches that slowly build up to give you the required patina. Oh how I laughed as, at first, areas of the paint steadfastly refused to budge, while other sections came off in huge slabs of white, like icebergs slipping from the face of a glacier. It didn't take me long to realise that this just wasn't working as advertised, so I stripped all the white off (lots of water and a scrubbing brush) reapplied the hairspray in heavier coats and then tried a different acrylic white. With some trepidation I started to scrub with a soft brush and to my surprise it actually started to look like it might work. Now it's in no way perfect and it's actually a long way from what I had in my mind but at least it eventually looked kind of how I wanted. The whole process does seem to be a bit random

to me though, I can tell I'm going to have to do some serious practising to get it anywhere near good enough. For now, though, I'm calling the paintwork done. Obviously, there's still a lot of detail painting to be completed, with the spinner in white and green, the oleo legs in RLM 02 and all the bombs and cradles in RLM 66. This takes time of course and as it progressed it started to look better but

And there you have it, the classic splinter scheme for Stukas and I'm about to totally trash it

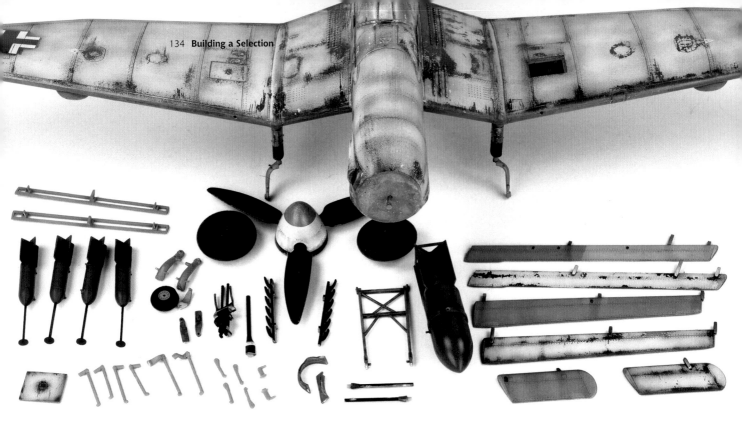

How many parts left? What have I been doing for the past couple of weeks? It's been a long, frustrating build

I opted to put the decals on first to spray the distemper around them; here you can see the modified fuselage cross, as I needed this simplified version

I'm afraid I will never like this one, as it's just not how I envisioned it looking.

Final Details

This is actually a big kit and it has a lot to do towards the end. I'd purposely left off the flaps and ailerons, knowing that the delicacy of the joints would hinder the build process, especially with the little mass balances and actuator linkages. But that's the least of it with this one, as the final build bit seemed to go on forever. Just check out the picture to see how much stuff is left to do. Personally, I despise rubber tyres, they just never look right and Trumpeter still insists on using them for some reason. The best way to get them looking better is to melt a flat spot on them with a hot knife, scuff them up a bit with some sand paper and paint them with matt grey acrylic.

The first attempt, this is actually White Acrylic from Hataka, on top of the hairspray coating… It didn't work

Once they are in place with the modified gear legs the model can finally stand on its own three feet. Even though there's still plenty to do, it's relatively straightforward and the additions of the bomb load and dive brakes make it look substantially more interesting. The final flat varnish pulls it all together quite nicely and then it's on to the final bits, which are the brake lines for the main wheels, the canopies and the aerial wire. The brake lines are just bent fuse-wire and the aerial wire is a single strand of fishing line with cyanoacrylate insulators and connections. That just leaves the canopies and both front and rear can be open or closed. I never like the rear one open because it covers the guns and looks a little odd to me, so that one stayed shut but the pilot's canopy is a different matter. This commendably clear section is moulded to be modelled in the closed position, so to get it open you have to slice out the aerial mast relief slot in the top and you basically have to force it down on the rails so it sits in the right spot. Thankfully the plastic Trumpeter use for their clear parts isn't too brittle and bends a little without cracking. Held in place with some cyanoacrylate all that

After a lot of cursing, I stripped the whole thing back to cammo and started over again with heavier coats of hairspray and Vallejo acrylics…seemed to work much better. But I'm not really happy with it. More practice needed for this style of finishing

was left was to touch up the paint around the cockpit opening and that's this Stuka ready for inspection.

Verdict

This is a big old kit, comes in a big old box and takes a lot of work to get it built. That's not to say any part of it is particularly difficult because the Trumpeter moulds are really good. There are some issues of shapes, with the prop blades and extended wing tips being the main culprits, but all in all it certainly looks like a late-war Stuka. The markings are good and other than my disappointment with my own inability to get the distemper finish right, this is heartily recommended for anyone looking for a big scale Ju 87.

Paints Used		
Gunze-Sangyo Mr Hobby Aqueous Color acrylic:		
H64 RLM 71	H65 RLM 70	H67 RLM 65
H70 RLM 02	H413 RLM 04	H416 RLM 66
Alclad 2 lacquer:		
ALC-600 Aqua Gloss		
Halfords acrylic (aerosol):		
Grey Plastic Primer		
Vallejo Model Air acrylic:		
71.001 White		
Xtracolor enamel:		
XDFF Matt Varnish		

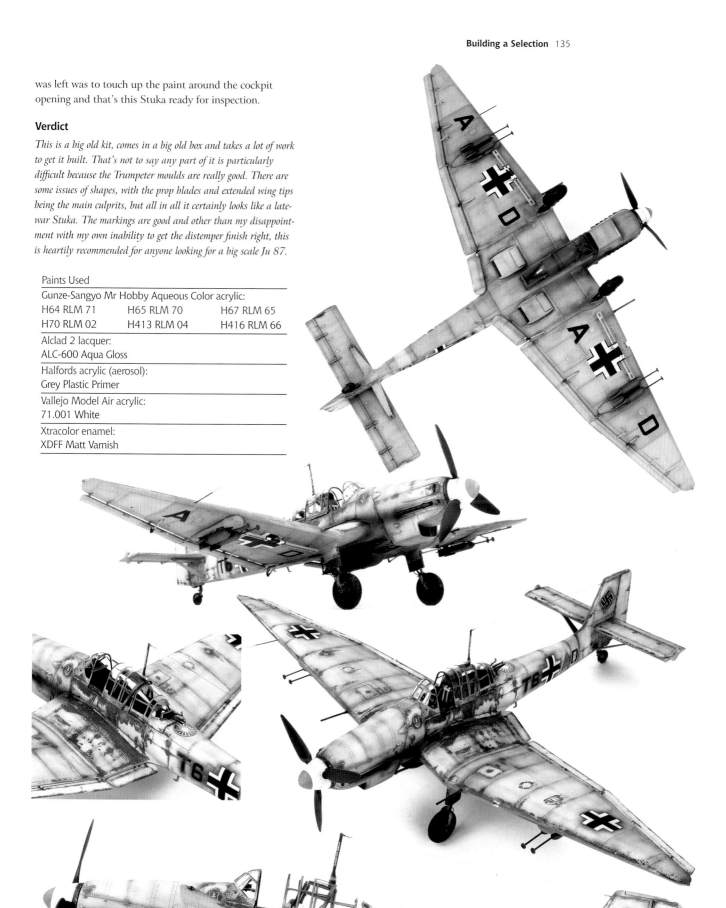

Chapter 8: **Building a Collection**

All artwork
© Juraj Jankovic 2020

With so many versions of the Ju 87 series as potential modelling subjects we thought it would be useful to show you the difference between each variant to assist you in making them.

Note: We have tried to keep this chapter to those machines that were actually built, however we have included a few projected versions simply because these have become commonplace in many accounts nowadays, regardless of the fact that no period documentary or photographic evidence exists to support them.

Prototypes

Ju 87 V1, W/Nr.4921, D-UBYR (Initial Form)

First Flight: 17th September 1935

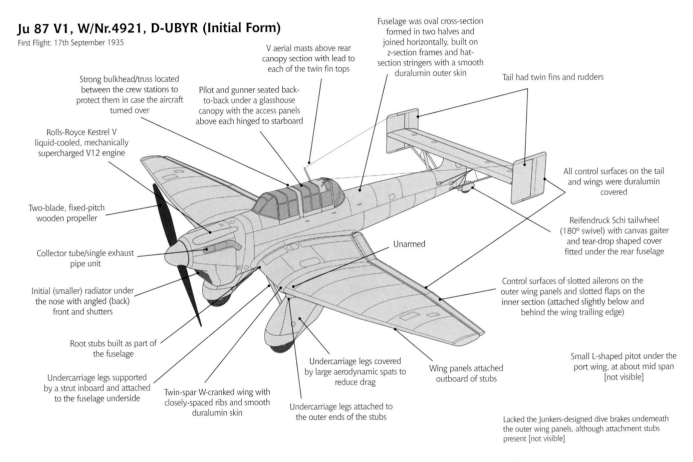

Strong bulkhead/truss located between the crew stations to protect them in case the aircraft turned over

V aerial masts above rear canopy section with lead to each of the twin fin tops

Pilot and gunner seated back-to-back under a glasshouse canopy with the access panels above each hinged to starboard

Fuselage was oval cross-section formed in two halves and joined horizontally, built on z-section frames and hat-section stringers with a smooth duralumin outer skin

Tail had twin fins and rudders

Rolls-Royce Kestrel V liquid-cooled, mechanically supercharged V12 engine

All control surfaces on the tail and wings were duralumin covered

Two-blade, fixed-pitch wooden propeller

Reifendruck Schi tailwheel (180° swivel) with canvas gaiter and tear-drop shaped cover fitted under the rear fuselage

Collector tube/single exhaust pipe unit

Unarmed

Initial (smaller) radiator under the nose with angled (back) front and shutters

Control surfaces of slotted ailerons on the outer wing panels and slotted flaps on the inner section (attached slightly below and behind the wing trailing edge)

Root stubs built as part of the fuselage

Undercarriage legs covered by large aerodynamic spats to reduce drag

Wing panels attached outboard of stubs

Small L-shaped pitot under the port wing, at about mid span [not visible]

Undercarriage legs supported by a strut inboard and attached to the fuselage underside

Twin-spar W-cranked wing with closely-spaced ribs and smooth duralumin skin

Undercarriage legs attached to the outer ends of the stubs

Lacked the Junkers-designed dive brakes underneath the outer wing panels, although attachment stubs present [not visible]

Ju 87 V1, W/Nr.4921, D-IFKQ (Revised Form)
Same as Ju 87 V1 (Initial Form) except:

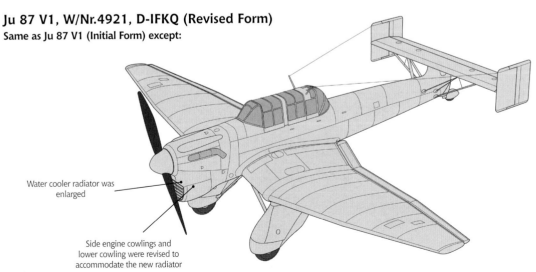

Water cooler radiator was enlarged

Side engine cowlings and lower cowling were revised to accommodate the new radiator

Ju 87 V2, W/Nr.4922, D-IDQR, re-registered D-UHUH 4th June 1937
First Flight: 25th February 1936
Similar to Ju 87 V1 except:

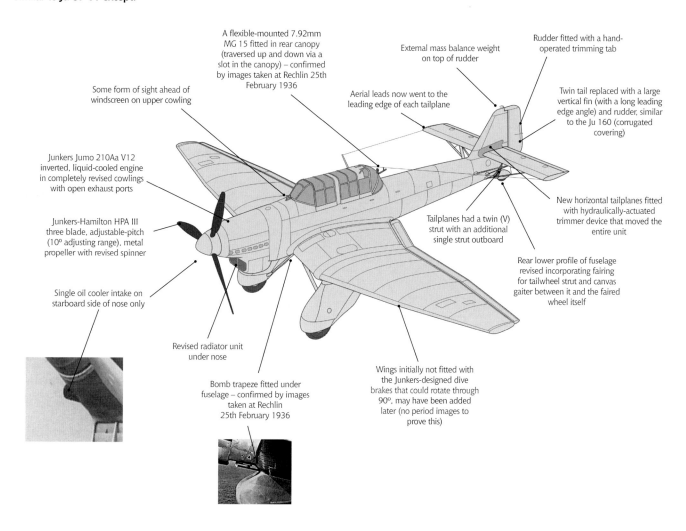

A flexible-mounted 7.92mm MG 15 fitted in rear canopy (traversed up and down via a slot in the canopy) – confirmed by images taken at Rechlin 25th February 1936

Some form of sight ahead of windscreen on upper cowling

External mass balance weight on top of rudder

Rudder fitted with a hand-operated trimming tab

Aerial leads now went to the leading edge of each tailplane

Twin tail replaced with a large vertical fin (with a long leading edge angle) and rudder, similar to the Ju 160 (corrugated covering)

Junkers Jumo 210Aa V12 inverted, liquid-cooled engine in completely revised cowlings with open exhaust ports

Junkers-Hamilton HPA III three blade, adjustable-pitch (10° adjusting range), metal propeller with revised spinner

Tailplanes had a twin (V) strut with an additional single strut outboard

New horizontal tailplanes fitted with hydraulically-actuated trimmer device that moved the entire unit

Single oil cooler intake on starboard side of nose only

Rear lower profile of fuselage revised incorporating fairing for tailwheel strut and canvas gaiter between it and the faired wheel itself

Revised radiator unit under nose

Bomb trapeze fitted under fuselage – confirmed by images taken at Rechlin 25th February 1936

Wings initially not fitted with the Junkers-designed dive brakes that could rotate through 90°, may have been added later (no period images to prove this)

Ju 87 V3, W/Nr.4923, D-UKYQ
First Flight: 27th March 1936
Similar to the V2 except:

Rudder and vertical fin enlarged to increase stability (resulting in it projecting aft of where the rear fuselage ended on the V2)

Tailplanes now only have a twin V-shaped support strut

Same Jumo 210Aa engine but thrust-line was lowered slightly to give better view over the nose

Tailplanes now squared off (the V2 had rounded ends), with the end plates that would be common to the design on the tips at the tailplane/elevator hinge

Engine cowling redesigned due to lower thrust-line

Revised tailwheel cover, canvas gaiter and fairing in lower/rear fuselage

Ventral radiator shape revised

Still no dive brakes fitted under wings, although the mounts for them can be seen [Not shown]

Landing light installed at mid-span in the leading edge of the port wing

First prototype to be fitted with FuG VIII radio [Not shown]

Ju 87 V4, W/Nr.4924, D-UBIP (Initial Form)

First Flight: 20th June 1936

Same as Ju 87 V3 except:

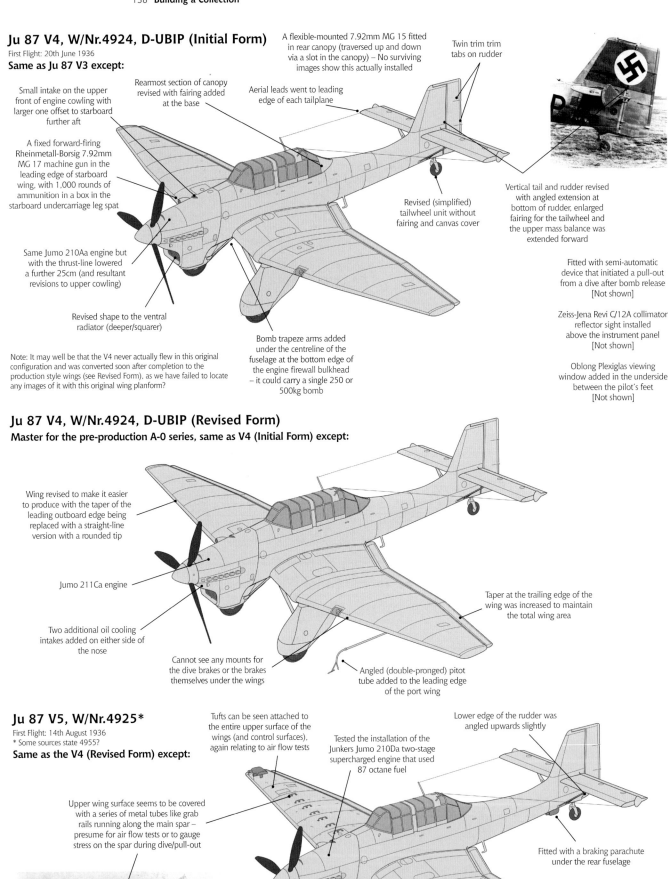

Small intake on the upper front of engine cowling with larger one offset to starboard further aft

A fixed forward-firing Rheinmetall-Borsig 7.92mm MG 17 machine gun in the leading edge of starboard wing, with 1,000 rounds of ammunition in a box in the starboard undercarriage leg spat

Same Jumo 210Aa engine but with the thrust-line lowered a further 25cm (and resultant revisions to upper cowling)

Revised shape to the ventral radiator (deeper/squarer)

Note: It may well be that the V4 never actually flew in this original configuration and was converted soon after completion to the production style wings (see Revised Form), as we have failed to locate any images of it with this original wing planform?

Rearmost section of canopy revised with fairing added at the base

A flexible-mounted 7.92mm MG 15 fitted in rear canopy (traversed up and down via a slot in the canopy) – No surviving images show this actually installed

Aerial leads went to leading edge of each tailplane

Twin trim trim tabs on rudder

Revised (simplified) tailwheel unit without fairing and canvas cover

Bomb trapeze arms added under the centreline of the fuselage at the bottom edge of the engine firewall bulkhead – it could carry a single 250 or 500kg bomb

Vertical tail and rudder revised with angled extension at bottom of rudder, enlarged fairing for the tailwheel and the upper mass balance was extended forward

Fitted with semi-automatic device that initiated a pull-out from a dive after bomb release [Not shown]

Zeiss-Jena Revi C/12A collimator reflector sight installed above the instrument panel [Not shown]

Oblong Plexiglas viewing window added in the underside between the pilot's feet [Not shown]

Ju 87 V4, W/Nr.4924, D-UBIP (Revised Form)

Master for the pre-production A-0 series, same as V4 (Initial Form) except:

Wing revised to make it easier to produce with the taper of the leading outboard edge being replaced with a straight-line version with a rounded tip

Jumo 211Ca engine

Two additional oil cooling intakes added on either side of the nose

Cannot see any mounts for the dive brakes or the brakes themselves under the wings

Taper at the trailing edge of the wing was increased to maintain the total wing area

Angled (double-pronged) pitot tube added to the leading edge of the port wing

Ju 87 V5, W/Nr.4925*

First Flight: 14th August 1936

* Some sources state 4955?

Same as the V4 (Revised Form) except:

Upper wing surface seems to be covered with a series of metal tubes like grab rails running along the main spar – presume for air flow tests or to gauge stress on the spar during dive/pull-out

Tufts can be seen attached to the entire upper surface of the wings (and control surfaces), again relating to air flow tests

Tested the installation of the Junkers Jumo 210Da two-stage supercharged engine that used 87 octane fuel

Lower edge of the rudder was angled upwards slightly

Fitted with a braking parachute under the rear fuselage

Enlarged oil cooler intakes on either side of nose, below propeller with pronounced exhaust fairing just behind them

Static pitot head at the end of each prong

Fitted with braking parachutes in pods above each wing tip

A-Series

Ju 87A-0

Ten built (W/Nrs: 0001 to 0011, D-IEAA to D-IEAK)

Same as the Ju 87 V4 (Revised Form) except:

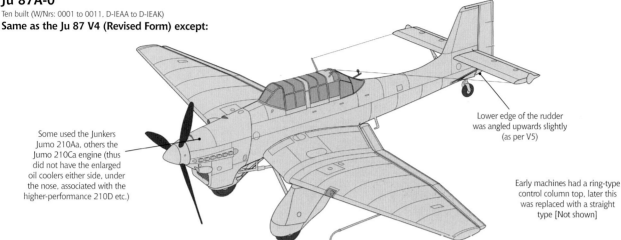

Some used the Junkers Jumo 210Aa, others the Jumo 210Ca engine (thus did not have the enlarged oil coolers either side, under the nose, associated with the higher-performance 210D etc.)

Lower edge of the rudder was angled upwards slightly (as per V5)

Early machines had a ring-type control column top, later this was replaced with a straight type [Not shown]

Ju 87A-1

Ten built (W/Nrs: 0012 to 0021, D-IEAU to N/K)

Similar to Ju 87A-0 except:

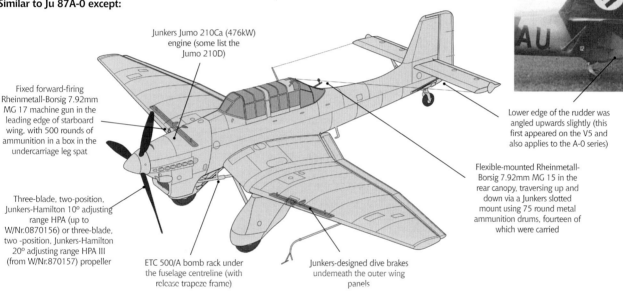

Junkers Jumo 210Ca (476kW) engine (some list the Jumo 210D)

Fixed forward-firing Rheinmetall-Borsig 7.92mm MG 17 machine gun in the leading edge of starboard wing, with 500 rounds of ammunition in a box in the undercarriage leg spat

Three-blade, two-position, Junkers-Hamilton 10° adjusting range HPA (up to W/Nr.0870156) or three-blade, two -position, Junkers-Hamilton 20° adjusting range HPA III (from W/Nr.870157) propeller

ETC 500/A bomb rack under the fuselage centreline (with release trapeze frame)

Junkers-designed dive brakes underneath the outer wing panels

Lower edge of the rudder was angled upwards slightly (this first appeared on the V5 and also applies to the A-0 series)

Flexible-mounted Rheinmetall-Borsig 7.92mm MG 15 in the rear canopy, traversing up and down via a Junkers slotted mount using 75 round metal ammunition drums, fourteen of which were carried

Ju 87A-2

Basically the same Ju 87A-1 except:

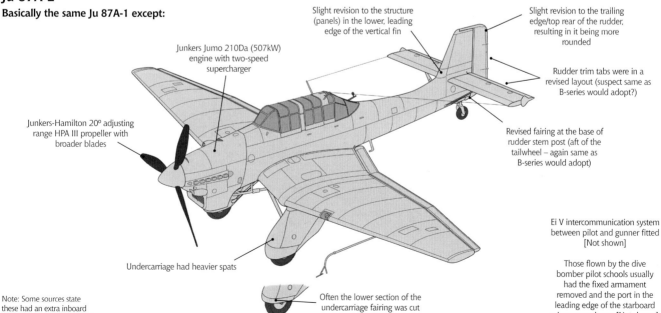

Junkers Jumo 210Da (507kW) engine with two-speed supercharger

Junkers-Hamilton 20° adjusting range HPA III propeller with broader blades

Undercarriage had heavier spats

Note: Some sources state these had an extra inboard undercarriage support strut, but no period images support this?

Often the lower section of the undercarriage fairing was cut back to give better clearance around the tyre

Slight revision to the structure (panels) in the lower, leading edge of the vertical fin

Slight revision to the trailing edge/top rear of the rudder, resulting in it being more rounded

Rudder trim tabs were in a revised layout (suspect same as B-series would adopt?)

Revised fairing at the base of rudder stem post (aft of the tailwheel – again same as B-series would adopt)

Ei V intercommunication system between pilot and gunner fitted [Not shown]

Those flown by the dive bomber pilot schools usually had the fixed armament removed and the port in the leading edge of the starboard wing covered over [Not shown]

B-Series

Ju 87 V6, W/Nr: 0870027, D-IDJU

First Flight: 14th June 1937
Basically, an A-1 except:

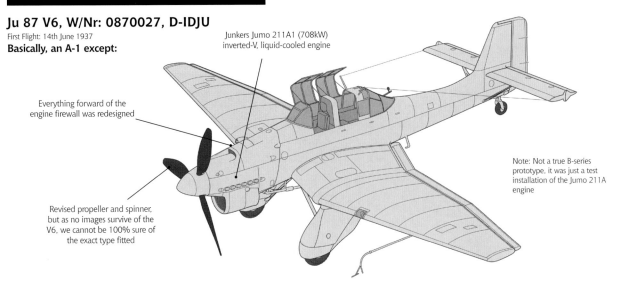

Junkers Jumo 211A1 (708kW) inverted-V, liquid-cooled engine

Everything forward of the engine firewall was redesigned

Revised propeller and spinner, but as no images survive of the V6, we cannot be 100% sure of the exact type fitted

Note: Not a true B-series prototype, it was just a test installation of the Jumo 211A engine

Ju 87 V7, V8 & V9, W/Nrs: 0870028, 4926 & 4927, D-IDFS, None & D-IELZ

First Flight: 23rd August 1937 (V7), 11th November 1937 (V8) and 16th February 1938 (V9, which was re-registered as WL-IELZ 16th October 1939)
Same as V6 except:

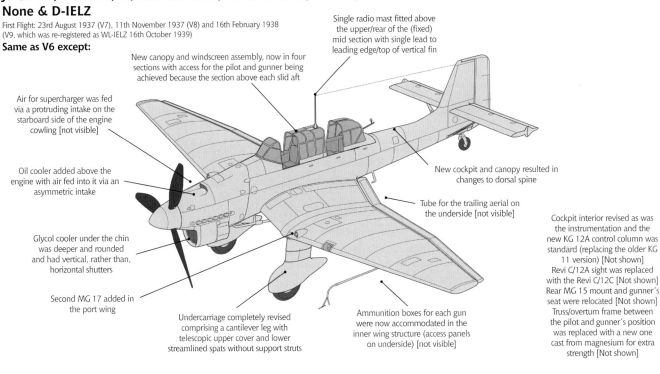

New canopy and windscreen assembly, now in four sections with access for the pilot and gunner being achieved because the section above each slid aft

Single radio mast fitted above the upper/rear of the (fixed) mid section with single lead to leading edge/top of vertical fin

Air for supercharger was fed via a protruding intake on the starboard side of the engine cowling [not visible]

Oil cooler added above the engine with air fed into it via an asymmetric intake

Glycol cooler under the chin was deeper and rounded and had vertical, rather than, horizontal shutters

Second MG 17 added in the port wing

Undercarriage completely revised comprising a cantilever leg with telescopic upper cover and lower streamlined spats without support struts

New cockpit and canopy resulted in changes to dorsal spine

Tube for the trailing aerial on the underside [not visible]

Ammunition boxes for each gun were now accommodated in the inner wing structure (access panels on underside) [not visible]

Cockpit interior revised as was the instrumentation and the new KG 12A control column was standard (replacing the older KG 11 version) [Not shown]
Revi C/12A sight was replaced with the Revi C/12C [Not shown]
Rear MG 15 mount and gunner's seat were relocated [Not shown]
Truss/overturn frame between the pilot and gunner's position was replaced with a new one cast from magnesium for extra strength [Not shown]

Ju 87B-0

Ten built (D-IELX (first))
Same as V7 to V9 except:

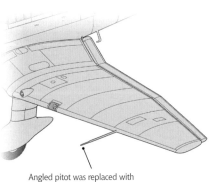

Angled pitot was replaced with a straight one in the leading edge of the port wing

Ju 87B of Schul-Sturzkampfgeschwader 102 at Deutsch-Broad being loaded with a 250kg bomb

Ju 87B-1 – Early Production
Same as B-0 except:

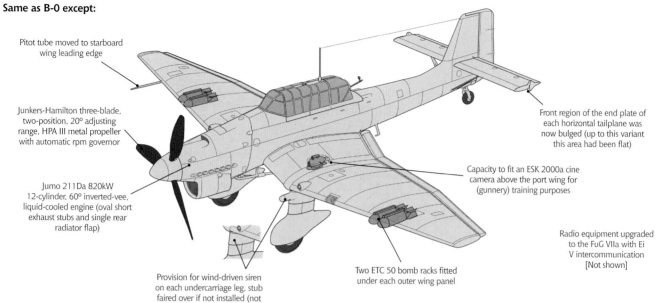

Pitot tube moved to starboard wing leading edge

Junkers-Hamilton three-blade, two-position, 20° adjusting range, HPA III metal propeller with automatic rpm governor

Jumo 211Da 820kW 12-cylinder, 60° inverted-vee, liquid-cooled engine (oval short exhaust stubs and single rear radiator flap)

Provision for wind-driven siren on each undercarriage leg, stub faired over if not installed (not all machines had it installed)

Two ETC 50 bomb racks fitted under each outer wing panel

Front region of the end plate of each horizontal tailplane was now bulged (up to this variant this area had been flat)

Capacity to fit an ESK 2000a cine camera above the port wing for (gunnery) training purposes

Radio equipment upgraded to the FuG VIIa with Ei V intercommunication [Not shown]

Ju 87B-1 – Mid Production
Same as B-1 – Early Production except:

Segmented, hinged, movable cooling flaps on the rear underside of the radiator cowling

Ju 87B-1 – Late Production
Same as B-1 – Early Production except:

Note: Both the early (single) and mid (segmented) cooling flaps at the rear of the radiator can be seen on machines with these revised exhausts, so it's more likely that the cowls and exhaust stacks were retrofitted on early and mid production machines, rather than this being a distinct production batch (we just called it 'late' for means of identification)

Ejector exhausts with associated revisions to the surrounding cowling area

Ju 87B-1 Trop
Same as B-1* except:
*Features dependent on the base airframe

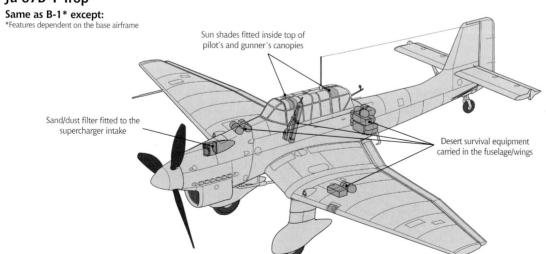

Sun shades fitted inside top of pilot's and gunner's canopies

Sand/dust filter fitted to the supercharger intake

Desert survival equipment carried in the fuselage/wings

Ju 87B-2
Basically similar to the Ju 87B-1 except:

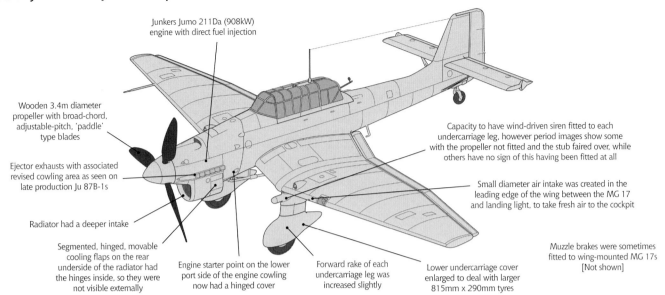

Junkers Jumo 211Da (908kW)
engine with direct fuel injection

Wooden 3.4m diameter
propeller with broad-chord,
adjustable-pitch, 'paddle'
type blades

Ejector exhausts with associated
revised cowling area as seen on
late production Ju 87B-1s

Radiator had a deeper intake

Segmented, hinged, movable
cooling flaps on the rear
underside of the radiator had
the hinges inside, so they were
not visible externally

Engine starter point on the lower
port side of the engine cowling
now had a hinged cover

Forward rake of each
undercarriage leg was
increased slightly

Lower undercarriage cover
enlarged to deal with larger
815mm x 290mm tyres

Capacity to have wind-driven siren fitted to each
undercarriage leg, however period images show some
with the propeller not fitted and the stub faired over, while
others have no sign of this having been fitted at all

Small diameter air intake was created in the
leading edge of the wing between the MG 17
and landing light, to take fresh air to the cockpit

Muzzle brakes were sometimes
fitted to wing-mounted MG 17s
[Not shown]

Ju 87B-2 (Late production)
Same as Ju 87B-2 except:
Revised armour around the rear gun position, in two styles:

Additional plates added to rear lower
corner of rear canopy plus armoured
MG 15 mount installed from Ju 88

Additional armour plates
added on either side of the
lower corner of the rear canopy

Trailing aerial mast was
removed from the underside

FuG 25 IFF was installed, with
associated flexible rod antenna
under aft fuselage (offset
slightly to port)

All seem to have had the Peil
G.IV D/F loop in the blister in
place of the trailing aerial mast

A Ju 87B-2 with the T6 codes of II./StG 2 in France in 1940 with netting applied over the fuselage and wing crosses to make them less obvious from the air

Ju 87B-2 T6+FA of Geschwader Stab StG 2 after a forced landing in France

Ju 87B-2 Trop
Same as Ju 87B-2 except:

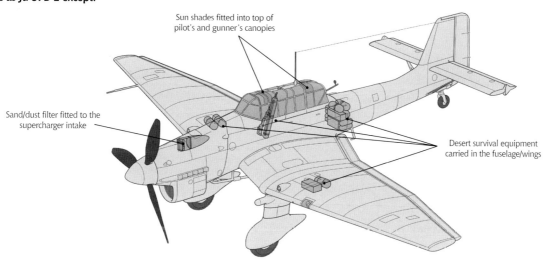

Sun shades fitted into top of pilot's and gunner's canopies

Sand/dust filter fitted to the supercharger intake

Desert survival equipment carried in the fuselage/wings

Ju 87B-2 Trop (Late production)
Same as Ju 87B-2 (Late production) except:

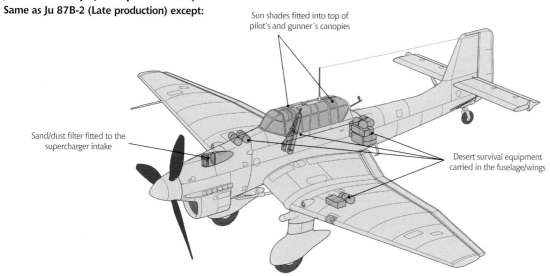

Sun shades fitted into top of pilot's and gunner's canopies

Sand/dust filter fitted to the supercharger intake

Desert survival equipment carried in the fuselage/wings

R-Series

Ju 87 V15, V16, V17* & V18*, W/Nr: 087031 (V15), 0870279 (V16) & N/K (V17 & V18), D-IGHK (V15), GT+AX (V16) & None (V17 & V18)

* Not known if the V17 & V18 were ever actually built
** The only known image of the V15 does not show it with drop tanks fitted

Same as B-1 except:

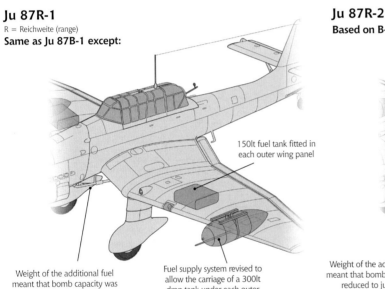

Suspect they tested the fitment of additional fuel tanks in the outer wing panels

And/or the carriage of a 300lt drop tank under each wing**

Ju 87R-1

R = Reichweite (range)
Same as Ju 87B-1 except:

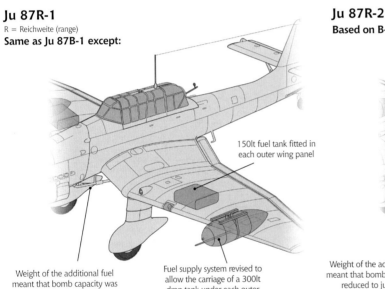

150lt fuel tank fitted in each outer wing panel

Weight of the additional fuel meant that bomb capacity was reduced to just 250kg

Fuel supply system revised to allow the carriage of a 300lt drop tank under each outer wing panel

Ju 87R-2

Based on B-2 except:

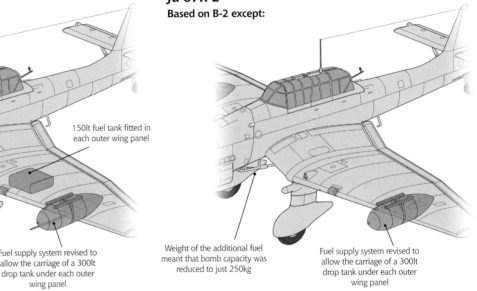

Weight of the additional fuel meant that bomb capacity was reduced to just 250kg

Fuel supply system revised to allow the carriage of a 300lt drop tank under each outer wing panel

Ju 87R-2 (Late production)

Same as B-2 (Late production) except:

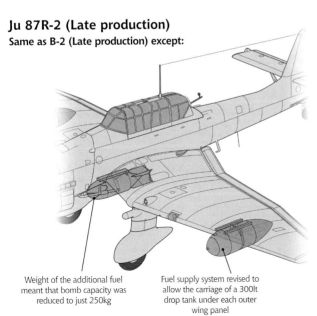

Weight of the additional fuel meant that bomb capacity was reduced to just 250kg

Fuel supply system revised to allow the carriage of a 300lt drop tank under each outer wing panel

Ju 87R-3

Same as R-2 except:

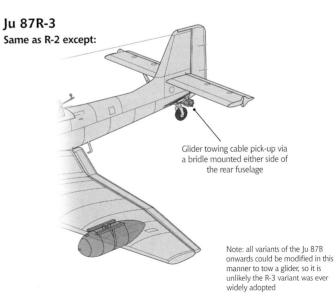

Glider towing cable pick-up via a bridle mounted either side of the rear fuselage

Note: all variants of the Ju 87B onwards could be modified in this manner to tow a glider, so it is unlikely the R-3 variant was ever widely adopted

Ju 87R-4
Same as Ju 87R-2 except:

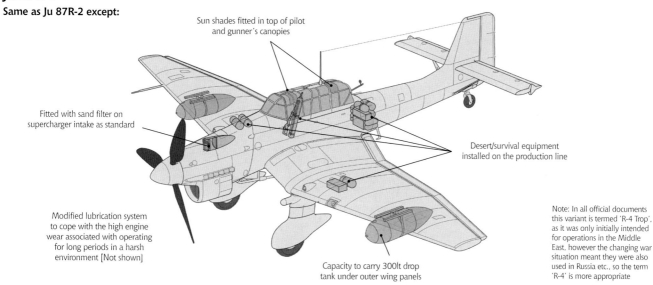

Sun shades fitted in top of pilot and gunner's canopies

Fitted with sand filter on supercharger intake as standard

Desert/survival equipment installed on the production line

Modified lubrication system to cope with the high engine wear associated with operating for long periods in a harsh environment [Not shown]

Capacity to carry 300lt drop tank under outer wing panels

Note: In all official documents this variant is termed 'R-4 Trop', as it was only initially intended for operations in the Middle East, however the changing war situation meant they were also used in Russia etc., so the term 'R-4' is more appropriate

Ju 87R-1 Trop
Same as Ju 87R-1:
Retrospectively modified (at manufacturer or unit level) for operations in the Middle East

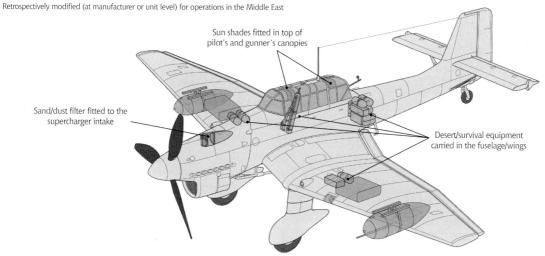

Sun shades fitted in top of pilot's and gunner's canopies

Sand/dust filter fitted to the supercharger intake

Desert/survival equipment carried in the fuselage/wings

Note: There are no references to the 'R-1 Trop' in any official manuals etc.

Ju 87R-2 Trop
Same as the Ju 87R-2:
Retrospectively modified (at manufacturer or unit level) for operations in the Middle East

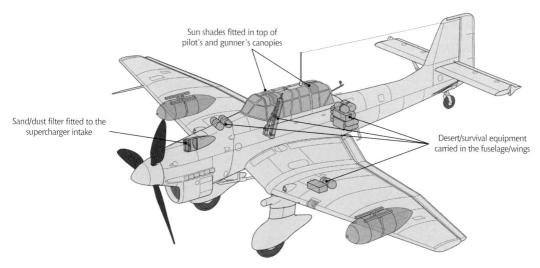

Sun shades fitted in top of pilot's and gunner's canopies

Sand/dust filter fitted to the supercharger intake

Desert/survival equipment carried in the fuselage/wings

D-Series

Ju 87 V21, V22, V23, V24, W/Nrs. 0870536 (D-INRF), 0870540 (SF+TY), 0870542 (PB+UB) and 0870544 (BK+EE)
Based on Ju 87B except:

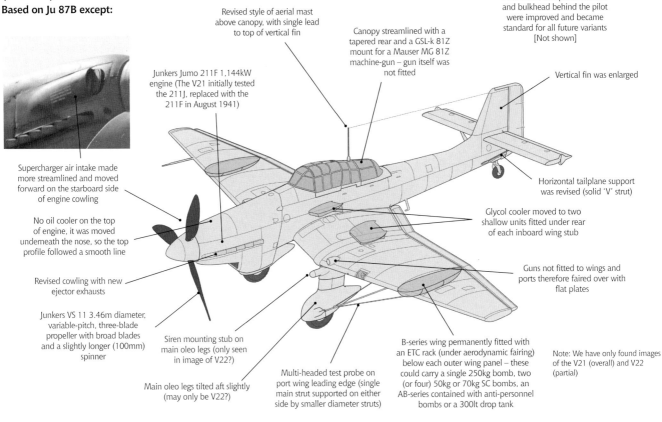

Pilot's seat, cockpit sides, floor and bulkhead behind the pilot were improved and became standard for all future variants [Not shown]

Revised style of aerial mast above canopy, with single lead to top of vertical fin

Canopy streamlined with a tapered rear and a GSL-k 81Z mount for a Mauser MG 81Z machine-gun – gun itself was not fitted

Junkers Jumo 211F 1,144kW engine (The V21 initially tested the 211J, replaced with the 211F in August 1941)

Vertical fin was enlarged

Supercharger air intake made more streamlined and moved forward on the starboard side of engine cowling

Horizontal tailplane support was revised (solid 'V' strut)

No oil cooler on the top of engine, it was moved underneath the nose, so the top profile followed a smooth line

Glycol cooler moved to two shallow units fitted under rear of each inboard wing stub

Revised cowling with new ejector exhausts

Guns not fitted to wings and ports therefore faired over with flat plates

Junkers VS 11 3.46m diameter, variable-pitch, three-blade propeller with broad blades and a slightly longer (100mm) spinner

Siren mounting stub on main oleo legs (only seen in image of V22?)

Main oleo legs tilted aft slightly (may only be V22?)

Multi-headed test probe on port wing leading edge (single main strut supported on either side by smaller diameter struts)

B-series wing permanently fitted with an ETC rack (under aerodynamic fairing) below each outer wing panel – these could carry a single 250kg bomb, two (or four) 50kg or 70kg SC bombs, an AB-series contained with anti-personnel bombs or a 300lt drop tank

Note: We have only found images of the V21 (overall) and V22 (partial)

Ju 87 V21 with skis
Same as Ju 87 V21 to V24 except:

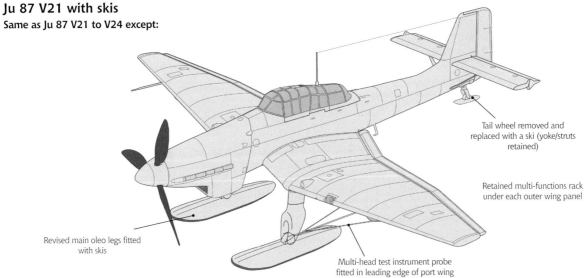

Tail wheel removed and replaced with a ski (yoke/struts retained)

Retained multi-functions rack under each outer wing panel

Revised main oleo legs fitted with skis

Multi-head test instrument probe fitted in leading edge of port wing

Ju 87 V21 (D-series prototype) SF+TY

Ju 87D-1
Same as the V21 to V24 except:

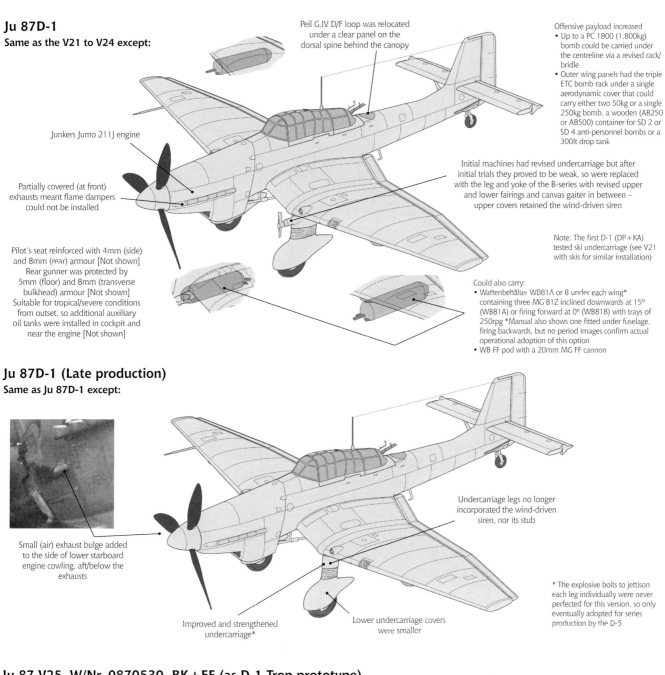

Peil G.IV D/F loop was relocated under a clear panel on the dorsal spine behind the canopy

Junkers Jumo 211J engine

Partially covered (at front) exhausts meant flame dampers could not be installed

Pilot's seat reinforced with 4mm (side) and 8mm (rear) armour [Not shown]
Rear gunner was protected by 5mm (floor) and 8mm (transverse bulkhead) armour [Not shown]
Suitable for tropical/severe conditions from outset, so additional auxiliary oil tanks were installed in cockpit and near the engine [Not shown]

Offensive payload increased
• Up to a PC 1800 (1,800kg) bomb could be carried under the centreline via a revised rack/ bridle
• Outer wing panels had the triple ETC bomb rack under a single aerodynamic cover that could carry either two 50kg or a single 250kg bomb, a wooden (AB250 or AB500) container for SD 2 or SD 4 anti-personnel bombs or a 300lt drop tank

Initial machines had revised undercarriage but after initial trials they proved to be weak, so were replaced with the leg and yoke of the B-series with revised upper and lower fairings and canvas gaiter in between – upper covers retained the wind-driven siren

Note: The first D-1 (DP+KA) tested ski undercarriage (see V21 with skis for similar installation)

Could also carry:
• Waffenbehälter WB81A or B under each wing* containing three MG 81Z inclined downwards at 15° (WB81A) or firing forward at 0° (WB81B) with trays of 250rpg *Manual also shows one fitted under fuselage, firing backwards, but no period images confirm actual operational adoption of this option
• WB FF pod with a 20mm MG FF cannon

Ju 87D-1 (Late production)
Same as Ju 87D-1 except:

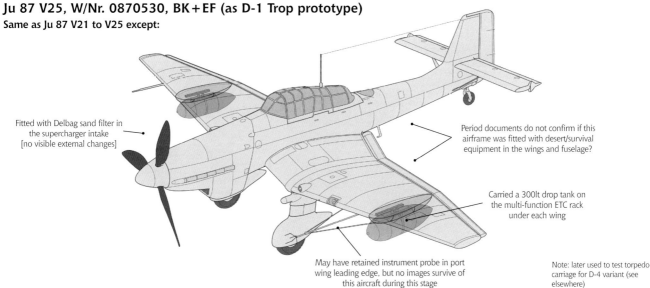

Small (air) exhaust bulge added to the side of lower starboard engine cowling, aft/below the exhausts

Improved and strengthened undercarriage*

Lower undercarriage covers were smaller

Undercarriage legs no longer incorporated the wind-driven siren, nor its stub

* The explosive bolts to jettison each leg individually were never perfected for this version, so only eventually adopted for series production by the D-5

Ju 87 V25, W/Nr. 0870530, BK+EF (as D-1 Trop prototype)
Same as Ju 87 V21 to V25 except:

Fitted with Delbag sand filter in the supercharger intake [no visible external changes]

Period documents do not confirm if this airframe was fitted with desert/survival equipment in the wings and fuselage?

Carried a 300lt drop tank on the multi-function ETC rack under each wing

May have retained instrument probe in port wing leading edge, but no images survive of this aircraft during this stage

Note: later used to test torpedo carriage for D-4 variant (see elsewhere)

Ju 87D-2
Was intended to be as per the D-1 but with revised armament – not proceeded with (note some sources state this was a glider-towing variant, but all D-series could be modified to tow gliders)

Ju 87D-3
Same as the D-1 (Late production) except:

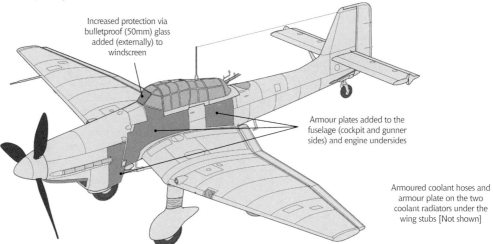

Increased protection via bulletproof (50mm) glass added (externally) to windscreen

Armour plates added to the fuselage (cockpit and gunner sides) and engine undersides

Armoured coolant hoses and armour plate on the two coolant radiators under the wing stubs [Not shown]

Ju 87D-3 (Late production)
Same as Ju 87D-3 except:

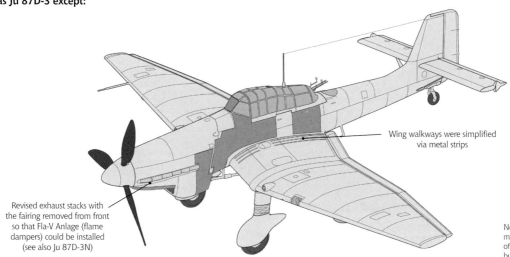

Wing walkways were simplified via metal strips

Revised exhaust stacks with the fairing removed from front so that Fla-V Anlage (flame dampers) could be installed (see also Ju 87D-3N)

Note: Intended to have 100% mass-balanced ailerons instead of original three-position system, but this was not adopted for series production until the D-5

Ju 87D-3N
Same as D-3 (Late Production) except:

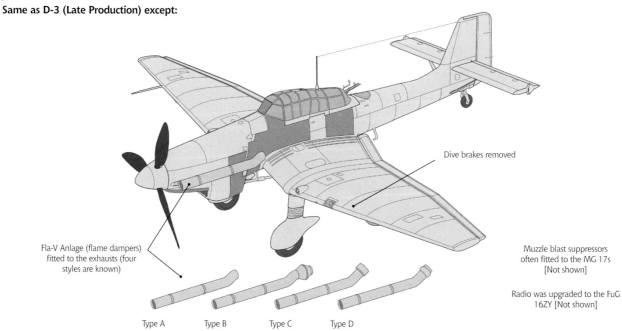

Dive brakes removed

Fla-V Anlage (flame dampers) fitted to the exhausts (four styles are known)

Muzzle blast suppressors often fitted to the MG 17s [Not shown]

Radio was upgraded to the FuG 16ZY [Not shown]

Type A   Type B   Type C   Type D

Ju 87D-3Ag

Ag = Agentenflugzeug (agent's aircraft)
Same as Ju 87D-3 (Late Production) except:

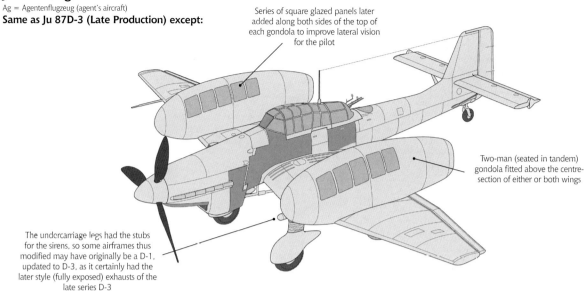

Series of square glazed panels later added along both sides of the top of each gondola to improve lateral vision for the pilot

Two-man (seated in tandem) gondola fitted above the centre-section of either or both wings

The undercarriage legs had the stubs for the sirens, so some airframes thus modified may have originally be a D-1, updated to D-3, as it certainly had the later style (fully exposed) exhausts of the late series D-3

Ju 87 V25, W/Nr. 0870530*, BK+EF

* Some sources state W/Nr.48928
Same as Ju 87 V21 to V25 except:

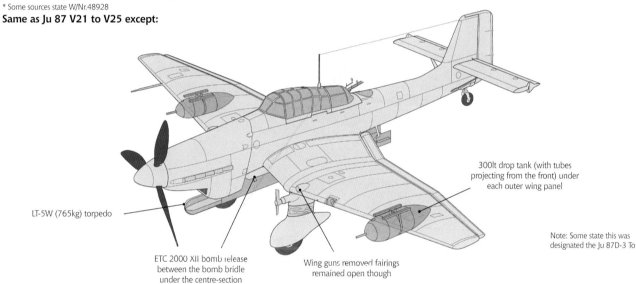

300lt drop tank (with tubes projecting from the front) under each outer wing panel

LT-5W (765kg) torpedo

ETC 2000 XII bomb release between the bomb bridle under the centre-section

Wing guns removed fairings remained open though

Note: Some state this was designated the Ju 87D-3 To

Ju 87D-4

Based on Ju 87 D-3 (Late production) airframe except:

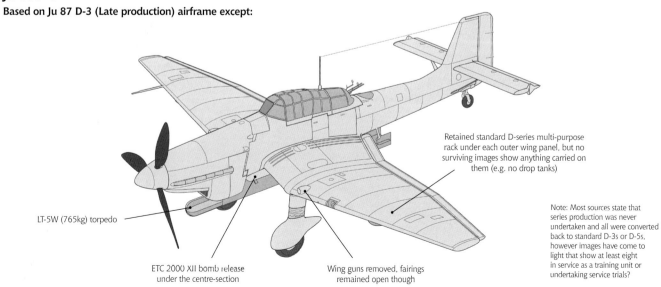

Retained standard D-series multi-purpose rack under each outer wing panel, but no surviving images show anything carried on them (e.g. no drop tanks)

LT-5W (765kg) torpedo

ETC 2000 XII bomb release under the centre-section

Wing guns removed, fairings remained open though

Note: Most sources state that series production was never undertaken and all were converted back to standard D-3s or D-5s, however images have come to light that show at least eight in service as a training unit or undertaking service trials?

Ju 87D-5
Same as the Ju 87D-3 except:

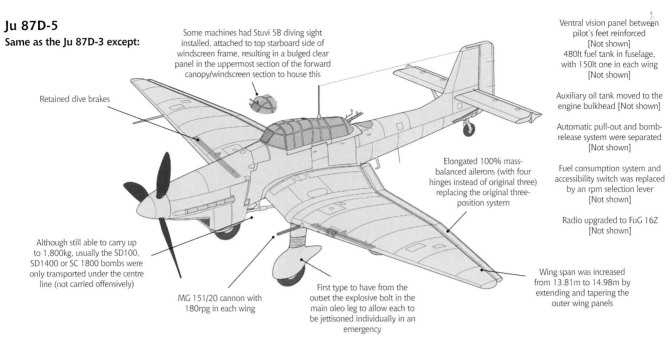

Some machines had Stuvi 5B diving sight installed, attached to top starboard side of windscreen frame, resulting in a bulged clear panel in the uppermost section of the forward canopy/windscreen section to house this

Retained dive brakes

Ventral vision panel between pilot's feet reinforced [Not shown]
480lt fuel tank in fuselage, with 150lt one in each wing [Not shown]

Auxiliary oil tank moved to the engine bulkhead [Not shown]

Automatic pull-out and bomb-release system were separated [Not shown]

Fuel consumption system and accessibility switch was replaced by an rpm selection lever [Not shown]

Radio upgraded to FuG 16Z [Not shown]

Elongated 100% mass-balanced ailerons (with four hinges instead of original three) replacing the original three-position system

Although still able to carry up to 1,800kg, usually the SD100, SD1400 or SC 1800 bombs were only transported under the centre line (not carried offensively)

MG 151/20 cannon with 180rpg in each wing

First type to have from the outset the explosive bolt in the main oleo leg to allow each to be jettisoned individually in an emergency

Wing span was increased from 13.81m to 14.98m by extending and tapering the outer wing panels

Ju 87D-5 (Late production)
Same as the Ju 87D-5 except:

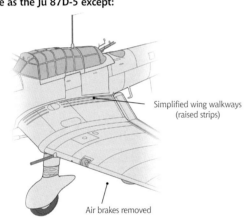

Simplified wing walkways (raised strips)

Air brakes removed

Ju 87D-5s newly delivered to the Eastern Front with temporary chalk-based paint applied with brush or broom, both have SB250 containers under the wings while the one in the foreground has an SC250 bomb under the fuselage

Ju 87D-5N
Same as the Ju 87D-5 (Late production) except:

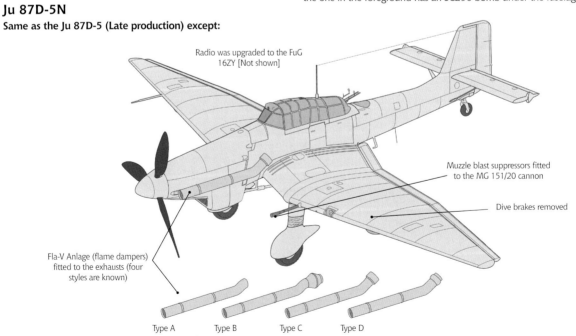

Radio was upgraded to the FuG 16ZY [Not shown]

Muzzle blast suppressors fitted to the MG 151/20 cannon

Dive brakes removed

Fla-V Anlage (flame dampers) fitted to the exhausts (four styles are known)

Type A   Type B   Type C   Type D

Ju 87D-6
Was intended to be the 'rationalised' version, with electrical system, bomb release switching and similar equipment significantly simplified – not proceeded with

Ju 87D-7
Same as Ju 87D-1 except:

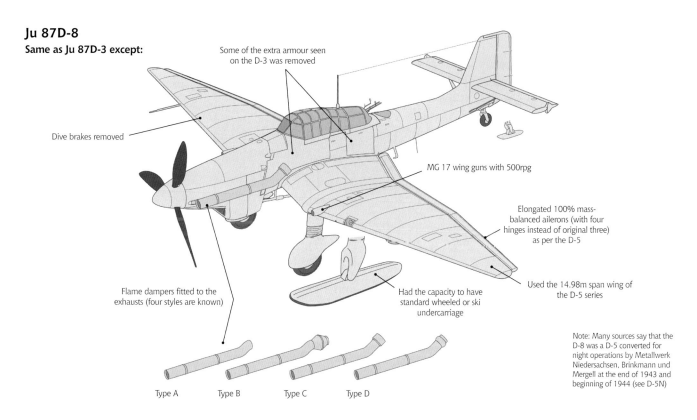

Used the 14.98m span wing of the D-5 series

Jumo 211P (1,118kW) engine

MG 151/20 cannon with 180rpg in each wing

Elongated 100% mass-balanced ailerons (with four hinges instead of original three) as per the D-5

Muzzle blast suppressors fitted to the MG 151/20 cannon

Had the capacity to have standard wheeled or ski undercarriage

Flame dampers fitted to the exhausts (four styles are known)

Type A Type B Type C Type D

Note: Unknown how far the engine, flame dampers and muzzle suppressor upgrade went . Many sources say that the D-7 was a D-3 converted for night operations by Metallwerk Niedersachsen, Brinkmann und Mergell at the end of 1943 and beginning of 1944 (See D-3N)

Ju 87D-8
Same as Ju 87D-3 except:

Some of the extra armour seen on the D-3 was removed

Dive brakes removed

MG 17 wing guns with 500rpg

Elongated 100% mass-balanced ailerons (with four hinges instead of original three) as per the D-5

Flame dampers fitted to the exhausts (four styles are known)

Had the capacity to have standard wheeled or ski undercarriage

Used the 14.98m span wing of the D-5 series

Type A Type B Type C Type D

Note: Many sources say that the D-8 was a D-5 converted for night operations by Metallwerk Niedersachsen, Brinkmann und Mergell at the end of 1943 and beginning of 1944 (see D-5N)

A Ju 87D-8 of NSG2 captured at Straubing, Germany in May 1945 with a wooden container pod under the fuselage

G-Series

Ju 87G-1
Rebuilt from/same as Ju 87D-3 except:

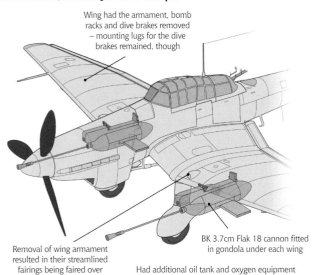

Wing had the armament, bomb racks and dive brakes removed – mounting lugs for the dive brakes remained, though

Removal of wing armament resulted in their streamlined fairings being faired over

BK 3.7cm Flak 18 cannon fitted in gondola under each wing

Had additional oil tank and oxygen equipment of the D-3 series removed [Not shown]

Ju 87G-2
Rebuilt from/same as Ju 87D-5 except:

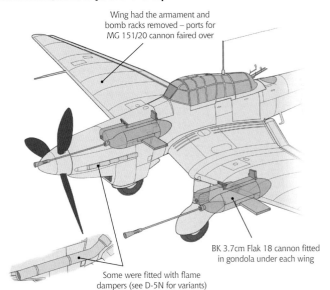

Wing had the armament and bomb racks removed – ports for MG 151/20 cannon faired over

BK 3.7cm Flak 18 cannon fitted in gondola under each wing

Some were fitted with flame dampers (see D-5N for variants)

Trainers

Ju 87H-1
Converted from/same as Ju 87D-1 except:

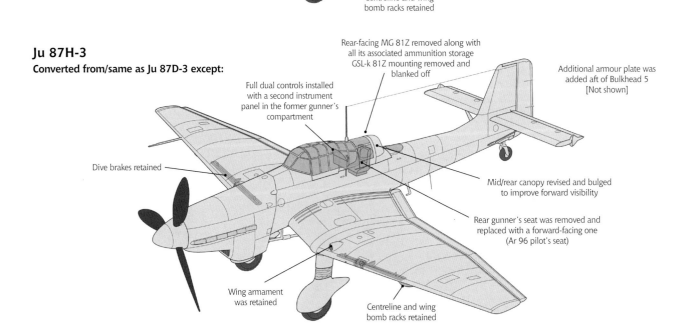

Full dual controls installed with a second instrument panel in the former gunner's compartment

Dive brakes retained

Rear-facing MG 81Z removed along with all its associated ammunition storage GSL-k 81Z mounting removed and blanked off

Additional armour plate was added aft of Bulkhead 5 [Not shown]

Mid/rear canopy revised and bulged to improve forward visibility

Rear gunner's seat was removed and replaced with a forward-facing one (Ar 96 pilot's seat)

Wing armament was retained

Centreline and wing bomb racks retained

Ju 87H-3
Converted from/same as Ju 87D-3 except:

Full dual controls installed with a second instrument panel in the former gunner's compartment

Dive brakes retained

Rear-facing MG 81Z removed along with all its associated ammunition storage GSL-k 81Z mounting removed and blanked off

Additional armour plate was added aft of Bulkhead 5 [Not shown]

Mid/rear canopy revised and bulged to improve forward visibility

Rear gunner's seat was removed and replaced with a forward-facing one (Ar 96 pilot's seat)

Wing armament was retained

Centreline and wing bomb racks retained

Ju 87H-5
Converted from/same as Ju 87D-5 except:

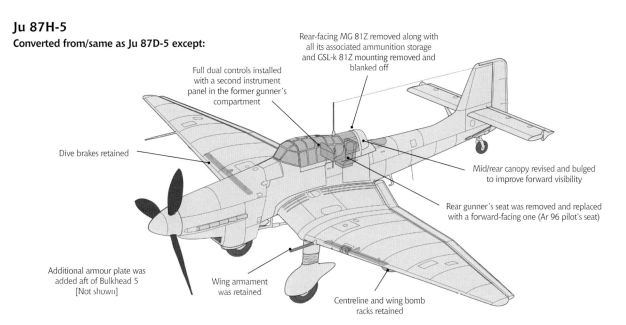

Full dual controls installed with a second instrument panel in the former gunner's compartment

Rear-facing MG 81Z removed along with all its associated ammunition storage and GSL-k 81Z mounting removed and blanked off

Dive brakes retained

Mid/rear canopy revised and bulged to improve forward visibility

Rear gunner's seat was removed and replaced with a forward-facing one (Ar 96 pilot's seat)

Additional armour plate was added aft of Bulkhead 5 [Not shown]

Wing armament was retained

Centreline and wing bomb racks retained

Ju 87H-7
Converted from/same as Ju 87D-7 except:

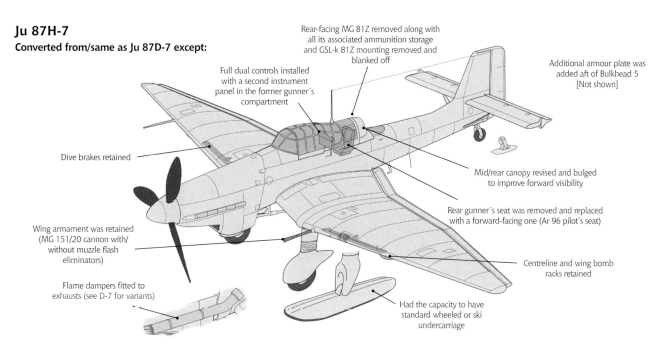

Rear-facing MG 81Z removed along with all its associated ammunition storage and GSL-k 81Z mounting removed and blanked off

Full dual controls installed with a second instrument panel in the former gunner's compartment

Additional armour plate was added aft of Bulkhead 5 [Not shown]

Dive brakes retained

Mid/rear canopy revised and bulged to improve forward visibility

Rear gunner's seat was removed and replaced with a forward-facing one (Ar 96 pilot's seat)

Wing armament was retained (MG 151/20 cannon with/ without muzzle flash eliminators)

Centreline and wing bomb racks retained

Flame dampers fitted to exhausts (see D-7 for variants)

Had the capacity to have standard wheeled or ski undercarriage

Ju 87H-8
Converted from/same as Ju 87D-8 except:

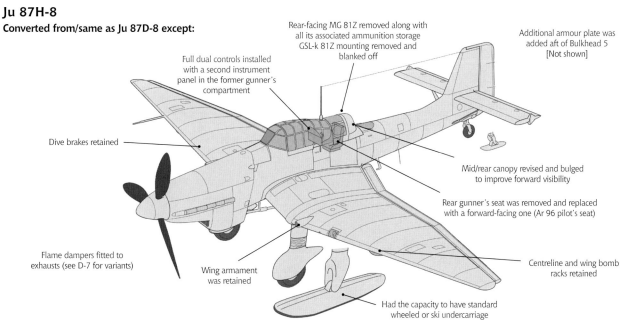

Rear-facing MG 81Z removed along with all its associated ammunition storage GSL-k 81Z mounting removed and blanked off

Full dual controls installed with a second instrument panel in the former gunner's compartment

Additional armour plate was added aft of Bulkhead 5 [Not shown]

Dive brakes retained

Mid/rear canopy revised and bulged to improve forward visibility

Rear gunner's seat was removed and replaced with a forward-facing one (Ar 96 pilot's seat)

Flame dampers fitted to exhausts (see D-7 for variants)

Wing armament was retained

Centreline and wing bomb racks retained

Had the capacity to have standard wheeled or ski undercarriage

Projects

Ju 87 V10, W/Nr: 4928, D-IHFH (later TK+HD)
Same as Ju 87B-0 except:

No gun in rear canopy

Fuselage strengthening associated with deck landings

Arrestor hook under rear fuselage

Looks to be a guard frame in front of the tailwheel?

Wing span reduced to 13.00m

Catapult launching gear pick-ups under fuselage

Guns in wings removed and blisters capped in wing leading edge

Ju 87 V11, W/Nr: 4929, D-ILGM (later TV+OV)
Same as the Ju 87 V10 except:

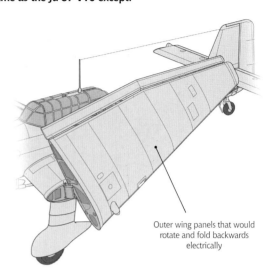

Outer wing panels that would rotate and fold backwards electrically

Ju 87C-0
Same as Ju 87 V11 except:

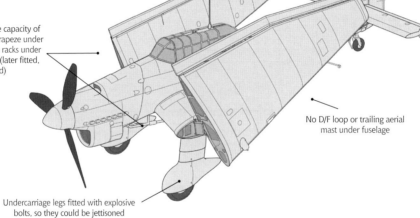

Would have had full armament (MG 15 in rear canopy and MG 17 in each wing)

Also retained ordnance capacity of the B-series, with rack/trapeze under main fuselage and two racks under the outer wing panels (later fitted, when needed)

No D/F loop or trailing aerial mast under fuselage

Two rubber floatation bags were fitted in the fuselage with two more inside the leading edge of each wing [Not shown]

Carried survival equipment including life rafts, presume in fuselage [Not shown]

Undercarriage legs fitted with explosive bolts, so they could be jettisoned individually in an emergency

Ju 87C-1
Based on Ju 87B-1:

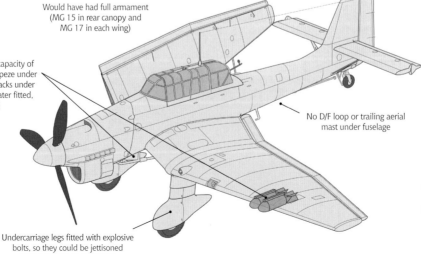

Would have had full armament (MG 15 in rear canopy and MG 17 in each wing)

Also retained ordnance capacity of the B-series, with rack/trapeze under main fuselage and two racks under the outer wing panels (later fitted, when needed)

No D/F loop or trailing aerial mast under fuselage

Undercarriage legs fitted with explosive bolts, so they could be jettisoned individually in an emergency

Two rubber floatation bags were fitted in the fuselage with two more inside the leading edge of each wing [Not shown]

Carried survival equipment including life rafts, presume in fuselage [Not shown]

Ju 87C-2
Based on Ju 87B-2:

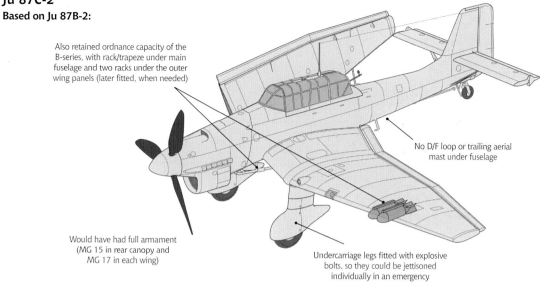

Also retained ordnance capacity of the B-series, with rack/trapeze under main fuselage and two racks under the outer wing panels (later fitted, when needed)

No D/F loop or trailing aerial mast under fuselage

Two rubber floatation bags were fitted in the fuselage with two more inside the leading edge of each wing [Not shown]

Carried survival equipment including life rafts, presume in fuselage [Not shown]

Would have had full armament (MG 15 in rear canopy and MG 17 in each wing)

Undercarriage legs fitted with explosive bolts, so they could be jettisoned individually in an emergency

Ju 87E-1

Projected 'navalised' version of the D-series. It was never proceeded with:

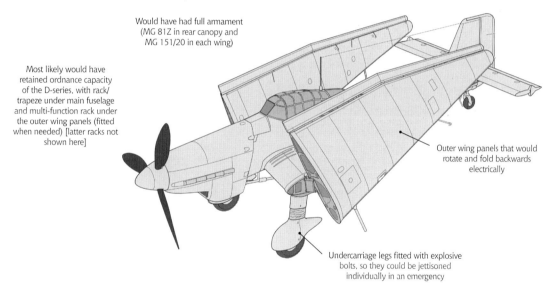

Would have had full armament (MG 81Z in rear canopy and MG 151/20 in each wing)

Most likely would have retained ordnance capacity of the D-series, with rack/ trapeze under main fuselage and multi-function rack under the outer wing panels (fitted when needed) [latter racks not shown here]

Outer wing panels that would rotate and fold backwards electrically

Two rubber floatation bags were fitted in the fuselage with two more inside the leading edge of each wing [Not shown]

Carried survival equipment including life rafts, presume in fuselage [Not shown]

Undercarriage legs fitted with explosive bolts, so they could be jettisoned individually in an emergency

Ju 87B with Jumo 213E (Ju 87F-related)
Same as Ju 87B-2 except:

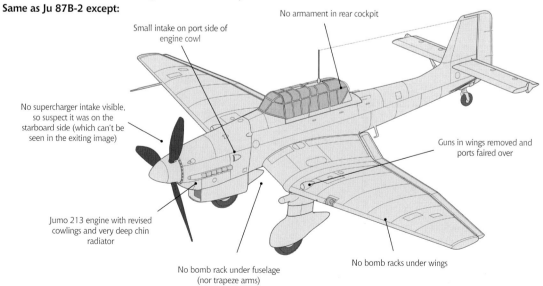

No armament in rear cockpit

Small intake on port side of engine cowl

No supercharger intake visible, so suspect it was on the starboard side (which can't be seen in the exiting image)

Guns in wings removed and ports faired over

Jumo 213 engine with revised cowlings and very deep chin radiator

No bomb rack under fuselage (nor trapeze arms)

No bomb racks under wings

Note: Only one partial image of a single airframe at Kirchheim exists, so there may well have been more converted in this way and/or other revisions that cannot be seen in the image

Ju 87F

Improved version of the D-series
(shown here with Stuvi sight etc., as per D-5 series)

New wing design (suspect this was the one used on the Ju 187/287, with the undercarriage that rotated through 90° into wells and traditional flaps and ailerons built in along the trailing edge)

Jumo 213 engine with revised cowlings and ventral radiator

Modifications of the initial design led to this later being given a whole new designation: Ju 187 (see elsewhere)

Ju 187

Developed from the aborted Ju 87F

Remote-controlled gun turret installed aft of the canopy that housed one MG 151/20 cannon and one MG 131 13mm machine gun

Two-seat cockpit canopy looks slightly shorter than original Ju 87-series, but has two hinged (to starboard) access panels much like the Ju 87A-series

Sighting unit (like that seen on the Ju 388) for remote-controlled turret installed aft of rear canopy

Heavy armour protection similar to that seen on the Ilyushin Il-2 Sturmovik

Jumo 213A engine with revised cowlings

Fixed armament comprised a forward-firing 20mm cannon, probably firing through the drive-shaft of the engine

Suspect the oil cooler (radiator) was situated under the nose, as there is a pronounced angled profile to the cowling in this region that is not usually associated with the Jumo 213 installation

Although not shown on the wind tunnel model, suspect dive brakes would have been installed under the wings

Bomb load was shown externally and at least 1.000kg going by diameter of bomb

Retractable undercarriage, the legs rotated through 90° back into underwing fairings (these remained attached at the outer wing panel/inner stub junction, so that area was covered with a bulge at the leading edge – to cover rotating gears at the top of the leg?)

Two ETC 50 racks for 50 or 70kg bombs under each outer wing panel (not shown on wind tunnel model)

Whilst many say that this had a fin and rudder assembly that could be rotated through 180° the only known image of a wind tunnel model clearly shows the fitment of support struts for the tailplanes, which would make rotating the whole tail problematic (struts would end up on top of the tailplanes). Careful study of the image of the wind tunnel model clearly shows the fillet at the base of the vertical fin still in place above the fuselage and a lot of filler around the fin/rudder that is located below the fuselage. It is our belief therefore that this original incarnation of the Ju 187 had a conventional vertical fin and rudder, but as is so often the case, the only surviving image shows it after modification testing the effects of a tail underneath the fuselage, which would then be developed further into the completely rotatable tail unit of the Ju 287

Note: Information about this type is confused, as the original Ju 287 was a development of the Ju 187 before its number was given to the twin jet engined bomber with forward-swept wings we all know. Above is therefore based on the one known image of the wind-tunnel model of the Ju 187 in its original form, see the Ju 287 for what most people think of as the 'Ju 187'!

Ju 287

Continued development of the Ju 187

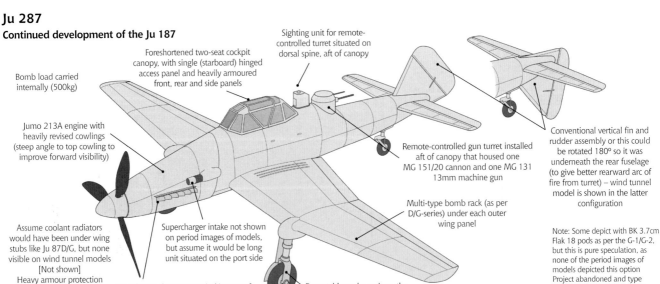

Bomb load carried internally (500kg)

Foreshortened two-seat cockpit canopy, with single (starboard) hinged access panel and heavily armoured front, rear and side panels

Sighting unit for remote-controlled turret situated on dorsal spine, aft of canopy

Jumo 213A engine with heavily revised cowlings (steep angle to top cowling to improve forward visibility)

Assume coolant radiators would have been under wing stubs like Ju 87D/G, but none visible on wind tunnel models [Not shown]

Heavy armour protection similar to that seen on the Ilyushin Il-2 Sturmovik [Not shown]

Supercharger intake not shown on period images of models, but assume it would be long unit situated on the port side

No exhausts shown on period images of models, but assume exposed versions on each side as per Fw 190D etc.

Remote-controlled gun turret installed aft of canopy that housed one MG 151/20 cannon and one MG 131 13mm machine gun

Multi-type bomb rack (as per D/G-series) under each outer wing panel

Retractable undercarriage, the legs rotated through 90° back into underwing fairings

Conventional vertical fin and rudder assembly or this could be rotated 180° so it was underneath the rear fuselage (to give better rearward arc of fire from turret) – wind tunnel model is shown in the latter configuration

Note: Some depict with BK 3.7cm Flak 18 pods as per the G-1/G-2, but this is pure speculation, as none of the period images of models depicted this option Project abandoned and type number given to Junker's twin jet engined, forward-swept wing bomber programme

Chapter 9:   **In Detail**

What follows is an extensive selection of images and diagrams that will help you understand the physical nature of the Ju 87 series.

This section includes photographic coverage of the few preserved Ju 87 airframes around the world; those featured are as follows:

- Ju 87G-2 at the RAF Museum, Hendon
- Ju 87R-2 W/Nr.5954 at the Museum of Science & Industry, Chicago
- Ju 87R-2 WNr.6234 being restored by the Flying Heritage & Combat Armor Museum in the USA
- Ju 87B-2 W/Nr 870406 at the Yugoslav Aeronautical Museum, Belgrade (tail only)

All photos ©R.A. Franks unless otherwise noted

Cockpit Interior

This is the instrument panel and control column etc. in the mock-up of the V1

Again, this is from the mock-up of the V1, but it shows the radio equipment on the centre bulkhead; the tube unit sticking up from the floor on the left of the gunner's seat is for the trailing aerial

Here you have the rear gun position in the mock-up of the V1, you can see the slot for the MG 15 plus how originally all the glazed panels were flat, to stop distortion

This image shows the starboard front cockpit sidewall of the A-series

Anschlußdose zur Beheizung des Atemschlauches – Junction box for heating the breathing tube
Rohr zur Führung des Atemschlauches – Tube for guiding the breathing tube
Rohrlagerung für Sender und Empfänger – Plug storage for transmitter and receiver
Höhen-atmer HLA 732 – HLA 732 breathing apparatus

Leitungs-kupplung LK 11 – Cable coupling LK 11
Winkel für Kabelbefestigung – Bracket for cable attachment
Gummiband und Spannband – Elastic band and tension band
Leichtmetallflaschen mit Anschlußstutzen – Light metal (oxygen) bottles with connecting pieces

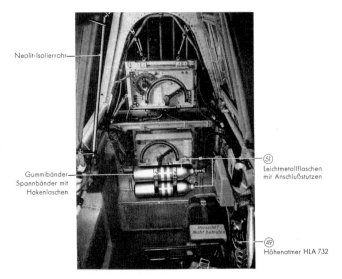

This image from the manual shows the port sidewall of the front cockpit

Druckknopf DK-IX für Bomben-auslösung – Push button for DK-IX bomb release
Heizregler – Heating controller
Navigations-tasche – Navigation bag

Kartenkasten – Card case
Zünder-umformer ZUK 455 – Igniter converted ZUK 455

This is the radio equipment set-up in the A-series

Neolit-Isolierrohr – Neolit insulating tube (for aerial lead)
Gummibänder Spannbänder mit Hackenlaschen – Rubber and metal tension bands with heel tabs
Leichtmetallflaschen mit Anschlußstutzen –

Light metal (oxygen) bottles with connecting pieces
Höhenatmer HLA 732 – HLA 732 breathing apparatus

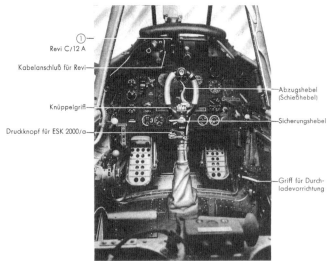

Although this image from the A-series manual shows the gun and camera related controls, it also gives a nice overall view of the forward region of the front cockpit

Revi C/12A – Revi reflector gunsight C/12A
Kabelansluß für Revi – Cable connection for Revi
Knüppelgriff – Control column
Druckknopf für ESK 2000/a – Push button for ESK 2000/a (gun camera)

Abzugshebel (Schießhebel) – Trigger (gun firing lever)
Sicherungshebel – Safety lever
Griff für Durch-ladevorrichtung – Handle for through-loading device

This is the image that got Trumpeter confused, it claims to show the radio installation in an A-series, but in fact it shows a mock-up of such an installation; the roll-over frame is wooden and the sender (S.5) and receiver (E.3) are mock-ups

This is the port sidewall of the rear (gunner's) cockpit region

Reißkupplung LK I f/g – Tear coupling LK I f/g
Isolierstück (nicht sichtbar) – Insulating piece (not visible)
Isolierplatten – Insulating panels
Heizregler – Heating controller

Stecker F 22 – Connector F 22
Stecker F 20 – Connector F 20
Kabel-halterung – Cable holder
Leitungs-kupplung LK II – Cable coupling LK II
Kabel-halterung – Cable holder

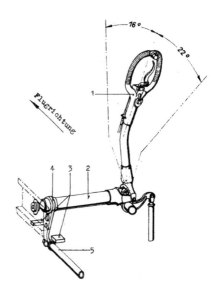

This is the original KG 11A control column with the round yoke, as used in the prototype and A-0 series

1. Steuerknüppel – Control column
2. Querwelle – Cross shaft
3. Anschläge – Stops
4. Hebel – Lever
5. Stoßstange – Connecting rod (literally = bumper)

This is the starboard sidewall of the rear (gunner's) cockpit region

Atemschlauch – Breathing tube
Brust bzw Rückenlehne – Chest or back rest (strap)
Höhenatmer HLA 732 – HLA 732

breathing apparatus
Beauchgurt Bagu 2 – Abdominal (waist) belt Bagu 2

An overall shot of the instrument panel in a production A-series, you can see the original round top of the control column, plus those rather clunky-looking rudder pedals

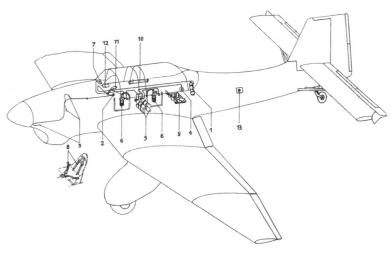

Safety equipment (inc. oxygen system) diagram for the A-1

1. Feuerlöschmittelbehälter – Extinguisher
2. Feuerlöschhahn – Fire valve
3. Sprühdüsen – Spray nozzles
4. Außenbordanschluß für Sauerstoff – Outboard connection for oxygen
5. Sauerstoff-Leicht-metallflaschen – Oxygen light metal bottles
6. Höhenatmer mit Atemschlauch – Breather with breathing tube
7. Sauerstoff-Druckanzeige – Oxygen pressure display
8. Bauch- und Schultergurt Führersitz – Abdominal (waist) and shoulder seat belts for pilot
9. Bauchgurt Schützensitz – Abdominal (waist) belts for rear gunner
10. Brust- und Rückenlehne Schützensitz – Chest and back rest strap for rear gunner
11. Leuchtpistole – Flare gun
12. Leuchtmunition – Flare gun ammunition
13. Sanitätspack – First Aid pack

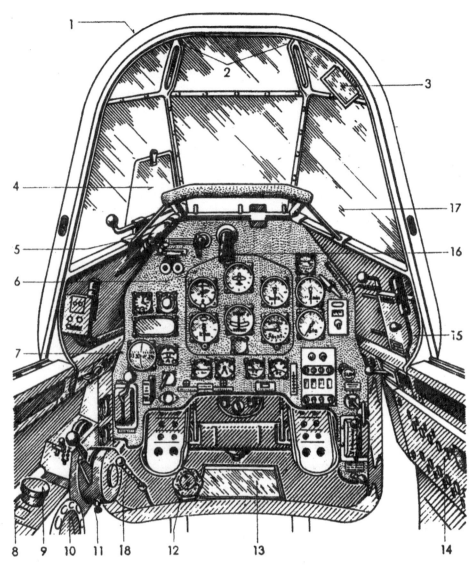

This diagram shows the equipment in the front cockpit of the B-2

1. festes Führerraumdach – Fixed cabin roof
2. Haltegriffe – Grab handles
3. Rückblickspiegel – Rearview mirror
4. vordere Klappe – Front (clear view) flap*
5. Leuchtpistolen-Einbau – Flare gun installation
6. elastisches Gerätebrett – Elastic-mounted equipment board (flying panel)
7. festes Gerätbrette – Fixed instrument panel
8. Schaltkasten – Control box
9. Seitenrudertrimmung – Rudder trim
10. Höhenrudertrimmung – Elevator trim
11. Schaltkasten für Luftdrosselregelung – Throttle box
12. Handrad für Bodenfenster – Handwheel for floor window
13. Bodenfenster mit Abdeckblende – Floor window with cover
14. Schalttafel mit Selbstschalter – Control panel with automatic switch
15. Leuchtoatronenkasten – Cockpit light
16. Belüftungsdüse mit Polster – Air vent with pad
17. zusätzliche Belüftungsregelung – Additional ventilation control

*We have only seen this on B-2 Trops and R-series airframes?

A nice period overall image of the instrument panel etc. in the B or R series

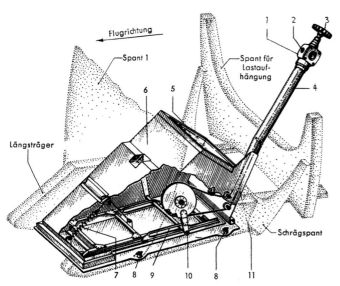

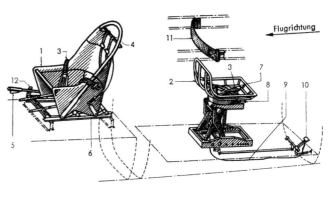

This is the ventral viewing panel in the floor of the Stuka and seen here in a diagram from the B-2 manual

1. Verstellgetriebe – Variable speed gear
2. Schauloch – Inspection hole
3. Handrad mit Buchse – Handwheel with socket
4. Führungsrohr – Guide tube
5. Plexiglas-Scheibe – Plexiglass pane
6. Kasten – Box
7. Entlastungsfeder für Klappe – Relief spring for flap
8. Topfverschluß – Rivet

9. Abdeckblende – Cover panel
10. Seilscheibe mit Kurbel – Pulley with crank
11. Seilzug – Cable
Längsträger – Side member
Spant 1 – Frame 1
Flugrichtung – Flight direction
Spant für Lastaufhängung – Frame for load suspension
Schrägspant – Bevel frame

The pilot and gunner's seats, taken from the B-2 manual

1. Führersitz – Pilot's seat
2. Schützensitz – Gunner's seat
3. Bauchgurt – Abdominal (waist) belt
4. Schultergurt – Shoulder strap
5. Hebel zum Verstellen des Sitzes – Lever for adjusting the seat
6. Hebel zum Verstellen des Schultergurtes – Lever for adjusting the shoulder strap
7. Auslösung für Fusstritt – Trigger for strap release
8. Knopf zum Drehen des Sitzes – Knob for rotating the seat
9. Bowdenzug – Bowden cable
10. Fußhebel zum Verstellen des Schützensitzes – Foot lever to adjust the gunner's seat
11. Brustlehne – Back or chest rest (strap)
12. Festlegestift – Locking pin

Rudder pedals from the B-1 manual, but this style also applies to the A-series

1. Lagerbock – Bearing block
2. Fußtritt – Foot plate
3. Fußpumpe – Foot pump
4. Anschluß für Öldruckleitung – Connection for oil pressure line
5. Rückholfeder – Return spring

6. Kolben – Piston
7. Rückenflugventil – Reverse travel valve
8. Entlüfttungsschraube – Vent screw
9. Füllschraube – Filling screw

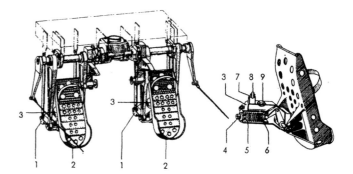

This is the instrument panel for the B-2

1. Druckknöpfe für Kühlerklappen-betätigung – Push buttons for radiator flap actuation
2. Verdunkler – Dimmer switch
3. Borduhr – Clock
4. Bediengerät für Peilanlage – Control device for DF system
5. Höhenmesser – Altimeter
6. Nahkompaß – Compass
7. Druckmesser für Drucköl der Landeklappenbetätigung – Pressure gauge for oil of flap actuation
8. Druckmesser für Drucköl deer Höhenflossenbetätigung – Pressure gauge for oil of the elevator control
9. Volt-Amperemeter – Volt meter
10. Netzausschalter – Ignition switch
11. Umschalter für Kraftstoff-vorratsmesser – Switch for fuel level meter
12. Merkleuchte für Kraftstoffrest (L. Behälter) – Low fuel indicator (left tank)
13. Kraftstoffvorrotsmesser – Fuel reserve meter
14. Merkleuchte für Kraftstoffrest (R. -Behälter) – Low fuel indicator (right tank)
15. Doppeldruckmesser für Schmier- und Kraftstoff – Double pressure gauge for oil and fuel

16. Anzeigegerät für Funknavigation – Display device for radio navigation
17. elektrisches Schmierstoff-Doppelthermometer – Electric double oil thermometer
18. Schauzeichen für Staurohr – Indictor pitot tube
19. elecktrisches Kühlstoffthermometer – Electric coolant thermometer
20. Statoskop-Variometer – Statoscope variometer
21. Ladedruckmesser – Boost pressure gauge
22. Drehzahlmesser – Tachometer
23. Stellungsanzeiger für Kühlerklappen – Radiator flap position indicator
24. Fahrtmesser – Trip meter
25. Wendezeiger – Turn indicator
26. 'Patin'-Führertochterkompaß – Pilot's 'Patin' compass
27. Kontakt-Höhenmesser – Contact altimeter
28. elastisches Gerätebrett – Elastic (shock-mounted) instrument panel
29. festes Gerätebrett – Fixed instrument panel

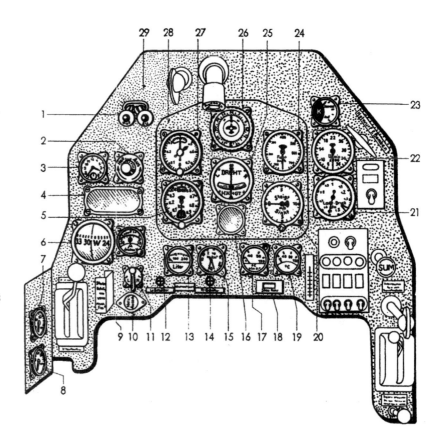

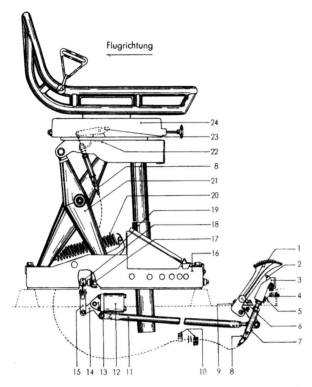

Flugrichtung

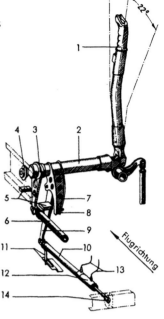

This KG 12 control column with the straight top, as used from the B-series

1. Steuerknüppel – Control column
2. Querwelle – Cross shaft
3. Hebel – Lever
4. Lagerung – Mounting point
5. Anschläge – Stops
6. Stoßstange – Connecting rod (literally = bumper rod)
7. Hebel – Lever
8. verstellbare Anschlagschraube – Adjustable stop screw
9. Anschlaghebel – Stop lever
10. Betätigungszylinder – Actuating cylinder
11. Führungsstift – Guide pin
12. Einziehstrebe – Retracting strut
13. Schlauch für Öldruckleitung – Hose for hydraulic line
14. Lagerung – Mounting point

This is a close-up diagram of the gunner's seat from the B-series manual

1. Fußtritt – Foot pedal
2. Raste – Rest
3. Lagerung für Raste – Rest mount
4. Ösenschraube – Eyebolt
5. Zugfeder – Tension spring
6. Welle – Pivot
7. Stellbolzen – Set bolts
8. Bowdenzug – Bowden cable
9. Lagerung – Storage
10. Schelle – Clamp
11. Zugstange – Drawbar
12. Füllstück – Filling piece
13. Hebellagerung – Lever position
14. Winkelhebel – Angle lever
15. Druckstange – Push rod
16. Rahmen – Frame
17. Rastbolzenverriegelung – Locking pin
18. Doppelhebel – Double lever
19. Federhaken – Spring hook
20. Zugfeder – Tension spring
21. Vorderstütze – Front support
22. Bowdenzughalterung – Bowden cable bracket
23. Hebel – Lever
24. Sitzoberteil – Seat support frame top

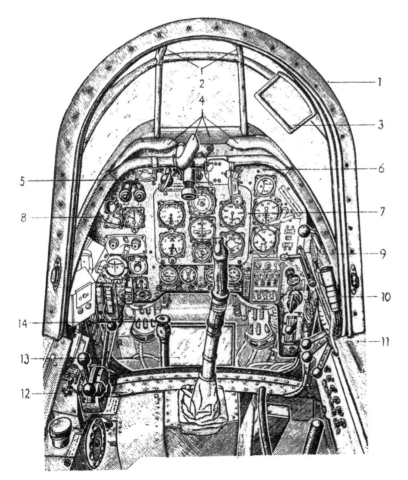

This is often listed as a B-series cockpit, but a look at the windscreen shape tells you this is the later style canopy, couple this with the odd crash-bar and non-standard frames and grab handles and it is most likely this is one of the B-series airframes used as D-series prototype

This diagram shows the equipment in the front cockpit of the D-1

1. Festers Führerraumdach – Fixed cabin roof (e.g. windscreen)
2. Haltegriffe – Grab handles
3. Rückblickspiegel – Rearview mirror
4. Scheobenspülanlage – Windscreen heating system
5. Verstellung der Scheibenspülanlage – Adjustment for windscreen heating system
6. Festes Gerätebrett – Fixed instrument panel
7. Elastisches Gerätebrett – Elastic-mounted equipment board (flying panel)
8. Leuchtpistolen-Halterung – Flare pistol holder
9. Leuchtpatronenkasten abwerfbar – Flare cartridge case can be ejected
10. Führerraumbeleuchtung – Cockpit light
11. Oberholm – Canopy sill
12. Träger I – Carrier I
13. Bodenfenster mit Abdeckblende – Floor window with cover
14. Handrad für Bodenfenster – Handwheel for floor window

This is the instrument panel in the Ju 87G-2 in the RAF Museum, which was converted from a D-5

Once again this is the RAF Museum's G-2 and this is the upper windscreen area with the rearview mirror and grab handles visible; no gunsight is installed, but you can see the mount and bumper pad in the middle of the image

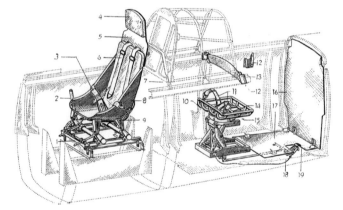

The pilot and gunner's seats, taken from the D-1 manual

1. Führersitz – Pilot's seat
2. Handhebel – Hand lever
3. Bauchgurt – Abdominal (waist) belt
4. Kopfpolster – Head cushion
5. Kopfschutz-Panzerplatte – Head protection armour plate
6. Schultergurt – Shoulder strap
7. Überschlagspant – Rollover frame
8. Gepanzererter Führersitz – Armoured pilot's seat
9. Hebel zum Verstellen des Schultergurtes – Lever for adjusting the shoulder straps
10. Schützensitz – Gunner's seat
11. Bauchgurt Abdominal (waist) belt
12. Halterung für Brustlehne – Bracket for chest rest (belt)
13. Brustlehne – Chest rest (belt)
14. Auslösung für Fußtritt – Release for kicking (?)
15. Verriegelungsknopf – Locking button
16. Panzerplatte am Hilfsspant hinter Spant 5 – Armour plate on the auxiliary frame behind Frame 5
17. Panzerplatte aug dem Fußboden – Armour plate on the floor
18. Bowdenzug – Bowden cable
19. Fußhebel zum Verstellen des Schützensitzes – Foot pedal to adjust the gunner's seat

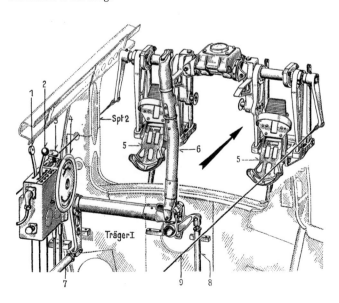

This diagram from the D-1 manual shows the later style of rudder pedals fitted to the D and G series

1. Schalthebel für Sturzflugbremse – Lever for dive brakes
2. Schalthebel für Verstellklappen und Höhenflosse – Lever for adjustable flaps and fin
3. Handrächen für Seitenhilfsruder-Verstellung – Rudder (thumb) adjuster
4. Handrad für Höhenhelfsruder-Verstellung – Handwheel for elevator adjustment
5. Fußtritt für Seitensteuerung – Rudder pedals
6. Steuerknüppel – Control column
7. Stoßstange zum Höhenruder – Connection rod to elevator
8. Stoßstange zum Querruder – Connection rod to ailerons
9. Seil zum Seitenruder – Control cable to rudder

This is the port sidewall of the G-2 at the RAF Museum, the trim wheel and throttle box being the main items in this region

This is the starboard sidewall of the G-2 at the RAF Museum, this area is mainly dominated by the large electrical distribution panel

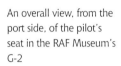

An overall view, from the port side, of the pilot's seat in the RAF Museum's G-2

The upper head armour in the RAF Museum G-2

This period image shows the radio equipment and solid bulkhead armour of a D-5

This period image shows the starboard side of the rear D-5 cockpit, with the radio equipment to the left and the VK5a switchboard and battery on the sidewall alongside

This is the radio equipment in the G-2 at the RAF Museum

This is the area directly above the radio equipment inside the RAF Museum's G-2, showing the style of head armour installed in this particular machine (the holes probably signify equipment that is no longer installed on this bulkhead – see the period image of the D-5 earlier in this section)

Unlike the earlier A, B & R series, the radio bulkhead is suspended by tubes to the inside of the canopy framework, as seen here with the RAF Museum's G-2; earlier variants had the unit suspended/dampened with bungees

This is the upper area to the port side of the radio equipment in the G-2 at Hendon

This is the lower area to the port side of the radio equipment in the G-2 at Hendon

This is the rear gunner's sidewall on the port side of the G-2 at Hendon and you can see the Morse key to the left and the back/chest strap in the middle

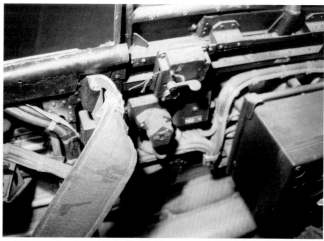

Moving slightly forward from the previous shot, you can see the intercomm toggle switchbox ahead of the back/chest strap and the radio box seen in a previous image on the far right

The starboard side of the rear gunner's position is pretty clear, as seen in this shot of the G-2 in the RAF Museum; the rear bulkhead is to the right and the reddish colour is Waxoil, a preservative

This is the area directly below the radio equipment in the G-2 at Hendon, this region is normally covered but this does allow you to see the big hoop casting for the wing spars and hydraulics etc.

This is the lower region of the rear bulkhead in the G-2 at Hendon, the box-shaped object on the floor past the bulkhead is, I think, the base of the FuG 25 IFF antenna, which has been removed and stowed loose at some stage in this aircraft's life

This is the foot pedal on the port side of the floor in the rear cockpit of the G-2 at Hendon, this allows the rear gunner to adjust the height of his seat

If you move up the rear bulkhead this is all you see in the RAF Museum's G-2, as the canvas bag for the spent cartridges, ammunition boxes and everything else associated for the rear MG 81Z have been removed from this machine when it was mocked-up as a B for the Battle of Britain movie in 1969

This is a view from the top down on the rear gunner's seat in the G-2 at Hendon, with the lap straps draped across it

This is the gunner's seat in the G-2 at Hendon with the lap straps removed, so you can see the tubular structure of the seat itself and the hydraulic column in the centre on which it is mounted; you can also see the back/chest support strap in place across the top of the image

Canopy

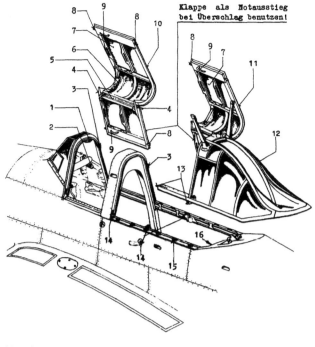

This period shot shows the canopies of the V4 from the starboard side, with the hinged sections open and the sliding panes in each fixed element slid fully back. Note the grab handles below the windscreen (only seen on the prototypes) and the various scoops and outlets on the engine cowls

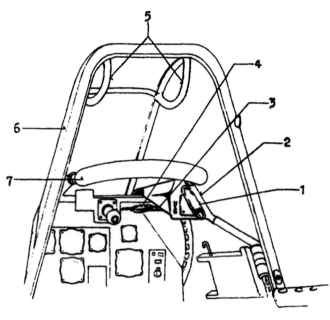

This is the main canopy elements of the A-1

1. Haltegriffe – Grab handles
2. Handgriff für Notabwurf – Handle for emergency release
3. Lagerhaken – Bearing hook
4. Scharnierbolzen – Hinge pin
5. Führerraumüberdachung – Cabin roofing
6. Rückspiegel – Rearview mirror
7. Schiebefenster – Sliding window
8. Riegel – Latch
9. Handgriff – Handle
10. Klappe der Führerraumüberdachung – Flap of the main canopy
11. Klappe der Schützenraumüberdachung – Flap of the gunner's canopy
12. Schützenraumüberdaschung – Rear gunner's fixed canopy section
13. Bolzen und Haken – Bolt and hook
14. Halterungen – Mounts
15. Auflagerstücke – Support pieces
16. Notabwurfhebel – Emergency release lever

Klappe als Notausstieg bei Überschlag benutzen! – Use the flap as an emergency exit in the event of a rollover!

Hand grips etc. in the front cockpit of the A-1

1. Handgriff – Handle
2. Befestigungsbock – Mounting bracket
3. Drahtseil – cable (literally 'wire rope')
4. Seilrolle – Pulley
5. Haltegriff – Grab handle
6. Fester Teil des Führerraumdaches – Fixed part of the cab roof
7. Kopfschutzpolster – Head protection pad

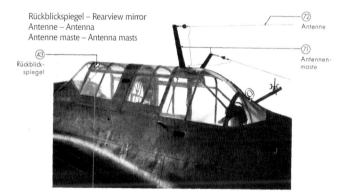

Rückblickspiegel – Rearview mirror
Antenne – Antenna
Antenne maste – Antenna masts

Canopy and antenna system of the A-series, note that the two antenna leads meet on the centre canopy frame via another ceramic insulator. You can also see the handgrip that pulls out in front of the hand-hold on the fuselage side

This combined period set of images from the type brochure shows how the two elements of the canopy for the A-series could be removed. Note the First Aid symbol on one of the rear panels, denoting this was a prototype because production machines had the First Aid kit in the port side of the rear fuselage

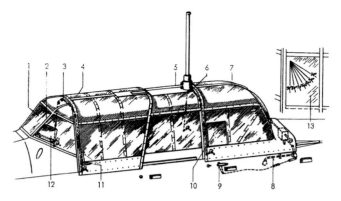

The canopy diagram from the B-2 manual

1. vorderes festes Dach – Front fixed roof (windscreen)
2. Stirnscheibe (Verbundglas) – Face plate (laminated glass)
3. Seilzug für Notabwurf – Cable for emergency release
4. Schiebedach über Führersitz – Sliding canopy (literally 'sunroof') over pilot's seat
5. Seilzug für Notabwurf – Cable for emergency release
6. Schiebedach über Schützensitz -Sliding canopy over the gunner's seat
7. Handgriff zum Öffnen von innen – Handle for opening from the inside

9. Handgriff zum Öffnen von außen – Handle for opening from the outside
10. Schiebefenster – Sliding window
11. Handgriff zum Öffnen – Handle for opening
12. vordere Klappe mit Verriegelung – Clear view (hinged) panel with lock*
13. Winkelskala für Sturzflug am Schiebedach (4) rechts – Angle scale for dive on the sunroof (4) on the right
*Note that this tends to be in those machines operating in hot climates (e.g. Italy, Sicily and Middle East)

In this period image of an A-1 you can see the hinged sections open, plus the vertical bars ('bird cage') directly behind the pilot's head within the fixed rollover structure that was standard for the A-series

This shows the canopy opening handle from the B-1 manual

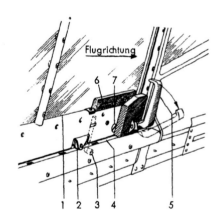

1. Rahmen am Führerraumdach – Frame on the cockpit canopy
2. Laufrolle – Roller
3. Gegenrolle – Counter roller
4. Laufschiene – Running track
5. Handgriff – Handle
6. Schild "Gesichert" – 'Secure' sign
7. Schlitzscheibe – Slotted disc 1. Rahmen am Führerraumdach – Frame on the cockpit canopy
2. Laufrolle – Roller
3. Gegenrolle – Counter roller
4. Laufschiene – Running track
5. Handgriff – Handle
6. Schild "Gesichert" – 'Secure' sign
7. Schlitzscheibe – Slotted disc

This period image taken from the back seat of a B or R-series Stuka clearly shows the 'V' shape created by the support tubes behind the pilot, plus the rearview mirror in the top right-hand of the windscreen and, just visible, the opening clear view panel that can partially be seen above the pilot's left shoulder; this latter feature was usually confined to those machines used in hotter climates, such as Italy, Sicily and the Middle East etc.

This image shows a Regia Aeronautica Ju 87B's rear canopy with the MG 15 (fitted with the spent cartridge bag) and the standard original style of un-armoured circular panel in which the gun is mounted

A nice period image of a new B-series machine at Junkers, clearly shows the original un-armoured circular panel for the gun mount/ring – note also the raised flange in the upper frame of the rear canopy that is common to all B- and R-series machines

After experience in combat many B- and R-series machines adopted the armoured style of gun ring seen on the Ju 88A, plus additional armour plate was added inside the lower quarter panel of the rear canopy, as seen here in this close-up

The new style of canopy for the D-series was first tested on B-series prototypes, such as this machine (W/Nr.2291)

Another view of the new style canopy on W/Nr.2291 shows what elements of the frames were inside and what were on the exterior. At this stage the canopy lacks the aerial mast but does have a slightly shallower vertical flange on the upper frame of the aft canopy section; the final cupola for the MG 81Z is not fitted either

This view of the D-series canopy from the front of test airframe W/Nr.2291 shows the curved nature of the windscreen and the small flat panel in its centre, most elements would be revised in some way for production as this prototype installation lacks armour of any kind

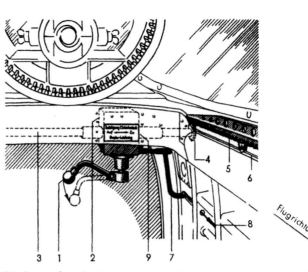

This diagram from the B-1 manual shows the rear canopy operating handle

1. Handkurbel – Hand crank
2. Kegelradgetriebe – Bevel gear
3. Hohlwelle – Hollow shaft
4. Zahnrad – Gear
5. Zahnstange – Rack
6. Laufschiene – Running track
7. Hebel zur Außenbetätigung – Lever for external actuation
8. Bowdenzug zur Außenbetätigung – Bowden cable for external operation
9. Schild für Betätigung des Schiebedaches – Sign for actuation of the sliding canopy

In tropical conditions fabric sun screens were installed above both the pilot and gunner, inside the canopy, as seen here in this period shot of such an installation in the pilot's canopy section; note that they run on tubes along their sides and fix in place with press-studs along the horizontal frames, quite a complex system

This is an overall view of the port side of the canopy on the G-2 at the RAF Museum, which is converted from a D-5 and has the additional frames in the lower section of the pilot's sliding canopy sections, with a sliding panel above that

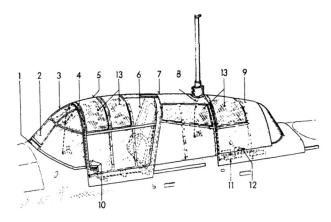

This diagram shows the production style of canopy adopted for the D (and later G) series

1. Spülluftklappe – Purge air flap
2. Hauptsichtscheibe (Panzerglas) – Main viewing window (bulletproof)
3. Vorderes festes Dach – Front fixed roof (windscreen)
4. Seilzug für Notabwurf – Cable for emergency release
5. Schiebedach über Führersitz – Sliding canopy (literally 'sunroof') over pilot's seat
6. Überschlagspant – Rollover frame
7. Festes Dach über Schützensitz – Fixed canopy over gunner's seat
8. Seilzug für Notabwurf – Cable for emergency release
9. Schiebedach über Schützensitz – Sliding canopy over the gunner's seat
10. Handgriff zum Entriegeln des

Schiebedaches über Führersitz außen und innen – Handle for unlocking the sliding canopy via the pilot's seat outside and inside
11. Handgriff zum Entriegeln des Schiebedaches über Schützensitz von innen – Handle for unlocking the sliding canopy from the inside of the gunner's position
12. Handgriff zum Entriegeln des Schiebedaches über Schützensitz von außen – Handle for unlocking the sliding canopy from the outside of the gunner's position
13. Gardinen – Curtains (sun screens)

The poor lighting at the RAF Museum makes it difficult to photograph the aircraft, especially when the G-2 was in the Battle of Britain Museum building (as here), so please excuse the poor clarity, but this does show the external armoured glass panel added to the windscreen of the D and G-series

This diagram shows additional cabin ventilation and comes from the D-series manual

1. Feste Klappe – Fixed flap
2. Belüftungsklappe – Ventilation flap
3. Rastlager – Control lever stop
4. Stoßstange – Control lever
5. Luftkasten – Air box
6. Luftrohr – Air pipe
7. Rohrschelle – Pipe clamp
Stellung zu – Position to (e.g. closed)
Stellung auf – Position up (e.g. open)

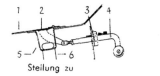

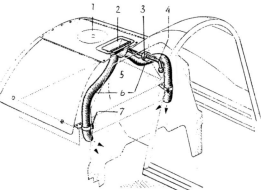

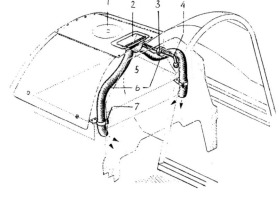

This diagram from the D-5 manual deals with set-up marks for alignment in the longitudinal axis, but is shows the revised rollover frame and head armour used in the D-series; note that there are a number of alternative styles for the head armour, so check period images

1. Spant 3 – Frame 3
2. Rüstmarken für Querachse – Set-up marks for the transverse axis
3. Panzerschutz – Armour protection

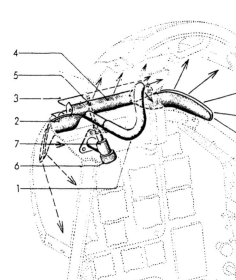

This diagram shows the 'window washing' (e.g demisting hot-air) system and comes from the D-series manual

1. Luftleitrohr – Air conduit
2. Luftleitstutzen – Air conduit supports
3. Spülluftklappe – Flush air flap
4. Luftleitblech – Air conduit
5. Bediengestänge – Operating rods
6. Rändelschraube – Latch screw
7. Bock – Operating rod support (literally 'trestle')

Main & Aft Fuselage

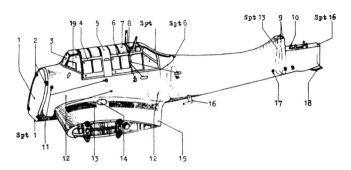

This diagram shows the main fuselage assembly of the A-series

1. Brandschott – Fire bulkhead
2. Anschlußpunkte für Triebwerksgerüst – Connection points for engine bearers
3. Stirnscheibe – End plate
4. Einsteigklappe für Führerraum – Pilot's canopy
5. Überschlagspant (Spt 3) – Rollover frame (Frame 3)
6. Einsteigklappe für Schützenraum – Gunner's canopy
7. Plexiverglasung – Perspex glazing
8. Haltergriffe – Hand holds (literally 'holder handles')
9. Stehbolzen – Stud
10. Gabel – Fork
11. Hißösen – Hoisting points
12. Ösen für Gräting – Eyelets for ladder (literally 'grating')
13. Auftrittsbelag – Anti-slip surface
14. Kraftstoffeinguß – Fuel filler point
15. Tragwerkmittelstück – Structural centre piece
16. Fußraste – Footrest
17. Hebeöffnung – Lift opening
18. Notspörn – Emergency tail bumper
19. Sichtklappe – Viewing flap
Spt = Spant (Frame)

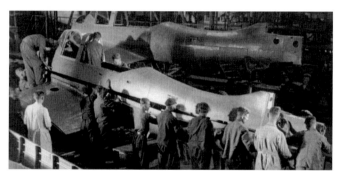

Here is the upper half of the fuselage being joined to the lower, again this is an A-series airframe

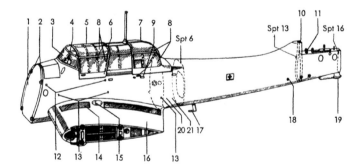

This diagram shows the main fuselage assembly of the B-series

1. Brandschott – Fire bulkhead
2. Anschlußpunkte für Triebwerksgerüst – Connection points for engine bearers
3. Stirnscheibe (Verbundglas) – Face plate (laminated glass)
4. vordere Klappe (Klappfenster)- Front flap (hinged window)
5. Schiebedach für Führerraum – Pilot's sliding canopy
6. Überschlagspant – Rollover frame
7. Schiebedach über Schützensitz – Gunner's sliding canopy
8. Plexiverglasung – Perspex glazing
9. Haltegriffe – Handles
10. Anschluß für Seitenflosse – Connection for fin
11. Anschluß für Höhenflosse – Connection for tailplanes
12. Hißösen – Hoisting points
13. Ösen für Laufleiter (Gräting) – Eyelet for ladder (literally 'grating')
14. Auftrittsbelag – Anti-slip surface
15. Kraftstoffeinguß – Fuel filler point
16. Tragwerkmittelstück – Structural centre piece
17. Auftritte – Step
18. Hebeöffnung – Lift (trestle) opening
19. Notspörn – Emergency tail bumper
20. Außenbordanschluß für Sauerstoff – Outboard connection for oxygen
21. Außenbordanschluß Elt-Anlage – Outboard connection for electrical system
Spt = Spant (Frame)

This period image shows how the fuselage was built in upper and lower halves, then joined together; this is an A-series airframe

Once the two fuselage halves are joined the unit moves along the assembly line to be kitted out – this image was taken at Dessau in 1938

The fuselage of the B (and R) series was made in the same way as the A-series, with upper and lower halves that were then joined together

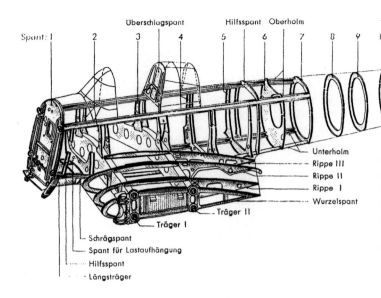

Spant: 1   2   Überschlagspant   3   4   Hilfsspant   Oberholm   5   6   7   8   9   10   11   12   13   14   15   16   Horizontalspant

Unterholm
Rippe III
Rippe II
Rippe I
Wurzelspant
Träger II
Träger I
Schrägspant
Spant für Lastaufhängung
Hilfsspant
Längsträger

Although the title is much more complex, this diagram from the D-1 manual shows the main frames and ribs in the fuselage and inboard wing stubs

Spant 1 – Frame 1
Überschlagspant – Rollover frame
Hilfsspant – Auxiliary frame
Oberholm – Upper beam
Horizontalspant – Horizontal frame
Unterholm – Lower beam
Rippe III – Rib III
Rippe II – Rib II
Rippe I – Rib I
Träger II – Carrier II (rear wing spar pick-up)
Träger I – Carrier I (front wing spar pick-up)
Längsträger – Side member
Hilfsspant – Auxiliary frame
Spant für Lastaufhängung – Frame for load suspension
Schrägspant – Bevel frame

This close-up shows the First Aid box in the port side of the rear fuselage of the B (and R) series; this is covered with a fabric panel that is ripped off in an emergency using the tape you can see casting a shadow to the right of the red cross marking

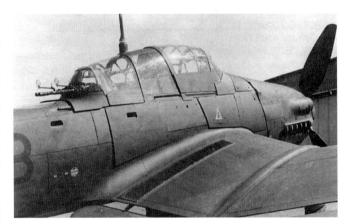

This image shows how the appliqué armour could be added to the fuselage sides on the D- (and G-) series), this also shows how such armour was also added to the canopy. Not all machines adopted this amount of armour and there are various combinations as a result

Once again apologies for the poor lighting, this shot of the RAF Museum's G-2 shows the flare pistol opening on the port side of the fuselage. Note how the upper cowling is not flush with the surrounding skins

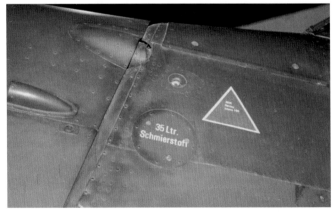

Below the windscreen on the port side of the RAFM G-2 is the oil filler cover marked as '35 Ltr. Schmierstoff' (35 litres of lubricant). The brown triangle above it denotes the type of oil to be used. The bulge you can see in the upper edge of the engine cowl is to clear the ball joint for the upper engine bearer pick-up

Moving back to the trailing edge of the wing on the port side here is the crew access step, there is another one on the opposite side of the fuselage

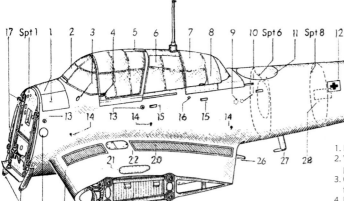

This diagram shows the main fuselage assembly of the D-series

1. Klappen – Flaps
2. Vorderes festes Führerdach – Front fixed pilot's roof (windscreen)
3. Öffnung für Leuchtpistole – Opening for flare pistol
4. Handgriff zum Öffnen des Schiebedaches von außen – Handle for opening the canopy from the outside
5. Schiebedach über Führersitz – Canopy over pilot's seat
6. Festes Dach hinter Führersitz – Fixed canopy over pilot's seat
7. Schiebedach über Schützensitz – Canopy over gunner's seat
8. Handgriff zum Öffnen des Schiebedaches von außen – Handle for opening the canopy from the outside
9. Außenbordanschluß für Sauerstoff – Outboard connection for oxygen
10. Außenbordanschluß 'Elektrisches Bordnetz" – Outboard connection for 'electrical wiring'
11. Wanne mit Plexiglasscheibe für Peilrahmen – Plexiglass cover over DF loop
12. Sanitätspack – First Aid pack
13. Heißpunkt – Hoisting points
14. Ösen für Laufleiter – Eyelet for ladder
15. Haltegriffe – Grab handles
16. Handgriff, einschiebbar – Handle, insertable

17. Kugelverschraubung für Triebwerksgerüst – Ball screw connection for engine bearers
18. Ausleger für Ablenkgabel – Pick-up for bomb trapeze
19. Außenbordanschluß für Schmierstoff – Oil filler point
20. Auftrittbelag – Anti-slip panels
21. Klappe für Restwamanlage des Kraftstoffes – Flap for low fuel warning system
22. Klappe für Kraftstoffeinguß – Fuel filler point
23. Fahrgestell-Anschluß – Undercarriage connection
24. Kugelverschraubung für Tragflügel – Socket for wing (spar) pick-up
25. Wurzelspant – Root rib
26. Ausleger für innere Verstellklappe – Boom for inner (flap) adjustment
27. Auftritt – Step
28. Klappe für Unterbringung des Notantennenmastes – Flap for housing the emergency antenna mast
29. Hebeöffnung – Trestle hole
30. Gabelköpfe für Höhenflossen-Strebenanschluß – Fork heads for horizontal tailplane support connection
31. Notsporn – Emergency tail bumper
Spt = Spant (Frame)

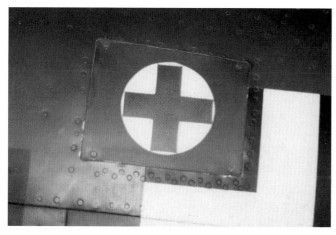

Further back still on the port fuselage is this access panel for the First Aid kit – we are not 100% sure the cover is authentic, as usually on earlier variants this area was covered with a tear-off fabric patch to ease access

Right towards the back of the fuselage, on both sides of all variants, is this tube to allow a bar to be passed through the fuselage to trestle the aircraft for things like gun alignment etc. 'Hier Aufbocken' basically means 'jack up here'

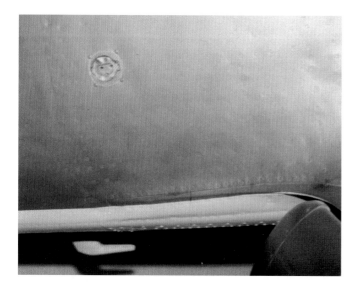

This is the external electrical connector on the starboard side, just aft of the wing trailing edge and seen here on the RAFM's G-2

This diagram from the D-1 manual shows how the external electrical connector should look, complete with hinged cover and data placard ahead of it

Engine & Cowls

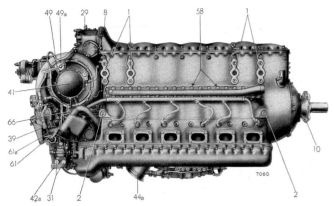

Views from Junkers showing the Jumo 211F and J engine

The port side view of the Jumo 211B/D at Gatow, Berlin *(©George Papadimitriou)*

A close-up of the supercharger intake on the starboard rear of the Jumo 211F in Munich *(©George Papadimitriou)*

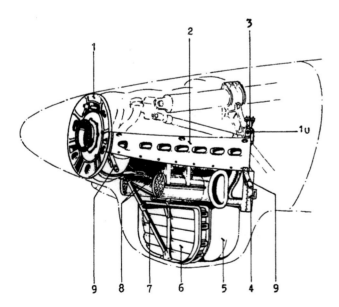

This diagram shows the cowling frames for the A-series

1. Ringspant – Ring frame
2. Auspuffwanne – Exhaust pan
3. Auflager für obere Haube – Support for upper cowling
4. Kühlerspant – Radiator frame
5. Wasserkühler – Coolant radiator
6. Kühlerklappen – Radiator flaps
7. untere Strebe – Lower strut
8. obere Strebe – Upper strut
9. Hebelverschluß – Lever lock (cowling)
10. Sechskantbolzen – Hexagon bolt

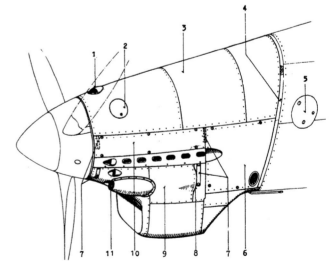

These are the cowling elements for the A-series

1. Belüftung für Lichtmaschine – Alternator cooling air intake
2. Klappe für Kühlstoffeingunß – Coolant filler point access cover
3. obere Haube – Upper cowling
4. Düsenspalt – Cowling gap (rubber)
5. Klappe für Schmierstoffeinguß – Oil filler access panel
6. seitliche Klappe hinten – Rear side cowling
7. Hebelverschluß – Lever lock (cowling)
8. untere Haube – Lower cowling
9. seitliche Klappe vorn – Front/side cowling
10. seitliche Klappe vorn – Front/side cowling
11. Lufteintritt für Ölkühler – Air inlet for oil cooler

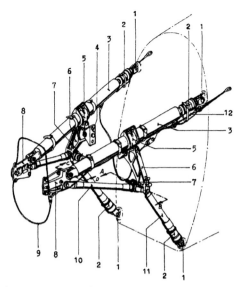

A nice starboard shot of the exposed engine on one of the A-0s sent to Spain for evaluation during the Spanish Civil War with 29•3 visible in the background

These are the engine bearers of the A-series

1. Rumpfanschlußpunkt (Gabelgelenk) – Fuselage connection point (fork joint)
2. JFM-Federpaket – JFM spring package
3. Biegungsträger – Load-bearing beam
4. Anschlußstück – Connector (engine)
5. Trägeroberteil – Carrier top
6. Trägerunterteil – Carrier base
7. Gelenkstab – Joint rod
8. Knotenstück – Front (engine) bracket
9. Motorsicherung – Engine earth wire
10. vordere Strebe – Front strut
11. untere Strebe – Lower strut
12. Dehnungsstab – Extension rod

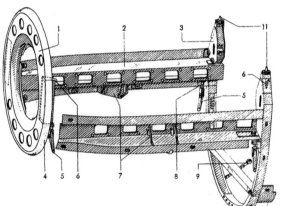

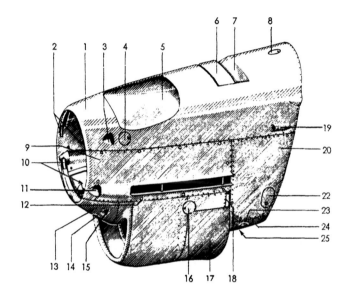

These are the cowling frames for the B-1

1. Ringspant – Ring frame
2. Auspuffwanne – Exhaust pan
3. hinterer Spant – Rear frame
4. Auflagefläche – Contact surface
5. Hebelverschluß für Kühlerverkleidung – Radiator cover lever lock
6. Verschlußhaken für obere Haube – Locking hook for the upper cowling
7. Aufhängebock für Kühler – Hanging bracket for the coolant radiator
8. Führungsstift für Kühlerverkleidung – Radiator cowl guide pin
9. Lasche zum Filtergehäuse – Tab for the filter housing
10. Schweißstück zum Ansetzen des hinteren Haubenteiles – Welding piece for attaching the rear cowl
11. Führungsstift für obere Haube – Guide pin for the upper cowling

These are the cowling elements for the B-1

1. obere Verkleidungshaube – Upper cowling
2. Hebelverschluß der oberen Verleidungshaube – Lever lock for upper cowling
3. Belüftung – Cooling air intake
4. Deckel für Kühlstoffeinguß – Coolant filler cap
5. Kühllufteintritt zum Schmierstoffkühler – Cooling air inlet to the oil cooler
6. Spreizklappe zur Regelung der Schmierstofftemperatur – Moving flap for regulating the oil temperature
7. Kühlluftaustritt vom Schmierstoffkühler – Cooling air outlet from the oil cooler
8. Deckel zum Einguß für Hydrauliköl – Hydraulic oil filler cap
9. linke Seitenklappe – Left side panel
10. Hebelverschluß der Kühlerverkleidung – Radiator cover lever lock
11. Kühlluft zur Auspuffwanne – Cooling air inlet to the exhaust pan
12. Schnellverschlüsse – Quick fasteners
13. Kühlerverkleidung – Radiator cover
14. Deckel für Warmluft im Winterflugbetrieb – Cover for warm air in winter flight operations
15. Belüftung – Cooling air intake
16. Deckel (zur Gelenkwelle der Speizklappenbetätigung – nicht mehr eingebaut – Cover (for the propeller actuating shaft – no longer installed)
17. Spreizkragen – Radiator (exhaust) flap
18. Sicherungsdeckel von Hebelverschluß – Safety cover for lever lock
19. Hutze für Generatorbelüftung – Cooling air intake (generator)
20. linke hintere Klappe – Left rear panel
22. Deckel zu den Handgriffen für Anlasserkupplung und Bürstenabheber – Access panel for starter handle pick-up
23. Außenbordanschluß für elektr. Anlassen – Outboard connector for electric start
24. hinterer Haubenteil – Rear cowling part
25. Deckel im hinteren Haubenteil zum Warmschmierstoff-Auffüllanschluß – Access panel in the rear cowling for draining hot lubricant

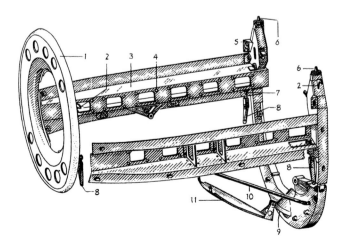

The cowling frames for the B-2 are slightly different from the B-1

1. Ringspant – Ring frame
2. Verschlußhaken für obere Haube – Locking hook for the upper cowling
3. Auspuffwanne – Exhaust pan
4. Aufhängebock für Kühler – Hanging bracket for the coolant radiator
5. Hinterer Spant-Oberteil – Rear bulkhead, top
6. Führungsstifte für obere Haube – Guide pins for the upper cowling
7. Führungsstift für Kühlerverkleidung – Radiator cowl guide pin
8. Hebelverkleidung für Kühlerverkleidung – Lever locks for radiator cowling
9. Hinterer Spant-Unterteil – Rear bulkhead , bottom
10. Strebe – Support strut
11. Abdeckblech – Cover plate

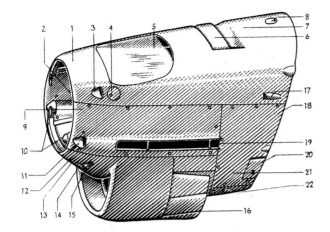

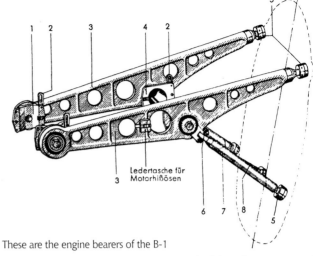

The cowling elements of the B-2 differs slightly from the B-1

1. obere Verkleidungshaube – Upper cowling
2. Hebelverschluß der oberen Verleidungshaube – Lever lock for upper cowling
3. Belüftung – Cooling air intake
4. Deckel für Kühlstoffeinguß – Coolant filler cap
5. Kühllufteintritt zum Schmierstoffkühler – Cooling air inlet to the oil cooler
6. Spreizklappe zur Regelung der Schmierstofftemperatur – Moving flap for regulating the oil temperature
7. Kühlluftaustritt vom Schmierstoffkühler – Cooling air outlet from the oil cooler
8. Deckel zum Einguß für Hydrauliköl – Hydraulic oil filler cap
9. linke Seitenklappe – Left side panel
10. Hebelverschluß der Kühlerverkleidung – Radiator cover lever lock
11. Kühlluft zur Auspuffwanne – Cooling air inlet to the exhaust pan
12. Schnellverschlüsse – Quick fasteners
13. Kühlerverkleidung – Radiator cover
14. Deckel für Warmluft im Winterflugbetrieb – Cover for warm air in winter flight operations
15. Belüftung – Cooling air intake
16. Spreizklappen – Radiator (exhaust) flap
17. Hutze für Generatorbelüftung – Cooling air intake (generator)
18. linke hintere Klappe – Left rear panel
19. Kühlluftaustritt deer Auspuffwanne – Cooling air outlet from the exhaust
20. Deckel zu den Handgriffen für Anlasserkupplung und Bürstenabheber – Access panel for starter handle pick-up
21. Außenbordanschluß für elektrisches Anlassen – Outboard connector for electric start
22. hinterer Haubenteil – Rear cowling part

These are the engine bearers of the B-1

1. vordere Lagerung – Front (engine) mount
2. Hißöse – Heat-resistant eyelet
3. Motorträger – Engine bearer
4. hintere Lagerung – Rear (engine) mount
5. Kugelverschraubung – Ball screw connection (firewall)
6. Zweitkantbolzen – Support strut upper bolt
7. Abstützstrebe – Support strut
8. Diagonalstrebe – Diagonal strut
Ledertasche für Motorhißösen – Leather bag for engine heat-resistant eyelets

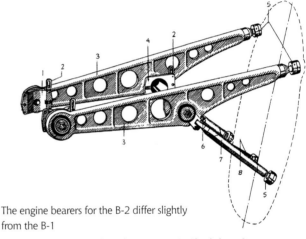

The engine bearers for the B-2 differ slightly from the B-1

1. vordere Lagerung – Front (engine) mount
2. Hißöse – Heat-resistant eyelet
3. Motorträger – Engine bearer
4. hintere Lagerung – Rear (engine) mount
5. Kugelverschraubung – Ball screw connection (firewall)
6. Zweitkantbolzen – Support strut upper bolt
7. Abstützstrebe – Support strut
8. Diagonalstrebe – Diagonal strut

A lovely port side view of the engine of a B-1, note the oval exhausts stubs and the narrow style of radiator

A factory shot of B-1s having final checks and adjustments done prior to a test flight at Bremen-Lemwerder

Another period shot of an early B-series undergoing adjustments, the narrow style of radiator with the shutters in the fully open position, plus the screen visible in the supercharger intake are of note

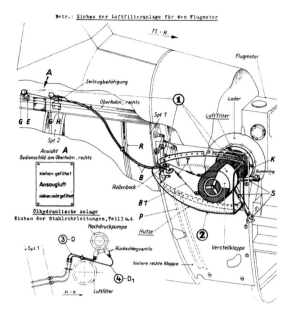

This modification sheet shows the tropical filter installation for the B-2 and R-series

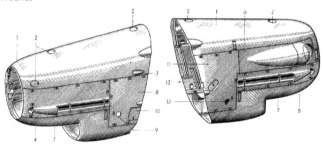

This diagram shows the left and right of the engine cowlings for the D and G-series

1. Obere Motorverkleidung – Upper engine cowling
2. Handlochdeckel (zum Auffüllen von Kühlund Schmierstoff sowie Drucköl) – Access cover (for filling coolant, lubricant and hydraulic oil)
3. Hutze für Generatorbelüftung – Air intake for cooling generator
4. Seitliches Klappenblech links – Side panel, left
5. Seitliches Klappenblech rechts – Side panel, right
6. Luftansaugstutzen (rechts) mit Verkleidung) – Air intake panel (right) with cladding)
7. Untere Motorverkleidung – Lower engine cowling
8. Hintere Klappe, links – Rear panel, left
9. Ausschnitt für elektrischen Außenbordanschluß – Cut-out for electrical outboard connection
10. Verschlußklape mit Riegel – Closure panel with latch
11. Hintere Klappe rechts – Rear panel, right
12. Handlochklappe für Kaltstart – Access panel for cold start
13. Ausschnitt für Motorbelüftungsleitung – Cut-out for engine ventilation line

The Jumo 211J of a D-1 being inspected by British personnel in North Africa, showing some nice detail like the exhausts, lower radiator and the fluid reservoirs on the top and side of the engine *(©British Official)*

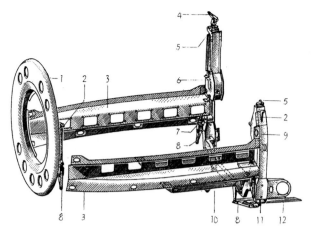

These are the cowling frames for the D-series and thus also apply to the G-series

1. Ringspant – Ring frame
2. Verschlußhaken für obere Verkleidung – Locking hook for upper cowling
3. Auspuffwanne – Exhaust pan
4. Hebel-Spannverschluß – Lever latch (cowling)
5. Führungsstifte für obere Verkleidung – Guide pins for upper cowling
6. Hinterer Spant rechts – Rear frame, right
7. Führungsstifte für untere Verkleidung – Guide pins for lower cowling
8. Hebel-Spannverschluß für Verkleidung – Lever latch for side panels
9. Hinterer Spant links – Rear frame, left
10. Lagerbrücje für Kühleraufhängung – Bearing bracket for radiator suspension
11. Anschlagschraube – Stop screw
12. Halterung des Leitbleches – Bracket for the guide plate

There are the engine bearers for the D and G series

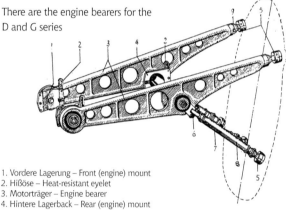

1. Vordere Lagerung – Front (engine) mount
2. Hißöse – Heat-resistant eyelet
3. Motorträger – Engine bearer
4. Hintere Lagerback – Rear (engine) mount
5. Kugelverschraubung – Ball screw connection (firewall)
6. Gabellager – Fork bearing
7. Abstützstrebe – Support strut
8. Diagonalstrebe – Diagonal strut
9. Sechskantschraube – Hexagon screw

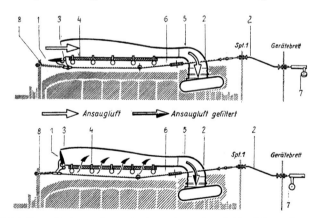

This is the revised supercharger intake on the starboard side of the engine cowling for the D and G series

1. Klappe – Flap
2. Bowdenzug – Bowden cable
3. Ansaugschacht – Intake duct
4. Luftfilter – Air filter
5. Krümmer am Lader – Manifold on the supercharger intake
6. Seilrolle – Pulley
7. Bedienhebel im Führerraum – Control lever in the pilot's cockpit
8. Zugfeder – Tension spring

Stellung: Ansaugluft nicht gefiltert – Position: intake air not filtered
Ansaugluft – Air intake
Ansaugluft gefiltert – Air intake filtered
Gerätebrett – Equipment board
Stellung: Ansaugluft gefiltert – Position: intake air filtered
Spt – Spant (Frame)

These are the ejector exhausts of the G-2 at Hendon, but they also apply to the D-series, there's no prominent weld seam but they do have the Junkers company logo as raised detail at the front of each pipe

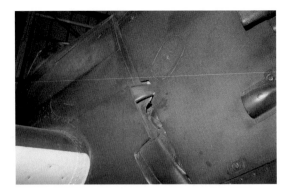

This is the engine ventilation pipe that projects on the starboard side of the rear of the engine cowls, seen here on Hendon's G-2, but also applicable to the D-series. Check period images though, as there are variations

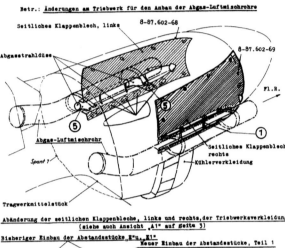

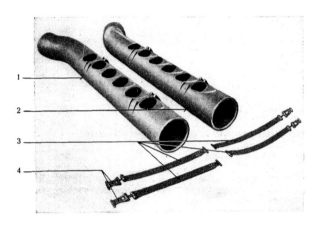

This diagram from the D-series manual shows the construction of each flame damper pipe

1. Mischrohr rechts – Exhaust tube, right
2. Mischrohr links – Exhaust tube, left
3. Spannband – Tension strap
4. Spannschloß – Tunbuckle

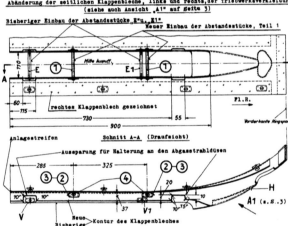

Flame dampers – this modification sheet shows the installation of flame dampers for the B-2. R-2 and R-4 variants, although you will rarely see images of such an installation on these variants

This is the prototype installation of the flame dampers, seen on D-5 W/Nr.1921

There are four styles of flame damper, this is one, with the bulged collar around the outlet and seen here on a D-3 of NSGr 9

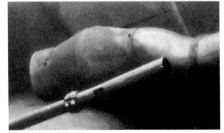

And another style, this time with this expand/contract section just before the outlet, seen on a D-5 of NSGr.9 in Italy in August 1944

Here is another type, this time with a flared outlet, seen on a D-5 of NSGr 9; note the diffuser/spark grill in the outlet

Radiator

The chin-mounted radiator of the Stuka went through a lot of changes initially, here you can see the slanted unit first used on the V1 with its Kestrel engine

The radiator of the V3 looks similar to the V2, but is slightly deeper around the front

The radiator on the V1 was insufficient and caused the engine to overheat, so it was greatly enlarged, as seen here

The V4 had a much deeper lip to the front of the radiator unit and, we suspect, a larger unit overall

The installation of the Jumo in the V2 led to the adoption of another complete revision to the radiator

By the V5 you are starting to see the shape associated with the production variant, note the oil cooler intake at the top, with its exhaust further aft on the cowl

Nice clear shot of the radiator under the nose of one of the A-0s sent for evaluation in Spain, note the oil cooler intake at the top, with a smaller scoop above that and the intake at the front of the exhausts to cool the manifold

The radiator unit itself under the cowls of the A-series looked like this

This is the lower chin cowling off an A-series

Under the cowling of the B-series you had the radiator unit itself slung below the engine, this is the early thin style unit, used on the B-1 series

With the B-series the radiator was enlarged and the oil cooler moved to the top of the cowling, this resulted in this 'big grin' intake with the shutters seen here fully closed

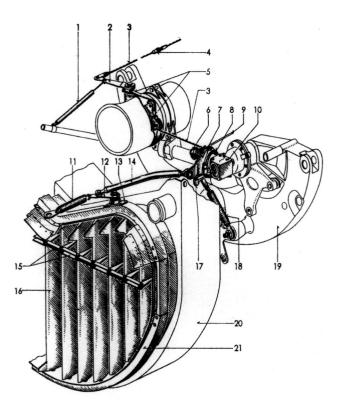

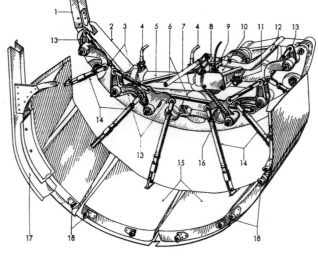

This diagram shows the aft radiator flaps, as seen on the B-2 and R-series

1. Hinterer Spant, Oberteil – Rear frame, upper part
2. Hinterer Spant. Unterteil – Rrear frame, lower part
3. Bedienstange – Control rod
4. Hochdruckschlaich – High pressure hose
5. Spreizklappenzylinder – Spreading flap cylinder
6. Hauptbedienstange – Main control bar
7. Bedienstange für Kühlerklappen – Operating rod for radiator flaps
8. Hebel für Kühlerklappenverstellung – Radiator flap adjustment lever
9. Potentiometer – Potentiometer
10. Kegelradgetriebe (Antrieb) – Bevel gear (drive)
11. Antriebshebel – Drive lever
12. Lagerbock – Bearing block
13. Hebel fur Speizklappenbetätigung – Lever for flap actuation
14. Stoßstange mit Schnelltrennstelle – Connecting rod with quick release
15. Spreizklappe – Spreading flap
16. Zugfeder – Tension spring
17. Spant 3 (Untere Haube) – Frame 3 (lower cowling)
18. Lagerbock (mit Kugellager) – Bearing block (with ball bearing)

This diagram shows the radiator shutter system and applies to the B and R-series

1. Zugfeder – Tension spring
2. Winkelhebel – Angle lever
3. Drahtseil (Notzug) – Cable (emergency operation)
4. schnell trennbare Seilkupplug – Quick cable release coupling
5. Seilumlenkung – Cable deflection
6. Druckfeder – Compression spring
7. Hebel mit Kupplungsnocken – Lever with clutch cam
8. Kupplungsring – Coupling ring
9. Bedienstange für Schmierstoffilter – Operating rod for oil filter
10. Winkelgetriebe – Bevel gear

11. Zugfeder – Tension spring
12. Verstellhebel – Adjustment lever
13. Lagerflansch (mit Kuggelager) – Bearing flange (with ball bearing)
14. Bedienstange – Operating rod
15. Laschen mit bolzen – Tabs with bolts
16. Kühlerklappen – Radiator flap
17. Puffer – Buffer
18. Zugfeder – Tension spring
19. hinterer Spant, Unterteil – Rear bulkhead, lower part
20. Kühlstoffkühler – Radiator
21. Kühlerklappenrahmen – Radiator flap frame

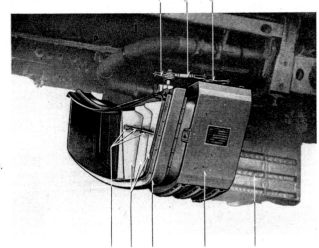

The D and G series adopted a completely new set up, with the coolant radiator relocated under the wings and the oil cooler moved under the nose, this diagram shows the oil cooler from the port side with the cowls off

1. Verstellhebel – Adjustment lever
2. Bedienstange – Operating rod
3. Hebel – Lever
4. Hebelblech mit Laschen – Lever plate with tabs

5. Kühlerklappen – Radiator flaps
6. Rahmen – Frame
7. Schmierstoffkühler – Oil cooler
8. Ladenuftkühler – Air cooler

Here is a view into the intake under the nose of the G-2 at Hendon, note the shutters on the oil cooler element to the right are open, plus the round access panel in the cowling; there is another version that lacks this access panel, so check images

A closer look into the chin intake on Hendon's G-2, the air cooler is to the left with the oil cooler and shutters on the right

Propeller & Spinner

All the prototypes used variations of the Hamilton-Junkers propeller and from the V4 the metal, three-blade, two-position, 10° adjusting range HPA II was used, as seen here on an A-0 tested in Spain

The propeller changed during the A-2 production, which initially started with the same unit as used by the A-0 and A-1s (up to W/Nr.0870156), but from W/Nr.870157 a 20° adjusting range HPA III propeller was used, as seen here on an A-2 used by the Luftwaffe Medical Department

There seems to be much confusion with regard to the propeller type used from the B-series, as many list the HPA III, others the VS 5 (which some state is the HPA III) and some the VS 11. The B-1 certainly had a propeller with a blade profile that is slightly flatter and thus wider, with the tip less pointed than the previous type

The B-2 adopted the broader bladed VS 11 propeller, as seen here with one being built at Bremen

The D and G series used the wide wooden blades of the VS 111 propeller, as seen here on a D-5 of 3./StG 3 at Immola in July 1944 (©SA Kuva)

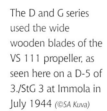

This is the spinner on the G-2 at Hendon, the manner in which the spinner is held on to the backplate is not seen in any period images, so we suspect it is a modification that has been made post-war during its various restorations. The hole in the centre of the spinner was usually filled with a bung

There is quite a gap between the front of the engine cowl and the back of the spinner backplate with the D and G series, as seen here on Hendon's G-2

Oil System

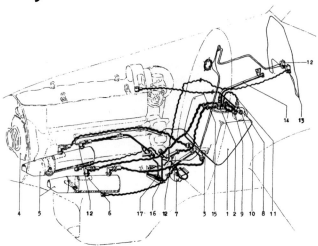

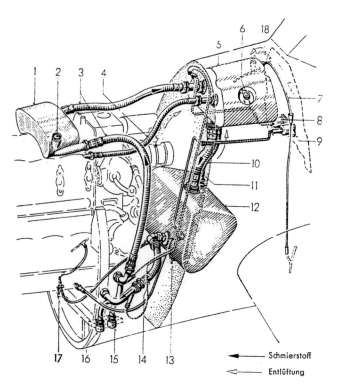

This diagram shows the overall oil system of the A-series

1. Schmierstoffbehälter – Oil reservoir
2. Behälterkopf – Container head
3. Sum-Ablaßventil – Sump drain valve
4. Motor – Motor
5. Kühler links und rechts – Cooler left and right
6. Überdruckventil 5kg/cm2 – Pressure relief valve 5kg/cm2
7. Ventilbatterie – Valve battery
8. Außenbordfüllanschluß – Outboard filler point
9. Fülleitung – Filling pipe
10. Überlaufleitung – Overflow line
11. Entlüftungsleitung – Vent line
12. Schmierstoffthermometer für Ein- und Austritt – Oil thermometer for entry and exit
13. Druckmesser für Kraft- und Schmierstoff – Pressure gauge for fuel and oil
14. Peilstab – Dipstick
15. Entlüftung – Venting
16. Füll- und Ablaßventil – Filling and drain valve
17. Ablaßventil – Drain valve

The oil system for the R-series is slightly different, due to the higher oil consumption in a hotter climate

1. Schmierstoffkühler – Oil cooler
2. Überdruckventil – Pressure relief valve
3. Rücklaufleitung – Return line
4. Entlüftungsleitung vom Motor – Vent line from engine
5. Zusatz-Schmierstoffbehälter – Additional oil reservoir
6. Einfüllverschraubung mit Peilstab – Filler cap with dipstick
7. Entlüftungsleitung (nur bei R-1) – Ventilation line (only with R-1)
8. Doppeldruckmesser für Schmierstoff-Ein- und Austritt – Double pressure gauge for oil inlet and outlet
9. Doppeldruckmesser für Schmierstoff-Kraftstoff – Double pressure gauge for oil and fuel
10. Entlüftungsleitung vom Hauptbehälter – Vent line form the main tank
11. Zulaufleitung – Inlet line
12. Haupt-Schmierstoffbehälter – Main oil reservoir
13. Ablaßventil – Drain valve
14. Vorlaufleitung – Flow line
15. Schmierstoff-Ablaßventil – Oil drain valve
16. Schmierstoff-Auffüll- und Ablaßventil – Oil fill and drain valve
17. Durchgangshahn für Kaltstart-einrichtung – Control tap for cold start device
18. Entlüftungsleitung (nur bei R-2) – Ventilation line (only for R-2)

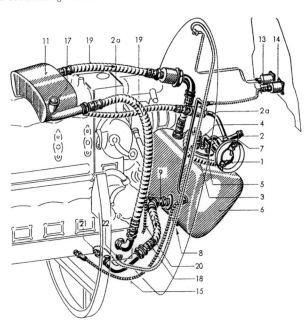

This is the oil system for the B-series

1. Außenbordfüllanschluß – Outboard filler point
2. Entlüftungsleitung vom Behälter zum Außenbordfüllanschluß – Vent line from tank to outboard filler point
2a. Entlüftungsleitung vom Motor zum Außenbordfüllanschluß – Vent line from engine to outboard filler point
3. Fülleitung – Filler pipe
4. Überlaufleitung – Overflow line
5. Behälterkopf – Container head
6. Schmierstoffbehälter (Inhalt 55 liter, Auffüllmenge 47 liter) – Oil container (content 55 litres, filling quantity 47 litres)
7. Peilstab – Dipstick
8. Ablaßventil-Sum – Sump drain valve
9. Krümmer mit ringdüse – Manifold with ring nozzle
10. Schmierstoffkühler – Oil cooler
13. Doppelthermometer für Ein- und Austrittstemperatur – Double thermometer for inlet and outlet temperature
14. Doppeldruckmesser für Kraft- und Schmierstoff – Double pressure gauge for fuel and oil
15. Scmierstoffdruckmesserleitung – Oil pressure line
17. Überdruckventil – Pressure relief valve
18. Vorlaufleitung – Flow line
19. Rücklaufleitung – Return line
20. Kraftstoffleitung für Kalstart – Fuel line for cold start
21. Thermometer-Anschluß für Schmierstoffeintritt – Thermometer connection for oil inlet
22. Thermometer-Anschluß für Schmierstoffaustritt – Thermometer connection for oil outlet

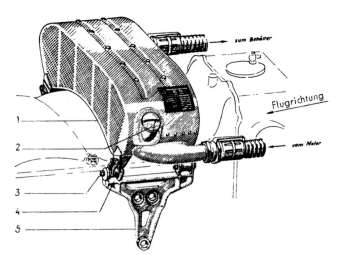

This the actual oil cooler for the B and R-series

1. Schmierstoffkühler – Oil cooler
2. Überdruckventil 4 atü – Pressure releif valve (4 atmospheres)
3. Sechskantbolzen – Hexagon bolt
4. Anschlußlager – Junction bearing
5. Lagerung – Mounting bracket

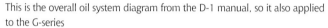

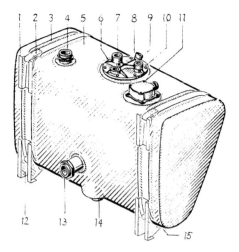

This is the overall oil system diagram from the D-1 manual, so it also applied to the G-series

This diagram shows the oil reservoir on the side of the engine for the D/G series, but the key also includes all those items missed from the previous diagram's key because this is the quoted 'Figure 14'

Kennzeichen der Einzelteile der Abbildung 15 – Identification of the individual parts in Figure 15
Einzelteile 1 bis 26 siehe vorhergehende Seite bzw. Abbildung 14 – Individual parts 1 to 26 see previous page or Figure 14

27. Rücklaufleitung von Motor zum schmierstoffkühler – Return line from motor to oil cooler
28. Geber für Schmierstoff-Eintrittstemperatur – Oil inlet temperature sender
29. Schmierstoff-Druckmesserleitung – Oil pressure gauge line
30. Schmierstoff-Vorlaufleitung – Oil feed line
31. Kraftstoffleitung für Kaltstart – Fuel line for cold start
32. Rücklaufleitung vom Schmierstoffkühler zum Schmierstoff-Hauptbehälter – Return line from the oil cooler to the main oil reservoir
33. Schmierstoffleitung vom Schmierstoff-Zusatzbehälter auf dem Motor zum Schmierstoff-Entnahmebehälter – Oil line from the additional oil reservoir on the engine to the oil removal reservoir
34. Druckluftleitung für Schmierstoff-Zusatzbehälter auf dem Motor – Compressed air line for additional oil container on the engine

35. Druckluftleitung (Ladeluft) vom Motor zur Ventilbatterie – Compressed air line (charge line) from the engine to the valve manifold
36. Entlüftungsleitung vom Motor zum Schmierstoff-Hauptbehälter – Vent line from the engine to the main oil reservoir
37. Schmierstoffleitung vom Schmierstoff-Zusatz-behälter auf der Steuerbrücke zum Schmierstoff-Hauptbehälter – Oil line from the additional oil reservoir to the main oil reservoir
38. Schmierstoff-Fülleitung – Oil filling line
39. Bediengestänge der Ventilbatterie (zum Schmierstoffumpumpen) – Control linkage of the valve manifold (for oil circulation)
40. Ventilbatterir der Umpumpanlage – Valve battery for the circulation system
41. Druckausgleichventil und Druckregler – Pressure compensation valve and pressure regulator
42. Stoßdraht für Ventilbatterir-Betätigung (Schmierstoffumpumpen) – Push wire for valve battery actuation (oil pumps)
43. Schalthebel für Schmierstoff-Neben-behälter auf der Steuerbrücke – Shift lever for oil sub-tanks on the instrument pane;

1. Oberer Befestigungsbock (am Spant 1) – Upper mounting bracket (on Frame 1)
2. Spannband – Tension strap
3. Polsterung – Pad (strap retaining)
4. Anschlußstutzen für Rückleufleitung – Connection piece for return line
5. Schmierstoff-Entnahme-Behälter (Inhalt 35 liter Schmierstoff) – Oil removal container (contents 35 litres of oil)
6. Stutzen für Auffülleitung – Connector for filling line
7. Stutzen für Zilaufleitung – Nizzle for pipeline
8. Stutzen für Peilstab – Connector for dipstick
9. Stutzen für Entlüftungsleitung – Vent pipe connection
10. Schmierstoff-Behälterkopf – Oil reservoir head
11. Elektr. Geber für Vollstandwarnung – Electrical sensor for full warning
12. Unterer Befestigungsbock (am Spant 1) – Lower bracket (on Frame 1)
13. Anschlußstutzen für Vorlaufleitung – Connection piece for flow line
14. Ablaßventil (SUM) – Drain valve (sump)
15. Spannverschluß – Tension lock

Fuel System

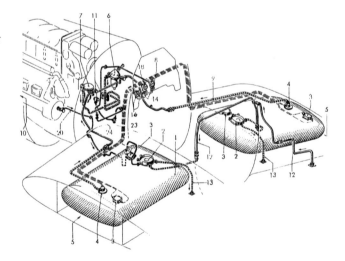

This is the fuel system diagram for the B-series

1. Behälter (je 240 Liter) – Container (240 litres each)
2. Behälterkopf mit Füllanschluß und Atmungsventil – Container head with filling connection and breathing valve
3. Vorratsgeber – Sensor
4. Elektr. Behälterpumpe mit Rückschlablaß – Electric pump with non-return valve
5. FBH-Armatur – FBH valve
6. FB-Armatur – FB valve
7. Doppeldruckmesser – Double pressure meter
8. Entnahmeleitung – Extraction line
9. Kraftstoffentlüfter – Fuel vent
10. Kraftstoff-Doppelförderpumpe – Double fuel feed pump

12. Behälterbelüftung – Tank ventilation
13. Überlaufleitung – Overflow line
14. Merkleuchte für Reststandsanzeige (je Behälter 30 liter) – Indicator light for remaining level indicator (30 litres per container)
16. Schalter für Inhaltsanzeigegät – Contents indicator switch
18. Inhaltsanzeigegerät – Contents display device
20. Entlüfterleitung – vent line
23. T-Stück für Kaltstartanlage – T-piece for cold start system
24. Sicherheitsdrossel – Safety choke

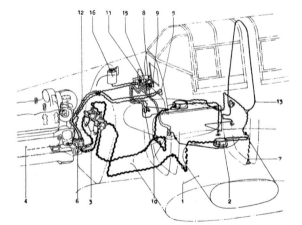

This diagram shows the fuel system of the A-series

1. Kraftstoffbehälter (200l inhalt) – Fuel tank (200lt contents)
2. Tankkopf mit Füllanschluß – Tank head with filling connection
3. FBH-Armatur – FBH valve
4. Motor – Motor
5. Differenzdruckmesser 0-0.5kg/cm2 – Differential pressure meter 0-0.5kg/cm2
6. Doppelkraftstoffpumpe – Dual fuel pump
7. Überlaufleitung am Tankkopf – Overflow line on the tank head
8. Inhaltsanzeige – Content display

9. Doppel-Dreiwegehahn – Double three-way valve
10. Membran-Rückschlagventil – Membrane check valve
11. Luftpumpe – Air pump
12. Laderdruckleitung – Charger pressure line
13. Behälterbelüftung – Reservoir ventilation
14. Einspritzpumpe (Sum) – Injection pump (sump)
16. Einspritzkraftstoffbehälter – Injection fuel tank

Although not the best quality image, this does at least show how the outer panels of the wing rotated through 90° before they could be folded back along the fuselage on the C-series

In this close-up of an image of a Ju 87B from 2./StG 2 forced down over the UK in 1940 you can clearly see the MG fairing on the left and the hole in the leading edge of this port wing, which took air for cockpit ventilation

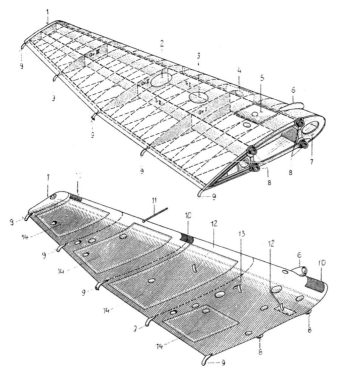

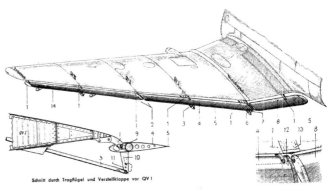

Details of the wing, flaps and ailerons of the D and G series

Schnitt durch Tragflügel und Verstellklappe vor QV1 – Section through wing and adjustment flap in front of QV1
1. Ausleger – Outrigger (mounting bracket)
2. Einstellmarken – Setting marks
3. Stißstange für mittlere Verstellklappe – Actuating rods for the middle flap
4. Mittlere Verstellklappe – Middle flap
5. Trimmklappe – Trim tab
6. Stoßstange für innere Verstellklappe – Actuating rod for inner flap
7. Hebel für innere Verstellklappe – Lever for inner flap

8. Innere Verstellklappe – Inner flap
9. Lagerung der mittleren Verstellklappe – Pivot for middle flap
10. Hebel für mittlere Verstellklappe – Lever for the middle flap
11. Loch für Prüfvorrichtung – Hole for tester
12. Lagerung an der mittleren Verstellklappe – Pivot for the middle flap
13. Spaltverkleidung – Gap (wing joint) cladding
14. Äußere Verstellklappe = Querruder – Outer flap = Aileron

This diagram shows the structure of the outer wing panels for the D (and G) series

1. Endklappe – End cap
2. Deckel für Kraftstoffbehälter-Auffüllkopf – Cover for fuel tank filler head
3. Deckel für Kraftstoffbehälter-Entnahmekopf – Cover for fuel tank head removal
4. Scheinwerfer – Landing light
5. Deckel über starrer Schußwaffe – Cover over the fixed machine-gun
6. MG-Verkleidung – MG fairing
7. Wurzelspant – Root rib
8. Kugelverschraubung – Ball screw connector
9. Ausleger – Outrigger

10. Aufstellversteifung – Reinforcing
11. Staurohr – Pitot tube
12. Auslegung für Sturzflugbremse – Operating strut for dive brake
13. Lagerung für Sturzflugbremse – Retraction (storage) strut for dive brake
14. Klappen für Wartung und Prüfung – Access panel for maintenance and testing
Rechte Tragflügel-Unterseite – Starboard wing, underside
Linke Tragflügel-Oberseite – Port wing, top

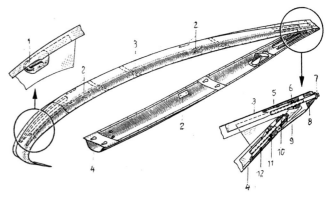

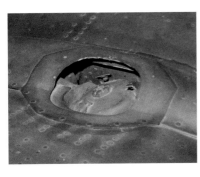

With the wing joint fairing on the D and G series, you get this panel towards the front, which covers the top of the undercarriage strut – it would usually have a cover over it, but it's missing on the RAF Museum's G-2

All variants have a fairing that covers the joint between the inner stub wing and the outer panel, and this diagram for that comes from the D/G series manual

1. Haken – Hook
2. Beilage (Vulkanfiber) – Padding (vulcanised fibre)
3. Oberes Verkleidungsblech – Upper panel
4. Unteres Verkleidungsblech – Lower panel
5. Spannstück – Clamping piece
6. Spannmutter – Lock nut
7. Spannschraube – Tension screw
8. Brücke – Bridge

9. Spannschraube – Tension screw
10. Spannlager-Zwischenstück – Radial insert spacer
11. Spannmutter – Lock nut
12. Spannstück – Clamping piece

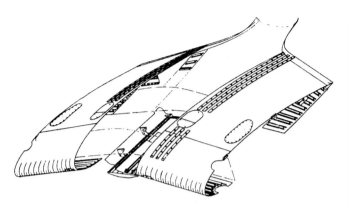

This diagram shows the simplified wing root anti-slip ribs that were introduced with the late production D-3

The landing light is installed in the port leading edge, as seen here on the G-2 at Hendon

The lighting at Hendon does not make photographing their G-2 easy, but in this instance the high contrast does nicely pick out the ribs added at each wing root to act as an anti-slip surface (from one who has worked on this aircraft, I can assure you it does not work unless you have really good grippy soles on your boots, as that wing slopes very sharply at the rear!)

The only real revision to the Stuka's wing was the extended tip seen here and used on all D-5-based derivatives; note the dotted-outline stencil on the leading edge over one of the reinforced panels

Dive Brakes

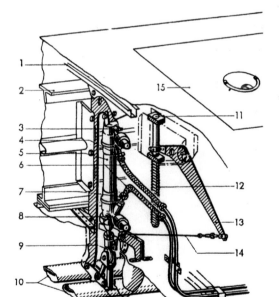

This is the dive brake actuating system diagram and it is the same for the A, B, C and R, plus early D-series

1. Hilfsrippe – Auxiliary rib
2. Träger 1 – Spar 1
3. Entlüftungsschraube, oben – Vent screw, top
4. Anschluß M 16 x 1,5 – Connector M 16 x 1.5
5. Einziehstrebe mit Verriegelung – Retracting strut with lock
6. Drucköllleitung – Hydraulic oil line
7. Anschluß M 14 x 1,5 – Connector M 15 x 1.5

8. Entlüftungsschraube, unten – Vent screw, under
9. verstellbarer Ösenkopf – Adjustable eyelet head
10. Bremsklappe – Dive brake flap
11. Anzeigebolzen – Indicator bolt
12. Feder – Spring
13. Winkelhebel – Angle lever
14. Seilzug – Cable
14. Deckel in Flügel-Oberhaut – Cover in outer skin

This period image shows the dive brakes in the stowed position under the wing of an early B-series

The dive brakes retained on some D-series machines, as seen here on a D-5 with 3./SG3 in 1944, were basically unchanged from those used on the earlier variants (©SA-Kuva)

While this shows the dive brakes in their extended position, again on the wings of an early B-series

Control Surfaces

This close-up of the V4 after modification to the production style wing, shows the 'Junkers wing' with the ailerons and two-section inboard flaps mounted behind and below the trailing edge

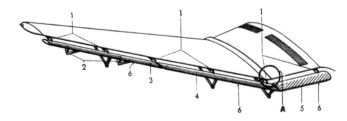

This shows the control surfaces for the A, B and R series wing

1. Ausleger – Outrigger (mounting)
2. Gewichtsausgleich – Mass balance weight
3. Querruder (äußere Verstellklappe) – Aileron (outer flap)
4. mittlere Verstellklappe (Tf) – Middle flap (Tf)
5. innere Verstellklappe (tm) – Inner flap (Tm)
6. Bügelstreifen – Trailing edge strips

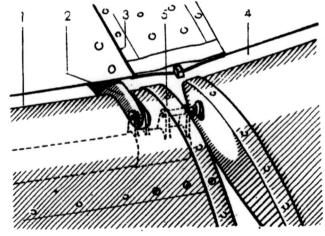

This is a close-up of the area 'A' from the control surfaces diagram of the A, B and R-series

1. mittlere Verstellklappe – Middle flap
2. Ausleger am Flügel – Mounting point on the wing
3. Spaltverkleidung – Gap cladding (wing joint)
4. innere Verstellklappe – Inner flap
5. Lagerung an mittlerer Verstellklappe – Internal spar/linkage in the middle flap

It is difficult to find any good image of the control surfaces on the wing of the B-series, this close-up of the first B-0 (D-IELX) does shows both the ailerons and both inner flap sections with their associated linkage; note how the mass balance weights point upwards at the tips

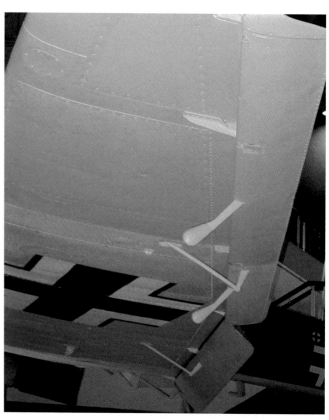

A view along the trailing edge of the port wing on the G-2 at Hendon allowing you to see the linkage and balance weights for the aileron, as well as the two inboard linkage rods for the inner flap sections (©Bryan Ribbans)

This close-up from a D-5 of 1./SG3 in 1944 clearly shows the extended wing tip and aileron, as well as the linkage and mass balance weights for the latter (©SA-Kuva)

This is the linkage to the inner flap section, again seen here on Hendon's G-2

Here is a close-up of one of the mass balance weights (which are set at a flatter angle than those on the A/B/R series) plus the linkage to the aileron on Hendon's G-2

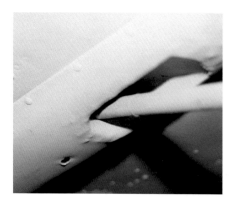

Most of the control linkage rods go into open holes in the wing undersurface, but the one that hits the joining fairing between the inner stub and outer wing panel goes into this little recessed region first

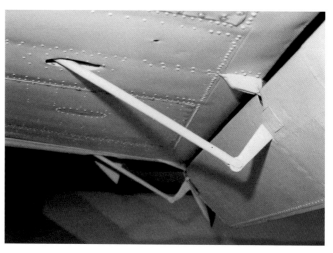

This is the linkage for the middle flap sections on the G-2 at Hendon

Vertical Fin & Rudder

This is the fin and rudder on the V4, you can see the original square profile to the top of the rudder, which is also narrower than production versions would be and the revised lower profile of the rudder and corresponding area of the rear fuselage

This combined image shows the original (A-1) square shape at the top/rear of the rudder on the A-series, with the later production (A-2) machines having the region rounded and the rudder chord increased

An overall view of the port side of the vertical fin, rudder and tailplanes of a B-series airframe currently on display in Belgrade (©George Papadimitriou)

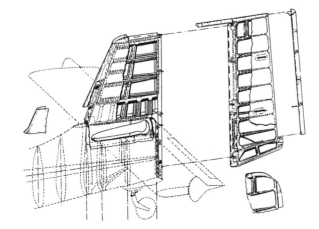

This diagram shows the construction of the A-series fin and rudder, with the scrap-view in the bottom right hand corner depicting the revision to the profile of the top of the rudder in later machines

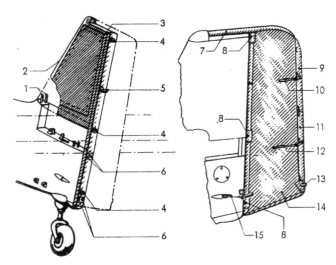

This diagram shows the fin and rudder assembly of the B and R series

1. Stehbolzen am Spant 13 – Bolt on Frame 13
2. Seitenflosse – Vertical fin
3. Deckel – Outer skin
4. Ausleger – Mounting bracket
5. Hebellager für Steuerung – Lever bearing for control
6. Schraubenbolzen am Spant 16 – Screw bolts on Frame 16
7. Gewichtsausgleich – Mass balance weight
8. Ausleger – Mounting point/hinge
9. Trimmklappe – Trim tab
10. Stoßstange für Trimmklappe – Trim tab actuating rod
11. Hilfsruder – Balance tab
12. Stoßstange für Hilfsruder – Balance tab actuating rod
13. Hecklicht – Tail light
14. Seitenruder – Rudder
15. Seilzug für Seitenruder – Operating cable for rudder

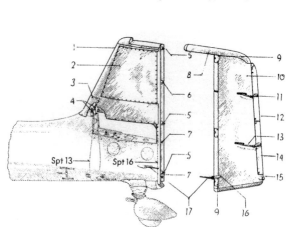

This diagram shows the fin and rudder assembly of the D and G series

1. Seitenflosse – Vertical fin
2. Deckel – Outer skin
3. Verkleidungskappe – Fairing cap
4. Stehbolzen am Spant 13 – Bolt on Frame 13
5. Ausleger – Mounting bracket
6. Hebellager für Steuerung – Lever bearing for control
7. Schraubenbolzen am Spant 16 – Screw bolts on Frame 16
8. Gewichtsausgleich – Mass balance weight
9. Verkleidungsbleche – Cladding sheets
10. Seitenruder – Rudder
11. Stoßstange für Trimm- und Ausgleichruder – Linkage for trim tab
12. Trimm- und Ausgleichruder – Trim and balance tabs
13. Stoßstange für Ausgleichruder – Linkage for balance tab
14. Ausgleichruder – Balance tab
15. Hecklicht – Tail light
16. Riderhebel – Operating lever
17. Seilzug für Seitenruder – Rudder control cable

Tailplanes & Elevators

A shot of the tailplane on the V2, complete with the three support struts, note also the corrugated skin of the rudder

This is another view of the tail on the V2, but this closer shot allows you to see the flange underneath the tailplane associated with the fact that the incidence of the whole unit could be adjusted through a set range

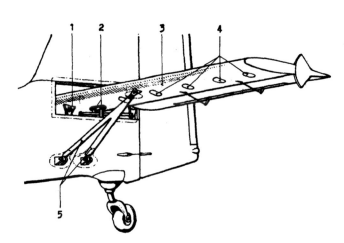

This diagram shows the tailplanes of the A-series

1. Gebellager – Bearing
2. Höhenflossenverstellspindel – Tailplane adjustment screw
3. Hüohenflosse – Tailplane
4. Deckel – Access panel
5. V-Strebe – V-strut

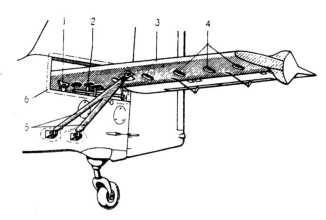

The diagram of the tailplanes for the B-series only differs in a few areas, such as the profile to the tailplane tip and the guide plate at the tailplane/ elevator hinge point

1. Gebellager – Bearing
2. Stoßstange vom Verstellgetriebe – Tailplane incidence adjustment
3. Höhenflosse – Tailplane
4. Deckel für Wartung – Access panel for maintenance
5. V-Strebe – V-strut
6. Flossenverkleidung – Cover for tailplane mounting area (not fitted)

A close-up of the tailplane and elevators of the Ju 87B tail unit displayed in Belgrade, note the maker's plate on the elevator end plate and the linkage underneath for the two trim tabs (©George Papadimitriou)

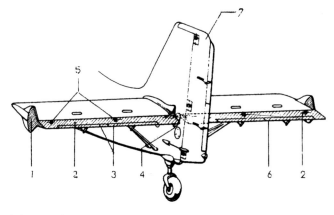

A diagram of the elevators for the B and R series

1. Gewichtsausgleich – Mass balance weight
2. Höhenruder – Elevator
3. Höhenruder-Trimmklappen – Elevator trim tabs
4. Flanschverschraubung – Flange screw connection
5. Ausleger – Mounting/hinge point
6. Hilfsruder – Balance tab (literally 'auxiliary rudder')
7. Seitenruder – Rudder

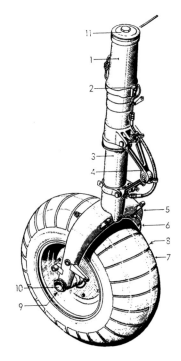

A period image from Junkers showing the main oleo leg and wheel in position attached to the wing stub of a B-series airframe; note the undercarriage covers in the background and the gaiter fitted to the oleo slider, even when it is then protected by the undercarriage covers

Sadly there seems little information about these Ju 87B spats that are decorated with characters from the Popeye cartoon – of interest though are the 'step plates' welded to the top of each, a non-standard modification and the cut-out added to gain access to the valve stem without the need to remove the whole cover (©SA-Kuva)

This diagram shows you the production style oleo leg for the D- and G-series with the 90mm slant forward in the lower yoke

1. KPZ-Außemrohr- KPZ (shock absorber) outer tube
2. Keil – Wedge
3. KPZ-Innenrohr – KPZ (shock absorber) inner tube
4. Lenkerpaar – Compression linkage
5. Radgabel – Wheel fork
6. Bremsölleitung – Brake fluid line
7. Laufrad – Wheel
8. Bremsschild – Brake plate
9. Aufbockfläche – Jacking point
10. Steckachse – Through axle
11. Deckel für Fahrgestellanschluß – Cover for undercarriage attachment

A nice close-up of the diving duck emblem of the undercarriage cover of a Ju 87B operated by 239a Squadriglia, 97° Gruppo, Regia Aeronautica. The stencil ' Nur Kurze Schraube' means 'Short screw only', as that fixing could not have screw-thread exposed inside, because the lower cover telescopes up inside it as the oleo leg is compressed

(©R.J. Caruana)

This modification sheet shows the difference between the B-series undercarriage on the left (used by initial D-1s) and the revised one on the right (to become standard for the D/G series) and comes from the D-1 manual

Betr: Austausch des bisherigen Ju 87D-1 Fahrgestelles nach Änderungsanweisung Ju 87 Nr.2002 gegen das neue mit un 90mm nach hinten verlegter Radusche und der dadurch bedingten Abänderung der unteren hinteren Fg-Verkleidung Linke Fahrgestellhälfte gezeichnet, rechte sinngemäß – Replacement of the previous Ju 87D-1 article according to the Ju 87 Nr.2002 change instruction with the new one moved 90mm to the rear and the resulting change in the lower Fg panelling Neue Ausführung des Fahrgestelles mit um 90mm nach hinten verlegter Radachse – New version of the undercarriage with the wheel axle moved 90mm to the rear Rumpf – BE – Hull – BE (fuselage centreline) Mit Luftschraube – With propeller Deckel für Fg-Anschluß – Cover for the undercarriage connection Lärmgerät 'L' – Siren 'L' (literally 'noise device') Fahrgestellanschluß – Undercarriage connection Bremsölleitung – Brake oil line Obere Fg-Verkleidung – Upper Fg panelling KPZ-Federbein – KPZ shock absorber

Schutzhülle 'Z' – Protective cover 'Z' Steckachse – Through axle Spornlage – Spur position Laufrad (Bremsrad mit Bereifung) – Wheel (brake hub with tyre) Untere vordere Fg-Verkleidung unverändert – Lower front Fg panel unchanged Untere hintere Fg-Verkleidung n.Z. 8-87.251-01 – Lower rear panel trim n.a 8-87.251-01 Bisherige Ausführung des Ju 87D-1 Fahrgestelles nA. Ju 87 Nr 2002 – Previous version of the Ju 87D-1 undercarriage NA. Ju 87 Nr.2002 Rumpf – BE – Hull – BE (fuselage centreline) Mitte Luftschraube – With propeller Fahrgestellhälfte nach Z.8-2682 A-1 – Half of the undercarriage according to Z.8-2682 A-1 Stützzylinder – Support cylinder Träger I – Carrier (spar) I Federweg – Travel Spornlage – Spur position Laufrad – Wheel Untere hintere Fg-Verkleidung n.Z.8-87.227-01 – Lower rear panel trim N/A.8-87.227.01

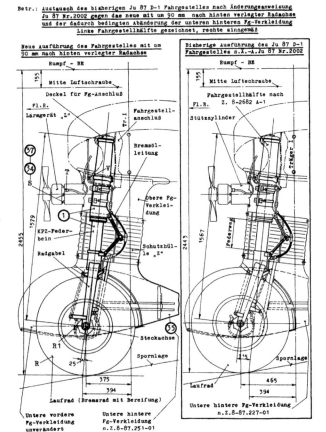

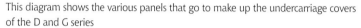

This diagram shows the various panels that go to make up the undercarriage covers of the D and G series

1. Obere Fahrgestellverkleidung (rechte Hälftel) – Upper undercarriage trim (right half)
2. Obere Fahrgestellverkleidung (linke Hälftel) – Upper undercarriage trim (left half)
3. Oberer Spant – Mittlere-Fahrgestellverkeidung – Upper frame – middle undercarriage trim
4. Schutzhülle – Mittlere-Fahrgestellverkeidung – Protective cover – middle undercarriage trim
5. Federspant – Mittlere-Fahrgestellverkeidung – Spring frame – middle undercarriage trim
6. Unterer Spant – Mittlere-Fahrgestellverkeidung – Lower frame – middle undercarriage trim
7. Anschlußstück – Connector
8. Untere vordere Fahrgestellverkleidung – Lower front undercarriage panel
9. Schnellverschluß – Quick release
10. Tragspant – Support frame
11. Untere hintere Fahrgestellverkleidung – Lower rear undercarriage trim

A period shot showing the outer wing panel being fitted to a D-5, which allows you to see the exposed undercarriage leg, its attachment for the wing stub and how the gaiter fits between two support frames attached to the oleo leg itself, not the covers

Whilst the G-2 at Hendon was being dismantled a while back it afforded you a view of the wing root and the oleo leg and its attachment

(©Bryan Ribbans)

On the Eastern Front or any region with snow or mud, the gaiter, its support frames and the lower undercarriage covers were often removed completely, as seen here on a D-3 of 7./ StG 1 in Russia

Here is another view of the oleo leg and wheel on Hendon's G-2, taken in the 1990s, which does allow you to see the frames that hold the gaiter over the slider element of the oleo (the vertical pins ensure the unit remains parallel during operation so that the gaiter does not pop off)

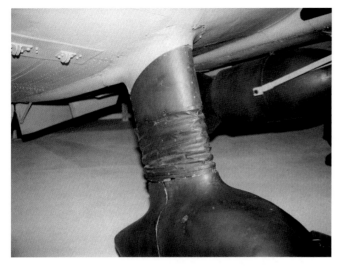

With the gaiter and covers in place the D and G undercarriage looks like this (note that Hendon's G-2 here has at some stage had the gaiters painted the same colour as the upper surfaces, whilst they should be similar in colour to waxed cotton)

With the D-series skis were first tested with the V21, D-INRF, seen here after one leg collapsed on landing

On the outer face of each lower undercarriage cover on the G-2 at Hendon is the stencil ' Reifendruck bis 5t Fluggew. 4 -0,3 atü Refendruck über 5t Fluggew. 4 +0.3 atü fl. Drucköl', which means ' Tyre pressure up to 5t flight weight 4 -0.3 atm Tyre pressure over 5t flight weight 4 +0.3 atm fl. pressure oil'

From the B-series onwards the Stuka main and tail undercarriage could be changed to skis. Here you can see Ju 87B-2/U4 DJ+FU during tests with skis

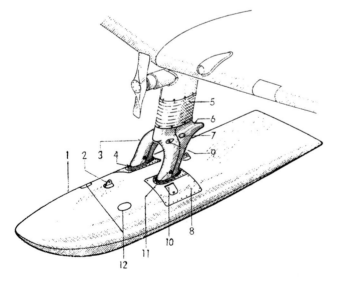

This diagram from the D-1 manual shows the ski for the main undercarriage leg

1. Fahrgestellkufe – Undercarriage skid
2. Transportbeschlag – Transport fitting
3. Untere vordere Verkleidung – Lower front panel
4. Abdichtung – Sealing
5. Mittlere Fahrgestellverkleidung – Middle undercarriage trim
6. Untere hintere Verkleidung – Lower rear panel
7. Deckel vor Befestigungsschrauben – Cover in front of fastening screws
8. Verkleidungsdeckel – Fairing cover
9. Schellverschluß – Quick release
10. Klappdeckel – Hinged cover
11. Bolzen mit Gewindestück – Bolt with threaded piece
12. Handlochdeckel über vorderen Federstrebenanschluß – Hand hold cover over front spring strut connection

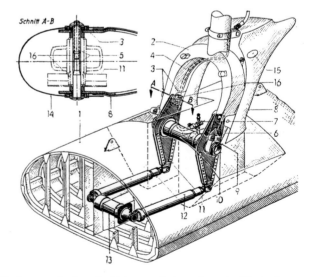

This diagram, also from the D-1 manual, shows the main ski's structure

1. Fahrgestellkufe – Undercarriage skid
2. Radgabel – Wheel fork
3. Befestigungslasche – Fastening tab
4. Bremsölleitung – Brake fluid line
5. Bolzen mit Gewindestück – Bolt with threaded piece
6. Flanschbutchse mit Lagerbüchsen – Flange bush with bearing bushes
7. Verschlußkappe – Fastening bracket
8. Untere hintere Fahrgestellverkleidung – Lower rear undercarriage trim
9. Sechskant-Gewindemutter – Hexagon nut
10. Steckachse – Through axle
11. Hebel – Lever
12. Federstrebe – Spring strut
13. Lager mit Achse für Federstrebenanschluß – Bearing with axle for spring strut connection
14. Untere vordere Fahrgestellverkleidung – Lower front undercarriage panel
15. Deckel vor Befestigungsschraube für hintere Verkleidung – Cover in front of fastening screw for rear panel
16. Bremszapfen mit Stein an beiden Gabelarmen – Brake pin with block on both fork arms
* Note that 8 is rarely seen fitted in period photographs

Tailwheel

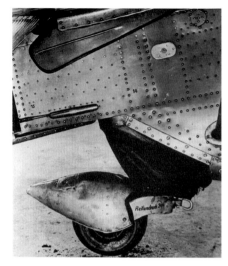

This shows the tailwheel unit on the V2 prototype, D-UHUH, W/Nr.4922 as photographed at Rechlin in January 1936

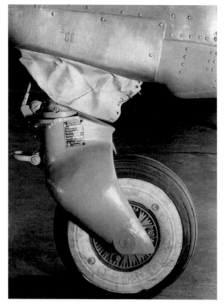

This diagram shows the other style of tail wheel with the heavy cast yoke seen on B and R-series airframes

An overall view from the starboard side of the tailwheel on the G-2 at Hendon – the stencil above states the tyre pressure is 2.6 atü (40psi)

The A-series adopted an exposed tailwheel unit, as seen here on Ju 87A-1 52+C24 of 4./StG 165

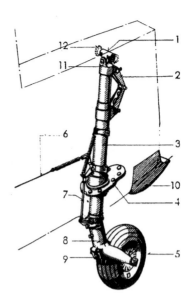

This diagram can be found in both the A and B-series manual

1. Federbeinlagerung – Suspension strut mounting
2. Lenker – Compression linkage
3. Federbein – Shock absorber
4. Rumpflager – Fuselage mounting bracket
5. Spornrad 350x135 – Tail wheel 350x135
6. Seilzug – Cable
7. Feststellvorrichtung – Locking device
8. Spornradgabel – Tail wheel fork
9. Schleppöse – Towing eyelet
10. Notsporn – Tail bumper
11. Büsche – Bushes
12. Büsche mit Bund – Bushes with a flange

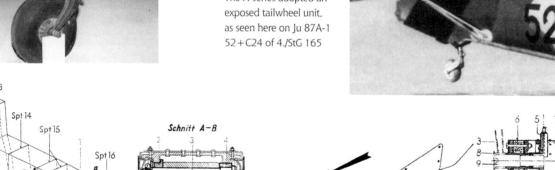

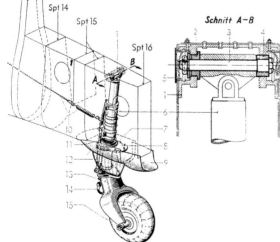

This is the tailwheel adopted for the D and G series

1. Obere Federbeinlagerung – Upper strut mounting
2. Feste Busche – Fixed bushes
3. Lagerbolzen – Bearing pin
4. Lose Buchse – Loose socket
5. Deckel – Cover
6. KPZ-Federbein KPZ shock absorber
7. Untere Federbeinlagerung – Lower strut mounting
8. Lagerplatte – Bearing plate
9. Notsporn – Tail bumper
10. Seilzug mit Feder – Cable with spring
11. Betätigungsstange – Actuating rod
12. Spornsack mit Verkleidungsblechen – Tail wheel strut gaiter
13. Spornradgabel – Tail wheel fork
14. Schleppöse – Towing eyelet
15. Spornrad – Tail wheel

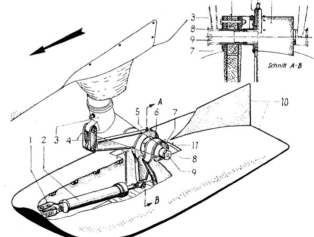

Once again, all versions from the B-series could have skis fitted in place of wheels and this diagram shows the unit fitted in place of the tailwheel

1. Lagerung für Federstrebe – Bracket with spring strut
2. Federstrebe – Spring strut
3. Spornradgabel – Tail wheel fork
4. Lenker – Bracket
5. Lenkerhebel – Bracket lever
6. Lagerbock – Bearing block
7. Lagerbusche – Bush
8. Schraubbuchse – Screw bushing
9. Steckachse – Through axle
10. Spornkufe mit Leitflosse – Ski with guide fin
11. Verkleidung – Fairing

Armament – Fixed

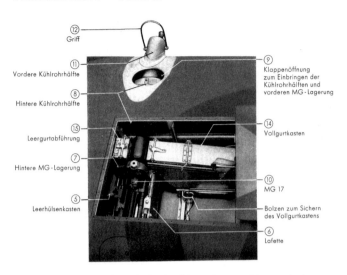

⑫ Griff

⑪ Vordere Kühlrohrhälfte

⑧ Hintere Kühlrohrhälfte

⑮ Leergurtabführung

⑦ Hintere MG-Lagerung

⑤ Leerhülsenkasten

⑨ Klappenöffnung zum Einbringen der Kühlrohrhälften und vorderen MG-Lagerung

⑭ Vollgurtkasten

⑩ MG 17

Bolzen zum Sichern des Vollgurtkastens

⑥ Lafette

This is an overall view, from the back, of the MG 17 machine-gun in the starboard wing of the A-series

5. Leerhülsenkasten – Empty cases
6. Lafette – Gun carriage
7. Hintere MG-Lagerung – Rear MG mounting
8. Hintere Kühlrohrhälfte – Rear cooling pipe half
9. Klappenöffnung zum Einbringen der Kühlrohrhälften und vorderen MG-Lagerung – Flap opening for inserting the cooling tube halves and front MG bearer

10. MG 17 – MG 17
11. Vordere Kühlrohrhälfte – Front cooling pipe half
12. Griff – Handle
14. Vollgurtkasten – Full ammunition belt box
15. Leergurtabführung – Empty ammunition belt discharge
Bolzen zum Sichem des Vollgurtkastens – Bolt to secure the full belt box

This image from the A-series manual shows the empty cartridge belt box in the starboard undercarriage spat, which is accessed from the inner face

Leergurstkasten – Empty cartridge belt box
Rastbolzen – Locking bolt

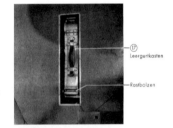

⑰ Leergurtkasten

Rastbolzen

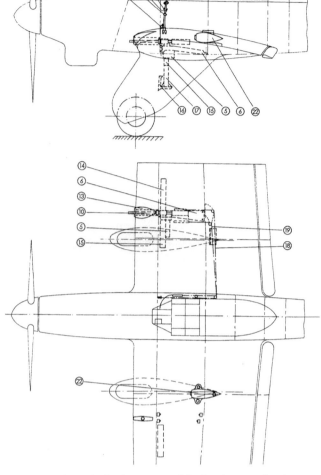

⑱ ③ ⑲ ⑳ ①

⑯ ⑰ ⑮ ⑤ ⑥ ㉒

⑭ ⑥ ⑬ ⑩ ⑤ ⑮ ⑲ ⑱

㉒

This diagram shows the fixed armament of the A-series, as well as the installation of a gun camera

Führerraum – Pilot's Cockpit
1. Reflexvisier C/12A – Gunsight Revi C/12A
2. Seilrollen für Betätigung des MG 17 – Wire pulley for operating MG 17
3. Betätigung des ESK 2000/a – Operation of the ESK 2000/a (gun camera)
Tragwerkmittelstück und rechter Flügel – Structural centrepiece (fuselage) and starboard wing
4. Seilrollen *f*ur Betätigung des MG 17 – Wire pulley for actuating MG 17
5. Leerhülsenkasten – Empty case
6. Lafette – Gun carriage
7. Hintere MG-Lagerung – Rear MG bearer
8. Beide Kühlrohrhälten – Both cooling tube halves
9. Vordere MG-Lagerung – Front MG bearer
10. MG 17 – MG 17
11. Vordere Kühlrohrhälften – Front cooling pipe halves

12. Handgriff – Handle
13. Verkleidung über Külrohrhälften – Fairing over the cooling tube halves
14. Vollgurtkasten – Full (ammunition) belt box
15. Leergurtabführung – Empty (ammunition) belt discharge
16. Lagerung für Leergurtkasten – Storage for empty (ammunition) belt box
17. Leergurtkasten – Empty (ammunition) belt box
Betätigung für MG 17 – Actuation for MG 17
18. Durchladevorrichtung – Loading device
19. Sicherung – Fuse
20. Abzug – Trigger
21. Verkleidungen – Fairings
Linker Flügel – Left wing
22. ESK 2000/a – ESK 2000/a gun camera

This photo from the A-series manual shows the access panel under the starboard wing, outboard of the undercarriage (note dive brake to right) that allowed all the spent cartridges collected in a box in the wing to be removed

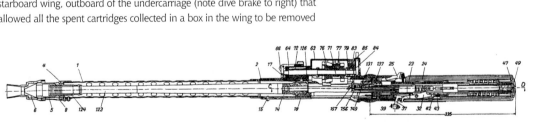

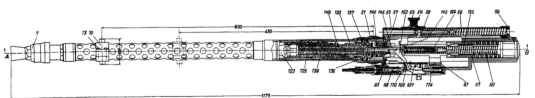

Up to the D-5 the fixed armament of the Stuka was one (A-series) or two (B, R, C and early D) MG 17s

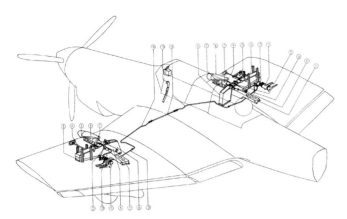

This diagram from the B-series manual shows the MG 17 in the port wing with the fairing removed

7. Kühlrohr (hintere Hälfte) – Cooling pipe (rear half)
7. Kühlrohr (vordere Hälfte) Cooling pipe (front half)
8. Verkleidung mit Gummipuffer – Fairing with rubber buffer

MG 17 – MG 17 machine-gun
Griff – Handle
Klappe für MG-Wartung – MG maintenance flap
Kupplung (P 23/24) – Clutch (P 23/24)
Kupplung (P 18/19) – Clutch P18/19)

This diagram shows the fixed armament of the B-series, so also applies to the R-series

Tragflügel (Linker & Rechter) – Wing (Left & Right)
1. Lafette mit Leerhülsenkasten – Carriage with empty (ammunition) case box
2. Vordere Lagerung – Front (MG) mounting
3. Hintere Lagerung – Rear (MG) mounting
4. Machinengewehr MG 17 – MG 17 machine-gun
5. Vollgurtkasten – Full (ammunition) belt box
6. Leergurtkasten – Empty (ammunition) belt box
7. Kühlrohr – Cooling pipe
8. Verkleidung – Fairing
9. Ziellinienprüferlagerung – Alignment tester storage
Rumpf – Fuselage
10. Knüppelgriff KG 12A – Control Column KG 12A
Preßluftanlage (Linker Tragflügel) – Compressed air system (Left wing)
11 Preßluftflasche mit Druckminderer DHAG

2 – Compressed air bottle with pressure regulator DHAG 2
12. Zentraufülleitung im linken Tragflügel – Charging (compressed air) line in the left wing
13. Epad-Schlauch – Epad tubing
Preßluftanlage (Rechter Tragflügel) – Compressed air system (Right wing)
14. Preßluftflasche mit DHAG 2 – Compressed air bottle with DHAG 2
15. Außenbordanschluß SUM 668 FC – SUM 668 FC outboard connector
16. Zentralfülleitung im rechten Tragflügel – Charging (compressed air) line in the right wing
17. Epad-Schlauch – Epad tubing
Rump – Fuselage
18. Zentralfülleitung im Rumpf und Stumpfe – Central filling line in the fuselage and wing stubs

This is the wing gun of the B-series, viewed from the side

Flugrichtung – Flight direction
1. Lafette mit Leerhülsenkasten – Mounting with spent cartridge case storage
3. Hintere Lagerung – Rear bearer
4. MG 17 – MG 17 machine-gun
5. Vollgurtkasten – Full (ammunition) belt box

6. Leergurtkasten – Empty (ammunition) belt box
Hebelbolzen – Lever bolt

For alignment of the fixed guns on the B (and R) series, this special tool was used combined with special equipment in the cockpit

Abdeckblech – Cover plate
Ziellinienprüfer – Gun alignment tester

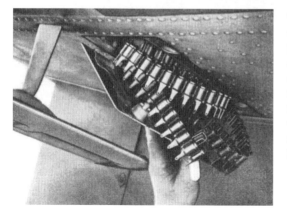

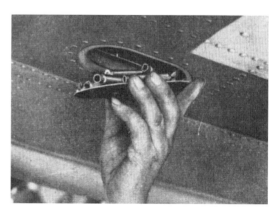

With the B (and R) series the spent ammunition belts were collected in a box in the wing and emptied by opening this access panel on the underside of the wing, outboard of the undercarriage (note dive brake to left)

The spent cartridge cases were also collected in the wing, and emptied out by opening this smaller access panel under the wing, further outboard of the spent belt one

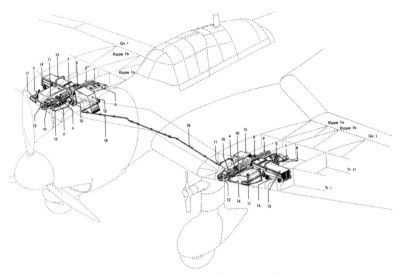

This diagram shows the fixed armament system of the D-1 to D-3 series

1. Preßluftflasche – Compressed air bottle
2. Preßluft-Außenbordanschluß PLA 6 – Compressed air bottle outboard connection PLA 6
3. Lafette – Gun carriage
4. Vordere MG-Lagerung – Front MG mount
5. Hintere MG-Lagerung – Rear MG mount
6. Lagerbock für vordere MG-Lagerung – Bearing block, MG front mount
7. Hülsenableitung – Sleeve (chute spent cartridges)
8. Flaschenlagerung – Bottle storage
9. MG 17 – MG 17 machine-gun
10. Kühlrohr – Cooling pipe

11. Verkleidung – Fairing
12. Kappe mit Pappscheibe – Cap with cardboard disc
13. Vollgurtkasten – Full (ammunition) belt box
14. Lagerung für Vollgurtkasten – Mount for full (ammunition) belt box
15. Leergurtgliederkasten – Empty (ammunition) belt link box
16. Hülsenfangbeutel – Bag catcher (spent cartridges)
17. Ziellinienprüferrohr – Gun alignment tester tube
18. Zentralfüllleitung – Central charging (compressed air) line

Here an armourer loads a belt of ammunition into the MG 17 of a D-3, note the extended fairing for the barrel in the wing leading edge that differed from that used by the A to D-1

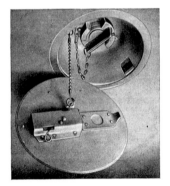

This is a close-up of the compressed air charger point for the MG 17s listed as ' Compressed air bottle outboard connection PLA 6' in the previous diagram

This nice shot of a late series D-5 operated by 3./SG3 at Immola in July 1944 being refuelled clearly shows the MG 151/20 barrels projecting from the wing, the canvas sleeve at the base (torn in this instance) and the rubber cap put over the barrel tip to stop dust etc. going down it whilst it taxies etc. (©SA-Kuva)

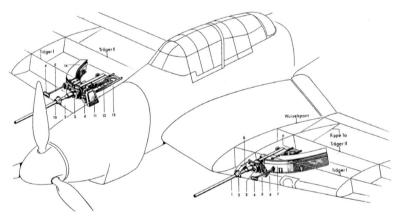

With the D-5 the fixed armament in the wing was upgraded to the 20mm MG 151, as seen in this installation diagram from the manual

1. MG 151/20 links – MG 151/20 left
2. Abdichtung – Canvas sleeve (seal)
3. Vordere lagerung der StL 151/9 – Front mounting StL 151/9
4. Klappe – Flap
5. Aufnahme-Rohr für Ziellinienprüfer – Pick-up for the gun alignment tester
6. Hülsenableiter – Sleeve (spent cartridge) guide
7. Gurtkasten links – (Ammunition) Belt box on the left
8. Gurtgliederabführung linkgs – Empty (ammunition) chute, left

9. Lagerung links – Left mounting
10. MG 151/20 rechts – MG 151/20 right
11. Gurtgliederabführung rechts – Belt links discharge on the right
12. Hineter Lagerung des StL 151/9 – Rear mounting StL 151/9
13. Lagerung rechts – Right mounting
14. Gurtkasten rechts – (Ammunition) belt box on the right

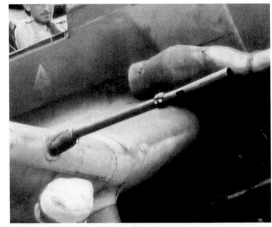

When used for night harassment operations, the barrels of the MG 151/20 were often fitted with flash eliminators, as seen on the D-5N of NSGr 9 in Italy in 1944

Armament – Rear Cockpit

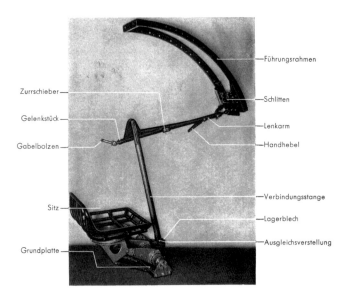

This image shows the seat and gun slot for the A-series

Grundplate – Base plate
Sitz – Seat
Gabelbolzen – Clevis bolt
Gelekstück – Joint piece
Zurrschieber – Stowage slide
Führungsrahem – Guide frame
Schlitten – Carriage (gun)

Lenkarm – Control arm
Handhebel – Hand lever
Verbindindungsstange – Connecting rod
Lagerblech – Bearing plate
Ausgleichsverstellung – Compensation adjustment

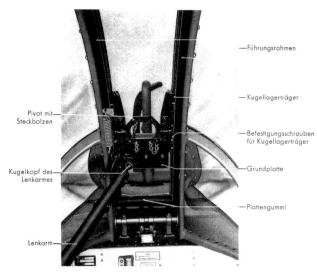

Führungsrahmen und Schlitten
(gegen Flugrichtung gesehen)

This is the actual gun mount and guide rail system in the A-series

Führungsrahmen und Schlitten (gegen Flugrichtung gesehen) – Guide frame and slide (seen against the direction of flight)
Lenkarm – Control arm
Kugelkopf des Lenkarmes – Ball head of the control arm
Pivot mit Steckbolzen – Pivot with pin

Führungsrahem – Guide frame
Kugellagerträger – Ball bearing support
Befestigungsschrauben für Kugellagerträger – Fixing screws for the ball bearing supports
Grundplatte – Base plate
Plattengummi – Plate rubber

Often quoted as showing the rear gun position in the A-series, this is most likely a mock-up in an early prototype, as the canopy frames and flat nature of much of the glazing do not match that of production A-series machines; the overall layout is still correct though, including the ammunition storage and spent ammo drum bag (the spent cartridges in this instance were held in the canvas bag just visible under the gun itself, while production machines had a concertina-type bag/tube)

Once again this is a poor quality image, this time from the manual, but it does show the fitment of the gun, the actual concertina-type bag/tube for spent cartridge cases below the MG 15, the 'floating' sight in place of a traditional bead sight at the front of the barrel and, as a bonus, the central insulation mount for the aerial leads

Once again not a great image, but this does clarify the shape of the concertina-style bag/tub attached to the bottom of the MG 15 to collect spent cartridges, while the 'waste bin' unit seen on the port sidewall is just for empty ammunition drums (so they aren't loose, rolling about on the floor)

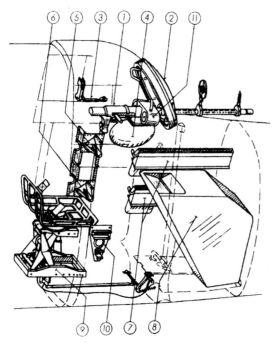

Here you can see how the saddle-type ammunition drums were stored on the starboard sidewall in the B (and R) series

Trommelträger unten – Ammunition drum carrier, bottom
Trommelschienen – Ammunition drum rails
Trommelträger oben – Ammunition drum carrier, top
Doppeltrommel – Double ammunition drum
MG 15 – MG 15 machine-gun
Hülsensack n.A. – Spent cartridge bag n.A.
Zurrbügel – Stowage bracket

Doppeltrommeln – Double ammunition drum
Schnellverschluß des Leertrommelsackes – Quick release of the empty ammunition drum bag
Leertrommelsack – Empty ammunition drum bag

This diagram shows the rear gun installation for the B-series

1. Machinengewehr MG 15 – MG 15 machine-gun
2. Kleine-Linsen-Lafete LLK – Small lens (gun) mount LLK
3. Zurrbügel – Stowage bracket
4. Hülsensack n.A – Spent cartridge bag n.A.
5. Trommelträger oben – Ammunition drum carrier, top
6. Trommelträger unten – Ammunition drum carrier, bottom
7. Trommelschienen – Ammunition drum rails
8. Leertrommelsack – Empty ammunition drum bag
9. Schützensitz – Gunner's seat
10. Bordtasche – Board plate
11. Doppeltrommeln – Double ammunition drum

A nice external view of the B and R-series rear gun position taken from the manual. Note the vertical flange in the upper canopy frame

MG-Lagerkugel – Machine-gun mounting ball
MG 15 – MG 15 machine-gun
Visierteile – Gun sights

Schienbedach über dem Schützen – Canopy frames over the gunner
Flugrichtung – Flight direction

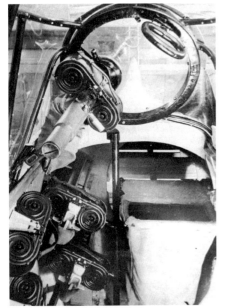

A period image showing the MG 15, mounting ring, ammunition drum and spent drum storage for the B and R series; the gun is locked in the stowed position to the starboard side and you can see the concertina-style spent cartridge bag slightly squashed under the gun itself

This is the port side of the gunner's position

Fußhebel für Schützensitzverstellung – Foot pedal for gunner's seat adjustment
Leertrommelsack – Empty ammunition drum bag

Schnellverschluß für Leertrommelack – Quick release for empty ammunition drum bag
Bordtasche – Board plate
Schützensitz – Gunner's seat

In this image from the B-series manual you can see the small bag used for spent cartridges seen on many B and R series machines in place of the concertina-style bag/tube

Hülsensack n.A. – Spent cartridge bag
Zurrbügel – Stowage bracket
MG 15 – MG 15 machine-gun
Doppeltrommel – Double ammunition drum
Einbauring am Schiededach über dem Schützen – Installation ring in the rear canopy

above the gun
Kleine-Linsen-Lafette LLK – Small lens mount (machine-gun) LLK
Markierung für Zurrstellung des Lafette – Alignment mark on mount when stowing the gun

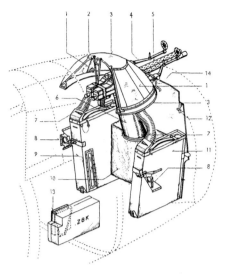

Some later B and R-series machines adopted the armoured style of gun mount lens, as used by the Ju 88 and seen here in the Ju 88R of the RAF Museum

This is the MG 81Z rear gun installation of the D and G series

1. Panzerschild – Armoured shield
2. Zurrung – Gun stowage arm
3. Gleitschienenlafette – Slide rail mount
4. Visierarm – Ring and bead sight arm
5. MG 81Z – MG 81Z twin machine-gun
6. Hülsenschlauch – Sleeve spent cartridges
7. Gurtführungsschalauch 81 – Ammunition belt guide
8. Gurtkastenlagerung – Ammunition belt storage box
9. Gurtkasten rechts – Ammunition belt box, right
10. Hülsen- und Leergurtsack – Sleeve and empty belt sack
11. Gurtkasten links – Ammunition belt box, left
12. Visierhalterung – Armour plate mount
13. Bordtasche – Board bag
14. Schußabweiser – Armour plate

The next series of images taken in 1998, show the MG 81Z mount from the G-2 at Hendon when found in the Reserve Collection and prior to it being reinstalled in the aircraft

Detail of the mount for the MG 81Z itself, plus the ring and bead sights; note the profile on the upper decking region that stopped the guns being able to hit any region of the tail

Overall shot of the cupola as a whole from the top starboard side

Looking down onto the MG 81Z mount with the roller that runs along the profile on the decking to ensure the guns cannot be lowered enough when fired to hit any part of the tail

A view inside the MG 81Z cupola showing the mounting gears around the bottom and the handle on the starboard side that locks the gun in position

With the cupola on its back edge you can see the stowage bracket in the middle and the wire emergency release chord around the rear frame

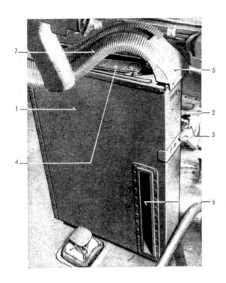

This image from the D-series manual shows the ammunition box on the port side of the rear fuselage

1. Gurtkasten – Ammunition belt box
2. Gustkasten-Lagerung – Ammunition belt box mounting bracket
3. Klinkenhebel – Latch lever
4. Deckel – Lid
5. Zuführhals – Ammunition feed neck
6. Schauglas – Contents sight glass
7. Gurtführungsschalauch 81 – Ammunition belt guide

This image from the D-series manual shows the MG 81Z mounting
1. Gleitschienenlafette – Slide rail mount
2. MG 81Z – MG 81Z twin machine-gun
3. Gurtführungsschlauch 81 – Belt guide hose
4. Hülsenableiter 81Z – Sleeve arrester 81Z
5. Leergurtführung – Empty belt guide
6. MG-Lagerung – MG stowage
7. Hülsenschlauch – Sleeve hose

A period view looking directly back at the MG 81Z installation, the lack of the gun profile and wheel under the gun mount, probably means this shows the installation in one of the early D-series prototypes

A period image from the port side of the MG 81Z installation in a D with the late VE42 style ring and bead sights installed

An unusual field modification, showing a D with a hand-operated machine-gun added to each side of the mid-canopy section, with each looking to have an armoured plate on the inside mounted above the gun's breech

Armament – BK 3.7cm

A close-up of the BK 3.7 cannon under the wing of a Ju 87G-1 used by 10.(Pz)/SG3; note the retention of the brackets for the dive brakes under the wing, denoting this is an early test machine

A view from the front of the BK cannon under the wing of a G-2 captured at Pilzen in 1945 – the front fairing has been removed exposing the cannon itself inside *(©USAAF)*

A view from the right side of the BK cannon under the wing of a G-series

The BK cannon had two of these six-round Wolfram-core 37mm shell clips loaded via the starboard side chute

Patronenrahmen

This image from the G-2 manual shows the cartridge frame in the side of the gondola

Close-up view from the right front of a BK cannon under the port wing of a Stuka; the hole in the front of the upper fairing is a fresh air intake

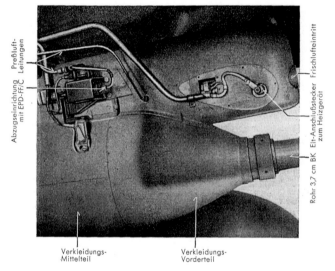

Preßluft-Leitungen

Abzugseinrichtung mit EPD-FF/C

Verkleidungs-Mittelteil

Verkleidungs-Vorderteil

Rohr 3,7 cm BK   Elt-Anschlußstecker zum Heizgerät   Frischlufteintritt

Not a great image, but this close-up from the manual shows you what all the pipework etc. is about on the starboard side of the cannon gondola

Verkleidungs-Mittelteil – Fairing, middle
Verkleidungs-Vorderteil – Fairing, front
Abzugsein richtung mit EPD-FF/C – Trigger device with EPD-FF/C
Preßluft-Leitungen – Compressed air lines

Rohr 3,7cm BK – Barrel 3.7cm BK
Elt-Anschlußstecker zum Heizgerät – Electrical connector to the heater
Frischlufteintritt – Fresh air intake

Looking up under the starboard wing of the G-2 at Hendon you can see the front and rear pick-up brackets to take the mounting for the cannon gondola; sadly, the Museum does not have the cannon to fit out this machine

Ordnance

This diagram shows the centreline rack and trapeze for the A-series, with both 250kg and 500kg bombs illustrated

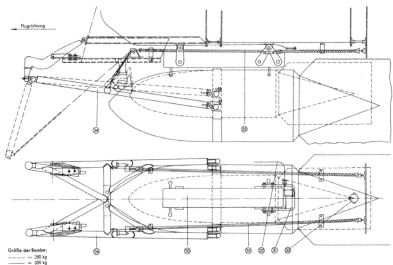

Here the lugs on the strap around the bomb are engaged with the hooks in the end of each arm of the trapeze under an A-series

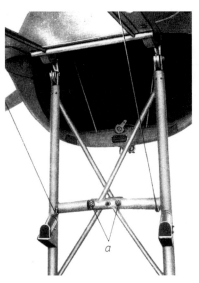

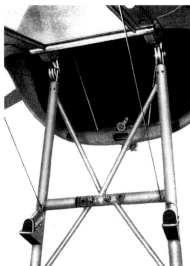

This is the trapeze set up for the A-series to take a 250kg bomb

This is the trapeze set up for the A-series to take a 500kg bomb

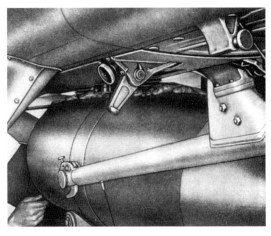

Next the ETC rack is connected and the sway braces on either side adjusted to keep the bomb stable

This is the ETC 500 IX ejector rack fitted under the fuselage of the Ju 87A with the surround cover removed

Rückfeder für Bowdenzug- Spring for Bowden cable
Befestigungsschelle – Mounting clamp
Führungsrohre – Guide tubes
Zünderleitung – Detonator wire

Auslöse- bzw. Rückmeldeleitung – Tripping or feedback line
Abzweigdose – Junction box

Once in place, the locking pin is pushed in on either side of the bomb

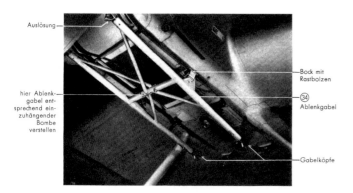

This is an overall view of the trapeze under the A-series

Auslösung – Release
hier Ablenkgabel entsprechend einzuhägender Bombe verstellen – Adjust the trapeze (literally 'deflecting fork') here according to the bomb to be lifted

Bock mit Rastbolzen – Block with locking pin
Ablenkgabel – Trapeze
Gabelköpfe – Clevises

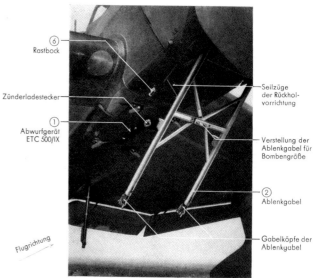

This is the rack and trapeze under the B series

Flugrichtung – Flight direction
Abwurfgerät ETC 500/IX – Ejector device ETC 500/IX
Zünderladestecker – Ignition charging plug
Rastbock – Trapeze rest/latch
Gabelköpfe der Ablenkgabel – Clevis on the trapeze

Ablenkgabel – Trapeze (literally 'deflection fork')
Verstellung der Ablenkgabel für Bombengröße – Adjustment of the trapeze for bomb size
Seilzüge der Rückholvorrichtung – Retractable cables

Overall view of the centreline of an A-series (note u/c support struts on either side, so not a B-series as many claim), in which you can see the trapeze, ETC rack, sway braces and the sighting window

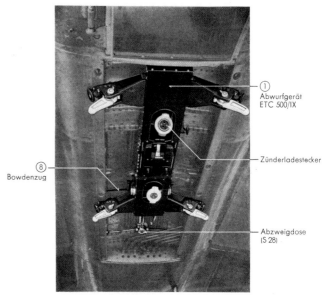

This is a view of the ETC 500/IX rack with the cover plate removed under the B-series, looking aft

Bowdenzug – Bowden cable
Abzweigdose (S28) – Junction box (S28)
Zünderladestecker – Igniter charger plug

Abwurfgerät ETC 500/IX – Ejector device ETC 500/IX

A 500kg bomb being loaded underneath the B-series

Schildzapfen – Guide plate pin
Fügrungszapfenband – Guide pin band
Geräteschloß – Locking device
Gabelköpfe der Ablenkgabel geöffnet – Open heads of the trapeze
Bomben-beladewagen (LWC) – Bomb loading trolley (LWC)

500kg Bombe – 500kg bomb
Flugrichtung – Flight direction
Ablenkgabel in den Rastböcken eingerastet – Trapeze with latching blocks locked in place

A close-up of the bomb attachment under the B-series

Gabelköpfe der Ablenkgabel – Clevis on the trapeze
Führungszapfenband – Guide pin band
Geräteschloß – Locking device
Zünderladestecker – Igniter charging plug

Flugrichtung – Flight direction
500kg bomb – 500kg bomb
Ablenkgabel – Trapeze
Abwurfgerät ETC 500/IX – Ejector device ETC 500/IX

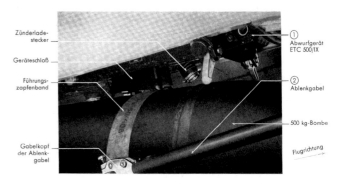

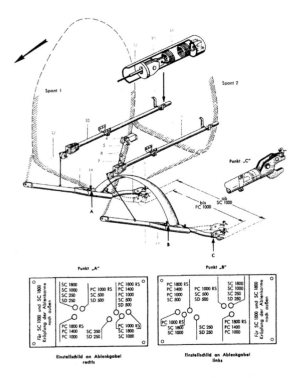

The D series adopted this style of bomb trapeze

1. Ablenkgabel – Trapeze
2. Ablenkarm – Trapeze arm
3. Gabelkopf – Vlevis
4. Halterung – Bracket
5. Riegel – Latch
6. Querträger der Ablenkgabel – Cross member of the trapeze
7. Ring – Ring
8. Zugdraht für Entriegelung – Pull wire for unlocking
9. Rohr links – Pipe, left

10. Rohr rechts, Pipe, right
11. Zugfeder – Tnesion spring
12. Seilzug – Cable
13. Einstellschild links – Setting sign, left
14. Einstellschild rechts – Setting sign, right
15. Auslösung für Gabelkopf – Release for fork head
Einstellschild an Ablenkgabel rechts – Adjustment placard on the trapeze, right
Einstellschild an Ablenkgabel links – Adjustment placard on the trapeze, left

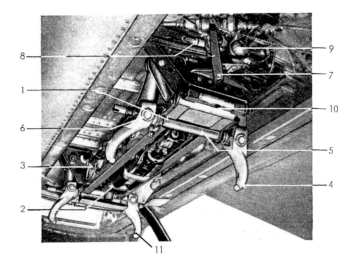

This is what the 1000/500 IXB bomb rack of the D-series looks like with the covers off, looking forward

1. Lastenträger – Load carrier
2. Schloßlafette – Lock carriage
3. Steckbolzen – Plug pin
4. Hintere Pratze – Rear claw
5. Pratzenlagerung für kleine Bombe – Bracket for small bombs
6. Fallenbolzen – Drop bolts
7. Notzung-Anschluß – Emergency connector
8. Anschluß für Zünderanlage – Connection

for igniter system
9. Anschluß für Auslöseanlage – Connection for release system
10. Pratzenlagerung für große Bombe – Big bomb claw storage
11. Vordere Pratze – Front claw

Not a particularly clear image, but this shot from the D-5 manual shows the centreline rack with the cover plate in place.

1. linke Verkleidung – Left panel
2. Lastenträger – Load carrier
3. rechte Verkleidung – Right panel

4. Schnellverschluß – Quick release
5. hintere Verkleidung – Rear panel

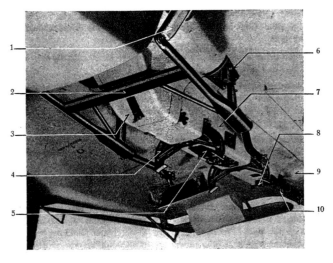

This photo from the D-5 manual shows the LT Rüstsatz (upgrade) set for the carriage of a torpedo, fitted to the underside of the fuselage

1. Ausleger – Outrigger
2. Ablenkgabel – Trapeze
3. Verkleidung vom – Front panel
4. Abstützung – Support
5. PVC 1006B – PVC 1006B (rack)
6. Verrieglungsbock – Locking stand

7. Verkleidung mitte – Centre panel
8. Tiefenruder-Einstellung – Rudder setting
9. Verkleidung hinten – Rear panel
10. Winkelschuß-Einstellung – Release angle setting

Nice overall view of a 500kg bomb being loaded under a D-5 of 1./SG3 at Immola on the 28th June 1944; the revised shape of the trapeze is quite clear (©SA-Kuva)

This diagram from the D-1 manual shows all the free-fall weapons combinations that the type could carry and this also applies to the D-3

Bemerkung: Die hintem Pratzen (17) am Lasterträger für Schloßlafette 1000/500/XIB werden bie Beladung der ETC 50/VIII dTp in der Rüstkiste aufbewahrt. Bei Abbau der Traggerüste für ETC 50/VIII dTp sind diese ebenfalls in der Rüstkiste an Stelle der entnommenen Traggerüste für Kraftstoffbehälter unterzubringen – Note: The rear claws (17) on the fuselage mount for the carrier ETC 1000/500/XIB are stored in the set-up box when the ETC 50/VIII dTp is loaded. When dismantling the support frames for the ETC 50/VIII dTp, these must also be accommodated in the set-up box instead of removed support frames for the fuel tanks

Abwurfwaffen am Tm – Freefall weapons at 'A'
1. Tragkörper – Carrier
2. Pratzen vom – Front claws
3. Steckbolzen – Plug pin
4. Schloßlafette 1000/5000/XIB – Lock mounting 1000/500/XIB
5. Pratzen hinten – Rear claws
6. Notzug-Anschluß – Emergency release connection
7. Schloß 500/XII – Carrier 500/XIII
8. Schloß 2000/XIII – Carrier 2000/XIII
Abwurfwaffen am Tf – Freefall weapons at 'B'
9. Pratzen vom – Front claws
10. Rohrrahmen innen – Interior frame
11. Lastenträger – Load carrier
12. Rohrrahmen außen – Tubular frame, outside
13. Traggerüst – Supporting structure
14. ETC 50/VIII dTp innen – ETC 50/VIII dTp, outside
15. Schloßlafette 1000/500/XIB im Lastenträger – Lock mounting 1000/500/XIB on the load carrier (beam)
16. ETC 50/VIII dTp außen – ETC 50/VIII dTp, outside
17. Pratzen hinten – Rear claws
18. Verkleidung – Fairing
19. Schloß 500/XII – Carrier 500/XII
250kg-Bombe Einsatz des Schloß 500/XIIC Schloßlafette Einsatz der 1000/500/XIB – 250kg bomb use the 500/XIIC carrier or the 1000/500/XIB
50kg Bombe bie Einsatz der ETC 50/VIII dTp – 50kg bombs when using the ETC 50/VIII dTp
8 = Schloß 2000/XIII für SC1000 bis SC 1800 Bombe – Carrier 2000/XIII for SC1000 to SC1800 bomb
7 = Schloß 500/XIIC für 250-bis 500kg Bombe – Carrier 500/XIIC for 250 and 500kg bombs

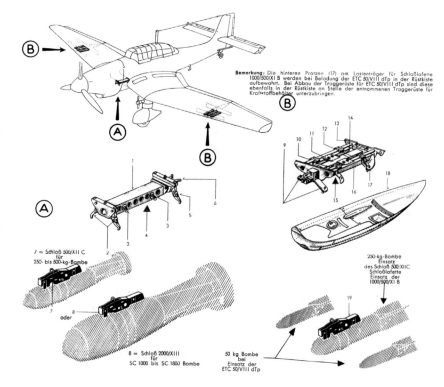

This diagram comes from the D-1 manual and shows all the free-fall weapons combinations that the type could carry

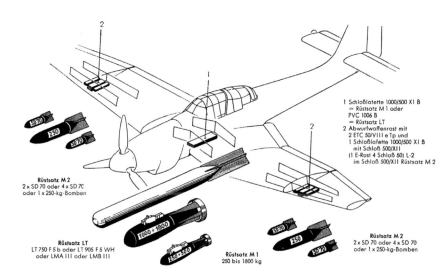

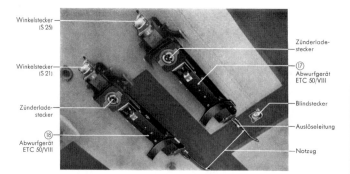

This image from the B-series manual shows the ETC 50 VIII rack under the starboard wing from below, looking aft

Abwurfgerät ETC 50/VIII – Ejector device (bomb rack) ETC 50/VIII
Zünderladestecker – Igniter charging plug
Winkelstecker (S21) – Angled plug (S21)
Winkelstecker (S25) – Angled plug (S25)
Notzug – Emergency release

Auslöseleitung – (Bomb) Release line
Blindstecker – Dummy plug
Abwurfgerät ETC 50/VIII – Ejector device (bomb rack) ETC 50/VIII

Here are two SC50 bombs on the ETC racks under the wing of a B-series airframe, note the 'Jericho Trumpet' whistles fitted in between the bomb fins

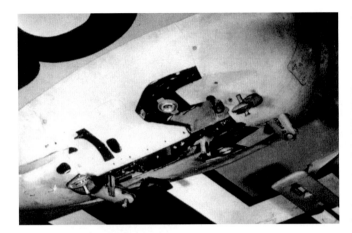

The D series adopted this multi-function bomb rack under each outer wing panel, which could carry 2x 50kg (or 70kg) bombs or a single 250kg bomb

Armourers load a bomb onto the centre carrier element of the multi-function rack under the wing of a D-5 operated by SG3 from Immola in 1944 (©SA-Kuva)

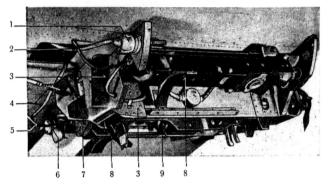

The multi-function bomb rack was installed on most D-series machines, but it was still a Rüstsatz (conversion set), this image from the manual shows the carrier without the outer cover fitted

1. Anschlußstecker für Bomben-Auslöseanlage – Connector for bomb release system
2. Bowdenzug f.r. ETC50 – Bowden cable outer ETC 50
3. Traggerüst – Support structure
4. Stoßstange – Bumper
5. Bowdenrust f.lk. ETC 50 – Bowden cable inner ETC 50
6. Anschlußstecker für Bomben Zünderanlage – Connector for bomb detonator system
7. Notzug-Anschluß – Emergency release connection
8. ETC 50/VIIIeTp – ETC 50/VIII eTp (bomb rack)
9. Schloßlafette 1000/5000/XIB – Carrier 1000/500/XIB

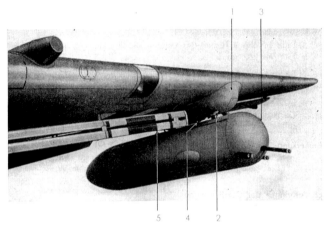

The outer racks could also take a WB81 weapons case, the first version being the 'A', which had the three MG 81Zs angled down at 15° as seen here

1. Bombenträger – Bomb rack
2. Abstützung – Support
3. Zusatz-Waffenbehälter – Additional weapon case
4. Aufhänge-Öse – Suspension eyelet
5. Anschlußkabel – Connection cable

As this Ju 87D-5 (6G+IM) from 4./SG1 backs away from the camera it affords a view of the underside with three SC250 bombs, one on each rack and all of them fitted with Dinort fuse extenders

A view into the interior of a WB81A container, showing the hinged access panel on the side and, on the upper back, the electrical connection socket on the outside

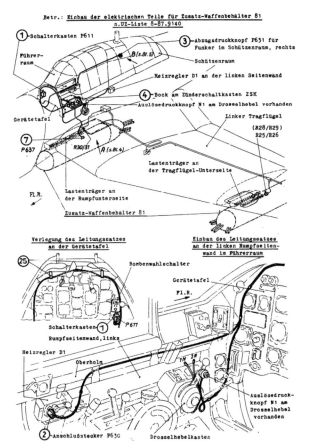

The other type of additional weapons container was the WB81B as seen here, which had the MG 81Zs all pointing directly ahead

This modification sheet for the D-series shows the installation of WB81 additional weapons containers, including one rear-firing one under the fuselage that we have never actually seen any period images to prove was ever adopted operationally?

Betr.: Einbau der elektrischen Teile für Zusatz-Waffenbehälter 81 n. UZ-Liste 8-87.9140 – Re.: Installation of electrical parts for additional weapons case 81 according to UZ list 8-87.9140
Schalterkasten P611 – Switch box P611
Führerraum – Pilot's cockpit
Gerätetafel – Device board
Abzugsdruckknopf P631 für Funker im Schützenraum, rechts – Trigger button P631 for radio operators in the gunner's cockpit, right
Schützenraum – Gunner's cockpit
Heinzregler D1 an der linken Seitenwand – Heinz controller D1 on the left sidewall
Bock am Züderschlaltkasten ZSK – Switchbox ZSK
Auslösedruckknopf N1 am Drosselhebel vordhanden – Trigger button N1 is on the throttle lever
Linker Tragflügel – Left wing

Lastenträger der Tragflügel-Unterseite – Load carrier (rack) on the underside of the wing
Lastenträger an der Rumpfunterseite – Load carrier (rack) on the underside of the fuselage
Zusatz-Waffenbehälter 81 – Additional weapon case 81
Einbau des Leitungssatzes an der linken Rumpfseitenwand im Führerraum – Installation of the wiring harness on the left fuselage sidewall in the pilot's cockpit
Gerätetafel – Instrument panel
Drosselhebelkasten – Throttle lever
Anschlußstecker P630 – Connector P630
Oberholm – Upper spar
Heinzregler D1 Rumpfseitenwand, links – Regulator box D1 fuselage sidewall, left
Verlegung des Leitungssatzes an der Gerätetafel – Layout of the wiring harness on the instrument panel
Schalterkasten – Switchbox
Bombenwahlschalter – Bomb selector switch

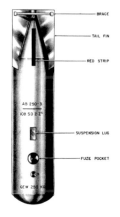

This illustration shows the AB250 container, there are a number of different versions, this being the -3 version marked for 108x SD2 bomblets

The Abwurfbehälter (air-dropped container) series could also be carried by the Stuka, either under the fuselage as here, or under each wing. This photo shows an AB500, containing either 392x SD1 or 111x SD4 anti-personnel bomblets, being winched up under the fuselage of a D-5

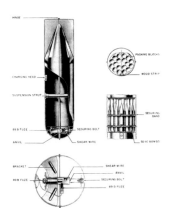

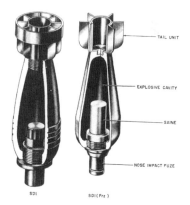

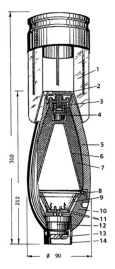

The other type of bomblet used in the AB-series container was the SD-4

1. Leitwerk – Tail
2. Bodenschruabe – Base plate
3. Zündmittle – Igniter agent
4. Zündlagung – Igniter cap
5. Bombenkörper – Bomb body
6. Einlage – Enclosure
7. Sprengstoff – Explosives
8. Zuleitungsdrähte – Lead wires
9. Kunststoffhalter – Plastic holder
10. Bombenkopf – Bomb head
11. Kontakstift – Contact pin
12. Zünderkörper – Fuse body
13. Turbinenkopf – Rotor head
14. Gewindering – Thread ring

This is the one version of the AB500 container

The SD1 1kg Splitterbombe was used in the AB-series containers

The Versorgungsbomben (provisions bombs) were also often carried under the outer wings of the D-series, usually this type with the four small metal fins at the back

Although the Stuka could carry such ordnance as the PC1800 and PC100 (as seen here), these were usually only carried for transportation, as they slowed the Stuka down so much they were too dangerous to carry operationally

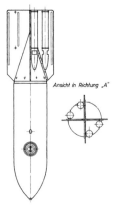

This diagram shows the SC50 fitted with the 'Jericho Trumpet' whistles; note that these are fitted on opposite sides, to make the bomb spin during descent and make the whistles even louder

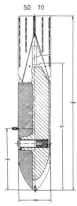

This is an SD70 bomb, as often used in place of the 50kg version

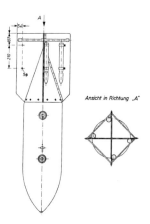

This shows an SC 250 bomb fitted with 'Jericho Trumpets'; note how these are fitted further out on the fins, but again opposite so as to spin the bomb as it drops

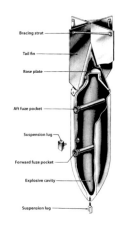

Cross-section of a typical SC 250 bomb

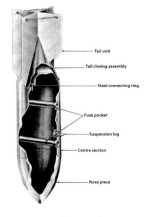

Cross-section of a typical SC 500 bomb

This is a 'Dinort rod' fuse extender and although this shows the type usually associated with the 50 and 70kg bomb, this type can also be seen used on 250kg bombs with the Stuka

Armourers of SG3 unloading 250kg bombs at Immola on the 28th June 1944, note the variety in bomb body and tail colours and the fitment of 'Jericho Trumpet' whistles between the fins of most of them (©SA-Kuva)

Sighting

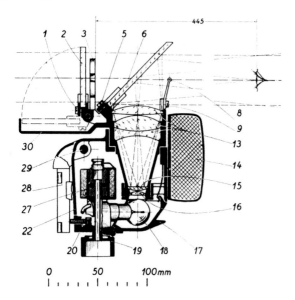

A period image from the manual of the Revi C/12A gunsight

The A-series of the Stuka used the Revi C/12A gunsight as seen in this sectional diagram

The B and D series used the Revi C/12D gunsight, as seen in this diagram from the D-1 manual

1. Revi – Revi gunsight
2. Gerätetafel – Instrument panel
3. Tragbogen – Supporting beam
4. Lagerung – Mounting
5. Schwenkplatte – Swivel plate
6. Anschluß-Stecker – Connection plug
7. Anschluß-Leitung – Connection cable
8. Anschluß-Steckdose – Connecting socket

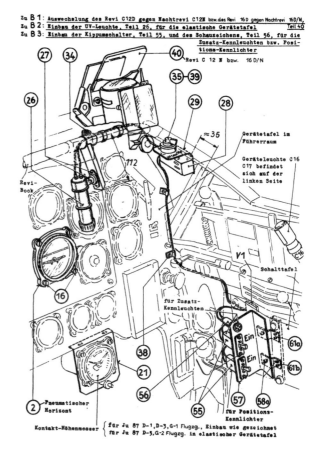

The Revi C/12D and 16D were used by the D-series, but these were replaced with the DN version for night operations by the D-3N, D-5N, D-7 & D-8, as seen in this modification sheet

B1: Auswechslung des Revi C12D gegen Nachtrevi C12N bzw. des Revi 16D gegen Nachtrevi 16D/N teile 40 – Replacement of the Revi C12D for Nachtrevi C12N or the Revi 16D with Nachtrevi 16D/N parts 40
B2: Einbai der UV-Lauchte, Teile 26, für die elastische Gerätatafel – Installation of the UV lamp, part 26, for the flexible device panel
B3: Einbau der Kippumschalter, Teile 55, und des Schauzeichens, teile 56, für die Zusatz-Kennleuchten bzw. Positions-Kennlichter – Installation of the toggle switch, part 55, and the indicator, part 56, for the additional or position lights
Gerätetafel im Führerraum – Instrument panel in the pilot's cockpit

Geräteleuchte C16 C17 befindet sich auf der linken Seite – Device light C16, C17 is on the left side
Schalttafel – Switchboard
für Zusatz-Kennleichten – for additional features
für Positions-Kennlichter – for position lights
Kontakt-höhenmesser – für Ju 87D-1, D-3, G-1 Flugzeug. Einbau wie gezeichnet – für Ju 87D-5, G-2 Flugzeug in elastischer Gerätetafel – Contact altimeter – for Ju 87D-1, D-3, G-1 aircraft, installation as shown – for Ju 87D-5, G-2 aircraft in an flexible device panel
Pneumatischer Horizont – Pneumatic horizon

Although this is a Revi 16B, it does give an overall impression of the type used by the D-series

Drop Tanks

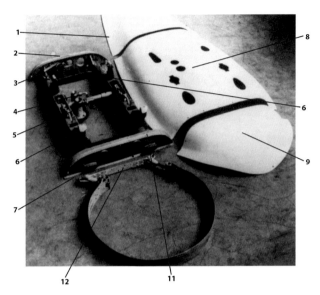

Ground-crewmen lift and attach a 300 litre drop tank under the starboard wing of an R-1

This is the mounting rack, cover and retaining ring for the standard 300 litre drop tank, as used on the D series

1. Verkleidung hinten – Rear panel
2. hintere Abstützung – Rear support
3. Notzug-Anschluß – Emergency jettison connection
4. Gebläseluft-Anschluß – Compressed air connection
5. Kraftstoff-Entnahme-Anschluß – Fuel feed connection
6. Behälter-Abwurfgerät – Container ejector
7. vordere Abstützung – Front support
8. Verkleidung Mitte – Centre panel
9. Verkleidung vom – Front panel
10. Trägerrost – Carrier frame
11. Spannband mit Spannschloß – Tension strap with turnbuckle
12. Spannband – Tension strap

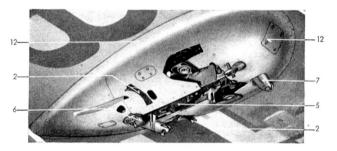

This is a 300lt tank under the wing of an R-series airframe, the lugs on each side pick up via the ETC 50 racks, whilst the retaining strap is held by the bomb release shackle on the outer ETC 50 rack; there is no cover over the racks with the system used by the B and R-series

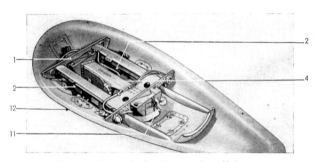

Traggerüst vollständig; vor dem Einbau

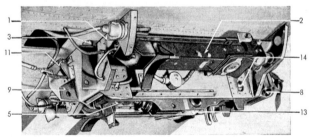

Traggerüst an rechter Flügel-Unterseite angeschlossen

These two illustrations from the D-1 manual show the interior of the fairing and the multi-purpose rack

Traggerüst vollständig; vor dem Einbau – Complete support structure; before installation
1 – hintere Abstützung – Rear support
2. ETC 50/VIIIeTp – Rack ETC 50/VIIIeTp
4. Scloßlafette 1000/500/IXB – Lock carriage 1000/500/IXB
11. Notzunganschluß – Emergency release connection
12. Verkleidung – Fairing
Traggerüst an rechter Flügel-Unterseite angeschlossen – Support frame connected to the right underside of the wing

1. Anschlußstecker für Bomben-Auslöseanlage – Connector for bomb release system
2. ETC 50/VIIIeTp – Rack ETC 50/VIIIeTp (right)
3. Traggerüst – Support structure
5. ETC 50/VIIIeTp – Rack ETC 50/VIIIeTp (left)
8 – vordere Abstützung – Front support
11. Stoßstange – Connecting rod
13. Schloßlafette 1000/500/XIB – Lock carriage 1000/500/IXB

From the D-1 manual this shows the production standard drop tank rack

2. ETC 50/VIII dTp – Rack ETC 50/VIII dTp
5. Schloßlafette 1000/500/IXB – Lock carriage 1000/500/IXB
6. Hintere Pratze – Rear claw
7. Vordere Pratze – Front claw
12. Verkleidung – Fairing

This diagram from the D-1 manual shows the typical 300 litre drop tank

1. Abwerfbarer Außenbehälter (Inhalt 295 Liter) – Removable outer container (contents 295lt)
2. Einfüllkopf – Filler cap
3. Vorderer Stützklotz – Front support block
4. Aufhängeöse – Suspension eyelet
5. Hinterer Stützklotz – Rear support block
6. Kraftstoff-Entnahme-Anschluß – Fuel supply connection
7. Gebläseluft-Anschluß – Compressed air connection
8. Entnahmerohr – Sample tube
9. Spannband mit Spannschloß – Strap with turnbuckle
10. Ablaßverschraubung – Drain screw connection
11. Endkappe – End cap
12. Gummiband – Rubber band

Radio & IFF

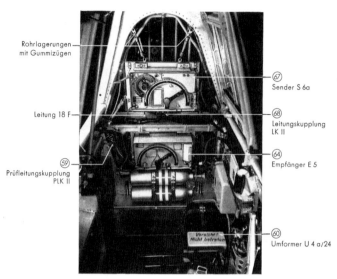

Rohrlagerungen
mit Gummizügen

Leitung 18 F

Prüfleitungskupplung
PLK II

⑥⑦ Sender S 6a
⑥⑧ Leitungskupplung
LK II
⑥④ Empfänger E 5
⑥⓪ Umformer U 4 a/24

This image from the manual shows the radio equipment in the A-series

Prüfleitungskupplug PLK II – Test line coupling
PLK II
Leitung 18F – Line 18F
Rohrlagerungen mit Gummizügen – Support
bearers (bungie)

Sender S6a – Transmitter S6a
Leitungskupplung LK II – Cable coupling LK II
Empfänder E5 – Receiver E5
Umformer U4 a/24 – Converter U4 a/24

Schelle
Karabinerhaken
Vereisungsschutzkörper
⑦① Antennenmaste
⑦⓪ Halterung
für Antennenmaste
⑦② Doppelantenne
⑥⑥ Antennendurchführung
D J 3

Not a great quality image, but this shot from the manual of the A-series clearly shows how the twin aerial leads go through the top of the canopy via a ceramic insulator

Halterung für Antennenmaste – Holder for
antenna masts
Antennenmaste – Antenna masts
Vereisungsschutzköper – Frost protection cup
Karabionerhaken – Snap hook

Schelle – Clamp
Doppelantenne – Dual antenna
Antennendruchführung DJ3 – Antenna feed-
through (insulator) DJ3

This image from the A-series manual shows how each antenna lead attaches to the leading edge of the horizontal tailplane

Zugfeder – Tensions spring
Schäkel – Shackle
Ösenbolzen – Eyebolt

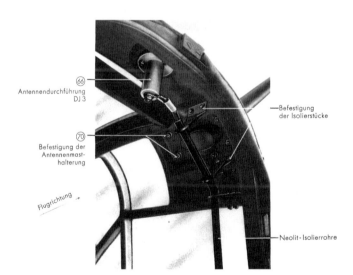

⑥⑥ Antennendurchführung
D J 3

⑦⓪ Befestigung der
Antennenmast-
halterung

Flugrichtung

Befestigung
der Isolierstücke

Neolit-Isolierrohre

Zugfeder
Schäkel
Ösenbolzen

This image from the A-series manual shows now where the aerial lead goes once inside the canopy

Flugrichtung – Flight direction
Befestigung der Antennenmasthalterung –
Attachment to the antenna mast bracket
Antennendurchführung DJ 3 – Antenna

feed-through DJ3
Befestigung der Isolierstücke – Fastenings
for the insulating piece
Neolit-Isolierrohre – Neolit insulating pipe

Sadly, we could find no illustrations of the B/R series radio installation in the manuals, so this is the overall layout for the D and G series. It also highlights the FuG 25 IFF antenna under the rear fuselage, the Peil G.IV D/F loop on the dorsal spine behind the rear cockpit and how the single radio antenna lead attaches to the vertical fin

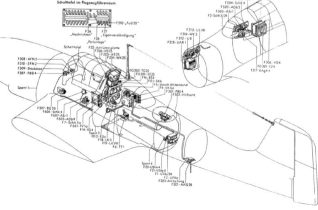

Anschluß-
kupplungen

Verteiler-
kasten

Vorschalt-
widerstand

This shows the radio equipment on the starboard sidewall of the D-series rear cockpit

Verteilerkasten – Distribution box
Anschlußkupplungen – Couplings
Vorschaltwiderstand – Ballast resistor

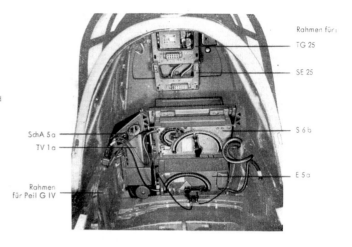

Rahmen für:

TG 25

SE 25

SchA 5a
TV 1a

S 6 b

E 5a

Rahmen
für Peil G IV

This diagram from the D-1 manual shows the S6b transmitter and E5a receiver, along with mounting frames for various other radio and direction-finding controls

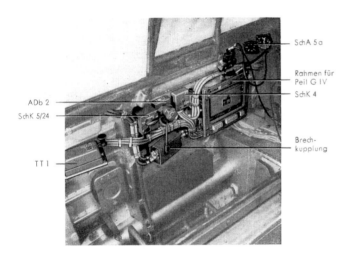

SchA 5a

Rahmen für
Peil G IV

SchK 4

ADb 2

SchK 5/24

Brech-
kupplung

TT 1

While this shows the port side in the rear cockpit of the D-series

An overall shot of the radio equipment on the mid-bulkhead of the G-2 at Hendon

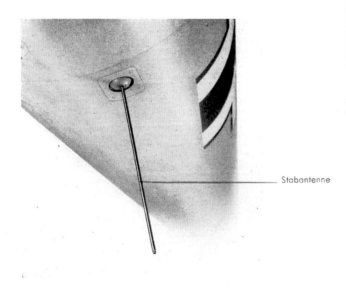

Stabantenne

This diagram shows the location of the FuG 25 IFF rod antenna and comes from the D-1 manual, but applies to all variants fitted with this system

In this shot underneath one of the torpedo-carrying D-series prototypes you can clearly see the IFF rod antenna offset to port under the rear fuselage

Camera

The A-series had no in-built camera, but this ESK 2000/a gun camera could be fitted above the port wing if needed

Flugrichtung – Flight direction
Grundplatte – Base plate
ESK 2000/a – ESK 2000/a gun camera

Stecker – Plug
Spaltverkleidu – Gap cladding (inner/outer wing joint)

This diagram from the D-series manual shows the controls etc. in the cockpit for the Robot camera in the wing

1. Leitungen des Kabelstranges – Wires of the cable harness
2. Gerätetafel – Instrument panel
3. Abzugsleitungen – Extraction lines
4. Auslösedruckknopf N1 – Release push button N1
5. N-Leitungen (abgeklemmt) – N-lines (disconnected)

The B, R, D and G series all used a Robot camera in the leading edge of the port wing, in the image on the left you can just make out the cover plate over the lens aperture to the right of the MG 151/20 cannon on a D-5 operated by 3./SG3 in 1944 [arrowed], whilst the image on the right shows a 1./SG3 machine with the camera installed and the lens cover in situ [arrowed] (©SA-Kuva)

The other way to create in-flight footage of the Stuka was by fitting this cine camera mounted on a tripod in the rear gunner's position (we assume the gunner's seat and gun/ammunition etc. were removed, along with the entire rear canopy section)

This is how some of the in-flight footage of the Stuka was filmed, with a 16mm cine camera mounted to the siren stub on the port undercarriage leg

There were a few experiments with cameras on the Stuka, this one shows a camera installed on the port undercarriage upper leg and it was intended for target clarification, but never adopted

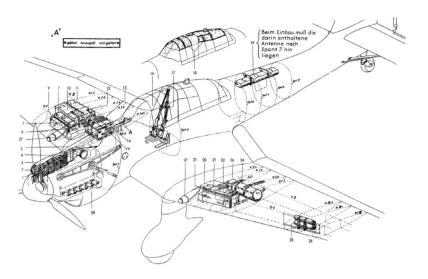

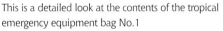

This diagram shows the placement of all the tropical equipment in the D-series

1. Zugfeder – Tension spring
2. Ansaugrohr – Intake pipe
3. Klemmbügel mit Rändelmulter und Gegenmutter – Clamping bracket with knurled shoulder and lock nut
4. Ansaugluft-Filter – Intake air filter
5. Tropen-Sanitätspackung – Tropical medical kit
6. Beutel für Verschlußkappen der Abgasstrahldüsen – Bags for exhaust stack caps
7. Gummimatratze – Rubber mattress
9. Bezug für Luftschraubenhaube, darin Eingewickelt: – Cover for propeller spinner, containing:
   1 Feststellvorrichtung für Seitenruder – Locking device for rudder
   1 Feststellvorrichtung für Höhenruder – Locking device for elevators
   1 Feststellvorrichtung für Querruder – Locking device for ailerons

1 Gummizug für Querruder – Elastic band for ailerons
2 Verankerungsösen – 2 anchor eyelets
10. Deckel – Lid
11. Bezug für Fahrgestell, Sporn und Stairohr – Cover for wheels, spur and dust pipe
12. Bezug für Motor, Führer- und Schützenraumdach – Cover for engine and pilot and gunner's canopies
13. Beitel mit Zeltstangen, Häringen usw. – Chisel with tent poles, tent pegs etc
14. Schlafsack – Sleeping bag
15. Moskitonetz – Mosquito net
16. Schrotdoppelflinte oder Drilling Kaliber 16 – Shotgun or triple calibre 16
17. Karabiner 98 – Rifle 98
18. Sonnenschutzgardinen – Sun screens
19. Notantennenmast – Emergency antenna mast
20. Deckel – Lid

21. Rucksack Nr.1 und 2 – Rucksack Nos.1 and 2
22. Tropen-Notausrüstung Sack Nr.2 – Tropical emergency equipment bag No.2
23. Werkzeugtaschen *für* Motor und Zelle – Tool bags for motor and cockpit
24. Tropen-Notausüstung Sack Nr.1 – Tropical emergency equipment bag No.1
25. Notsender – Emergency transmitter
26. Handlochdeckel – Handhole cover
27. Stutzkappe mit Pappeinlage für MG-Schußkanal – Cover with paper insert for MG barrel
28. Verschlußkappen der Abgasstrahldüsen – Exhaust stack caps

This is a detailed look at the contents of the tropical emergency equipment bag No.1

1. Stablampe – Flashlight
2. Kochgeschirr – Cookware
3. Büchse mit Notproviant – Rifle with emergency provisions
4. Buschmesser – Bush knife
5. Notsignalbehälter mit Leuchtpistole – Emergency signal container with flare pistol
6. 50 Schuß Schratmunition Kaliber

16 – 50 rounds of shotgun ammunition 16 calibre
7. Klappspaten – Folding spade
8 1/2 Pfund Salz in Schraubdose – 1/2 pound of salt in a screw-top can
9. Benzinkocher – Gas stove
10. 50 Schuß jagdmunition Kaliber 7,9 – 50 rounds of hunting ammunition, 7.9mm calibre

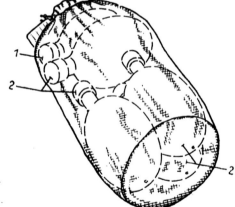

This is a detailed look at the contents of the tropical emergency equipment bag No.2

1. 1 Liter Benzin in gelber Feldflasche – 1 litre of gasoline in a yellow canteen
2. Wasserflasche zu 2 Liter – Water bottle, 2 litres

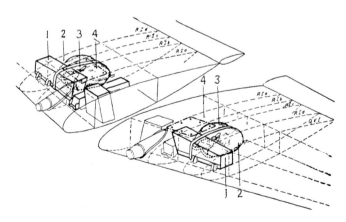

This diagram shows the placement of winter emergency equipment in the wings of the D-1 to D-4 and G-1

1. Vollgurtkasten (vor dem Anbringen des Rucksackes audbauen) – Full ammunition belt box (remove before attaching the backpack)
2. Rucksack mit Winter-Bordnotausrüstung –

Backpack with winter on-board emergency equipment
3. Zurrleine – Lashing line
4. Klappe – Flap

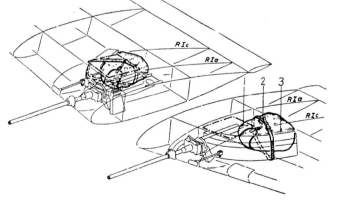

This diagram shows the placement of winter emergency equipment in the wings of the D-5 to D-8 and G-2

1. Rucksack mit Winter-Bordnotausrüstung – Backpack with winter on-board emergency equipment
2. Zurrleine – Lashing line
3. Vollgurtkasten – Full ammunition belt box

Towing Equipment

Here is a port side view of the towing attachment under the tail of a B-series

This shot shows the towing cable fed into position within the bridle under the tail of a B or R-series

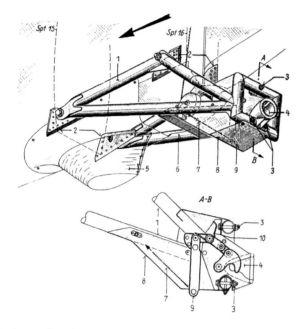

This diagram shows how the towing cable fits in the bridle

1. Bock – Bridle
2. Schleppkupplung – Tow coupling
3. Auslösehebel – Release lever
4. Seilzug – Cable
5. Seilrolle im Notsporn – Rope pulley in tail bumper
6. Seilrolle im Rumpfender – Rope pulley in end of fuselage

This diagram from the D-1 manual shows the towing bracket in detail and applies to the B and R series as well

1. Bock (für Schleppkupplung) – Bridle (for towing connection)
2. Verstärkungsblech – Reinforcing plate
3. Befestigungsschrauben – Fixing screws
4. Eingebaute Schleppkupplung – Built-in towing cable guide
5. Radspornverkleidung – Tailwheel leg trim
6. Notsporn – Tail bumper
7. Seilzug – Cable
8. Verkleidung für Schleppkupplung – Cover for towing cable
9. Hebel für Schleppkupplung – Lever for towing cable
10. Feder – Spring

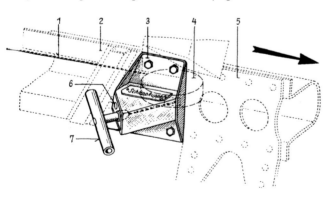

This diagram shows the tow cable release in the cockpit

1. Seilzug – Cable
2. Oberholm (links) – Upper beam (left)
3. Schutzkasten – Protection box
4. Seilrollenbock mit Larerung – Cable roller bracket with coating
5. Spant 2 – Frame 2
6. Führungsstück – Guide piece
7. Betätigungsgriff – Operating handle

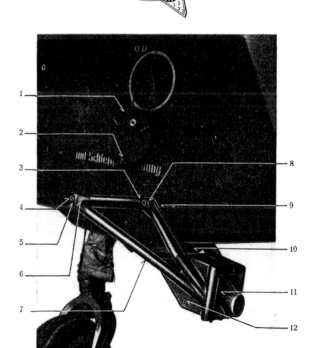

This is the 'Rüststaze S' (Upgrade kit S) installation

1. Handlochdeckel – Hand hole cover
2. Schnellverschluß – Quick release
3. Hinterer Befestigubgspunkt – Rear attachment point
4. Lagerplatte vorn – Front bearing plate
5. Sechskantbolzen – Hexagon bolt
6. Vorderer Befestigungspunkt – Front attachment point
7. Bock – Bridle
8. Kronenmutter – Crown nut
9. Lagerplatte hinten – Rear bearing plate
10. Notsporn – Tail bumper
11. Schleppkupplung – Two cable lead-in
12. Verkleidung – Fairing

HobbyBoss 80287

Hobbycraft HC1241

Italeri 070

Italeri 1292

Italeri 6805

Matchbox 40111

Modelist 207213

MPM 72010

Revell 04692

Special Hobby SH72136

Special Hobby SH72169

Zvezda 7306

Airfix A05100

Airfix A07114

Airfix A07115

Fujimi 7A-F13

Formaplane E10

Fujimi 351339 & F-17

Fujimi 7A-F14

Fujimi 7A-F15

- **Airfix** Ju 87B #Patt No.91 (1957) – Renumbered as #Patt No. 1395 in 1959, reissued as Patt No.91 in 1967, renumbered as #01011-3 in 1973 and reissued as a series 2 kit #N/K in early 1980
- **Airfix** Ju 87B Stuka #02049 -1 (1978) – *New tooling* – Renumbered as #9 02049 in 1983 as a Ju 87B-2 and as #02049 in 1986
- **Airfix** Ju 87B-1 #A03087 (2016) – *New tooling* – Issued as Junkers Ju 87R-1 & Gloster Gladiator Mk I as a 'Dogfight Double' (#A50179) in 2016
- **Airfix** 1/72nd Ju 87B/R #03030-0 (1979) – *New tooling* – Reissued, same kit number, in 198, in 2000 and 2005 as #03030, renumbered in 2008 as #A03030, reissued as #A03030 marked as 'Ju 87B' in 2010
- **Airfix** Ju 87B-2/R-2 Stuka #A03089 (2017) – Revised tooling
- **Airfix Corporation of America** Ju 87 Stuka #2-39 (1963)

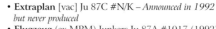

Astromodel (ex-Fujimi) 1/72nd Ju 87B/R built by Author in 1996

- **Airfix/Lodela** 1/72nd Ju 87B/R #03030 (200?)
- **Airfix/Tomy** Ju 87B #010011 (1976)
- **Airdoc** [res] Ju 87D/G #N/K (1998)
- **Astrokit** (ex-Fujimi) Ju 87B/R 'Desert Snake & *Regia Aeronautica*' #72101 (1996)
- **Aviastend** [vac] Ju 87B #N/K (1990s)
- **Aviastend** [vac] Ju 87D #N/K (1990s)
- **Bilek** (ex-Italeri) Ju 87B-2 Stuka #804 (1990s)
- **Bilek** (ex-Italeri) Ju 87R-2 Stuka #806 (1990s)
- **CMR** (ex-Czechmaster) [res] Junkers Ju 87A-1 #34 (late 1990s)
- **Continental Models** (ex-Airfix) Ju 87B #N/K (late 1950s)
- **Czechmaster** [res] Junkers Ju 87A-1 #N/K (late 70s – late 80s)
- **Cyber-Hobby/Dragon** Junkers Ju 87B Stuka #5054 – *Announced for 2010, new tooling, not released to date*

- **Extraplan** [vac] Ju 87C #N/K – *Announced in 1992 but never produced*
- **Flugzeug** (ex-MPM) Junkers Ju 87A #1017 (1992)
- **Frog** Ju 87G-1 #F195 (1968-1977)
- **Frog** 'Combat Series' Hurricane & Ju 87G #F510 (1969 – 1972)
- **Fujimi** Ju 87B/R 'Immelmann' #7A-F13 (1980s) – Reissued as #25013, renumbered #250137 & F-13 (2005)
- **Fujimi** Ju 87B 'Shark Mouth' #35133 (1993) – Renumbered #351339 & F-17 (2005)
- **Fujimi** Ju 87D-1 'Dora' #7A-F14 (late 1987) – Reissued as #25014, renumbered #250144 & F-14 (2005)
- **Fujimi** Ju 87D-5 'White Milk' #7A-F16 (late 1987) – Reissued as #25016 in 05/1998, renumbered #250168 & F-16 (2005)
- **Fujimi** Ju 87G-1 'Tankbuster' #7A-F15 (late 1987) – Reissued as #25015, renumbered #250151 & F-15 (2005)
- **Fujimi** Ju 87G-2 'Kanonenvogel' #7A-F17 (late 1987) – Reissued as #25017 and again in 09/1998 as #72061 (£10.99), renumbered #720616 & F-31 (2005)
- **Hasegawa** (ex-Frog) Ju 87G-1 #JS-044 (1967-1973/4)
- **Heller** Stuka-Junkers Ju. 87. B1 #L388 (1973) – Renumbered #388 in 1974, reissued as #388 mid-1979 and renumbered as #80388 in 1987
- **Heller** 'Bataille de France' set [inc. Ju 87B-1] #377 (1981) – Reissued in 1990 as #80377
- **Hi-Tech** [res/mtl/pe] Ju 87A #006 (1988)
- **HobbyBoss** Junkers Ju 87D-3 #80286 (2013) – *New tooling – 'Easy Assembly'*
- **HobbyBoss** Junkers Ju 87G-1 #80287 (2013) – *New tooling – 'Easy Assembly'*
- **Hobbycraft** Ju 87G #HC1241 (1987)
- **Hobby 2000** (ex-Fujimi) Ju 87D-1 'North Africa' #72019 (2020)
- **Hobby 2000** (ex-Fujimi) Ju 87D-3N/D-7 #72020 (2020)
- **Hobby 2000** (ex-Fujimi) Ju 87G-2 'Last Flight' #72021 (2020)
- **Hobby 2000** (ex-Fujimi) Ju 87G-2 'Winter 1944/45' #72022 (2020)
- **Idea** Ju 87G #AP013 (1980s) – *Same kit (box art) as Hobbycraft (#HC1241)*
- **InTech** (ex-Frog) Ju 87G-1 #04 (1992->)

- **Italeri** (ex-Zvezda) Ju 87 Stuka #045 – *Announced 1994, but never actually produced*
- **Italeri** Ju 87 B2/R2 #079 (1997) – Reissue in 2010 as #1292
- **Italeri** Ju 87 B2/R2 'Speciale Italia' #6805 (1999) – *Special Limited edition*
- **Italeri** Ju 87D-5/8 Stuka' #070 (1996) – Reissued in 2005 as a Ju 87D-5 (#1070)
- **Italeri** Ju 87G-2 'Kanonenvogel' #1221 (2001)
- **Keilkraft** Junkers Ju 87B #N/K (1958-1960) – *Planned but never released*
- **K&K** [vac] Junkers Ju 87B-2 #N/K (1992-1993)
- **Master Models** (ex-Czechmaster) [res] Junkers Ju 87A-1 #N/K (1991->)
- **Matchbox** Ju 87 'Stuka' #PK-111 (1975) – Reissued under Revell's control in 1991 as #40111
- **Mavi** (Model Aviation) [vac] Junkers Ju 87A/B Stuka #7036 (1993->)
- **Modelist** (ex-Academy) Ju 87G-1 #207213 (200?)
- **MPC** (ex-Airfix) Stuka Ju 87B #7004-70 (1965-1985) Also #2-0102, 2-1107 (Profile Series packaging in 1972), 2-7004 & #1-4203 (1982)
- **MPC** (ex-Airfix) Ju 87 Stuka with crewmen #02-102 (1976)
- **MPM** [ltd inj/pe/vac] Junkers Ju 87A-1 #72010 (1989)
- **Plasty Modelle** (ex-Airfix) Junkers Ju 87B #23 (50s-70s)
- **Polistil** Junkers Ju 87B #KA.4 – *Kit production ended in 1979*
- **Revell** (ex-Italeri) Ju 87B2/R2 #04620 (2001)
- **Revell** Ju 87B/R #H-149 (1977) – Reissued as #0149 in 1981 and as #4155 (Revell-Ceji packaging) in 1984

Notes

inj	– Injection Moulded Plastic
ltd inj	– Limited-run Injection Moulded Plastic
mtl	– White-metal (including Pewter)
pe	– Photo-etched (brass or steel)
res	– Resin
vac	– Vacuum-formed Plastic
(1999)	– Denotes date the kit was released
(1994->)	– Date denotes start of firm's activities, the exact date of release of this kit is however not known
ex-	– Denotes the tooling originated with another firm, the original tool maker is noted after the '-'

- **Revell** Ju 87 Tank Buster #H-142 (1975) – *Built D-5 or G-2 versions* – Reissued, same kit number, in 1978 – Reissued marked as Ju 87G-2 (but also still offering D-5 option) as #0142 in 1981, again as #4153 in 1984 (Revell Ceji packaging) and as a Ju 87D-5/G-2 #04153 in 1993
- **Revell** (ex-Frog) Junkers Ju 87G – *This kit was one of nineteen Axis types sold to Revell Inc by Novo in 1977, of which these eight (Bf 109F, Fw 190A, He 219A, Ju 87G, Me 262A. MC.202 and Zero) were not released by Revell as they already had their own mould for the types in their own range. Finally released in 2010 as Junkers Ju87G/D 'Tank Buster' #04692 and also released 2011 with paints and glue as a 'Gift Set' (64962), also this was apparently the Ju 87 in the Battle of Britain 'Icons of Aviation' set with the He 111/Hurricane/Spitfire in 2010 (#05711)*
- **Revell** (ex-Matchbox) Ju 87G-2 #04992 (2013)
- **Special Hobby** [ltd inj] Junkers Ju 87A Stuka 'Legion Condor' #SH72123 (2005)
- **Special Hobby** [ltd inj] Ju 87A Stuka 'Anton in Luftwaffe service' #SH72136 (2005)
- **Special Hobby** [ltd inj] Junkers Ju 87A Stuka 'In Foreign Service' #SH72169 (2008)
- **Storia dell'Aviazione** (ex-Airfix) Junkers Ju 87 #55 (1973 & 1977-78) – *Issued bagged along with a book on the subject by publishers Fabbri Editori on two occasions on the dates quoted*
- **Tamiya** (ex-Italeri) Ju 87B-2/R-2 Stuka #60776 (2007) – *Reissued in 2012*
- **Tamiya** (ex-Italeri) Ju 87G-2 #60735 (2002) – *Japanese market only*
- **Testors** (ex-Fujimi) Ju 87G-2 #342 (1988)
- **Testors** (ex-Heller) Ju 87B-2 #419 (1985)
- **Testors** (ex-Italeri) Junkers Ju 87 Stuka #0047
- **Testors** (ex-Italeri) Ju 87D-5 Stuka' #0070
- **Unicraft** [res] 1/72nd Junkers Ju 87 #N/K (2002/3)
- **UPC** (Universal Powermaster Corp.) (ex-Frog) Junkers Ju 87G #5053 (1969) – *All kit production ceased in the early 1970s*
- **Zvezda** Ju 87B #N/K – *Announced but never released (late 1990s)*
- **Zvezda** 1/72nd Ju 87B-2 #7306 (Announced 2013, released 2015) – *Snap-together kit*
- **Zvezda** 1/72nd Ju 87 with skis #7322 – *Announced for 2020 – Snap-together kit*
- **Zvezda** 1/72nd Ju 87G-2 #7261 – *Not released to date*

Italeri #070 1/72nd Ju 87D-5 built by Author in 1996

1/48th to 1/68th
All 1/48th scale unless otherwise stated

- **Airfix** Ju 87B-1 #A07114 (Announced 2015 released 2017) – *New tooling*
- **Airfix** Ju 87B-1 Stuka #A07114A (2019) – *Additional decal options compared with #A07114*
- **Airfix** Ju 87R-1 Stuka #05100-4 (1981) – *New tooling* – Renumbered as #9 05100 in 1983 (Ju 87B-2/R), reissued as #05100 in 1991 and in 09/2010 as #A05100
- **Airfix** Ju 87R-2/B-2 Stuka #A07115 (2017) – *Revised tooling (based on #A07114)*
- **Artiplast** (ex-Lindberg) Ju 87B Picchiatello #110 (1960s-1975) – *1/50th scale*
- **Bandai** (ex-Imai) Ju 87 Dive Bomber #8501 (1971) – *1/50th scale (Pin Point series)*
- **Bandai** (ex-Monogram) Junkers Ju 87G-1 #8926 (late 1970s) – *Issued in same packaging as Monogram edition*
- **Esci Junkers** Ju 87D – *There were rumours of this kit in 1979, but it was never produced/released*
- **Formaplane** [vac] Junkers Ju 87A-1 #PNE10 (1976 – mid-1990s) – *Range bought by Capital Models in 1983 and MHW Models in 1984*
- **Hasegawa** Ju 87B-2 Stuka #JT13 (1994)
- **Hasegawa** Ju 87B-2 'Desert Stuka' #JT16 (1994)
- **Hasegawa** Ju 87B-2 Stuka 'Izetta Die Letzte Hexe' #64740 (2016) – *Limited edition*
- **Hasegawa** Ju 87B-2/U-4 w/skis #JT111 (1995) – *Export market only*
- **Hasegawa** Ju 87B-2 Stuka w/skis #07317 (2012) – *Limited edition (resin parts of #JT111 replaced with injected plastic)*
- **Hasegawa** Ju 87B-2 'with SC250 Stabo bomb' #JT137 (1997) – *Limited edition (same box art etc as #JT13 with sticker on ends to denote addition of bombs)*

- **Hasegawa** Ju 87R-2 'Desert Snake' #JT114 (1996) – *Export market only* – Reissued as #07337 in 2013
- **Hasegawa** Ju 87B-2 'Hungarian AF' #JT128 (1996) – *Export market only*
- **Hasegawa** Ju 87B-2/R2 Stuka #JT153 (1998) – *Limited edition*
- **Hasegawa** Ju 87B-2 'Regia Aeronautica' #JT176 (1999) – *Limited edition*
- **Hasegawa** Ju 87B-2/R2 'Greece Theatre' #JT153 (1998) – *Limited edition*
- **Hasegawa** Ju 87C 'Graf Zeppelin' #09899 (2010) – *Limited edition*
- **Hasegawa** Ju 87D 'Regia Aeronautica' #09546 (2004) – *Limited edition*
- **Hasegawa** Ju 87D 'Rumanian Air Force' #09704 (2006) – *Limited edition*
- **Hasegawa** Ju 87D-1/D-3 #JT185 (1999)
- **Hasegawa** Ju 87D-3N Stuka 'NSGr.2' #07323 (2013) – *Limited edition*
- **Hasegawa** Ju 87D-4 'Torpedo Flieger' #09307 (1999) – *Limited edition*
- **Hasegawa** Ju 87D-4 'Torpedo Flieger 2' #09348 (2000) – *Limited edition*
- **Hasegawa** Ju 87D-5 #JT53 (1998)
- **Hasegawa** Ju 87D-8 'Night Attacker' #JT179 (1999) – *Limited edition*
- **Hasegawa** Ju 87G-1 'Kanonenvogel' #09370 (2001) – *Limited edition*
- **Hasegawa** Ju 87G-2 #JT54 (1998) – Reissued, same kit number, in 2001
- **Hasegawa** Ju 87G-2 'With Super-Detailed Gun Pods' #CH38 (1999) – *Limited edition*
- **Hasegawa** Ju 87G-2 Stuka 'Rudel' #07360 (2013) – *Limited edition*
- **Hasegawa** Hs 129B-1/2 & Junkers Ju 87G-2 'Tank Busters' #07409 (2015) – *Limited edition*
- **Hasegawa** Ju 87R-2 Stuka #JT15 (1995)
- **Hasegawa** Ju 87R-2 Stuka 'StG2' #09584 (2004) – *Limited edition (same box art as #07337)*
- **Hasegawa** Ju 87R-2 Stuka 'StG2 Immelmann' #09673 (2006) – *Limited edition*
- **Heller** (ex-Airfix) Ju 87R-2 'Hi-Tech Concept' #80541 (1992)
- **Hobbycraft** Ju 87G-1 Stuka #HC1512 (1980s) – Reissued as #HC1512 in 1989 and as #HC1515 in 1984
- **Idea** Ju 87G-1 Stuka #1512 (1980s) – *Copy of Monogram kit (also issued by Hobbycraft)*

Fujimi 7A-F16

Fujimi F-17

Hasegawa JT128

Hasegawa JT13

Hasegawa JT153

Hasegawa JT15

Hasegawa JT16

Hasegawa JT185

Hasegawa JT53

Heller 805411

Hobbycraft HC1512

Italeri 2690

Italeri 2709

Lindberg 70508

Monogram 6480

Monogram 85-5975

Revell 04564

Special Hobby SH48007

Special Hobby SH48007

21st Century Toys 22015

Hasegawa ST25

Hasegawa ST26

Revell 04711

Revell H-298

Trumpeter 03213

Trumpeter 03214

Trumpeter 03216

Trumpeter 03216

Trumpeter 03218

Airfix A18002A

Heller 80498

Trumpeter 02424

Trumpeter 02420

Trumpeter 02421

Airfix 18002-7

- **Imai** Ju 87B #808 (1965) – Reissued as #4512 – *1/50th scale*
- **Italeri** Ju 87B-2 Stuka #2690 (2010) – *New tooling*
- **Italeri** Ju 87B-2/R2 'Picchiatello' #2769 (2017)
- **Italeri** Ju 87D-5 Stuka #2709 (2012)
- **Italeri** Ju 87G-2 Stuka Kanonenvogel #2722 (2013)
- **JN Models** [res] Junkers Ju 87A #N/K (1989)
- **Lindberg** Ju 87B Stuka #524 (1955-1975) – Also #306M (included electric motor for propeller) and 3101M (1969, motorised), reissued #1505M, (1976 [motorised], some state #1504M?) #1505 & 2312 (1975-1990), then as #70508 (1990) and reissued in 2007 as #70508
- **Marusan**, (ex-Lindberg) Junkers Ju 87B Stuka #N/K (1950s-1970s) – *Quoted scale is accurate as possible, but does not reflect that stated on the box*
- **Model Toys** (ex-Lindberg) Ju 87B Stuka #524 (1956-1958)
- **Monogram** Ju 87G-1 #PA207 (1968) – Reissued in a Monogram-Mattel box as #6840 in 1970, reissued, same kit number, in standard Monogram box in 1973, 1975, 1979 and in 1999 (#85-0207) as a Limited Edition reissue with original box art in the 'Monogram Classics' series
- **Monogram** Stuka Ju 87D #6840 (1983) – *Revision of Ju 87G-1 kit (#6840)* – Reissued by Monogram Europe as Ju 87D-1 in 1992 (#74011)
- **Monogram** (ex-Hasegawa) 'Pro-Modeler' Ju 87R-2 #85-5975 (2002)
- **Otaki** Ju 87D #OA-20 (early 1960s-1985) – *1/68th scale*
- **MPM/CMK** [vac/ltd inj] 1/48th Junkers Ju 87A-1 #N/K – *Listed in 1992, release not confirmed (may in fact be 1/72nd scale version)*

- **Revell** (ex-Hasegawa) Ju 87B-2 Stuka #04564 (2001)
- **Revell** USA (ex-Monogram) Junkers Ju 87D Stuka #85-5250 (2007-2009) – *US market packaging, which differed from that used elsewhere by Revell AG*
- **Revell** USA (ex-Monogram) Stuka Ju 87G-1 Tank Buster #85-5270 (2016) – *US market packaging, which differed from that used elsewhere by Revell AG*
- **Scalecraft** Junkers Ju 87B Stuka #5510 (early 70s) – *1/50th scale* – Brand name used by KIM Toys, reappeared in USA under this brand in 1979
- **Special Hobby** [ltd inj/res] Junkers Ju 87A Stuka #SH48007 (2000)
- **Tamiya** (ex-Italeri) Ju 87B-2 Stuka w/Bomb Loading Set #37008 (2011) – *The bomb loader and figures was from their Fw 190F kit*
- **Toltoys** Junkers Ju 87B #N/K – *Announced 1957, never released*
- **USAirfix** (ex-Airfix) Junkers Ju 87B-2 #4804 – *Planned 1981, never released*
- **Vacukit** [vac] Junkers Ju 87A-1 #4503 (1987-early 90s)

Heller 1/48th Hi-Tech Ju 87 (#80541) built by Martin Sage in 1992

1/32nd

- **Blue Max** – *See Schmidt Modellbau*
- **Hasegawa** Junkers Ju 87D #ST26 (2007) – Reissue, same kit number, in 2018
- **Hasegawa** Junkers Ju 87D-4 'Torpedo Flieger' #08216 – *Announced 2011, not released to date*
- **Hasegawa** Junkers Ju 87D-5 'Winter Camouflage' #08189 (2008) – *Limited edition*
- **Hasegawa** 1/32nd Junkers Ju 87D-8 'Night Stuka' #08171 (2007) – *Limited edition*
- **Hasegawa** 1/32nd Junkers Ju 87G 'Kanonenvogel' #ST25 (2006) – *New tooling, first production run included a white-metal figure of Rudel and his dog –* Reissued, same number, in 2011 and due again in 2020
- **Horizon Conversions** [vac] Ju 87A #3229 (1985)
- **Idea** (ex-Revell) Ju 87G-1 #N/K (1980s)
- **Revell** Ju 87B Stuka Dive Bomber #H-298 (1969) – Reissued in 1984 as #4751 (Revell Ceji box) and in 1990 as #4796 (and/or #04796)
- **Revell** Ju 87B Stuka #H-153 (1971) – *Hungarian AF markings*
- **Revell** (ex-Hasegawa) Ju 87D Stuka #04711 (2008)

- **Revell-Japan** Ju 87B Stuka #H-298 (1970) – Reissued, same kit number (revised box art), in 1975
- **Revell/Congost** Ju 87B Stuka #H-298 (1970s)
- **Revell/Kikoler** Ju 87B Stuka #H-298 (1979)
- **Revell/Lodela** Ju 87B Stuka #H-298 (1969)
- **Revell/Lodela** Ju 87B 'Bombadero en Picada Stuka' #H-153 (1971)
- **Schmidt Vacu-Modellbau** [vac] Ju 87D #3211 (1984-2000) – *Issued under their Blue Max label*
- **Schmidt's Hobby Modellbau** [vac] Ju 87D #N/K (1980s)
- **Trumpeter** Ju 87A #03213 (2014)
- **Trumpeter** Ju 87B-2 #03214 (2012)
- **Trumpeter** Ju 87B-2/U4 #03215 (2013)
- **Trumpeter** Ju 87D #03217 (2016)
- **Trumpeter** Ju 87D-2 #TBA – *Announced for 2010, not released to date*
- **Trumpeter** Ju 87D-7 #TBA – *Announced for 2010, not released to date*
- **Trumpeter** Ju 87G-2 #03218 (2015)
- **Trumpeter** Ju 87R #03216 (2013)
- **21st Century Toys** Ju 87B/R Stuka #22015 (2007)

1/24th

- **Airfix** Ju 87B Stuka #18002-7 (Announced 1975, released 1976) – Reissued in 1996 as #18002 'Ju 87B-2 Stuka', reissued in 2005 as #A18002 and again in 2015 as #A18002A
- **Heller** (ex-Airfix) Ju 87B Stuka #80498 (1990)
- **MPC** (ex-Airfix) Ju 87B #2-3506 (1978) – Reissued as #1-4604 in 1982
- **Trumpeter** Ju 87A Stuka #02420 (2017)
- **Trumpeter** Ju 87B-2 Stuka #02421 (2019)
- **Trumpeter** Ju 87D-5 #02424 (2018)
- **Trumpeter** Ju 87G-2 #02425 (2019)

Hasegawa 1/32nd Ju 87D (#ST26) built by Steve Evans

Appendix: II Ju 87 Accessories & Masks

With a subject as popular as the Ju 87, the number of accessories produced over the years is such that we have had to limit this Appendix to just those that remain available as we write (February 2020). Our apologies for this, but there would have been simply too many to fit within the available space had we attempted to list all the accessories produced to date in this section.

1/144th

- **Master** [br] 3.7cm Flak 18 Gun Barrels for Ju 87G etc. #AM-144-005
- **Owl** [res] Uncovered Landing Gear for Ju 87D/G #OWLR44002 {Eduard}
- **Owl** [res] Uncovered Cannon Bk 37 for Ju 87G #OWLR44001 {Eduard}
- **RetroWings** [res] Ju 87 Stuka Cockpit Detail Set #RW44049 {Eduard}
- **RetroWings** [res] Ju 87C Conversion #RW44111 {Eduard}

1/72nd

- **Aires** [res/pe] Ju 87D/G Cockpit Set #7093 {Academy}
- **Aires** [res] Bordkanone 3.7cm Pods for Ju 87G #7095 {Academy}
- **Aires** [res/pe] Ju 87G Detail Set #7096 {Academy}
- **Aires** [res] Bordkanone 3.7cm x2 #7098
- **Aires** [res] Ju 87B-1 Stuka Control Surfaces #7363 {Airfix}
- **Airwaves** [pe] Ju 87B Detail Set #AC72038 {Fujimi} – *Also #AEC72038*
- **Airwaves** [pe] Ju 87B/C Detail Set #AEC72189 {Italeri}
- **AML** [vma] Ju 87B-1 Camouflage Pattern Masks #AMLM73030 {Airfix}
- **AML** [vma] Ju 87B-2 Camouflage Pattern Masks #AMLM73031 {Zvezda}
- **Blackbird Models** [res] Ju 87 Unspatted Undercarriage #72011 – *Due 2020*
- **CMK** [res/pe] Ju 87G Interior Detail Set #7054 {Academy}
- **CMK** [res/pe] Ju 87G Engine Set #7055 {Academy}

- **Eduard** [ma] Ju 87B Canopy & Wheel Masks #CX053 {Fujimi}
- **Eduard** [pe] Ju 87B-1 Interior 'Zoom' Detail Set #SS543 {Airfix}
- **Eduard** [pe] Ju 87B-1 Detail Set #73-543 {Airfix}
- **Eduard** [ma] Ju 87B-1 Canopy & Wheel Masks #CX436 {Airfix}
- **Eduard** [ma] Ju 87B-2 Canopy & Wheel Masks #CX443 {Zvezda}
- **Eduard** [ma] Ju 87B-2/R2 Interior 'Zoom' Detail Set #SS633 {Italeri}
- **Eduard** [ma] Ju 87B-2/R2 Canopy & Wheel Masks #CX513 {Airfix}
- **Eduard** [pe] Ju 87D Interior 'Zoom' Detail Set #SS133 {Italeri}
- **Eduard** [ma] Ju 87D/G Canopy & Wheel Masks #CX088 {Fujimi}
- **Eduard** [ma] Ju 87G Canopy & Wheel Masks #CX144 {Academy}
- **Eduard** [pe] Ju 87B-2/R2 Detail Set #73-633 {Airfix}
- **Falcon** [vac] Luftwaffe Fighters & Attack Aircraft, Clear-Vax Set No.5 – *Includes Ju 87B & D canopies* {Fujimi}
- **Kora Models** [res/dec] Ju 87B-2/U4 on Skis Conversion #CSD7266
- **Kora Models** [res/dec] Ju 87D V21 on Skis Conversion #CSD7267
- **Kora Models** [res/dec] Ju 87D-1 on Skis Conversion #CSD7268
- **Kora Models** [res/dec] Ju 87D-1/Trop on Skis Conversion #CSD7269
- **LF Models** [vma] Ju 87B/R Camouflage Masks #M7216 {Airfix/Italeri/Revell/Tamiya}
- **LF Models** [vma] Ju 87D/G Camouflage Masks #M7216 {Fujimi or Italeri}
- **Master** [br] 3.7cm Flak 18 Canon Barrels x2 #AM-72-090
- **Montex** [vma] Ju 87A Canopy & Wheel Masks #SM72142 {Special Hobby}
- **Montex** [vma] Ju 87B-1 Canopy & Wheel Masks #SM72274 {Airfix}
- **Montex** [vma] Ju 87B/R Canopy & Wheel Masks #SM72060 {Fujimi}
- **Montex** [vma] Ju 87G Canopy & Wheel Masks #SM72019 {Academy}

- **Montex** [vma] Ju 87G-2 Canopy & Wheel Masks #SM72061 {Fujimi}
- **Part** [pe] Ju 87B-2/R2 Detail Set #S72-101 {Italeri}
- **Part** [pe] Ju 87D-5 Detail Set #S72-102 {Italeri}
- **Part** [pe] Ju 87G-1 Detail Set #S72-202 {Academy}
- **Peewit** [vma] Ju 87B-1 Canopy & Wheel Masks #M72049 {Airfix}
- **Pmask** [vma] Ju 87B-1 Canopy & Wheel Masks #Pk72107 {Airfix}
- **Pmask** [vma] Ju 87B-2/R2 Canopy & Wheel Masks #Pk72136 {Airfix}
- **Pmask** [vma] Ju 87D/G Canopy & Wheel Masks #Pk72010 {HobbyBoss}
- **Pmask** [vma] Ju 87D/G Canopy & Wheel Masks #Pk72156 {Fujimi}
- **Quickboost** [res] Ju 87D-5N Night Exhausts Type B #QB72244 {Fujimi}
- **Quickboost** [res] Ju 87D-5N Night Exhausts Type C #QB72252 {Fujimi}
- **Quickboost** [res] Ju 87B/R Exhausts Type B #QB72259 {Fujimi}
- **Quickboost** [res] Ju 87D Exhausts – Early Version #QB72266 {Fujimi}
- **Quickboost** [res] Ju 87D Exhausts – Late Version #QB72267 {Fujimi}

Notes

If no intended kit is given the item is generic in fitment/use

ac – Clear Acetate Film
br – Brass (or aluminium)
bz – Bronze
dec – Decals
ma – Die-cut Self-adhesive Paint Masks [tape]
wm – White-metal (including Pewter)
pe – Photo-etched Brass
rb – Rubber
res – Resin
SA – Self-adhesive
vac – Vacuum-formed Plastic
{Academy} – Denotes the kit for which the set is intended

Aires 2068

Aires 7093

Eduard 72-133

Aires 7096

Quickboost QB72328

Quickboost QB72543

Quickboost QB72422

Quickboost QB72327

ExtraTech EX72144

Quickboost QB72323

Eduard 73-633

Quickboost QB72259

Master AM-72-090

Part S72-202

- **Quickboost** [res] Ju 87G Rudder #QB72323 {Academy}
- **Quickboost** [res] Ju 87D-5/D-8/G Compass #QB72327 {Fujimi}
- **Quickboost** [res] Ju 87G Correct Spatted Undercarriage #QB72328 {Academy}
- **Quickboost** [res] Ju 87G Propeller #QB72331 {Academy}
- **Quickboost** [res] Ju 87B/R Propeller w/tool #QB72422 {Fujimi}
- **Quickboost** [res] Ju 87 Seats with Safety Belts #QB72543
- **Quickboost** [res] Ju 87B Pitot Tube and Gun Barrels #QB72594 {Airfix}
- **Quickboost** [res] Ju 87B Exhausts #QB72595 {Airfix}
- **ReXX** [wm] Ju 87B Exhausts #72029
- **SBS Model** [res] Ju 87B Exhaust & Radiator Cowling Set #72053 {Airfix}
- **Squadron** [vac] Ju 87B Canopy #9136 {Fujimi}
- **Top Notch** [vma] Ju 87B/D/G/R Camouflage Pattern Masks #TNM72-M60
- **Yahu Models** [pe] Ju 87B-2 Instrument Panel #YMA7265 {Airfix, Italeri & Zvezda}
- **Yahu Models** [pe] Ju 87B-1 Instrument Panel #YMA7275 {Airfix}

1/48th

- **AIMS** [res] Replacement Radiator Intake for Ju 87B-1 & B-2 #48P008 {Airfix}
- **Aires** [res/pe] Ju 87B Cockpit Set #4026 {Hasegawa}
- **Aires** [res/pe] Ju 87D/G Cockpit Set #4119 {Hasegawa}
- **Aires** [res/pe] Ju 87D Gun Bays #4134 {Hasegawa}
- **Aires** [res/pe] Ju 87D Detail Set #4161 {Hasegawa}
- **Aires** [res/pe] Ju 87G 3.7cm BK Pods #4169 {Hasegawa}
- **Aires** [res] Bordkanone 3.7cm BK x2 #4178
- **Aires** [res/pe] Ju 87B Gun Bays #4306 {Hasegawa}
- **Aires** [res/pe] Ju 87D Air Coolers #4404 {Hasegawa}

- **Aires** [res/pe] Ju 87D Control Surfaces #4413 {Hasegawa}
- **AML** [vma] Ju 87B-1 Camouflage Pattern Masks #AMLM49033 {Airfix}
- **Blackbird Models** [res] Ju 87 Unspatted Undercarriage Legs #48002
- **Eduard** [ma] Ju 87B Canopy & Wheel Masks #EX048 {Hasegawa}
- **Eduard** [ma] Ju 87B Canopy & Wheel Masks #EX327 {Italeri}
- **Eduard** [pe] Ju 87B Detail Set 'Zoom' #FE200 {Hasegawa}
- **Eduard** [pe] Ju 87B Interior Detail Set #49-554 {Italeri}
- **Eduard** [pe/ma] Ju 87B-1 'Big Ed' Detail & Mask Set #BIG49166 {Airfix}
- **Eduard** [pe] Ju 87B-1 Interior Detail Set #49-800 {Airfix}
- **Eduard** [pe] Ju 87B-1 Seat Belts – Steel #49-801 {Airfix}
- **Eduard** [pe] Ju 87B-1 Interior Detail Set 'Zoom' #FE800 {Airfix}
- **Eduard** [ma] Ju 87B-1 Canopy & Wheel Masks #EX536 {Airfix}
- **Eduard** [pe] Ju 87B-2/R2 Detail Set #49-894 {Airfix}
- **Eduard** [pe] Ju 87B-2/R2 Detail Set 'Zoom' #FE894 {Airfix}
- **Eduard** [pe] Ju 87B-2/R2 Seat Belts – Steel #FE895 {Airfix}
- **Eduard** [ma] Ju 87B-2/R2 Canopy & Wheel Masks #EX589 {Airfix}
- **Eduard** [ma] Ju 87D Canopy & Wheel Masks #EX368 {Italeri}
- **Eduard** [ma] Ju 87D/G Canopy & Wheel Masks #EX089 {Hasegawa}
- **Eduard** [pe] Ju 87D-5 Interior Detail Set 'Zoom' #FE614 {Italeri}
- **Eduard** [pe] Ju 87G-2 Detail Set #49-324 {Hasegawa}
- **Eduard** [pe] Ju 87G-2 Detail Set 'Zoom' #FE324 {Hasegawa}
- **Falcon** [vac] Lufwaffe **Part** 2 #Clear-Vax Set No.16 – *Included canopies for Ju 87B [original Airfix] and Ju 87D/G [Monogram]*

- **LF Models** [vma] Ju 87B/R Camouflage Pattern Masks #M4819 {Airfix/Hasegawa/Italeri/Revell/Tamiya}
- **LF Models** [vma] Ju 87D/G Camouflage Pattern Masks #M4814 {Hasegawa/Italeri}
- **Master** [br] Flak 18 (37mm) Cannon Barrels #AM-48-024
- **Montex** [vma] Ju 87B Canopy & Wheel Masks #SM48033 {Revell}
- **Montex** [vma] Ju 87B Canopy, Wheel & Marking Masks #MM48033 {Revell}
- **Montex** [vma] Ju 87B Canopy & Wheel Masks #SM48334 {Italeri}
- **Montex** [vma] Ju 87B-1 Canopy & Wheel Masks #SM48464 {Airfix}
- **Montex** [vma] Ju 87B-1 Canopy, Wheel & Marking Masks #MM48464 {Airfix}
- **Montex** [vma] Ju 87D Canopy & Wheel Masks #SM48366 {Italeri}
- **Montex** [vma] Ju 87D/G Canopy & Wheel Masks #SM48048 {Hasegawa}
- **Montex** [vma] Ju 87D-5 Canopy, Wheel & Marking Options Masks #MM48366 {Italeri}
- **Montex** [vma] Ju 87G-2 Canopy, Wheel & Marking Options Masks #MM48048 {Hasegawa}
- **Montex** [vma] Ju 87B-2 Marking Options Masks #K48058 {Hasegawa/Revell}
- **Montex** [vma] Ju 87B-2 Marking Options Masks #K48103 {Hasegawa/Revell}
- **Montex** [vma] Ju 87D-3/D-5 Marking Options Masks #K48144 {Hasegawa}
- **Montex** [vma] Ju 87B-2 Marking Options Masks #K48172 {Hasegawa}
- **Montex** [vma] Ju 87B-2/R2 Marking Options Masks #K48211 {Italeri}
- **Montex** [vma] Ju 87G Marking Options Masks #K48185 {Hasegawa}
- **Montex** [vma] Ju 87B-1 Marking Options Masks #K48361 {Airfix}
- **New Ware** [ma] Ju 87B-1 Canopy (open & closed), Wheel & Marking Option Masks – Expert #NWAM0135 {Airfix}
- **New Ware** [ma] Ju 87B-1 Canopy (closed), Wheel & Marking Option Masks #NWAM0134 {Airfix}

AIMS 48PE008

Aires 4001

Aires 4134

Aires 4169

Aires 4238

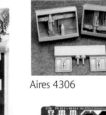
Aires 4306

Aires 4404

Eduard BIG4979

Aires 4413

Eduard 48-749

Aires 4413

Quickboost QB48305

AIRMO 48701

Quickboost QB48257

Eduard FE895

Quickboost QB48141

Eduard 49-614

Moskit 48-08

Quickboost QB48373

Quickboost QB48376

Quickboost QB48385

Quickboost QB48387

Quickboost QB48260

Quickboost QB48499

REXx 48 017

Quickboost QB48284

Quickboost QB48794

Reheat Models RH098

True Details 48050

Eduard 33055

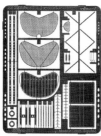

Eduard 32-323

Eduard 32-033

Eduard 33053

Eduard BIG3322

Eduard 33055

Eduard 32-751

- **New Ware** [ma] Ju 87B/R2 Canopy (closed), Wheel & Swastika Masks #NWAM0377 {Airfix}
- **New Ware** [ma] Ju 87B-2/R2 Canopy (closed), Wheel & Swastika Masks – Expert #NWAM0378 {Airfix}
- **Part** [pe] Ju 87B-2 Detail Set #S48-058 {Hasegawa}
- **Part** [pe] Ju 87D-5 Detail Set #S48-059 {Hasegawa}
- **Part** [pe] Ju 87B Canopy Frames #S48-060 {Hasegawa}
- **Pmask** [vma] Ju 87B-1 Canopy & Wheel Masks #Pk48093 {Airfix}
- **Pmask** [vma] Ju 87B-2 Canopy & Wheel Masks #Pk48044 {Italeri}
- **Pmask** [vma] Ju 87D/G Canopy & Wheel Masks #Pk48031 {Italeri}
- **Quickboost** [res] Ju 87B Exhausts #QB48095 {Hasegawa}
- **Quickboost** [res] Ju 87B-2 Gun Barrels #QB48141 {Hasegawa}
- **Quickboost** [res] Ju 87D/G Exhausts #QB48245 {Hasegawa}
- **Quickboost** [res] Ju 87 Uncovered Wheels #QB48257 {Hasegawa}
- **Quickboost** [res] Ju 87 Uncovered Wheels – Version II #QB48260 {Hasegawa}
- **Quickboost** [res] Ju 87D-5N Standard Night Exhausts #QB48280 {Hasegawa}
- **Quickboost** [res] Ju 87D-5N Night Exhausts – Type A #QB48284 {Hasegawa}
- **Quickboost** [res] Ju 87D-5N Night Exhausts – Type B #QB48292 {Hasegawa}
- **Quickboost** [res] Ju 87D-5N Night Exhausts – Type C #QB48305 {Hasegawa}
- **Quickboost** [res] Ju 87D-1/D-3 Exhausts – Early Type #QB48324 {Hasegawa}
- **Quickboost** [res] Ju 87B Exhausts #QB48368 {Italeri}
- **Quickboost** [res] Ju 87 MG Drum Magazines #QB48373 {Hasegawa}
- **Quickboost** [res] Ju 87 Gun Barrels #QB48376 {Italeri}
- **Quickboost** [res] Ju 87 Pitot Tube #QB48385 {Italeri}
- **Quickboost** [res] Ju 87B/R Propeller w/tool #QB48387 {Hasegawa}

- **Quickboost** [res] Ju 87B/R Propeller w/tool #QB48402 {Italeri}
- **Quickboost** [res] Ju 87B Seat with Safety Belts #QB48499 {Hasegawa}
- **Quickboost** [res] Ju 87B VS-11 Propeller w/tool #QB48787 {Airfix}
- **Quickboost** [res] Ju 87B Jumo Propeller w/tool #QB48788 {Airfix}
- **Quickboost** [res] Ju 87B Exhausts – Oval Type #QB48789 {Airfix}
- **Quickboost** [res] Ju 87B Seats with Safety Belts #QB48794 {Airfix}
- **Quickboost** [res] Ju 87B Exhausts #QB48842 {Airfix}
- **REXx** [wm] Ju 87B Exhausts #48017 {Italeri}
- **Squadron** [vac] Ju 87B Canopies #9522 {Original Airfix}
- **TopNotch** [vma] Ju 87B-G/R Camouflage Pattern Masks #TNM48-M60
- **True Details** [res] Ju 87B Wheels #48050 {Hasegawa}
- **Ultracast** [res] Ju 87B Exhausts #48101
- **Ultracast** [res] Ju 87D/G Exhausts #48102
- **Yahu Models** [pe] Ju 87B-1 Instrument Panel #YMA4856 {Airfix}

1/32nd

- **Aires** [res/vma] Ju 87G Wheels #2048 {Hasegawa}
- **Aires** [res/pe] Ju 87D/G Cockpit Set #2068 {Hasegawa}
- **Aires** [res/pe] Ju 87D/G Cockpit Set #2211 {Trumpeter}
- **Eduard** [pe/ma] Ju 87A 'Big Ed' Detail & Mask Set #BIG3351 {Trumpeter}
- **Eduard** [ma] Ju 87A Canopy & Wheel Masks #JX178 {Trumpeter}
- **Eduard** [pe] Ju 87A Detail Set #32-832 {Trumpeter}
- **Eduard** [pe] Ju 87A Seat Belts #32-833 {Trumpeter}
- **Eduard** [pe] Ju 87A Interior Detail Set 'Zoom' #33145 {Trumpeter}
- **Eduard** [ma] Ju 87B-2 Canopy & Wheel Masks #JX144 {Trumpeter}
- **Eduard** [pe] Ju 87B-2 Exterior Detail Set #32-323 {Trumpeter}

- **Eduard** [pe] Ju 87B-2 Seat Belts #32-753 {Trumpeter}
- **Eduard** [pe] Ju 87B-2 Interior Detail Set 'Zoom' #33113 {Trumpeter}
- **Eduard** [pe] Ju 87D Exterior Detail Set #32-167 {Hasegawa}
- **Eduard** [pe] Ju 87D Interior Detail Set #32-594 {Hasegawa}
- **Eduard** [pe] Ju 87D Interior Detail Set #32-749 {Trumpeter}
- **Eduard** [pe/ma] Ju 87D 'Big Ed' #BIG3254 {Hasegawa}
- **Eduard** [pe] Ju 87G Seat Belts #32-564 {Hasegawa}
- **Eduard** [ma] Ju 87D Canopy & Wheel Masks #JX063 {Hasegawa}
- **Eduard** [ma] Ju 87G Canopy & Wheel Masks #JX053 {Hasegawa}
- **Eduard** [ma] Ju 87G-2 Canopy & Wheel Masks #JX183 {Trumpeter}
- **Eduard** [pe] Ju 87G-2 Exterior Detail Set #32155 {Hasegawa}
- **Eduard** [pe] Ju 87G-2 Exterior Detail Set #32-378 {Trumpeter}
- **Eduard** [pe] Ju 87G-2 Interior Detail Set #32-561 {Hasegawa}
- **Eduard** [pe] Ju 87G-2 Interior Detail Set #32-847 {Trumpeter}

Notes
br – Brass (or aluminium)
bz – Bronze
inj – Injection-moulded plastic (ltd = limited-run)
ma – Self-adhesive Paint Masks (Kabuki Tape)
mtl – Metal (other than white-metal/pewter)
pe – Photo-etched Brass
pa – Paper (laser-cut)
rb – Rubber
res – Resin
SA – Self-adhesive
vac – Vacuum-formed Plastic
vma – Vinyl Self-adhesive Paint Masks
wm – White-metal (including Pewter)
{Academy} – Denotes the kit for which the set is intended

Eduard 32-751

Eduard 32-753

Master AM-32-014

Quickboost QB32022

Montex K32166

Eduard 32-335

Quickboost QB32046

Quickboost QB32047

Quickboost QB32074

Quickboost QB32076

Quickboost QB32080

Quickboost QB32073

Quickboost QB32081

Quickboost QB32085

Quickboost QB32181

Quickboost QB32137

Scale Aircraft
Conversions 32067

Quickboost QB32141

Schatton-Modellbau
3205

- **Eduard** [pe] Ju 87G-2 Seat Belts #32-848 {Trumpeter}
- **Eduard** [pe/ma] Ju 87G-2 'Big Ed' #BIG3241 {Hasegawa}
- **Eduard** [ma] Ju 87R Canopy & Wheel Masks #JX154 {Trumpeter}
- **Eduard** [pe] Ju 87R Exterior Detail Set #32-335 {Trumpeter}
- **Eduard** [pe] Ju 87R Ju 87R Seat Belts #32-768 {Trumpeter}
- **Eduard** [pe] Ju 87R Interior Detail Set 'Zoom' #33124 {Trumpeter}
- **Eduard** [pe/ma] Ju 87G-2 'Big Ed' Detail & Mask Set #BIG3357 {Trumpeter}
- **HGW Models** [pe/pa] Ju 87 Seat Belt Set #132042 {Hasegawa}
- **HGW Models** [pa/pa] Ju 87 Seat Harness Set #132592
- **Maketar** [ma] Ju 87B-2 Canopy & Marking Masks #MM32112K {Trumpeter #03214}
- **Maketar** [vma] Ju 87B-2 Canopy & Marking Masks #MM32112V {Trumpeter #03214}
- **Maketar** [ma] Ju 87B-2/U4 Canopy & Marking Masks #MM32111K {Trumpeter #03215}
- **Maketar** [vma] Ju 87B-2/U4 Canopy & Marking Masks #MM32111V {Trumpeter #03215}
- **Maketar** [ma] Ju 87D/G Canopy Masks #MMC002K
- **Maketar** [ma] Ju 87D/G Canopy Masks #MMC002V
- **Maketar** [ma] Ju 87D 'Desert Doras' Masks #MM32002V
- **Maketar** [ma] Ju 87D Canopy & Marking Masks #MM32097K {Hasegawa #ST26}
- **Maketar** [vma] Ju 87D Canopy & Marking Masks #MM32097V {Hasegawa #ST26}
- **Maketar** [ma] Ju 87G Canopy & Marking Masks #MM32092K {Hasegawa #ST25}
- **Maketar** [vma] Ju 87G Canopy & Marking Masks #MM32092V {Hasegawa #ST25}
- **MasterCasters** [res] Ju 87 'Jumo' Stamped Hollow Exhausts #MTS32090 {Hasegawa}
- **MasterCasters** [res] Ju 87 Correct Chord Propeller Blades #MTS32091 {Hasegawa}
- **MasterCasters** [res] Ju 87 Weighted Wheels #MTS32092 {Hasegawa}
- **Montex** [vma] Ju 87A Canopy & Wheel Masks #SM32157 {Trumpeter}

- **Montex** [vma] Ju 87A Canopy, Wheel & Marking Masks #MM32157 {Trumpeter}
- **Montex** [vma] Ju 87A Marking Masks #K32296 {Trumpeter}
- **Montex** [vma] Ju 87B Canopy & Wheel Masks #SM32040 {Revell}
- **Montex** [vma] Ju 87B Marking Masks #K32053 {Revell}
- **Montex** [vma] Ju 87B-2 Canopy & Wheel Masks #SM32130 {Trumpeter}
- **Montex** [vma] Ju 87B-2/R2 Marking Masks #K32236 {Trumpeter}
- **Montex** [vma] Ju 87B-2 Marking Masks #K32234 {Trumpeter}
- **Montex** [vma] Ju 87D Marking Masks #K32110 {Hasegawa}
- **Montex** [vma] Ju 87D-1 Marking Masks #K32166 {Hasegawa}
- **Montex** [vma] Ju 87D/G Canopy & Wheel Masks #SM32046 {Hasegawa}
- **Montex** [vma] Ju 87D/G Canopy & Wheel Masks #MM32046 {Hasegawa}
- **Montex** [vma] Ju 87G Canopy, Wheel & Marking Masks #MM32046 {Hasegawa}
- **Montex** [vma] Ju 87G Marking Masks #K32180 {Hasegawa}
- **Montex** [vma] Ju 87G Canopy, Wheel & Marking Masks #SM32161 {Trumpeter}
- **Montex** [vma] Ju 87G-2 Canopy & Wheel Masks #SM32161 {Trumpeter}
- **Montex** [vma] Ju 87R-2 Marking Masks #K32235 {Trumpeter}
- **Profimodeller** [br] Ju 87 Pitot Tube #320381 {Hasegawa or Trumpeter}
- **Quickboost** [res] Ju 87G Exhausts #QB32015 {Hasegawa}
- **Quickboost** [res] Ju 87D Propeller Blades #QB32022 {Hasegawa}
- **Quickboost** [res] Ju 87D Gun Barrels #QB32046 {Hasegawa}
- **Quickboost** [res] Ju 87D D/F Loop Antenna – Late #QB32047 {Hasegawa}
- **Quickboost** [res] Ju 87D/G VS 111 Wooden Propeller Blades #QB32063 {Hasegawa}
- **Quickboost** [res] Ju 87D-5N Standard Night Exhausts #QB32073 {Hasegawa}
- **Quickboost** [res] Ju 87D-5N Night Exhausts – Type A #QB32074 {Hasegawa}
- **Quickboost** [res] Ju 87D-1/D-3 Exhausts – Early #QB32076 {Hasegawa}

- **Quickboost** [res] Ju 87D-5N Night Exhausts – Type B #QB32079 {Hasegawa}
- **Quickboost** [res] Ju 87D-5N Night Exhausts – Type C #QB32080 {Hasegawa}
- **Quickboost** [res] Ju 87 Control Columns #QB32081 {Hasegawa}
- **Quickboost** [res] Ju 87 Gun Barrels #QB32085 {Hasegawa}
- **Quickboost** [res] Ju 87 Pitot Tube #QB32137 {Trumpeter}
- **Quickboost** [res] Ju 87B Exhausts #QB32139 {Trumpeter}
- **Quickboost** [res] Ju 87B Ammo Drums #QB32141 {Trumpeter}
- **Quickboost** [res] Ju 87G Exhausts #QB32181 {Trumpeter}
- **REXx** [wm] Ju 87D Exhausts #32004 {Hasegawa}
- **Scale Aircraft Conversions** [wm] Ju 87 Landing Gear #32067 {Trumpeter}
- **TopNotch** [vma] Ju 87B/D/G/R Camouflage Pattern Masks #TNM32-M60
- **Yahu Models** [pe] Ju 87D/G #YMA3244 {Hasegawa/Trumpeter}

1/24th

- **Airscale** [pe/dec] Ju 87 Instrument Panel Upgrade #PE24STU {Airfix}
- **Airscale** [dec] Ju 87 Instrument Panel #AS24JUA {Airfix}
- **AMS Resin** [res] Ju 87 Wheel Set #24004 {Airfix}
- **Montex** [vma] Ju 87B Canopy & Wheel Masks #SM24006 {Airfix}
- **Montex** [vma] Ju 87B Masking Masks #K24010 {Airfix}
- **Montex** [vma] Ju 87B-2 Masking Masks #K24035 {Airfix}
- **Montex** [vma] Ju 87B-2 Masking Masks #K24056 {Airfix}
- **Montex** [vma] Ju 87D-5 Canopy & Wheel Masks #SM24019 {Trumpeter}
- **Montex** [vma] Ju 87D-5 Canopy, Wheel & Marking Masks #MM24019 {Trumpeter}
- **TopNotch** [vma] Ju 87B-G/R Camouflage Pattern Masks #TNM24-M60

Appendix III: **Ju 87 Decals**

With a subject as popular as the Ju 87, the number of decal sheets produced over the years is such that we have had to limit this Appendix to a selection of those that remain in print as we write (03/2020). Our apologies for this, but there are simply too many to fit within the available space.

1/144th

Blue Rider
#MS-002 Slovak Air Force 1939-1944
Inc.
• Ju 87D-1, OK-XAC

HAD Models
#144046 – Hungarian Air Force Bf 109G-6,
Fw 190F-8 & Ju 87B-2
Inc.
• Ju 87B-2 'B601, Royal Hungarian Air Force, 1942
#144047 – Hungarian Air Force Bf 109G-6,
Fw 190F-8 & Ju 87B-2
Inc.
• Ju 87B-2 'B6+09, Royal Hungarian Air Force, Soviet Front, 1944

One Shot Decal
#HM-OS14409 Ju 87B-2/R2 B6+09 Hungarian Air Force
#HM-OS14410 Ju 87B-2/R2 208th Squadriglia, Regia Aeronautica

LF Models
#C4417 Ju 87D-5
• Ju 87D-5, 'White 30', Royal Bulgarian Air Force, Spring/Summer 1944
#C4418 Ju 87D-3
• Ju 87D-3, 'White 216', 216 Squadriglia, 121º Gruppo, Capua airfield, August 1943
• Ju 87D-3, 'Red IX', 216 Squadriglia, 121º Gruppo, Capua airfield, August 1943
#C4419 Ju 87R-2 Part 1
• Ju 87R-2 Trop, 'Yellow 209', 209 Squadriglia, 97º Gruppo, September 1941
• Ju 87R-2 Trop, above aircraft after capture by the RAF
#C4420 Ju 87R-2 Part 2
• Ju 87R-2, 237 Squadriglia, 96º Gruppo, March 1941
• Ju 87R-2, 237 Squadriglia, 96º Gruppo, Leece, winter 1940-41

MYK Design
#A-90 Ju 87R-2
#A-231 Ju 87D 'Eastern Front'

Owl Decals
#44002 Junkers at Night (Inc. Ju 87D & G-2)
• Ju 87G-2, W/Nr.494200, 4 Lft.Kdo 4, probably 10.(Pz)/SG2, May 1945
• Ju 87D-5(N)/D-8, W/Nr.142091, probably NSGr.4, Czechoslovakia, May 1945

Peddinghaus-Decals
#EP 1677 Ju 87B-2 Trop
#EP 2793 Ju 87 'Stuka des Sturzkampfgeschwader 2'

Print-Scale
#144-002 Ju 87 Stuka
• Ju 87A-1, 29•2 of Kampfgruppe 88, Legion Condor, Spain 1938
• Ju 87R-2, T6+AP flown by Staffelkapitän of 6./St.G 2 'Immelmann', summer 1940
• Ju 87B-1 of 6./St.G 1, France, 1940
• Ju 87B-1, S2+AC flown by the Kommandeur of II./St.G 77, Balkans, 1941
• Ju 87R-2, 6G+KT, 6. St.G 1, Mediterranean theatre, early 1941
• Ju 87B-1, J9+AL of 1.(St.)/Tr.Gr.189, France, May 1940
• Ju 87B-1, 35+G12, of 2./St.G 163 'Immelmann', Cottbus, February 1939
• Ju 87D-5, I/Sg 2 'Immelmann', Soviet Front, winter 1943-1944
• Ju 87D-3, 4./St G 2, Stalingrad, September 1942-February 1943
• Ju 87R-2 of 6./St.G 2 'Immelmann', Tmimi, Lybia 1941
• Ju 87B-2/Trop, III./St.G 1, North Africa, 1941
• Ju 87D-3, 2./NSG 2, Byelorussia. May 1944
• Ju 87G-2 of 10.(Pz)/SG 3, Lithuania, autumn 1944
#144-137 Ju 87 Stuka

1/72nd

Almark Decals
#C-4 Messerschmitt Bf 110 & Ju 87B
#C-6 Protection Flights
Inc.
• Ju 87B/R of 7./St.G.51, 6./St.G.1 & 96º Gruppo, Regia Aeronautica
#C-7 Early Stukas
• Ju 87B-2, W/Nr.0353, 236 Squadriglia, Comiso, September 1940
• Ju 87B-1, 6G+FR, 7./St.G.51. Germany, 1939
• Ju 87R-2, 6G+KT, 6./St.G.1, Eastern Front, spring 1942
#C-8 Tropical Stukas
• Ju 87R-4, L1+DW, 12.(Stuka)/LG1, Finland, 1942
• Ju 87B-2/Trop, S7+CM, 4./St.G.3, El Adam, mid-June 1942
• Ju 87R-2/Trop, T6+CP, 6./St.G.2

Blue Rider
#BR220 Slovak Air Force 1939-1944 Inc.
• Ju 87D-1, OK-XAC

CAM (Custom Aeronautical Miniatures)
#72045 Stuka!
• Ju 87R-2, A5+HH, 1./St.G.1, Bulgaria, 1941
• Ju 87B-2, T6+AN, 5./St.G.2, North Africa, 1941
• Ju 87B-2, T6+IR, 7./St.G.2, Russia, 1941-2
• Ju 87B-2, S7-BB, Stab 1./St.G.3 Libya, 1942

DR Casper
#72006 Forgotten Operations: Merkur, Crete, May 1941

Eagle Editions
#97 Ju 87G-2 Pt.1
• W/Nr.494110, Stab SG.2, Kitzingen, 8th May 1945, flown by Oberst. Hans-Ulrich Rudel
• W/Nr.494221, T6+NU, 10./SG 2
#98 Ju 87G Stuka
• Ju 87G-2, W/Nr.494200 Luftflotte 4, Pilsen, 1944
• Ju-87G-1, W/Nr. unknown, T6+BB, I./SG 2
#143 Junkers Ju 87B
• Ju 87B, T6+AN, 5./St.G.2, 2nd September 1941
• Ju 87B, 'Yellow G' of an unknown unit, winter 1941/2
#144 Ju 87B/R
• Ju 87B-2, T6+AK, St.G 2
• Ju 87B-2, FI+AN
• Ju 87R-2, T6+AC, Stab II./St.G. 2, Mediterranean, 1941
• Ju 87B-2, 'White 18', 209 Squadriglia, 96º Gruppo, Regia Aeronautica, September 1941

Exito Decals
#ED72004 Luftwaffe Ground Attackers Vol.1
Inc.
• Ju 87D-3, W/Nr.100082, T6+HN, 5./St.G.2, Achtirskaya, Russia, early summer 1942

HAD Models
#72081 Ju 87A/B (Hungary & Germany)

HR Model
#HRD7210 Ju 87D-5
• Ju 87D-5, OK-XAB, Slovakia, 1944

Kora Models
#DEC 72.054 Ju 87D-5 (Hungarian)
#DEC 72.075 Ju 87B-2/K-2 (Hungarian)
#DEC 72.122 Ju 87D-3 (Rumanian service)
#DEC 72.123 Ju 87D-5 (Rumanian service)
#DEC 72.124 Ju 87D-3 (Hungarian)
#NDT 72015 Ju 87B-1 'Condor Legion'

LF Models
#C7232 Ju 87D-5
Same option as #C4417
#C7233 Ju 87D-3
Same options as #C4418
#C7234 Ju 87R-2 Part I (RAF/Italian)
Same options as #C4419
#C7235 Ju 87R-2 Part II (Italian)
Same options as #C4420

Peddinghaus-Decals
#EP862 Ju 87 Standard Stencils
#EP1506 Ju 87T Maschine für den Flugzeugträger Graf Zeppelin
#EP1673 Ju 878G-2, 10.(Pz) SG2, 1945, Oblt. Hans Ulrich Rudel

CAM 72-045

Plastic Planet Club 72008

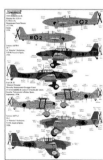
HAD Models 144047

Xtradecals X72274

Exito Decals ED48004

H Models Decals HMD48043

HAD Models 48081   Kora DEC 4834   Kora DEC 4862   Kora DEC 4863   ROP MNFD L48040   ROP MNFD L48041

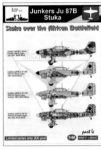

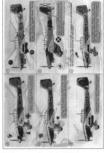
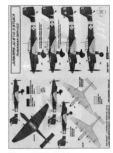

ROP MNFD L48042   ROP MNFD L48043   ROP MNFD48039   ROP MNFD48040   Print-scale 48-032   Kora DEC4861

#EP1676 Ju 87B-2/Trop 6./St.G2, Libya, July 1941, Hubert Pölz

Plastic Planet Club
#PPD-72008 Ju 87B over Mediterranean

Print-Scale
#72-014 Ju 87A/B/G Stuka
- Ju 87A-1, 29•2, Kampfgruppe 88, Legion Condor, Spain 1938
- Ju 87R-2, T6+AP flown by Staffelkapitän of 6./St.G 2, summer 1940*
- Ju 87B-1, 6./St.G 1, France, 1940*
- Ju 87B-1, S2+AC flown by the Kommandeur of II./St.G 77, Balkans, 1941*
- Ju 87R-2, 6. St.G 1, 6G+KT, Mediterranean theatre, early 1941*
- Ju 87R-2, S1+AB flown by Maj. Walter Sigel, Kommandeur of I./St. G3, Greece, 1941*
- Ju 87B-2, S2+DB, Stab I./St.G 77, Greece, spring 1941*
- Ju 87B-1, 35+G12, 2./St.G 163, Cottbus, February 1939*
- Ju 87B-1, J9+AL, 1.(St.)/Tr.Gr.189, France, May 1940*
- Ju 87B-2, F1+BD, Stab III./St.G 77, Crimea, spring 1942*
- Ju 87B-2 Trop, S1+GK, 2./St.G 3, Derna airfield, Libya, autumn 1941 – RLM 70/7179/65
- Ju 87B-2 Trop, III./St.G 1, North Africa, 1941- RLM 70/71/79/65
- Ju 87D-5, I./SG 2, Eastern Front, winter 1943-1944*
- Ju 87D-3, 4./St.G 2, Stalingrad. September 1942/ February 1943*
- Ju 87D-3, 2./NSGr 2, Byelorussia, May 1944*
- Ju 87G-2, 10.(Pz)/SG 3, Lithuania, Autumn 1944*
- Ju 87R-2, 6./St.G 2, Tmimi, Libya, 1941 – RLM 79/71/65
* All finished in RLM 70/71 over 65

ROP o.s.
#MNFD L72044 Ju 87B-1 'France Campaign Part 1'
- Ju 87B-1, 6G+JR, 8./St.G.51, Cologne-Wahn, May 1940
- Ju 87B-1, 6G+FS, 8./St.G.51, Cologne-Wahn, May 1940
- Ju 87B-1, T6+CA, Stab St.G.2, Cologne-Ostheim, May 1940
- Ju 87B-1, T6+FH, III./St.G2, Cologne-Ostheim, May 1940
#MNFD L72045 Ju 87B-2 'Battle of Britain Pt 1'
- Ju 87B-2, 6G+LT, 8./St.G.1, Norent-Fontes, France, August 1940

- Ju 87B-2, T6+HL, 3./St.G.2, Norrent-Fontes, August 1940
- Ju 87B-2, T6+GM, 4./St.G.2, Siegburg, May 1940
- Ju 87B-2, 6G+AT, 9./St.G.1, Norrent-Fontes, August 1940
#MNFD L72046 Ju 87B-2 'Stuka to East Part 3'
- Ju 87B-2, S7+DL, 3./St.G.3, Belica, Bulgaria, spring 1941
- Ju 87B-2, F1+AR, 7./St.G.77, Arad, Rumania, spring 1941
- Ju 87B-2, S7+DK, 2./St.G.3, Belica, Bulgaria, April 1941
- Ju 87B-2, S2+AB, HQ I./ST.G.77, Argos, Greece, May 1944
#MNFD L724047 Ju 87B-2/R2 'Stuka over the African Battlefield Part 4'
- Ju 87B-2, T6+IN, 5./St.G.2, Derna, Libya, July 1941
- Ju 87B-2, S1+GK, 2./St.G.3, Derna, Libya, 1941
- Ju 87B-2, S1+HK, 2./St.G.3, Derna, Libya, summer 1941
- Ju 87R-2, A5+EL, III./St.G.3, El Daba, Egypt, late 1942
#MNFD L72048 Ju 87B-1/B-2 'Stuka – Invasion of Russia Part 5'
- Ju 87B-1, 6G+CC, II./St.G.1, Eastern Front, 1941
- Ju 87B-1, 6G+AC, II./St.G.1, Eastern Front, September 1941
- Ju 87B-1, T6+CK, 2./St.G.2, Eastern Front, September 1941
- Ju 87B-2, T6+AD, III./St.G.2, Eastern Front, 1943
#MNFDL72049 Ju 87B-2 'Stuka in the Regia Aeronautica Part 6'
- Ju 87B-2, W/Nr.5794, 236th Squadriglia, 96° Gruppo autonomo bombardamento a tuffo, Corniso, Sicily, September 1940
- Ju 87B-2, flown by Capt. Raul Zucconi, 101° Gruppo autonomo bombardamento a tuffo, 1940
- Ju 87B-2, W/Nr.5763, 'White 209', 209th Squadriglia, 101° Gruppo autonomo bombardamento a tuffo, Derna, Libya, late summer 1940
- Ju 87B-2, 'White 208', 208th Squadriglia, 101° Gruppo autonomo bombardamento a tuffo, Sicily, April 1941

 # Xtradecals
#X72-118 Battle of Britain 70th Anniversary
Inc.
- Ju 87B-1, 6G+AT, 6./St.G.1, France, summer 1940
#X72-162 The Battle of Malta – Axis
Inc.
- Ju 87R-2, S7+KP, 6 Staffel, II./St.G.3, Sicily, Feb/ March 1941

#X72-223 Ju 87B/K/R Stuka
- Ju 87B-2, J9+BL, 9./St.G.I, Angers, France, summer 1940
- Ju 87B-2, T6+KL, 3./St.G.2, St Malo, France, August 1940
- Ju 87B-2 Trop, T6+MM, 4./St.G.2, Trimini, Libya, June 1941
- Ju 87B-2 Trop, S1+GK, 2./St.G.3, North Africa, 1941
- Ju 87B-2, S2+AC, II./St.G.77, Balkans, 1941
- Ju 87B-2, 'White 237', 237a Squadriglia, 96° Gruppo, Regia Aeronautica, Lecce-Galatina, Italy, autumn 1940
- Ju 87R-2, 'Black 239', 239a Squadriglia, 97° Gruppo, Regia Aeronautica, Lecce-Galatina, April 1941
- Ju 87R-2/K-2, B6+02 of the Training Unit Magyar Lëgierö, Veszpren, Hungary, 1943
- Ju 87B-2, W/Nr.0406, 5B+ER, NSGr.10, captured by Yugoslavian partisans, 12th February 1945
- Ju 878B-2, A5+HH, 1./St.G.1, Krainici, Bulgaria, April 1941
- Ju 87B-2, J9+HH, 7./St.G.1, Ostende, Belgium, January 1941
#X72-249 Ju 87B-1 Stuka
- Ju 87B-1, A5+DH, 1./St.G.1, September 1939
- Ju 87B-1, T6+BC, Stab./St.G.2, Bonn-Hangelar, 1940
- Ju 87B-1, T6+GM, 7./St.G.2, 1939
- Ju 87B-1, W/Nr.473, 6G+FS, 8./St.G.51, 1939
- Ju 87B-1, 6G+AR, 7./St.G.51, France, 1940
- Ju 87B-1, 6G+HR, 7./St.G.51, France, 1940
- Ju 87B-1, S1+AB, I./St.G.76, flown by Hptm. Walter Sigel, Battle of Poland, 1939
- Ju 87B-1, S2+AP, 6./St.G.77, Russia, July 1941
- B-1, S2+EP, 6./St.G.77, Battle of Britain, 1940
- B-1, L1+HU, IV./LG1
#X72-274 Spanish Civil War – Nationalist Fighter & Ground Attack Collection Pt.1
Inc.
Ju 87B-1, 29•7, 'Jolanthe' Stukakette 5.K/88, Spain, 1939
Ju 87A-1, 29•2, 'Jolanthe' Stukakette VJ/88, Spain, 1938

1/48th

Eagle Editions
#143 Junkers Ju 87B/B-2 'St.G.2'
Same options as 1/72nd scale version
#144 Ju 87B-2/R2 'St.G.2, St.G.77 & 96 Gruppo'
Same options as 1/72nd scale version

Exito Decals
#48004 Luftwaffe Ground Attackers Vol.1 (Inc. Ju 87D-3)
Same options as 1/72nd scale version

H-Model Decals
#HMD48043 Ju 87B/R Stencils
#HMD48044 Ju 87D/G Stencils

HAD Models
#48081 Ju 87A/B Stuka
#48187 – Hungarian Air Force Bf 109G-6, Fw 190F-8 & Ju 87D-5

Kora
#DEC 4833 Ju 87B-2/K-2 'Royal Hungarian A.F.'
#DEC 4834 Ju 87D-5 'Hungarian Air Force'
• Ju 87D-5, B7+03, 102/2, Eastern Front, summer 1944
• Ju 87D-5, B6+31, 2/2 Zumanóbombárzo Szazád, Eastern Front, August 1943
#DEC 1856 Ju 87R-2 'Bulgarian Eagles'
#DEC 4861 Ju 87B-2/R 'Rumanian Service'
#DEC 4862 Ju 87D-5 'Rumanian Service'
#DEC 4863 Ju 87D-3 'Hungarian Service'
• B.6+41, 2/2 Zumanóbombárzo Szazád, Eastern Front, 1943
• ZB+03, 102/2 Zumanóbombárzo Század, Eastern Front, 1943
#NDT 48032 Ju 87B-1 'Condor Legion'

LF Models
#C4810 Ju 87D-5
Same option as #C4417
#C4811 Ju 87D-3
Same options as #C4418
#C4812 Ju 87R-2
Same options as #C4419

Peddinghaus-Decals
#EP2762 Ju 87 'Snake -Stukas des Sturzkampf-Geschwaders 2'

Print-Scale
#48-032 Ju 87A/B/D/G Stuka
• Ju 87R-2, T6+AP flown by Staffelkapitän of 6./St.G 2, summer 1940*
• Ju 87R-2, 6./St.G 1, 6G+KT, Mediterranean theatre, early 1941*
• Ju 87D-5, J9+AL, 2 Pulk Szturmovy, Royal Bulgarian Air Force, summer 1944*
• Ju 87B-1, 6./St.G 1, France, 1940*
• Ju 87B-1, J9+AL, 1.(St.)/Tr.Gr.189, France, May 1940*
• Ju 87D-3, 4./St.G 2, Stalingrad. September 1942/ February 1943*
• Ju 87D-5, I./SG 2, Eastern Front, winter 1943-1944*
• Ju 87A-1, 29•2, Kampfgruppe 88, Legion Condor, Spain 1938
• Ju 87B-2 Trop, III/St.G 1, North Africa, 1941 – RLM 70/71/79/65
• Ju 87B-2, 209° Squadriglia, 96 Gruppo, Regia Aeronautica, Libya, September 1941*
* All finished in RLM 70/71 over 65

ROP o.s.
#MNFD48039 Ju 87B-1 'France Campaign Pt 1'
Same options as #MNFD L72044
#MNFD48040 Ju 87B-2 'Battle of Britain Part 1'
Same options as #MNFD L72045
#MNFD48041 Ju 87B-2 'Stuka- to East Part 3'
Same options as #MNFD L72046
#MNFD48042 Ju 87B-2/R2 'Stuka over the African Battlefield Part 4'
Same options as #MNFD L72047
#MNFD48043 Ju 87B-1/B-2 'Stuka – Invasion of Russia Part 5'
Same options as #MNFD L72048
#MNFD48044 Ju 87B-2 'Stuka in the Regia Aeronautica Part 6'
Same options as #MNFD L72049

Xtradecals
#X48-087 Battle of Britain – Luftwaffe
Same option as #X72-118
#X48-164 Ju 87B-1 Stuka
• Ju 87B-1, T6+BC, Stab./St.G.2, Bonn-Hangelar, 1940
• Ju 87B-1, T6+GM, 7./St.G.2, 1939
• Ju 87B-1, T6+EP, 6./St.G.2
• Ju 87B-1, T6+BS, 8./St.G.2
• Ju 87B-1, 6G+AR, 7./St.G.51, France, 1940
• Ju 87B-1, S1+AB, I./St.G.76, flown by Hptm. Walter Sigel, Battle of Poland, 1939
• Ju 87B-1, S2+EP, 6./St.G.77, Battle of Britain, 1940
• Ju 87B-1, S2+AP, 6./St.G.77, Russia, July 1941

1/32nd

CAM (Custom Aeronautical Miniatures)
#32143 Ju 87B-2/R2
• Ju 87B-2, A5+HH, 1./St.G.1, Bulgaria, 1941
• Ju 87R-2, T6+AN, 5./St.G.2, North Africa, 1941

Eagle Editions
#97 Ju 87G-2
Same options as 1/72nd scale version
#98 Ju 87G-1/G-2
Same options as 1/72nd scale version
#143 Junkers Ju 87B/B-2 'St.G.2'
Same options as 1/72nd scale version
#144 Ju 87B-2/R2 'St.G.2, St.G.77 & 96 Gruppo'
Same options as 1/72nd scale version

Kora Models
#DEC3203 Ju 87D-3 Rumanian Service
#DEC3204 Ju 87D-5 Rumanian Service
#DEC3209 Ju 87R-2 Bulgarian Service
#DEC3210 Ju 87D-5 Bulgarian Air Force

Owl Decals
#OWLD32005 Ju 87 Stuka at Night
• Ju 87G-2, W/Nr.494200, 4.Lf.Kdo, probably 10.(Pz)/SG.2, May 1945
• Ju 87D-5(N)/D-8, W/Nr.142091, probably NSGr.4, Czechoslovakia, May 1945
#OWLD32023 Ju 87D-5(N)/D-8
• Ju 87D-5(N)/D-8, W/Nr.142091, probably NSGr.4, Czechoslovakia, May 1945
#OWLD32024 Ju 87G-2 Stuka Nachtschlacht
• Ju 87G-2, W/Nr.494200, 4.Lf.Kdo, probably 10.(Pz)/SG.2, May 1945

Peddinghaus-Decals
#EP2479 Ju 87B-2/Trop 6./St.G2, Libya, July 1941, Hubert Pölz

Print-Scale
#32-019 Ju 87 Stuka Pt.1
• Ju 87A-1, 29•2, Kampfgruppe 88, Legion Condor, Spain, 1938
• Ju 87B-1, 6G+AT, 6./St.G.1, France, 1940
• Ju 87B-1, S2+AC, flown by the Kommandeur of II./St.G.77, Balkans, 1941
• Ju 87R-2, T6+AP, flown by the Staffelkapitan of 6./St.G.2, summer 1940
#32-020 Ju 87 Stuka Pt.2
• Ju 87R-2, 6G+KT, 6./St.G, Mediterranean theatre, early 1941
• Ju 87B-1, J9+AL, 1.(St)/Tr.G.189, France, May 1940
• Ju 87B-2, S2+DB, Stab. I./St.G.77, Greece, spring 1941
• Ju 87D-5, T6+BK, I./St.G.2, Eastern Front, winter 1943/44
• Ju 87B-2 Trop, A5+HL, III./St.G.1, North Africa, 1941
• Ju 87B-2 Trop, S1+GK, 2./St.G.3, Derna, Libya, autumn 1941
• Ju 87B-1, 35+G12, 2./St.G.163, Cottbus, February 1939

1/24th

CAM (Custom Aeronautical Miniatures)
#24003 Ju 87B-2/R2
Same options as #32143

Kora DEC3209

Eagle Cals 98 (32nd)

EagleCals 97 (32nd)

EagleCals 143 (48th)

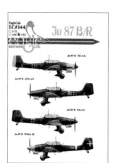
EagleCals 144 (32nd)

Kora DEC 3203

Kora DEC 3204

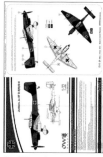
Owl Decals
OWLD32023

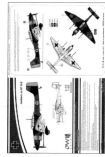
Owl Decals
OWLD32024

CAM 24-003

Appendix IV: **Bibliography**

The list below of Ju 87-related publications is as comprehensive as possible, but there are bound to be omissions so if you have amendments or additions, please contact the author via the Valiant Wings Publishing address shown at the front of this title.

Official Publications
- Ju 87A-1, Betriebsanweisung, 1937
- Ju 87A-1, Bewaffnung und Bordfunkanlage, LDv 577/1, 1938
- Ju 87A-1, Bombenausrüstung, LDv 576/2, 1940
- Ju 87A, Lichtbild-Lehrvortrag, 1938
- Ju 87B-1, Betriebsanweisung, 1939
- Ju 87B-1, Bedienungsvorschrift-Fl, LDvT 2087 B-1, 1942
- Ju 87B-1, Bordfunkanlage, LDv 577/2a, 1938
- Ju 87B-1, B-2, Bewaffnung, LDv 577/2, 1939
- Ju 87B-1 mit JUMO 211 A, Kurz-Betriebsanweisung, 1939
- Ju 87B-1, Ersatzteilliste, Werksausgabe, 1939
- Ju 87B-2, Betriebsanleitung, 1940
- Ju 87B-2, Kurz-Betriebsanleitung, 1940
- Ju 87B, Schusswaffe, LDv 576/3, 1938
- Ju 87B, Abwurfwaffe, LDv 576/4, 1938
- Ju 87B, Gerät und Sonderwerkzeug, 1940
- Ju 87R-1 Bedienungsvorschrift-Fl, 1942
- Ju 87R-2, Bedienungsvorschrift/Fl, LDvT 2087 R-2/Fl, 1941
- Ju 87B, D und R-Typen Änderungsanweisungen, 1941-1944
- Ju 87D-1, Flugzeug-Handbuch, D(Luft)T 2087 D-1, 1942-1943
- Ju 87D-1 trop, D-3 trop Bedienungsvorschrift/Fl, 1942
- Ju 87D-1 bis D-8, G-1, G-2, H-1 bis H-8, Bedienungsvorschrift/Fl, 1944
- Ju 87D-1, Schußwaffenanlage, LDVT 2087 D-1/Wa, 1942
- Ju 87D-1, Abwurfwaffenanlage, LDvT 2087 D-1/Bo, 1942
- Ju 87D-5, Flugzeug-Handbuch, D(Luft)T 2087 D-5, 1944
- Ju 87G-2, Flugzeug-Handbuch, 1944

Publications
- Camouflage & Markings of the Luftwaffe Aircraft Vol.2 Night Fighters, Bombers & Others, Model Art Special No.356 (Model Art Co., Ltd 1990)
- Cockpit Profile No.6 – Deutsche Flugzeugcockpits und Instrumentenbretter by P.W. Cohausz (Flugzeug Publikations GmbH 2000)
- Condor: The Luftwaffe in Spain 1936-1939 by P. Laureau (Hikoki Publications 2000 ISBN: 0-902109-10-4)
- Courage Alone: The Italian Air Force 1940-1943 by C. Dunning (Hikoki Publications 1998 ISBN: 1-902109-02-3. reprinted 2009 978-1-90210-909-1)
- Eagles of the Third Reich: Hitler's Luftwaffe by S.W. Mitcham (Airlife Publishing Ltd 1988/Guild Publishing Ltd 1989)
- Flugzueg Typenbuch (reprint of 1944 edition by J Beyer Verlag 1984 ISBN: 3-8805-051-0)
- German Aircraft of the Second World War by J.R.Smith & A.L. Kay (Putnam, 1972)
- German Anti-Tank Aircraft by J. Dressel & M. Griehl (Schiffer ISBN: 0-88740-520-7)
- Gli Stuka Della Regia by F. Becchetti & M. Gueli, Ali Straniere in Italia No.2 (La Bancarella Aeronautica 2003)
- Hungarian Air Force by G. Punka (Squadron/Signal Publications 1994 ISBN: 0-89747-349-3)
- Hungarian Eagles: The Hungarian Air Forces 1920-1945 by G. Sárhidai, G. Punka & V. Kozlik (Hikoki Publications 1996 ISBN: 0-9519899-1-X)
- Ju 87 – A Luftwaffe Profile No.5 (Schiffer)
- Ju 87 – Aero Series No.8 (Aero Publisher Inc., 1966)
- Ju 87 In Foreign Service by M. Wawrzynski, Red Series No.5107 (Mushroom Model Publications 2005, ISBN; 83-89450-17-8)
- Ju 87 Stuka by M.J. Murawski, Monografie Lotnicze No.19 (AJ Press 1994 ISBN: 83-86208-22-8)
- Ju 87 Stuka In Action No.73 by B. Filley (Squadron/Signal Publications 1986 ISBN: 0-89747-175-X)
- Ju 87 Stuka: Their history and how to model them by B. Robertson & G. Swanborough, Classic Aircraft No.5 (Patrick Stephens Ltd 1977 ISBN: 0-85059-193-7)
- Junkers Ju 87 by U. Elfrath (Schiffer ISBN: 0-88740-407-1)
- Junkers Ju 87 by M.J. Murawski, Monografie Loitnicze No.19 (AJ-Press)
- Junkers Ju 87 Stuka, Famous Airplanes of the World No.32 (Bunrin-do)
- Junkers Ju 87: Vom Original zum Modell by H. Erfurth (Bernard & Graefe Verlag 1999 ISBN: 3-7637-6017-2)
- Junkers Ju 87A Stuka, Famous Airplanes of the World No.84 (Bunrin-do)
- Junkers Ju 87 Stuka by A.W. Hall, Warpaint No.3 (Hall Park Books Ltd 1995/Warpaint Books Ltd)
- Junkers Ju 87 Stuka by R. Michulec & M. Willis, Orange Series No.6125 (Mushroom Model Publications 2008 ISBN: 978-83-89450-49-4)
- Junkers Ju 87 Vol.I by M.J. Murawski, Monograph No.25 (Kagero 2006 ISBN: 83-60445-08-7)
- Junkers Ju 87 Vol.II by M.J. Murawski, Monograph No.27 (Kagero 2006 ISBN: 83-60445-11-7)
- Junkers Ju 87 'Picchiatello' by M Di Terlizzi, Aviolobri Special No.2 (IBN Editore 2000 ISBN: 88-86814-58-1)
- Junkers Ju 87 Stuka by M. Bily (MBI/Sagitta, 1992)
- Junkers Ju 87 Stuka by M. Griehl: Part 1 – The Early Variants A, B, C and R, WWII Combat Aircraft Photo Archive No.5 (AirDOC Publications 2007 ISBN: 3-935687-44-3)
- Junkers Ju 87 Stuka by M. Griehl: Part 2 – The D Variant of the Luftwaffe Dive Bomber, WWII Combat Aircraft Photo Archive No.9 (AirDOC Publications 2011 ISBN: 978-3-935687-48-5)
- Junkers Ju 87 Stuka Vol.2 by F. Zoebel & J.M. Mathmann (Schiffer ISBN: 0-7643-0092-X)
- Junkers Ju 87 Monografie Lotnicze No.19 (AJ-Press)
- Junkers Ju 87 From 1936 to 1945 by H. Léonard, Planes & Pilots No.4 (Historie & Collections 2003 ISBN: 2-913903-53-3)
- Junkers Ju 87 1936-1945 by H. Léonard & A. Jouineau, Aircraft & Pilots (Historie & Collections 2004)
- Junkers Ju 87 Stuka by Alan W. Hall (Hall Park Books, 1996)
- Junkers Ju 87 Stuka by P.C. Smith (The Crowood Press 1998 ISBN: 1-86126-177-2)
- Junkers Ju 87 Stuka: A complete history by P.C. Smith (Crécy Publishing 2011 1998 ISBN: 978-0-85979-156-4)
- Junkers Ju 87 Stuka by R. Michulec & M. Willis, Yellow Series No.6125 (Mushroom Model Publications 2008, ISBN: 978-89450-49-4)
- Junkers Ju 87 Stuka by M. Derry & N. Robinson, Flight Craft No.12 (Pen & Sword Books Ltd 2017 ISBN: 978-152670-2623)
- Junkers Ju 87 Stukageschwader 1937-1941 by J. Weal, Osprey Combat Aircraft No.1 (Osprey Publishing/Reed International Books 1997 ISBN: 1-85532-636-1)

- Junkers Ju 87 – Stukageschwader of North Africa and the Mediterranean by J. Weal, Osprey Combat Aircraft No.6 (Osprey Publishing 1998 ISBN: 1-85532-722-8)
- Junkers Ju 87A by M. Griehl & J. Dressel, Luftwaffe Profile No.5 (Schiffer 1996 ISBN: 0-88740-920-2)
- Junkers Ju 87A by M. Griehl & J. Dressel, Flugzeug Profile No.2 (Flugzeug Publikations)
- Junkers Ju 87A, MPM Profile (MPM)
- Junkers Ju 87A & B by J.R. Smith, Profile No.76 (Profile Publications 1966)
- Junkers Ju 87A-C Stuka by W. Baczkowski, Typy Broni i Uzbrojenia 139 (TBiU)
- Junkers Ju 87D, Profile No.211 [Blue Series] (Profile Publications)
- Junkers Ju 87D/G, Aero Modelismo Anno IV No.3 (Delta, 1983)
- Junkers Ju 87D/G Variants by S.K. Mokwa, Top Drawings 7 (Kagero 2009 ISBN: 978-83-61220-43-5)
- Junkers Ju 87D/G Stuka, Aero Detail No.11 (Dai Nippon Kaiga Co., Ltd 1994 ISBN: 4-499-22634-1)
- Ju 87 Stuka In Action No.73 by B. Filley (Squadron/Signal Publications 1986 ISBN-0-89747-175-X)
- Kursk – The Air Battle: July 1943 by C. Berström (Classic Publications 2007 ISBN: 978-1-903223-88-8)
- Les Hydravions de la Luftwaffe Vol.1 by J-L Roba & M. Ledet, Collection Profils Avions No.15 (Lela Presse 2008 2-914017-47-2)
- Luftwaffe Camouflage and Markings 1935-1945 Vol.1 by K.A. Merrick (Kookaburra Technical Publications)
- Luftwaffe Camouflage and Markings 1935-1945 Vol.2 by K.A. Merrick (Kookaburra Technical Publications 1976)
- Luftwaffe Colours 1935-1945 by M. Ullmann (Hikoki Publications Ltd 2002/Crécy Publishing Ltd 2008 ISBN: 9-781902-109077)
- Luftwaffe Fledglings 1935-1945: Luftwaffe Training Units & their Aircraft by B. Ketley & M. Rolfe (Hikoki Publications 1996 ISBN: 1-9519899-2-8)

- Luftwaffe Im Focus, Edition No.2 (Start 2003 ISBN: 3-9808468-1-4)
- Luftwaffe Im Focus, Edition No.8 (Start 2005 ISBN: 3-9808468-8-1)
- Luftwaffe Im Focus Colour, Special No.1 (Start 2003 ISBN: 3-9808468-3-0)
- Luftwaffe in World War II Part 1, Aero Pictorials 1 (Aero Publishers Inc. 1968)
- Luftwaffe in World War II Part 2, Aero Pictorials 5 (Aero Publishers Inc. 1979 ISBN: 8168-0316-1)
- Luftwaffe over Britain: A Pictorial Essay on the German Luftwaffe's Combat Against Britian in World War 2, Combat Pictorial No.1 (Blandford Studio 1977 ISBN: 0-905948-00-9)
- Luftwaffe Warbirds Photo Album Vols.2, 3, 4, 5 & 6 Tank Magazine Special Issue (Delta Publishing 1992-1994)
- Photo Archive 1 – Luftwaffe Camouflage & Markings 1933-1945 by K.A. Merrick, E.J. Creek & B. Green (Midland Publishing 2007 ISBN: 1-85780-275-6)
- Regia Aeronautica: A Pictorial History of the Italian Air Force 1940-1943 Vol. 1 by C. Shores (Squadron/Signal Publications 1976 ISBN: 0-89747-060-5)
- Rumanian Air Force: The Prime Decade, 1938-1947 by D. Bernárd (Squadron/Signal Publications 1999 ISBN: 1-89747-402-3)
- Sojusznicy Luftwaffe cz.2 by J. Rajlich, W. Baczkowski, Z. Lalak & M.J. Murawski (Books International ISBN: 83-906942-2-0)
- St.G 2 'Immelmann' by M.J. Murawski, Lotnicze Miniatury No.21 (Kagero 2003 ISBN: 83-89088-95-9)
- Stuka by G. Adlers (Schiffer)

- Stuka by H. Leonard (Heimdal)
- Stuka at War by P.C. Smith (Ian Allan Ltd)
- Stuka! Junkers Ju 87 by Richard P. Bateson (Ducimus Books Ltd 1972)
- Stuka – Hitler's Lethal Dive Bomber by A. Smith, Images of War series (Pen & Sword Books 2013 ISBN: 978-18488-480-47)
- Stuka Ju 87 by Lt. Col. A.J. Barker, Warplanes in Colour No.6 (Arms & Armour Press 1980)
- Stuka Ju 87 by A. Vanags-Baginskis (Jane's Publsihing Co., Ltd)
- Stuka Pilot: The War Memoirs of Hans-Ulrich Rudel (Barbarossa Books 2007 ISBN: 9-7809-5387-779-9)
- The Bulgarian Air Force In Action During the Second World War (Air Power of the Kingdom of Bulgaria Part IV) by D. Nedialkov (Air Sofia)
- The Luftwaffe In Camera 1939-1942 by A. Price (Budding Books 2000 ISBN: 1-84015-111-0)
- The Warplanes of the Third Reich by William Green (Macdonald & Co Ltd, 1970)
- War Prizes: The Album by P. Butler (Midland Publishing 2006 ISBN: 1-85780-244-6)
- Wings of the Luftwaffe by Capt. Eric Brown (Airlife Publishing Ltd 1987, 1993 & 2000 ISBN: 1-85310-413-2)

Periodicals
- Luftfahrt International No.18 (Nov-Dec 1976), No.19 (Jan-March 1977), No.22 (July-August 1977), No.23 (Sept-Oct 1977) & No.27 (May-June 1978)
- Model Airplane International Vol.5 Iss.50 September 2009 & Vol.5 Iss.59 June 2010
- Replic Nos.37 & 83
- Wings of the Black Cross Nos.1, 2 & 3 by J. Crandall/M. Proulx (Eagle Editions Ltd)
- Scale Aircraft Modelling Vol.9 No.12 September 1987
- Scale Models, Vol.8 No.90 March 1977 & Vol.8 No.90 April 1977
- 21st Profile Vol.2 No.15 & Vol.2 No.17 (21st Profile Ltd ISSN: 0961-8120)

How most Stukas ended the war, this D-5 was found by American troops in a
wooded area alongside a make-shift airfield in Germany in 1945 *(©USAAF)*